GREAT EXPLORATIONS: AN AUSTRALIAN ANTHOLOGY

Edited by

JAN BASSETT

Melbourne
OXFORD UNIVERSITY PRESS
Oxford Auckland New York

OXFORD UNIVERSITY PRESS AUSTRALIA

Oxford New York
Athens Auckland Bangkok Bombay
Calcutta Cape Town Dar es Salaam Delhi
Florence Hong Kong Istanbul Karachi
Kuala Lumpur Madras Madrid Melbourne
Mexico City Nairobi Paris Port Moresby
Singapore Taipei Tokyo Toronto

and associated companies in
Berlin Ibadan

OXFORD is a trade mark of Oxford University Press

National Library of Australia
Cataloguing-in-Publication data:

Great explorations : an Australian anthology.

   Bibliography.
   Includes index.
   ISBN 0 19 553741 6.

   1. Australia — Description and travel — Sources.
   2. Australia — Discovery and exploration — Sources.
   3. Australia — History — Sources. I. Bassett, Jan, 1953– .

919.404

Edited by Katherine Steward
Cover design by Guy Mirabella
Typeset by Scriptorium Desktop Publishing Pty Ltd
Printed through OUP China
Published by Oxford University Press,
253 Normanby Road, South Melbourne, Australia

CONTENTS

Introduction   vii
Map of Australia   xvi
Editor's acknowledgments   xviii

PART ONE   AUSTRALIA   1

1   BY SEA   2
Alexander Vesper (dates unknown)   2
François Pelsaert (c. 1591–1630)   5
Abel Tasman (1603?–59)   9
William Dampier (1652–1715)   11
Willem de Vlamingh (1640–?)   16
James Cook (1728–79)   17
Kenneth Slessor (1901–71)   19
Matthew Flinders (1774–1814)   21
Ernestine Hill (1900–72)   22
Nicolas Baudin (1754–1803)   26
Phillip Parker King (1791–1856)   29
John Lort Stokes (1812–85)   33

2   THE EAST   39
William Clark (dates unknown)   39
John Price (c. 1779–?)   41
George Caley (1770–1829)   45
Gregory Blaxland (1778–1853)   47

CONTENTS

George Evans (1780–1852)   49

John Oxley (1785?–1825)   54

Hamilton Hume (1797–1873) and

    William Hovell (1786–1875)   60

Allan Cunningham (1791–1839)   62

3   THE SOUTH   65

Charles Sturt (1795–1865)   65

George Augustus Robinson (1788–1886)   68

Robert Lawrence (1808–33)   69

John Lhotsky (1795?–1865?)   74

Laurie Duggan (1949–   )   76

Richard Whately (1787–1863)   79

Thomas Livingstone Mitchell (1792–1855)   83

Anonymous   88

Joseph Hawdon (1813–71)   90

William Light (1786–1839)   93

Angus McMillan (1810–65)   97

Paul Edmund de Strzelecki (1791–1873)   102

Edward John Eyre (1815–1901)   104

Francis Webb (1925–73)   108

Geoffrey Dutton (1922–   )   109

Jane Franklin (1791–1875)   112

Georg Neumayer (1826–1909)   115

4   THE NORTH AND CENTRE   122

Charles Sturt (1795–1869)   122

Martin Thomas (1943–   )   125

John Ainsworth Horrocks (1818–46)   127

Thomas Livingstone Mitchell (1792–1855)   130

Ludwig Leichhardt (1813–48?)   134

A.B. Paterson (1864–1941)   138

Patrick White (1912–90)   139

Janis Balodis (1950–)   142

Charles Augustus FitzRoy (1796–1858)   145

Jackey Jackey (?–1854)   148

Ernest Favenc (1845–1908)   154

William John Wills (1834–61)   157

Catherine Martin (1847–1937)   159

Barry Oakley (1931–)   164

Alan Moorehead (1910–83)   168

William Landsborough (1825–86)   175

John McDouall Stuart (1815–66)   179

Archibald John Richardson (1837–1900)   181

Anne Robertson (1937–)   183

Charles Winnecke (1856–1902)   191

Anonymous   196

Ion Idriess (1889–1979)   198

Hedley Herbert Finlayson (1895–1991)   203

Arthur Groom (1904–53)   206

Barry Hill (1943–)   209

5   THE WEST   214

George Grey (1812–98)   214

Kevin Coate (?–)   218

Francis Thomas Gregory (1821–88)   224

John Forrest (1847–1918)   226

William Gosse (1842– 81)   230

Peter Egerton Warburton (1813–89)   232

Jules Verne (1828–1900)   234

Ernest Giles (1835–97)   237

Ray Ericksen (1919   )   239

David Carnegie (1871–1921)   241

Louis de Rougemont (1847–1921)   245

Robyn Davidson (1950–)   247

Robert Drewe (1943–)   250

PART TWO   NEW GUINEA   257

John MacGillivray (1821–67)   258
John Moresby (1830–1922)   259
J. A. Lawson (dates unknown)   263
Luigi D'Albertis (1841–1901)   266
Lawrence Hargrave (1850–1915)   267
George Ernest Morrison (1862–1920)   269
Anonymous   272
John Lindt (1845–1926)   275
Hubert Murray (1861–1940)   280

PART THREE   THE ANTARCTIC   283

Louis Bernacchi (1876–1942)   284
Douglas Mawson (1882–1958)   286
Eric Webb (dates unknown)   291
Frank Hurley (1885–1962)   296
Thomas Keneally (1935–   )   299
Phillip Law (1912–   )   301

Bibliography   305
Sources and acknowledgments   307
Index   315

INTRODUCTION

My constant companion while working on this anthology has been
Kathleen Fitzpatrick's *Australian Explorers: A Selection from their
Writings*, published by Oxford University Press in London in 1958, as
part of its World's Classics series. The copy in my possession still has
its saltbush-blue dust-jacket, with an illustration on the front by
William Stobbs. A quixotic figure, complete with staff, pointed beard,
and broad-brimmed hat, looking rather like Manning Clark in his later
years, strides into the desert, towards three smaller male companions
and two packhorses. All cast dark shadows across the stony ground.

Inside the densely packed little book are lengthy extracts from
journals and narratives written by eighteen of Australia's most famous
explorers, including Charles Sturt, Thomas Livingstone Mitchell,
George Grey, Edward John Eyre, Ludwig Leichhardt, and Peter
Egerton Warburton, men whose names have been etched on the minds
of generations of school students in this country. Writing out the above
list is enough to transport me back to a classroom in a Melbourne
primary school in the early 1960s, carefully tracing a map of Australia
from a Tasmania-less template, and marking in what others have since
called the explorers' 'ant-tracks'. I doubt that I understood much then
about the significance of their actions, but I knew one thing for
certain. These men were 'Heroes'.

The explorers represented in Fitzpatrick's collection form the back-
bone, so to speak, of this anthology, although the extracts that I have
chosen do not necessarily come from her sources, nor always recall the
same expeditions. Our books, of course, reflect their times, as well as
the anthologists' different prejudices and predilections. Kathleen Pitt
(later Fitzpatrick), who was born in the Victorian town of Omeo in
1905, studied at the University of Melbourne during the 1920s, where
her teachers included the historian Ernest Scott, whose own interest in
Australian exploration led to several publications, among them *The*

Life of Captain Matthew Flinders, R.N. (1914), *Australian Discovery by Sea* (1929), and *Australian Discovery by Land* (1929).[1] After further study at Oxford University, Fitzpatrick taught history at the University of Melbourne from 1930 to 1962, becoming associate professor in 1938. Although she had retired by the time that I first became a student in her old department in the early 1970s, her name remained well known. Following her death in 1990, an annual lecture in her memory was instituted in 1994.[2]

Our greatest difference lies in our attitudes towards the explorers' status. To Fitzpatrick all of the Australian explorers 'were heroes',[3] and she quotes with approval these words from one of their number, Ernest Giles: 'No work of fiction can excel, or even equal, in romantic and heart-stirring interest, the volumes worthy to be written in letters of gold, which record the deeds and sufferings of these noble toilers in the dim and distant field of discovery afforded by the Australian continent'.[4] Given the shifts in historical thinking that have taken place since the 1950s, it is not surprising that a group whom Fitzpatrick sees as 'Great Men of History', albeit with a few (sometimes literally) fatal flaws, should appear to me now as 'Dead White Males', whose behaviour spans the spectrum from admirable to despicable.

Confident in the assumption that her readers will know what she means by the term 'explorer', Fitzpatrick makes little attempt to define it. A quick look at her choices, however, reveals that she was employing a narrow definition of the word. Hers are all *deliberate* explorers, men who embarked on exploratory expeditions with particular purposes in mind, searching for fertile lands, following river systems, or pursuing scientific knowledge. Moreover, they are all leaders of these ventures, with the exception of William Wills, who was deputy to Robert O'Hara Burke. The only reason for this variation is that Burke's many failings included not bothering to keep a regular journal. While acknowledging that it 'is not easy to make a distinction between explorers and overlanders', Fitzpatrick excludes the latter from consideration, on the grounds that they were mainly concerned with extending private enterprise, whereas the former were, according to her, working for the public good.[5]

Fitzpatrick's focus is on explorers, mine more generally on exploration. To explore means, among other things, 'to travel extensively through (a country etc.) in order to learn or discover about it',[6] a definition that I have interpreted with a fair degree of latitude, while choosing the ninety very diverse extracts that make up this book. I was also influenced by the distinction that Paul Carter draws between exploration and discovery in his 'essay in spatial history', *The Road to Botany Bay* (1987). 'For, while discovery rests on the assumption of a world of facts waiting to be found, collected and classified ... exploration lays stress on the observer's active engagement with his environment', he writes.[7]

In addition to selections from the works of leading explorers, I have included pieces written by their more obscure fellows, such as John Price, who took part in, and recorded, two unsuccessful searches in 1798 for the 'New World', which convicts believed lay several hundred kilometres south-west of Sydney. The fineness of the line between overlanding and exploration becomes particularly apparent in the excerpt from a report by Archibald Richardson, a surveyor who accompanied the Jardine brothers on their famous trek to Cape York in 1864–65. Followers of earlier explorers occasionally make appearances, one of them being Melbourne University academic Ray Ericksen, whose 1967 'journey of discovery into the heartland of Australia' was inspired by the travels of Ernest Giles. At the risk of being seen to be using an oxymoron, I have added some accounts by 'accidental explorers', people who set out with quite different intentions, but, for whatever reasons, ended up becoming involved in some exploration. It is worth noting that the first long overland expedition made in Australia by Europeans, part of which is described here by a participant, William Clark, was undertaken by sailors seeking help after the *Sydney Cove* was wrecked in 1797. Writings *about* other explorers, by explorers and non-explorers alike, are also included in this anthology.[8]

Fitzpatrick's book, which is organised chronologically, begins with the crossing of the Blue Mountains in 1813 by Blaxland, Lawson, and Wentworth and concludes with Giles's discovery of Gibson's Desert and traverses of the continent in the mid-1870s, thus covering the period that probably could be described as the 'heroic', some might say 'hysterical', age of Australian land exploration. Fitzpatrick acknowledges doing Tasmania an 'injustice' by ignoring it, but gives no reason for doing so.[9] My boundaries are much broader. This book opens with a section on the exploration of Australia by sea (which is not part of Fitzpatrick's 'story'),[10] much of which occurred between the 1600s and 1800s. It then roughly follows the sweep of European exploration of Australia by land, with sections on 'The East', where most of the activity between the 1790s and 1820s happened, 'The South', where attention turned in the 1830s, 'The North and Centre', where many expeditions took place between the 1840s and 1860s (and later), and 'The West', the scene of much interest during the 1870s.

These geographical designations are loose, as indeed has been the explorers' use of such terms. Sometimes my positioning of particular extracts has been fairly arbitrary. Accounts of Eyre's 1841 trip across the Nullarbor could have gone into 'The West', but instead I put them into 'The South', because that expedition often is seen as belonging to the phase of 'opening up the south'. Towards the end of the nineteenth century, Australian explorers began to set their sights elsewhere, hence my inclusion of a section about the exploration of New Guinea, by Australians or people with Australian connections, particularly in the 1870s and 1880s. One of the more unusual associations involved the flamboyant Luigi D'Albertis, who flew both the Italian and New South Wales flags when he steamed up the Fly River in 1876. As Australians have also played a prominent role in Antarctic exploration since the turn of the century, there is a section on that 'accursed land'. Interestingly, when I mentioned to friends and colleagues that I was working on a project involving Australian explorers one of the most common responses was 'Oh, you mean people like Douglas Mawson'.

As William Stobbs's illustration suggests, the realm of exploration has largely been a 'man's world'. There are no female explorers in Fitzpatrick's collection, and only a handful in mine. Women have rarely had opportunities to participate in exploratory expeditions, but I also suspect that not many have been particularly keen on attempting 'to penetrate the interior', to borrow a term frequently used by male explorers, nor on the idea of racing one another across the country. That 'indefatigable traveller', Jane Franklin, wife of a lieutenant-governor of Van Diemen's Land (present-day Tasmania), probably counts as an explorer. Here, in a letter to her sister, she describes an arduous journey in which she took part in 1842. Another example is Robyn Davidson, who travelled across outback Western Australia in 1977, with only camels and a dog for company, after which she wrote *Tracks* (1980). Not only have female explorers been thin on the ground, but few female writers have been attracted to the subject, Fitzpatrick having been unusual in this regard. Although better known for her unrelated novel, *An Australian Girl* (1890), Catherine Martin wrote an epic poem about the Burke and Wills expedition, entitled *The Explorers* (1874), the first part of which I have reproduced. (I am indebted to Des Cowley, La Trobe rare books librarian at the State Library of Victoria, for alerting me to this and other sources.) Another woman represented in these pages is Ernestine Hill, herself a great traveller, whose works include a novel based on the life of Matthew Flinders, *My Love Must Wait* (1941).

Regrettably, few Aboriginal voices can be heard in this anthology. And yet, as Robin Hanbury-Tenison observes in his general *Oxford Book of Exploration* (1993), 'The real explorers were those who for tens of thousands of years before history began searched the world for uninhabited land'.[11] Some acknowledgment of these people is to be found in the first extract, a dreaming story told by Alexander Vesper. Since the 1600s, when the first known European contacts with Australia were made, explorers have been 'discovering' places where Aboriginal people had been living for thousands of years. Jackey Jackey, who participated in Edmund Kennedy's disastrous 1848 expedition, is one of numerous Aboriginal guides who have assisted European explorers, but is a rarity in having left a statement about his experiences. Descriptions of encounters with Aboriginal people are plentiful in explorers' journals, but often are difficult to interpret, given the distortions caused by the heavy weight of cultural baggage that the early explorers were carrying.

Fitzpatrick mentions Aborigines at the end of a long list of dangers facing explorers, including lack of water, food shortages, scurvy, eye trouble, and extremes of temperature, claiming that 'the early explorers of Australia were always in danger from the aboriginal people'.[12] Although she attempts to be even-handed, her sympathy clearly lies with the explorers, of whom she makes the following debatable claim: 'Probably no white men have ever admired the aborigines so much nor (in the main) treated them so humanely as the explorers'.[13] If this is true, it seems to be an appalling indictment of the rest of White Australian society. Despite the horrors of the past, one feels somewhat more optimistic about the present and future when one reads works, such as Barry Hill's recent book, *The Rock: Travelling to Uluru* (1994), which attempt to build bridges between Aboriginal and non-Aboriginal Australians.

Exploration has long been a powerful theme in Australian literature of various kinds. So, in addition to using explorers' journals, narratives, letters, addresses to learned societies, reports, and other works of non-fiction, I have also drawn upon fiction, drama, and poetry. Possibly the best-known novel in this field is Patrick White's *Voss* (1957), the main character of which is based, in part, upon the enigmatic Leichhardt, whose disappearance in the late 1840s remains one of the great mysteries of Australian history. Other works inspired by the same explorer include Janis Balodis's play *Too Young for Ghosts* (1985). Not surprisingly, the Burke and Wills fiasco, in particular, has provided the basis for many imaginative works, among them Barry Oakley's short story 'O'Hara 1861' (1959). Perhaps more unexpected is the fact that

Jules Verne's prolific output includes a novel entitled *Mistress Branican* (1891), in which the eponymous heroine follows Warburton's route from Alice Springs through the deserts of Western Australia, while searching for her long-lost husband. She seems to be capable of doing virtually everything that Warburton could do, if not backwards and in high heels, at least wearing the cumbersome garments of a nineteenth-century lady. Creative writings with their roots in the explorers' journals continue to be published, a recent example being Martin Thomas's unusual novel *The Roan* (1994), a blend of fact and fiction about a horse left in central Australia by Charles Sturt in 1844.

Indeed, it is not always easy to differentiate between fact and fiction in the texts represented here, even those purporting to be factual. Ion Idriess's highly popular work of faction, *Lasseter's Last Ride* (1931), is one of the more blatant exercises in myth-making. Many genuine incidents recorded in these sources also truly sound 'stranger than fiction'. Bizarre images, of the 'Across the Andes by Frog' sort, that jump to mind include the idiosyncratic Dr John Lhotsky enjoying an 'aerial bath' on his way from Sydney to the Australian Alps in 1834, poor John Ainsworth Horrocks being shot by his camel in 1846, the first animal of its kind to be used in Australian exploration, and Warburton, whom Fitzpatrick describes as a perfect representation of 'the Anglo-Indian colonel'[14] type, addressing members of the Royal Geographical Society in London in 1874 on the subject of eating camels (they taste like 'the contents of a carpenter's glue-pot').

Maybe inevitably, there have been hoaxes, one of the most extraordinary being that involving *The Adventures of Louis de Rougemont: As Told by Himself* (1899), in which the author states that he lived among Aboriginal people for some thirty years, after having been shipwrecked. Controversy raged over his claims, and he was soon exposed, by various critics, as a fraud. De Rougemont proved to be Swiss-born Henri Louis Grin, who had lived an unspectacular life in Australia between 1875 and 1897.[15] The similarities in tone to be found in many of the journals of the authentic explorers and the works of their fraudulent counterparts are enough to send shivers down the spine of the anthologist fearful of mistaking one for the other. I shall leave readers to speculate about the provenance of each of the following sub-headings: 'We begin another week badly', 'Curious mounds of stones', 'Aboo bitten by a small snake', 'Gluttony of the crew', 'Seized by an octopus', and 'All more or less knocked up'.[16]

My primary criterion for choosing extracts was intrinsic interest. Some of the explorers' journals have literary merit, but Fitzpatrick's claim that most of them are 'well-written'[17] seems overly generous. Perhaps it would be more accurate to say that overall they contain passages to suit almost all tastes. The works of fiction and poetry also fluctuate greatly in quality, there being a world of difference, for example, between Kenneth Slessor's fine poem, *Five Visions of Captain Cook* (1931), and the dreadful doggerel addressed to Mitchell as he set off on his third expedition, published in the *Sydney Gazette* in March 1836, the author of which sensibly remained anonymous. Many of the extracts, of course, describe incidents and events that are generally considered to be of historical significance, such as Paul Edmund de Strzelecki's naming of Mount Kosciusko, Australia's highest mountain, in 1840. All are taken from published sources, so that readers can follow up any if they wish to do so.

'The idea of exploration now seems, at best, an archaic notion, at worst a cultural shame', wrote Christine Thompson in 1994, in a favourable review of Hanbury-Tenison's *Oxford Book of Exploration*.[18] There remains, however, an enduring fascination about the subject, attested to by the continuing publication of facsimiles of early explorers' journals, literature inspired by them, and revisionist studies, the making of films and television programs about exploration, and the undertaking of expeditions following explorers' routes. Reading, or re-reading, the extracts collected here causes one to ponder a multiplicity of questions about, among other things, the ways in which the Australian colonies were settled, relationships between indigenous peoples and European explorers, interactions between humans and their environments, the development of various models of masculinity, and the powers of human endurance. Perhaps Francis Webb sums up part of the appeal of such sources in the introductory note to his poem *Eyre All Alone* (1961), based on Eyre's 1841 expedition, when he talks of 'seeing such a journey of discovery as suggestive of another which is common to us all'.

Paradoxically, the less the early explorers knew about Australia and its peoples, the more certain their views about them often were, some of which are perpetuated in Fitzpatrick's own writing. More recent explorers, physical and intellectual, equipped with far greater factual knowledge, have been much more obviously troubled by doubts and uncertainties. Fitzpatrick's anthology sometimes seems to me to be like a jigsaw, with a definite place for each piece, whereas mine is intended to be a kaleidoscope, albeit one with some of her jigsaw pieces. I have included glowing and murky, clear and hazy, large and small, tragic and comic, beautiful and ugly, serious and frivolous fragments. Depending partly on the order in which one reads them, they illuminate, contradict, overlap, confirm, and undermine one another. I hope that readers find the process of creating new patterns from them stimulating.

Jan Bassett

Note to readers

Original spellings have been retained in these extracts. Some footnotes and a minor amount of technical detail have been deleted. Present-day spellings are used in the map of Australia and in the index.

Notes

1 For further biographical details about Ernest Scott see Kathleen Fitzpatrick, 'Sir Ernest Scott', in *Australian Dictionary of Biography*, vol. 11, Geoffrey Serle (ed.), Melbourne University Press, Carlton, 1988, pp. 544–5, and Stuart Macintyre, *A History for a Nation: Ernest Scott and the Making of Australian History*, Melbourne University Press, Carlton, 1994.

2 For further biographical details about Fitzpatrick see her *Solid Bluestone Foundations*, Macmillan, Melbourne, 1983.

3 Kathleen Fitzpatrick (ed.), *Australian Explorers: A Selection from their Writings*, Oxford University Press, London, 1958, p. 27.

4 Fitzpatrick, *Australian Explorers*, p. 9.

5 Fitzpatrick, *Australian Explorers*, p. 18.

6 Joyce M. Hawkins (ed.), *The Oxford Reference Dictionary*, Clarendon Press, Oxford, 1986, p. 286.

7 Paul Carter, *The Road to Botany Bay: An Essay in Spatial History*, Faber & Faber, London, 1988 (1987), p. 25.

8 Full details of all the sources from which the extracts in this anthology were taken are given in the list of sources and acknowledgments at the back of the book.

9 Fitzpatrick, *Australian Explorers*, p. 27.

10 Fitzpatrick, *Australian Explorers*, p. 2.

11 Robin Hanbury-Tenison (ed.), *The Oxford Book of Exploration*, Oxford University Press, Oxford and New York, 1993, p. x.

12 Fitzpatrick, *Australian Explorers*, p. 8.

13 Fitzpatrick, *Australian Explorers*, p. 9.

14 Fitzpatrick, *Australian Explorers*, p. 28.

15 See B. G. Andrews, 'Louis de Rougemont', in *Australian Dictionary of Biography*, vol. 8, Bede Nairn & Geoffrey Serle (eds), Melbourne University Press, Carlton, 1981, p. 290.

16 The first and fourth sub-headings are the words of Luigi D'Albertis, the second those of George Grey, the third and sixth those of J. A. Lawson, and the fifth those of Louis de Rougemont, taken from the works listed under their names in the list of sources and acknowledgments.

17 Fitzpatrick, *Australian Explorers*, p. 28.

18 *Age*, 26 March 1994.

MAP

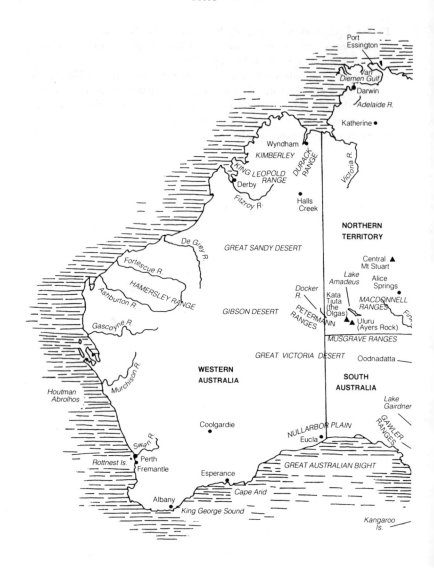

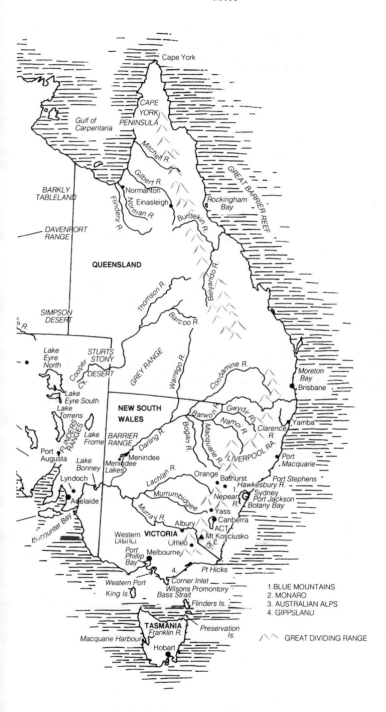

1. BLUE MOUNTAINS
2. MONARO
3. AUSTRALIAN ALPS
4. GIPPSLAND

/\^\ GREAT DIVIDING RANGE

EDITOR'S ACKNOWLEDGMENTS

I should like to thank Olga Abrahams, Janette Bomford, Nicholas Bomford, Jude Bourguignon, Debra Burgess, Alexa Burnell, Gillian Cardinal, Sonja Chalmers, David Collins, Geraldine Corridon, Des Cowley, Jill Davies, Andrew Demetriou, Dr Robin Gerster, Frank Lyons, Una Lyons, Dr Michael McKernan, Dr Ross McMullin, Neil McPhee, Professor Peter McPhee, Alan Mason, Guy Mirabella, David Preston, Sue Preston, Dr Carolyn Rasmussen, Maggie Richardson, Peter Rose, Richard Samson, Katherine Steward, Dr David Stockley, and Louise Sweetland for their much appreciated assistance. Without the support and encouragement of the late Dr Lloyd Robson during earlier stages of my career I would not have published this or any other book.

Part One

—

AUSTRALIA

1

BY SEA

ALEXANDER VESPER

(dates unknown)

Aboriginal elder. Vesper, from Woodenbong in north-east New South Wales, was said to be 'an almost inexhaustible source of Aboriginal traditions'. He told this story to the Jindyworobak poet Roland Robinson in the early 1960s. Aborigines in other parts of Australia have their own stories about how their ancestors arrived in this country.

'THE THREE BROTHERS'

This story is not a *butheram*. A *butheram* is a story that is given out by a being that lives in the mountains. This story has been handed down by the aborigines through their generations. This story cannot be altered.

I am sixty-seven years of age. I heard this story from my grandfather who was a full-blood of the Ngarartbul tribe near Murwillumbah. On my grandmother's side the tribe was Gullibul, from Casino and Woodenbong. I heard this story also from many old aborigines who came from other tribes.

The first finding of this unknown land, Australia, was made by three brothers who came from the central part of the world. The names of these three brothers were Mamoon, Yar Birrain and Birrung. They were compelled to explore for land on the southerly part of the world. They were forced out of the centre of the world by revolutions and warfare of those nations of the central part.

They came in a sailing ship. As they made direct for south, coming across and seeing different islands and seeing the people in these islands, they kept in the sea all the time until they came to Australia, to the eastern part of this continent.

Their first coming into the land was at Yamba Head, Clarence River. They anchored just on the mouth of the Clarence. This was the first landing of men in this empty continent. They camped, taking out of their empty ship all their camping belongings, such as a steel axe and many other things of the civilized race in the central part of the world.

After they had rested from the voyage, through the night a storm started to rise from the west. The force of wind broke the anchor and deprived them of the ship, which was driven out to sea and never seen again.

These three brothers each had a family of his own and they had their mother. Their three wives were with them. When they knew that the ship was gone, they reasoned among themselves and said, 'The only possible chance is to make a canoe and return from here from island to island.'

So they went up the Clarence River and they came across a black-butt tree. They stripped the bark off it, made a big fire, a long fire, and heated the bark until it was flexible, until you could bend it about as you pleased. Out of this fifteen to twenty feet long sheet of bark, they made a canoe. Three of these canoes were made.

They went back to their families and told them to get everything packed up as they were about to leave. Their families said, 'Yes, we'll pack up, but mother has gone out for some yams. She was looking for something to eat.' So they sang out. They searched along the beach, among the honey-suckle and the tea-tree along the coast, trying to find the old woman. But she had wandered too far out of the reach of their search. She thought within herself that her sons would not be able to make the canoes so quickly.

The three brothers said, 'Well, she might have died. We'll have to take back into the sea.' So they packed up. So they took to the ocean in the three canoes with the intention of returning where they came from.

After they got a distance out from Yamba Head, the old woman arrived back at the camp they had left. So she went up to the top of the hill and started singing out for them. And she saw them two to three miles out on the ocean.

She was trying to wave them back, but it seemed to be impossible for her to draw their attention. So she was angry with them. She cursed the families and said to the ocean to be rough. As she cursed them and spoke to the ocean to be rough, the ocean started to get fierce. As they attempted to continue on against the tempest they were driven back to the northern shore beyond Yamba. They were compelled to come in to land at the place which is now known as Evans Head.

They made the first settling place in Australia at Evans Head. One of the sons returned to Yamba when the ocean was calm and found the mother still alive. She had lived on yams. That is how Yamba got its name. Well, that word 'yam,' it comes from a civilized word. It means 'sweet spud.' So that word alone will give you a clue as to where those first people came from.

So, one brother went back to Yamba and brought the mother to Evans Head. When they settled there, in the process of time, they increased their families. One family race generated northwards on the Australian coast, one to the west and one to the south. As they were generating, they were keeping on extending, and they kept in touch with each other all the time.

As they went on in that manner they became tribal races, and the first language of their origin we call *Jabilum*, that means, 'The Originals.' Tabulum is the word the white man made out of this word. And the first language of these Jabilum was the Birrein tongue. And the second was Gumbangirr, of the Grafton tribe. Weervul is the Ballina lot. And Gullibul, that is between the two. Gullibul sprang out of the centre from Tweed Heads.

The race of the aborigines as it was continually generated had often a knowledge of the other races across the sea in the other islands. We call these islands Ngareenbil, that is, other countries that are not contactable to Australia. The coastal aboriginal often took a canoe to these islands and was married there.

And during the period of the increase of the aborigines, they started to make a tribal law which is notable through the other races in the world. And by these laws which they made they were able to check up on different things. They were compelled to use the stone tomahawk. They were made to climb trees after possums and hunt for food such as kangaroos, wallabies and many other things, such as fishes.

And as far as making weapons, they made shields, they made boomerangs, discovering and imitating swifts and swallows. They saw it was possible to make a boomerang take to the air and come back. And they made boomerangs for fighting, especially the straight boomerang which will cut through the air. Their shields, *buggarr*, came from the central part of the world. Also their spears. They never used the *woomera*, the spear-thrower. The spear they threw with their hand, holding the spear in the middle. In warfare they used mainly the shield and the boomerang.

Well, that's how the aborigines came to be in Australia. When they landed here there was no one because God had wiped out the whole of the earth in a great flood.

So, when Captain Cook came here there were about five hundred tribes in Australia. They were cut off in this country from all other civilizations. The *butheram* were living in the mountains in Australia before the three brothers came here. When the tribes became clever, they found the *butheram* here and made them their gods.

And when Captain Cook landed, he never fired a shot at the aborigines. The aborigines made friends with him because, they said 'This is one of our friends from the other part of the world.' Then Captain Cook returned to England and reported that he had found a great land in the south. And this is how the white man came here and settled, but our stories like the ones I tell to you are being forgotten by the last of our people.

It is good you have written some down. They will be remembered.

Roland Robinson, *The Man Who Sold His Dreaming* (1965)

FRANÇOIS PELSAERT

(*c.* 1591–1630)

Dutch East India Company officer. Pelsaert inadvertently became an explorer when his ship the Batavia, *sailing between Holland and Batavia (present-day Jakarta), struck a reef off the Houtman Abrolhos islands, about 75 kilometres from the Western Australian coast, in June 1629. Some of the 300-odd soldiers, crew, and passengers drowned, but the rest managed to reach nearby islands. Pelsaert sailed an open boat to Batavia for help. During his absence, mutiny broke out among the survivors on the islands, with much blood being shed. After his return, some of the mutineers were hanged on the spot; others were hanged in Batavia, and two were marooned in what is now Western Australia. Soon after the wreck occurred, Pelsaert explored part of the mainland, as he recorded in his journal, which forms the basis for this account.*

SEARCHING FOR WATER

Sail for the Mainland

Thereupon they commenced their voyage in the name of the Lord, and sailed into the open. In the afternoon they were in latitude 28 deg. 13 min. and shortly afterwards sighted the mainland, probably-about six miles north by west of their foundered ship, the wind blowing from the west. They were there in about 28 or 30 fathoms of water, wherefore in the evening they turned away from the land, but went near it again about midnight.

On the morning of the 9th they were still about three miles from the shore, the wind, with some rain, being mostly north-west. They guessed that during these 24 hours they had made from four to five miles in a north-westerly direction. The shore in these parts stretches mostly north-west and south-east; a bare and rocky coast, without trees, about as high as at Dover, in England. They saw an inlet and some low, sandy dunes, which they thought they could approach; but, coming close, they found that near the beach the breakers were very rough and that the sea rolled high on the land, so that they could not very well risk the landing; since the wind rose more and more.

In peril through the night

On the 10th they had to move about for a period of 24 hours on account of the strong wind and storm, which blew harder and harder from the nor-west, so that they were obliged to let go the sloop, which they had taken with them, and even to throw overboard some of their bread and other things that were in the way, as they could not otherwise bale out the water. In the night they were still in greater danger of sinking on account of the strong wind and the high seas. They had no means of keeping off the shore. They could carry no sail. They were at the mercy of the sea. That night a steady rain poured down, and they hoped that the people on the islands might also have some of it, and provide themselves with water.

On the 11th, it became calmer, and the wind turned to the west-south-west. They therefore turned northward, but the sea was just as rough and high.

On the 12th, at noon, the weather steadied down and cleared up. They were then at a latitude of 27 deg. They kept close to the shore, the wind being south-east, but they had no opportunity of nearing the land with the boat, for the breakers were too strong and the coast too steep and jagged, without any foreland or inlet, as is usually found on other coasts, so that it seemed to them, a bare and cursed country, devoid of green or grass.

On the 13th, at noon, they were at a latitude of 25 deg. 10 min. They found then that they had drifted north a good deal, and had doubled the cape, keeping mostly northward during these 24 hours, as the coast now stretched north-north-east and south-south-west. The rocks were of redstone, a good deal battered and broken. There was no foreland. These rocks were all along of very much the same height, and made landing impossible on account of the breakers and high seas.

On the 14th, in the morning, there was a gentle breeze, but during the day a calm set in. At noon they were in latitude 24 degs., keeping north with an east wind. The current still took them every day much round the north, greatly against their wish, for with but little sail they were close to the shore.

They see smoke on the shore

In the afternoon, seeing inland some smoke, they rowed thither, hoping to find an opportunity of landing. They were quite rejoiced, for they imagined that where there were people there would also be fresh water. Having reached the shore, they found the ground to be a steep and rough incline; stony and rocky, against which the breakers beat violently, so that they saw no means of landing. It made them very dejected, for they feared that they would have to depart without landing. At last six men, trusting themselves to their swimming powers jumped overboard, and reached the shore with great difficulty and peril, while the boat remained at anchor outside the breakers in 25 fathoms of water. The swimmers having reached the shore, looked the whole day for fresh water everywhere, till in the evening they became convinced that their search was vain.

They find people

They then happened upon four people, who were creeping towards them on their hands and feet. When one man, coming out of a hollow upon a height, suddenly approached them they leaped to their feet and fled full speed, which was distinctly observed by those in the boat. They were black savages, quite naked, leaving themselves uncovered like animals.

No fresh water

As those on the shore had spent the whole day without finding water, they swam aboard again towards evening being all a good deal hurt and bruised, since the breakers had dashed them roughly against the rocks. Then getting ready and lifting the grappling iron they started in search of a better opportunity, sailing along the coast all night with but little sail, and keeping outside the breakers.

On the morning of the 15th, they came to a point where a large reef extended at about a mile from the coast, and, so it seemed, another reef along the shore, so that they tried their best to steer between the two, for the water there appeared to be calm and smooth. But they did not find an entrance until the afternoon, when they saw an opening where there were no breakers. But it was very dangerous, very stony, and often not holding two feet of water. The shore here had a foreland of dunes about a mile broad, before the higher land was reached.

At last they find some

When they had gone ashore they commenced to dig holes in the said foreland, but found nothing except salt water. Some of them therefore went higher up and fortunately found some small hollows in a cliff, full of fresh water that the rain had left there. They quenched their great thirst greedily, for they had almost succumbed. Since they had left the ship they had been without wine or other drink, except a daily allowance of one or two cups of water. They also collected a fair provision, about 80 cans of water, remaining there the whole night. It seemed that the blacks had been there just before, for they found the bones of crabs and the ashes of the fire.

On the 16th, as soon as it was light, they resolved to go further inland, hoping to find more such hollows with fresh water in the mountains. But their search was vain, for they found that there had not been any rain in the mountains for a long time; nor was there any appearance of running water, for behind the mountain chain the country was flat again; bearing neither trees nor vegetation, nor grass, and being everywhere covered with high ant hills built of earth, which in the distance were not unlike Indian huts.

Great ant hills and multitudes of flies

There were also such multitudes of flies that one could not keep them out of one's mouth and eyes. They next saw eight black people, each carrying a stick in his hand. These approached them to a musket-shot's distance, but when they saw our people coming towards them they took to their heels, and would neither speak nor stop.

'The Abrolhos Tragedy', trans. Willem Siebenhaar (1897, first published in Dutch 1647)

ABEL TASMAN

(1603?–59)

Dutch mariner. In 1642, Tasman 'discovered' Van Diemen's Land, named it after the governor-general of the Dutch East Indies, and claimed it for the Dutch. Some of his men went ashore briefly, as he records in this 2 December entry in his journal. During a later voyage, Tasman charted part of the northern and north-western coast of Australia. Van Diemen's Land was renamed Tasmania after him in 1855.

VAN DIEMEN'S LAND VISIT

Early in the morning we sent our Pilot-Major Francoys Jacobsz Vissher in command of our pinnace, manned with 4 musketeers and 6 rowers, all of them furnished with pikes and side-arms, together with the cock-boat of the 'Zeehaen' with one of her second mates and 6 musketeers in it, to a bay situated north-west of us at upwards of a mile's distance, in order to ascertain what facilities (as regards fresh water, refreshments, timber, and the like) may be available there. About three hours before nightfall the boats came back, bringing various samples of vegetables, which they had seen growing there in great abundance, some of them in appearance not unlike a certain plant growing at the Cabo de Bona Esperance, and fit to be used as pot-herbs, and another species with long leaves and a brackish taste, strongly resembling persil de mer or samphire. The Pilot-Major and the second mate of the 'Zeehaen' made the following report, to wit: —

That they had rowed the space of upwards of a mile round the said point, where they had found high but level land, covered with vegetation (not cultivated, but growing naturally by the will of God), abundance of excellent timber, and a gently sloping watercourse in a barren valley, the said water, though of good quality, being difficult to procure, because the watercourse was so shallow that the water could be dipped with bowls only.

That they had heard certain human sounds, and also sounds nearly resembling the music of a trump or a small gong not far from them, though they had seen no-one.

That they had seen two trees about 2 or 2½ fathom in thickness, measuring from 60 to 65 feet from the ground to the lowermost branches, which trees bore notches made with flint implements, the bark having been removed for the purpose; these notches, forming a kind of steps to enable persons to get up the trees and rob the birds' nests in their tops, were fully 5 feet apart, so that our men concluded that the natives here must be of very tall stature, or must be in possession of some sort of artifice for getting up the said trees; in one of the trees these notched steps were so fresh and new that they seemed to have been cut less than four days ago.

That on the ground they had observed certain footprints of animals, not unlike those of a tiger's claws; they also brought on board certain specimens of animal excrements voided by quadrupeds, so far as they could surmise and observe, together with a small quantity of gum of a seemingly very fine quality, which had exuded from trees, and bore some resemblance to gum-lac.

That around the eastern point of this bay they had sounded 13 or 14 feet at high water, there being about 3 feet at low tide.

That at the extremity of the said point they had seen large numbers of gulls, wild ducks, and geese, but had perceived none farther inward, though they had heard their cries; and had found no fish except different kinds of mussels forming small clusters in several places.

That the land is pretty generally covered with trees, standing so far apart that they allow a passage everywhere, and a look-out to a great distance, so that when landing our men could always get sight of natives or wild beasts, unhindered by dense shrubbery or underwood, which would prove a great advantage in exploring the country.

That in the interior they had in several places observed numerous trees which had deep holes burnt into them at the upper end of the foot, while the earth had here and there been dug out with the fist so as to form a fireplace, the surrounding soil having become as hard as flint through the action of the fire.

A short time before we got sight of our boats returning to the ships, we now and then saw clouds of dense smoke rising up from the land, which was nearly west by north of us; and surmised this might be a signal given by our men, because they were so long coming back; for we had ordered them to return speedily, partly in order to be made acquainted with what they had seen, and partly that we might be able to send them to other points, if they should find no profit there, to the end that no precious time might be wasted. When our men had come on board again, we inquired of them whether they had been there and made a fire, to which they returned a negative answer, adding, however, that at various times and points in the wood they also had seen clouds of smoke ascending. So there can be no doubt there must be men here of extraordinary stature. This day we had variable winds from the eastward, but for the greater part of the day a stiff, steady breeze from the south-east.

The Discovery of Tasmania (1942)

WILLIAM DAMPIER

(1652–1715)

English mariner and writer. Dampier included the following description of the north-western coast of New Holland (present-day mainland Australia), which he and other buccaneers from the Cygnet *had visited in 1688, in his book entitled* A New Voyage Round the World *(1697), about his voyages to the Pacific (1686–91). He also wrote of his second visit to the same area, made during a later official British expedition, in* A Voyage to New Holland 1699 *(1703, 1709). Dampier's publications provoked much interest in the subject of New Holland.*

DAMPIER'S FIRST IMPRESSIONS OF NEW HOLLAND

The 4th Day of *January*, 1688, we fell in with the Land of *New-Holland* in the Lat. of 16 d. 50 m. having, as I said before, made our Course due South from the Shoal that we past by the 31st Day of *December*. We ran in close by it, and finding no convenient anchoring, because it lies open to the N.W. we ran along shore to the Eastward, steering N.E. by E. for so the Land lies. We steered thus about 12 Leagues; and then came to a Point of Land, from whence the Land trends East and southerly, for 10 or 12 Leagues; but how afterwards I know not. About 3 Leagues to the eastward of this Point, there is a pretty deep Bay, with abundance of Islands in it, and a very good place to anchor in, or to hale ashoar. About a League to the eastward of that Point we anchored *January* the 5th, 1688, two Mile from the Shore, in 29 Fathom, good hard Sand, and clean Ground.

New-Holland is a very large Tract of Land. It is not yet determined whether it is an Island or a main Continent; but I am certain that it joins neither to *Asia, Africa,* nor *America.* This part of it that we saw is

[11]

all low even Land, with sandy Banks against the Sea, only the Points are rocky, and so are some of the Islands in this Bay.

The Land is of a dry sandy Soil, destitute of Water, except you make Wells; yet producing divers sorts of Trees; but the Woods are not thick, nor the Trees very big. Most of the Trees that we saw are Dragon-Trees as we supposed; and these too are the largest Trees of any there. They are about the bigness of our large Apple-trees, and about the same heighth; and the Rind is blackish and somewhat rough. The Leaves are of a dark Colour; the Gum distils out of the Knots or Cracks that are in the Bodies of the Trees. We compared it with some Gum-Dragon or Dragon's Blood that was aboard, and it was of the same colour and taste. The other sort of Trees were not known by any of us. There was pretty long Grass growing under the Trees; but it was very thin. We saw no Trees that bore Fruit or Berries.

We saw no sort of Animal, nor any Track of Beast, but once; and that seemed to be the Tread of a Beast as big as a great Mastiff-Dog. Here are a few small Land-birds, but none bigger than a Black-bird; and but few Sea-fowls. Neither is the Sea very plentifully stored with Fish, unless you reckon the Manatee and Turtle as such. Of these Creatures there is plenty; but they are extraordinary shy; though the Inhabitants cannot trouble them much having neither Boats nor Iron.

The Inhabitants of this Country are the miserablest People in the World. The *Hodmadods* of *Monomatapa*, though a nasty People, yet for Wealth are Gentlemen to these; who have no Houses, and skin Garments, Sheep, Poultry, and Fruits of the Earth, Ostrich Eggs, &c. as the *Hodmadods* have: And setting aside their Humane Shape, they differ but little from Brutes. They are tall, strait-bodied, and thin, with small long Limbs. They have great Heads, round Foreheads, and great Brows. Their Eye-lids are always half closed, to keep the Flies out of their Eyes; they being so troublesome here, that no fanning will keep them from coming to one's Face; and without the Assistance of both Hands to keep them off, they will creep into ones Nostrils, and Mouth too, if the Lips are not shut very close; so that from their Infancy being thus annoyed with these Insects, they do never open their Eyes as other People: And therefore they cannot see far, unless they hold up their Heads, as if they were looking at somewhat over them.

They have great Bottle-Noses, pretty full Lips, and wide Mouths. The two Fore-teeth of their Upper-jaw are wanting in all of them, Men and Women, old and young; whether they draw them out, I know not: Neither have they any Beards. They are long-visaged, and of a very unpleasing Aspect, having no one graceful Feature in their Faces. Their

Hair is black, short and curl'd, like that of the Negroes; and not long and lank like the common *Indians.* The Colour of their Skins, both of their Faces and the rest of their Body, is Coal-black, like that of the Negroes of *Guinea.*

They have no sort of Cloaths, but a piece of the Rind of a Tree tied like a Girdle about their Waists, and a handful of long Grass, or three or four small green Boughs full of Leaves, thrust under their Girdle, to cover their Nakedness.

They have no Houses, but lie in the open Air without any covering; the Earth being their Bed, and the Heaven their Canopy. Whether they cohabit one Man to one Woman, or promiscuously, I know not; but they do live in Companies, 20 or 30 Men, Women, and Children together. Their only Food is a small sort of Fish, which they get by making Wares of Stone across little Coves or Branches of the Sea; every Tide bringing in the small Fish, and there leaving them for a Prey to these People, who constantly attend there to search for them at Low-water. This small Fry I take to be the top of their Fishery: They have no Instruments to catch great Fish, should they come; and such seldom stay to be left behind at Low-water: Nor could we catch any Fish with our Hooks and Lines all the while we lay there. In other Places at Low-water they seek for Cockles, Muscles, and Periwincles: Of these Shell-fish there are fewer still; so that their chiefest dependance is upon what the Sea leaves in their Wares; which, be it much or little they gather up, and march to the Places of their Abode. There the old People that are not able to stir abroad by reason of their Age, and the tender Infants, wait their return; and what Providence has bestowed on them, they presently broil on the Coals, and eat it in common. Sometimes they get as many Fish as makes them a plentiful Banquet; and at other times they scarce get every one a taste: But be it little or much that they get, every one has his part, as well the young and tender, the old and fee-ble, who are not able to go abroad, as the strong and lusty. When they have eaten they lie down till the next Low-water, and then all that are able march out, be it Night or Day, rain or shine, 'tis all one; they must attend the Wares, or else they must fast: For the Earth affords them no Food at all. There is neither Herb, Root, Pulse nor any sort of Grain for them to eat, that we saw; nor any sort of Bird or Beast that they can catch, having no Instruments wherewithal to do so.

I did not perceive that they did worship any thing. These poor Creatures have a sort of Weapon to defend their Ware, or fight with their Enemies, if they have any that will interfere with their poor Fishery. They did at first endeavour with their Weapons to frighten us, who lying ashore deterr'd them from one of their Fishing-places. Some of them had wooden Swords, others had a sort of Lances. The Sword is a piece of Wood shaped somewhat like a Cutlass. The Lance is a long strait Pole sharp at one end, and hardened afterwards by heat. I saw no Iron, nor any other sort of Metal; therefore it is probable they use Stone-Hatchets, as some *Indians* in *America* do ...

How they get their Fire I know not; but probably as *Indians* do, out of Wood. I have seen the *Indians* of *Bon-Airy* do it, and have my self tried the Experiment: They take a flat piece of Wood that is pretty soft, and make a small dent in one side of it, then they take another hard round Stick, about the bigness of one's little Finger, and sharpening it at one end like a Pencil, they put that sharp end in the hole or dent of the flat soft piece, and then rubbing or twirling the hard piece between the Palms of their Hands, they drill the soft piece till it smoaks, and at last takes Fire.

These People speak somewhat thro' the Throat; but we could not understand one word that they said. We anchored, as I said before, *January* the 5th, and seeing Men walking on the Shore, we presently sent a Canoa to get some Acquaintance with them: for we were in hopes to get some Provision among them. But the Inhabitants, seeing our Boat coming, run away and hid themselves. We searched afterwards three Days in hopes to find their Houses; but found none: yet we saw many places where they had made Fires. At last, being out of hopes to find their Habitations, we searched no farther; but left a great many Toys ashore, in such places where we thought that they would come. In all our search we found no Water, but old Wells on the sandy Bays.

At last we went over to the Islands, and there we found a great many of the Natives: I do believe there were 40 on one Island, Men, Women and Children. The Men at our first coming ashore, threatned us with their Lances and Swords; but they were frighted by firing one Gun, which we fired purposely to scare them. The Island was so small that they could not hide themselves: but they were much disordered at our Landing, especially the Women and Children: for we went directly to their Camp. The lustiest of the Women snatching up their Infants ran away howling, and the little Children run after squeaking and bawling; but the Men stood still. Some of the Women, and such People as could not go from us, lay still by a Fire, making a doleful noise, as if we had been coming to devour them: but when they saw we did not intend to harm them, they were pretty quiet, and the rest that fled from us at our first coming, returned again. This their place of Dwelling was only a Fire, with a few Boughs before it, set up on that side the Winds was of.

After we had been here a little while, the Men began to be familiar, and we cloathed some of them, designing to have had some service of them for it: for we found some Wells of Water here, and intended to carry 2 or 3 Barrels of it aboard. But it being somewhat troublesome to carry to the Canoas, we thought to have made these Men to have carry'd it for us, and therefore we gave them some old Cloaths; to one an old pair of Breeches, to another a ragged Shirt, to the third a Jacket that was scarce worth owning; which yet would have been very acceptable at some places where we had been, and so we thought they might have been with these People. We put them on them, thinking that this finery would have brought them to work heartily for us; and our Water being filled in small long Barrels, about six Gallons in each, which were made purposely to carry Water in, we brought these our new Servants to the Wells, and put a Barrel on each of their Shoulders for them to carry to the Canoa. But all the signs we could make were to no purpose, for they stood like Statues, without motion, but grinn'd like so many Monkeys, staring one upon another: For these poor Creatures seem not accustomed to carry Burthens; and I believe that one of our Ship-boys of 10 Years old, would carry as much as one of them. So we were forced to carry our Water our selves, and they very fairly put the Cloaths off again, and laid them down, as if Cloaths were only to work in. I did not perceive that they had any great liking to them at first, neither did they seem to admire any thing that we had.

At another time our Canoa being among these Islands seeking for Game, espy'd a drove of these Men swimming from one Island to another; for they have no Boats, Canoas, or Bark-logs. They took up Four of them, and brought them aboard; two of them were middle-aged, the other two were young Men about 18 or 20 Years old. To these we gave boiled Rice, and with it Turtle and Manatee boiled. They did greedily devour what we gave them, but took no notice of the Ship, or any thing in it, and when they were set on Land again, they ran away as fast as they could. At our first coming, before we were acquainted with them, or they with us, a Company of them who liv'd on the Main, came just against our Ship, and standing on a pretty high Bank, threatned us with their Swords and Lances, by shaking them at us: At last the Captain ordered the Drum to be beaten, which was done of a sudden with much vigour, purposely to scare the poor Creatures. They hearing the noise, ran away as fast as they could drive; and when they ran away in haste, they would cry *Gurry, Gurry*, speaking deep in the Throat. Those Inhabitants also that live on the Main, would always run away from us; yet we took several of them. For, as I have already observed, they had such bad Eyes, that they could not see us till we came close to them. We did always give them Victuals, and let them go again, but the Islanders, after our first time of being among them, did not stir for us.

When we had been here about a Week, we hal'd our Ship into a small sandy Cove, at a Spring-tide, as far as she would float; and at low Water she was left dry, and the Sand dry without us near half a Mile; for the Sea riseth and falleth here about five fathom. The Flood runs North by East, and the Ebb South by West. All the Neep-tides we lay wholly a-ground, for the Sea did not come near us by about a hundred Yards. We had therefore time enough to clean our Ships bottom, which we did very well. Most of our Men lay ashore in a Tent, where our Sails were mending; and our Strikers brought home Turtle and Manatee every Day, which was our constant Food.

While we lay here, I did endeavour to persuade our Men to go to some *English* Factory; but was threatned to be turned ashore, and left here for it. This made me desist, and patiently wait for some more convenient place and opportunity to leave them, than here: Which I did hope I should accomplish in a short time; because they did intend, when they went from hence, to bear down towards Cape *Comorin*. In their way thither they designed also to visit the Island *Cocos*, which lieth in Lat. 12 d. 12 m. North, by our Drafts; hoping there to find of that Fruit; the Island having its Name from thence.

A New Voyage Round the World (1729 edition, first published 1697)

WILLEM DE VLAMINGH
(1640–?)

Dutch mariner. While searching for a lost ship, de Vlamingh visited a small island off the west coast of New Holland, not far from present-day Perth, in December 1696. The sighting by his men of numerous quokkas (short-tailed wallabies), which they took to be rats, resulted in the place being named Rottnest (originally Rottenest) Island, after the Dutch word for 'rat nest'. De Vlamingh subsequently surveyed part of the mainland coast before departing for Batavia in February 1697.

A NEST OF RATS

[December] the 30th in the morning the wind southerly, slight top-gallant breeze, resolved together to send our boats ashore, to wit our and the hooker's longboats to sail round the island to search for any remains of lost sailors or anything else and our pinnace with our book-keeper and upper-steersman and the commander of the soldiers with 12 soldiers to go through the aforesaid island what might be on shore. And the small boat having come back on board towards evening, our bookkeeper reported that he and the people with him had gone through and searched everything thoroughly, and that of animals there is nothing there but bush rats of which they shot a few and brought with them on board and various trees with a pleasant fragrance. After seeking a long time, had finally found a place where they dug a hole from which they obtained fine fresh water, of which they brought a sample on board which I found very good. After sunset our under-steersman came back on board with our longboat, reported to have seen no remains or anything else of lost ships; the wind as above with topgallant breeze until the morning.

[December] the 31st Monday in the morning the wind from WSW to S, stiff topsail breeze. After breakfast I went ashore with our book-keeper and sent our longboat ashore with a party of hands to cut fire-wood which was to be had there in abundance and very fine of fragrance just like rosewood, of which I have had some in our own boat full taken on board, and let our bookkeeper examine the island further. On coming back reported to have found nothing more than related above. Back on board towards the evening the steersman who had been on board reported that he and all the crew had seen much smoke rise up on the mainland coast; by evening the wind as before until the morning.

Voyage to the Great South Land (1985, first published in Dutch 1976)

––––

JAMES COOK
(1728–79)

English navigator and cartographer. One of the best known of all British explorers, Cook led three major expeditions to the Pacific. In 1770, during the first (1768–71), he sailed north along the east coast of New Holland

and eventually claimed the eastern part of the continent for Britain at Possession Island. Along the way he made several landings, the first of which was at Botany Bay, where he stepped ashore in April.

BOTANY BAY

Sunday 29th — In the PM winds southerly clear weather with which we stood into the bay and Anchor'd under the South shore about 2 Mile within the entrence in 6 fathoms water, the south point bearing SE and the north point East. Saw as we came in on both points of the bay Several of the natives and a few hutts, Men, women and children on the south shore abreast of the Ship, to which place I went in the boats in hopes of speaking with them accompaned by Mr Banks Dr Solander and Tupia; as we approached the shore they all made off except two Men who seemd resolved to oppose our landing. As soon as I saw this I orderd the boats to lay upon their oars in order to speake to them but this was to little purpose for neither us nor Tupia could understand one word they said. We then threw them some nails beeds &ca a shore which they took up and seem'd not ill pleased in so much that I thout that they beckon'd to us to come a shore; but in this we were mistaken, for as soon as we put the boat in they again came to oppose us upon which I fired a musket between the two which had no other effect than to make them retire back where bundles of thier darts lay, and one of them took up a stone and threw at us which caused my fireing a second Musquet load with small shott, and altho some of the shott struck the man yet it had no other effect than to make him lay hold of a Shield or target to defend himself. Emmidiatly after this we landed which we had no sooner done than they throw'd two darts at us, this obliged me to fire a third shott soon after which they both made off, but not in such haste but what we might have taken one, but Mr Banks being of opinion that the darts were poisoned, made me cautious how I advanced into the woods. We found here a few Small hutts made of the bark of trees in one of which were four or five small children with whome we left some strings of beeds &ca. A quantity of darts lay about the hutts these we took away with us. Three Canoes lay upon the bea[c]h the worst I think I ever saw, they were about 12 or 14 feet long made of one peice of the bark of a tree drawn or tied up at each end and the middle kept open by means of peices of sticks by way of Thwarts.

After searching for fresh water without success except a little in a small hole dug in the sand, we embarqued and went over to the north point of the bay w[h]ere in coming in we saw several people, but when

we now landed there were no body to be seen. We found here some
fresh water which came trinkling down and stood in pools among the
rocks; but as this was troblesome to come at I sent a party of men a
shore in the morning to the place where we first landed to dig holes in
the sand by which means and a small stream they found fresh water
sufficient to water the ship. The strings of beeds &ca we had left with
the children last night were found laying in the hut this morning,
probably the natives were afraid to take them away. After breakfast we
sent some empty casks a shore and a party of men to cut wood and I
went my self in the Pinnace to sound and explore the Bay, in the doing
of which I saw several of the natives but they all fled at my approach.
I landed in two places one of which the people had but just left, as
there were small fires and fresh muscles broiling upon them — here
likewise lay vast heaps of the largest oyster shells I ever saw.

The Voyage of the Endeavour, *1768–1771* (1955)

KENNETH SLESSOR

(1901–71)

Australian poet and journalist. Slessor's Five Visions of Captain Cook, *first
published in 1931, is considered to be one of the most significant 'voyager'
poems in Australian literature. Partly based on Cook's journals, it opens with
the following portrait of the great seafarer.*

FROM 'FIVE VISIONS OF CAPTAIN COOK'

Cook was a captain of the Admiralty
When sea-captains had the evil eye,
Or should have, what with beating krakens off
And casting nativities of ships;
Cook was a captain of the powder-days
When captains, you might have said, if you had been
Fixed by their glittering stare, half-down the side,
Or gaping at them up companionways,
Were more like warlocks than a humble man —
And men were humble then who gazed at them,

Poor horn-eyed sailors, bullied by devils' fists
Of wind or water, or the want of both,
Childlike and trusting, filled with eager trust —
Cook was a captain of the sailing days
When sea-captains were kings like this,
Not cold executives of company-rules
Cracking their boilers for a dividend
Or bidding their engineers go wink
At bells and telegraphs, so plates would hold
Another pound. Those captains drove their ships
By their own blood, no laws of schoolbook steam,
Till yards were sprung, and masts went overboard —
Daemons in periwigs, doling magic out,
Who read fair alphabets in stars
Where humbler men found but a mess of sparks,
Who steered their crews by mysteries
And strange, half-dreaded sortilege with books,
Used medicines that only gods could know
The sense of, but sailors drank
In simple faith. That was the captain
Cook was when he came to the Coral Sea
And chose a passage into the dark.

How many mariners had made that choice
Paused on the brink of mystery! 'Choose now!'
The winds roared, blowing home, blowing home,
Over the Coral Sea. 'Choose now!' the trades
Cried once to Tasman, throwing him for choice
Their teeth or shoulders, and the Dutchman chose
The wind's way, turning north. 'Choose, Bougainville!'
The wind cried once, and Bougainville had heard
The voice of God, calling him prudently
Out of a dead lee shore, and chose the north.
The wind's way. So, too, Cook made choice,
Over the brink, into the devil's mouth,
With four months' food, and sailors wild with dreams
Of English beer, the smoking barns of home.
So Cook made choice, so Cook sailed westabout,
So men write poems in Australia.

Selected Poems (1977 edition)

MATTHEW FLINDERS

(1774–1814)

English navigator. Matthew Flinders and George Bass sailed around Van Diemen's Land in 1798–99, confirming the existence of a strait between it and New South Wales, now known as Bass Strait. Here Flinders gives some words of advice about that treacherous stretch of water. He subsequently circumnavigated the Australian continent (1801–03), charting large sections of the coast, after which he wrote A Voyage to Terra Australis *(1814).*

'BASS'S STRAIT'

The extensive passage which separates Van Diemen's Land from New Holland, was named Bass's Strait by governor Hunter. Mr Bass had visited the north side of it in an open whale boat, from Port Jackson, in January, 1797; and the magnitude of the swell which he found rolling in from the south-westward, strongly indicated its origin to be from the southern Indian Ocean; and came so strong in confirmation of the former suppositions of an existing strait, that His Excellency the governor, thought proper to order me in a vessel to ascertain its certainty, by sailing through it. It was with pleasure that I was able to associate Mr Bass in the expedition; but much more so, that our success enabled the governor to pay a just tribute to his personal exertions and correct judgment.

In giving some caution to those who may first sail through Bass's Strait, it is necessary to observe, that as several unknown isles and rocks may probably lie to the westward of Hunter's Isles; a ship should be cautious in running down the last two or three degrees of longitude, before she make the isles.

The latitude of 40° 20' is a proper parallel with a leading wind. After seeing Albatross Island, Three-hummock Island will immediately appear, and leave no doubt as to what land it is.

The land of considerable extent which is marked in the chart as uncertainly known, is represented to be low land. It was seen by Mr Reed, in the schooner Martha; but its longitude is very uncertain. The latitude of its south end may have some little reliance put in it.

With the wind to the northward of west, it would be as well to go to windward of Kent's Group; but after that, not to steer a more northerly course than north-east-by-east, until certain of being to the eastward of Cape Howe. In all cases, the long beach is to be avoided, even if it should be a weather shore at the time.

A ship bound to Port Jackson, and meeting with a foul wind, would find Hamilton's Road a convenient place to anchor in for a few days.

It may be necessary to observe to some, that I can by no means answer for there being no rocks or islands in the middle of the strait; or indeed in any of the blank places, except a few miles on each side of the *day* track. Islands and rocks must be expected to be fallen in with in other places; it therefore behoves every man who has the charge of a ship here, to run with caution in the day; and if he does run during a moon-light night, it should be under working sail, and with the best look-out. But with every advantage, it would be to hazardous to run before the wind in the night.

Observations on the Coasts of Van Diemen's Land, on Bass's Strait and its Islands, and on Part of the Coasts of New South Wales (1801)

———

ERNESTINE HILL

(1900–72)

Australian writer. Ernestine Hill's extensive travels in the outback provided her with the material for her best-known works, The Great Australian Loneliness *(1937) and* The Territory *(1951). She also travelled around Australia, in the wake of Flinders' navigation, as part of her preparation for writing her only novel, the wartime bestseller* My Love Must Wait *(1941), which was based on that navigator's life. Flinders' love did, indeed, have to wait. He and Ann Chappell married in 1801, expecting that she would accompany him on his forthcoming voyage, but the Admiralty refused her permission to go. The couple were to remain apart for the next nine years, during part of which time Flinders was imprisoned on Mauritius by the French. Hill, who seems to have become besotted with her subject, concludes the novel with a rather odd non-fiction eulogy, of which this forms part.*

REMEMBERING FLINDERS

A valuable *Life of Matthew Flinders* was written by the late Professor Ernest Scott, from wide research and all data then available, in 1914.

It was eight years later that Sir W. M. Flinders Petrie offered his grand-father's intimate diaries and letter-books to the archives of the first Australian State that would have the grace to perpetuate his memory in the erection of a statue. By this time we were 'Flinders-conscious', and competition was keen. New South Wales, in the interests of the Mitchell Library, storehouse of the nation's history, promptly produced an expensive effigy with more haste than thought. The bronze figure purporting to be Flinders that guards its portals to-day is a poor pre-sentation of a great sailor.

Not to be outdone, the other States followed. Melbourne, in an imaginative conception by the sculptor Web Gilbert, accorded him pride of the place in the city, beside St Paul's Cathedral, in contempla-tion of the vast railway station that bears his name. It was unveiled to an oratorio composed for the occasion, 'Let Us Praise Famous Men'.

In Adelaide, a more lifelike commemoration of 'the indefatigable Flinders', a sturdy young Lincolnshire sea-captain, his eyes a-dream of 'the vacant spaces of the map', was erected by public subscription, con-vened by the late Sir Frank Moulden, Mr A. S. Diamond and the late Fred Johns. Lord Tennyson, at one time Governor of South Australia, was a grandson of Flinders, and son of Alfred Tennyson, poet laureate of England.

The fatal Third Log-book, confiscated by Decaen, for which Flin-ders fretted to the end of his days, was lost for nearly 130 years. Its facts and fabric have gone to the making of this book. It was discovered in the London Records Office in 1927 by Miss Ida Leeson, Mitchell Librarian, in a miscellany of old mariners' manuscripts unclassified.

In all probability, it had been restored by the French Government to the British at the time when Phillip Parker King, who was to com-plete Flinders's unfinished work on the north and north-west coasts, made application for it in 1818. Recognized as a treasure, it was not generously presented to Miss Leeson by the Records Office, though the originals of the *Investigator's* first and second log-books are among the most carefully-guarded manuscripts of the Mitchell Library. Her share of the discovery she had made was a photostat copy.

Poring over the old letter-books and diaries—so much of emotion, so much of thought in the faded copper-plate handwriting of one who so loved the world—has been to me one of the rarest pleasures of the writing. Flinders forever lives in those sea-stained pages, the ink bronzed and burnished by time, of his own written word.

On his map of the new continent, on which he had inscribed a thousand names for friendship, for association, and in his humorous fancy, he claimed nothing for himself. The years between have given him tribute. Those who followed could never forget him.

From Cape Leeuwin nine thousand miles to the Wessel Islands, both commemorating the valiant Dutch sailors drifting down in olden day, from Flinders Bay in the south-west to Flinders River in Carpentaria, all the explorers since have paid him his due respect. Islands, headlands, inlets, and lighthouses innumerable hold memory of his epic work, notable among them the Flinders Passage, the channel he found in his nine days' travail through the Great Barrier Reef. The Flinders Ranges in South Australia, 300 miles from south to north, their colourful peaks majestic against the desert sky, are worthy monument. The tufted yellow *Flindersia*, that blows all over the continent, is one of the richest fodder grasses of a mighty pastoral land.

His name is a household word in our five capital cities, each of them having conferred it on one of the principal streets. The little towns are legion where you will find it. Australia's great naval training school in Victoria is the Flinders Base. Flinders Column, the tall white monolith on Mount Lofty, visible for sixty miles by day and night, is one of our great southern aviation lights, in this century a beacon to navigators of aerial seas. The most modern locomotive of Commonwealth railways, that glossy green giant, stream-lined in its strength, that swings the Spirit of Progress nightly between Melbourne and Sydney at seventy miles an hour, is the *Matthew Flinders*.

Even the blacks immortalized his memory. At the Wessel Islands, where he left the survey off the coast of Arnhem Land, there are caves with crude drawings of Stone Age Man, Old Masters in red ochre and pipe-clay depicting his redcoat marines with their white cross-bands. Mrs Daisy Bates, the famous 'White Mother of a Black Race', assures me that in her wanderings among the Bibbulmun aboriginal tribes of the south-west of Australia, an ancient native named Nebinyan danced for her the 'Kurranup' dance of Flinders's men, when he drilled them to amuse a simple, savage people of the woods of King George's Sound. That corroboree of the 'white brothers' had survived five generations.

In the windy solitudes of the Gulf of Carpentaria, on the brown crest of Observation Island, where, limping with illness, oppressed with fever and the knowledge that his ship was breaking, he discovered that his time-keepers were three degrees out of reckoning, I stood beside a little cairn of stones. It was erected there by Commander Bennett of HMAS *Geranium* in 1925, dedicated to Matthew Flinders's memory. As I travelled his ship-tracks all round Australia, visioning a new land through his eyes, I have noted no monument, no recognition, that would be dearer to him than that rough cairn of stones, where no ships pass to-day.

Still stands that chart of Carpentaria, the original lost in shipwreck, the duplicate compiled from stray notes and a genius of mathematic memory, as the only existing documentary knowledge of too-long-neglected shores.

For the rest, our one hundred and fifty years have seen a miracle of change. Leviathan ships of the world follow the track of *Tom Thumb* through Sydney Heads, to carry away thousands of Australia's sons fighting for Britain's empire.

Now the sandhills where he wandered, theodolite on shoulder, look down on pulsing cities and prosperous towns. Rarely did his instinct fail him in visions of the future. From Albany in the far south-west, to Cape York, the apex of the continent, a chain of great ports and happy havens was of his finding.

The one blind spot in his eye was for Australia's rivers. It is a curious fact that Flinders found none. He missed the mouth of the Murray, one of earth's greatest, though, as I have told in 'Fleur-de-Lis', its tumbled breakers were sighted. He missed the broad stream of the Clarence—though he anchored in its harbour—and passed unseeing, two thousand miles to the Roper, all the rich waterways of the east and the north coast that swing down from the Great Dividing Range to slink through sand-flats and sandhills into the sea. As one who knew only the free English rivers, he could not be prepared for such deception. But he was to circumnavigate Australia again after this preliminary survey. Let us remember that he left his work unfinished when he was only twenty-eight years old.

That was the most poignant sadness of his life.

In our brotherhood with America, Great Britain's eldest child, it is a fact too long forgotten that we claim the same birthplace. The square tower of Boston Stump looked down on the little ships that sailed to great beginnings; that low coast of East Anglia has mothered two great nations.

From there the Pilgrim Fathers buffeted the lonely sea in quest of God and freedom. From there the Whitby collier *Endeavour* followed a star of destiny to strange adventure. Banks, Bass, Flinders and Franklin dreamed of the Unknown in those tranquil Fenland villages, all within the throb of Boston bells.

And the greatest of these is Flinders, 'that obscure name', as he wrote to Sir Joseph, at last a 'ray of glory'. The map of Australia is his memorial. For his consuming love of this country, his great achievement when it was a shapeless bulk in the minds of men, un-lucky and unwanted, he will some day be crowned our national hero.

The soul of Matthew Flinders lives in every boy who points the prow of his little skiff to sea.

As the life's work of his illustrious grandson leads back across the age-old past to earth's beginning, so his life's work rolls as a crested wave to the triumphs of the timeless future.

While the old order crumbles in Europe, in the new world that we shall build, Australia, continent of his naming, faces the dawn.

My Love Must Wait (1942 edition, first published 1941)

———

NICOLAS BAUDIN

(1754–1803)

French navigator. Baudin led an expedition, generally considered to be fairly unsuccessful, which charted parts of the coasts of Van Diemen's Land and New Holland between 1801 and 1803. In April 1802 he unexpectedly met Matthew Flinders on the coast of present-day South Australia, at a place which the latter man named, for obvious reasons, Encounter Bay.

AN 'AGREEABLE MEETING'

At daybreak on the 18th [8 April] we stood in for the coast in order to continue our work. But it was ten o'clock before we could begin, as we found ourselves further off shore than our overnight depth had seemed to indicate. We steered North-East to within a short league of the land. This brought us into another broad, deep bay with as little of interest as those we had visited up to that time. To get out of it, we had to steer successively from North-East to North-West by West. The entire stretch of coast that we have examined since yesterday consists solely of sand-hills and inspires nothing but gloom and disappointment. Quite apart from the unpleasant view that it offers, the sea breaks with extraordinary force all along the shore, and two or three swells preceding the breakers indicate that there is a bar there which must reach at least half a mile out to sea.

The look-out men at the mast-heads and the curious who wanted to climb up there reported that the hinterland was nothing but arid sand for as far as the eye could see, with no vegetation.

The coast that we explored on this day had, however, an advantage over that of yesterday: the water was much deeper and the bottom regular. Although only a bare league off shore, we never had less than 16 fathoms when doubling the points of the small coves along it and 19 to 20 on either side of them.

At midday the latitude observed was 36° 1' 10" and the chronometer put us in 137° 9' 40" of longitude.

In the afternoon we continued along a stretch of coast consisting entirely of sand-hills. But towards three o'clock we began to see some high terrain which looked as if it must be pleasant. Shortly after, we sighted a ship which we thought at first could only be the *Naturaliste*, for we were far from thinking that there would be any other Europeans in this region and at this time of the year. Nevertheless, we were greatly mistaken, for as we drew near her, we realised from her masts and size that she was not our consort. Finally, at five o'clock, when we were both able to see each other clearly, this ship made a signal which we did not understand and so did not answer. She then ran up the English flag and shortened sail. We, for our part, hoisted the national flag, and I braced sharp up to draw alongside her. As they spoke us first, they asked what the ship was. I replied that she was French. Then they asked if Captain Baudin was her commander. I was very surprised, not only at the question, but at hearing myself named as well. When I said yes, the English ship brought to. Seeing her make ready to send a boat across, I likewise brought to to wait for it. The English captain, Mr Flinders (the very one who discovered the strait which should bear his name, but which has most inappropriately been called Banks Strait), came aboard, expressed great satisfaction at this agreeable meeting, but was extremely reserved on all other matters. As soon as I learnt his name, I paid him my compliments and told him of the pleasure that I had in making his acquaintance, etc. I informed him of all that we had done up till then in the way of geographical work. As it was already late, Mr Flinders said that if I were willing to stand off and on till dawn, he would return the following day and give me various pieces of information concerning the coast that he had examined from Cape Leeuwin as far as here. I was very gratified by his proposal and we agreed to remain together during the night. The weather was very fine.

On the morning of the 19th [9 April], seeing that Mr Flinders was making ready to come aboard again, as he had said he would the day before, I hove to once more to await him. He arrived at half past six, accompanied by the same person as on the earlier occasion. As he was much less reserved on this second visit than before, he told me that his ship was the Investigator and that he had left Europe about eight months after I had. He also told me that he had begun his exploration of the coast of New Holland at Cape Leeuwin. He had visited the Isles of St Peter and St Francis, as well as all the coast up to the point of our meeting. In addition, he informed me of the lay-out of a port that he had discovered on an island. This latter was only 15 or 20 leagues from where we were, and he had named it Kangaroo Island because of the great numbers of that animal that he found there. According to his report, the island is long, high and extensive, and there is a good passage between it and the mainland. He stayed six weeks there and so had time to examine it well.

Before we separated, Mr Flinders gave me several charts published by Arrowsmith since our departure. As I told him of the accident that had befallen my dinghy and asked him to give it all the help he could if he should chance to meet it, he told me of a similar misfortune that had happened to him, for he had lost eight men and a boat on his Kangaroo Island. His companion ship had also been separated from him during the equinoctial gale, part of which I had weathered in Bass Strait and the remainder outside. Upon leaving, Mr Flinders said that he was going to make for the strait and try to find some land which was said to exist between the Hunter Group and the place that they have named Western Port. We parted at eight o'clock, each wishing the other a safe voyage.

There was little wind for the rest of the day. Sometimes we were even becalmed and at the mercy of the current, which carried us towards the coast, then only a league off. After sighting our points of the previous day, we sailed along the high land that we had seen a little before sunset. The coast in this part, if not extremely pleasant, was at least preferable to the region of sand-hills that we had just left.

At midday the latitude observed was 35° 36', but this was very uncertain. At three o'clock we sighted the island and islets spoken of by Mr Flinders. I proceeded so as to run in for the channel separating them from the mainland, but since the slight wind blowing did not allow me to do this before dark, I went about at five o'clock to stand out to sea.

Coasting the mainland during the day, we sighted three islets or rocks lying such a short way out, that to see them, it was necessary to be as close in as we were. If becalmed, one could anchor there in 24 or 21 fathoms, for the bottom is sandy and good — a rather rare thing between here and the Promontory. At sunset we could still see Mr Flinders' ship running on the South-westerly leg.

Until midnight the winds were South to South-South-East and rather fresh, but then they moderated, and shortly after, we went on the landward leg.

The Journal of Post Captain Nicolas Baudin, trans. Christine Cornell *(1974)*

―――

PHILLIP PARKER KING

(1791–1856)

Australian hydrographer. Phillip Parker King, the son of Philip Gidley King, was born on Norfolk Island. After being educated in England, he entered the navy in 1807. King surveyed parts of the Australian coast between 1818 and 1822. Here he describes helping John Oxley in 1819 to chart Port Macquarie, which the latter had 'discovered' and named after the then governor in the previous year. After surveying the southern coasts of South America from 1826 to 1830, King returned to New South Wales in 1832, where he later became commissioner of the Australian Agricultural Company.

CHARTING PORT MACQUARIE

The next morning we anchored off Port Macquarie; and, whilst the Lady Nelson was beating up to an anchorage, Lieutenant Oxley accompanied me in the whale-boat to examine the entrance.

In pulling in we got among the sand rollers on the north side, on which the sea broke so heavy as at one time to endanger the boat's upsetting; but fortunately we escaped with only the loss of an oar; after contending for some time against the tide, which was ebbing with great strength, we landed on the south side; when we were met by five natives, who had been watching us all the morning, and had not been backward in their invitations and entreaties for us to land. At first they kept aloof until approached by Lieutenant Oxley, whom they soon recognised: after a short interview, in which they appeared to place the greatest confidence in all our movements, we ascended the hill to observe the channel over the bar; the water of which was so clear, that the deepest part was easily seen. As this was the principal object, we did not delay longer on shore than was necessary, and upon our return sounded the depth of water upon the bar and in the channel, the particulars of which are detailed upon the plan of the harbour.

The next morning the two vessels were warped into the port; and, by eleven o'clock, were anchored within a few yards of the south shore, and secured to trees near the beach, close to a fresh water stream which ran into the sea.

The following day we pulled three or four miles up the river; on the way up two natives were seen in a canoe, but on our approach they landed to avoid us, and quickly disappeared. The boat was kept in mid-stream, and we passed by without taking any notice of them. Half a mile further on we put ashore on the south bank, and took bearings to fix the position of our station and the direction of the next reach upwards, which appeared to be about three miles long, and half a mile broad. We then returned to the cutter, and on the 14th Lieutenant Oxley and Mr Roe accompanied me in one of our boats upon the examination of the river.

After reaching our former station on the south bank, we proceeded up the long reach towards Black-man Point, on which a tribe of natives were collected: the river is here divided into two streams; we followed that which trended to the westward, as it appeared to be the most considerable. At the end of the next reach the river is again divided into two branches, and as the southernmost was found, upon trial, to be the shoalest, the other was followed. On our left was a small contracted arm, which probably communicates with the lagoon on Rawdon Island; here we landed to examine the trees which so thickly and beautifully cover both banks: several sorts of large growth were noticed, among which was a tree of the *trichilliea*, nat. ord. Juss. (*trichillia glandulosa*,) which the colonists have flattered with the name of rose-wood, and a *ficus* of gigantic growth, both of which are very abundant. We landed at Point Elizabeth, and walked a mile back through a fine open country, well timbered and richly clothed with luxuriant grass, and apparently much frequented by kangaroos.

From the edge of the bank Mount Cairncross, a remarkable round-topped hill, which is conspicuously seen from the coast over the entrance of the port, appeared over the next reach, and formed a rich picturesque back-ground for the view.

After refreshing ourselves, we re-imbarked, and passed on our right a shoal inlet, in which we saw a native's weir, for the purpose of taking fish; it was formed by sticks stuck in the mud, and so close as to prevent the retreat of such as were inside: three miles above this we landed on an open grassy spot on the south bank, and pitched our tent for the night.

About half an hour before we landed, we heard the voices of natives in the woods; who, after we passed by, embarked in two canoes and followed us for some distance, but the near approach of night obliged us to look out for a convenient spot to encamp upon; so that the natives, finding they were unattended to, soon gave up their pursuit.

In the morning, before we embarked, our barica was filled at a water-hole close at hand; on walking about a quarter of a mile back, we came to the borders of a large circular plain, about one mile in diameter, covered with reeds and other indications of its being a morass or lagoon.

We then pursued our way up the river; it soon trended sharply round to the S.E., and joined the main stream, which we had unknowingly left the preceding evening. There we had to unload and drag the boat over a fall; but, as the ascent was not more than ten or twelve inches, no difficulty was experienced in effecting it. Whilst thus employed, we were visited by ten natives, some of whom, by being painted and ornamented in a remarkable manner, were recognised as those who followed us last evening: their timidity was at first very great, but our conduct gave them confidence, and they very soon came to the boat, and assisted in launching her into deeper water, for which service they were presented with fishing hooks and lines, which they gladly received. Every thing we said or did was repeated by them with the most exact imitation; and indeed they appeared to think they could not please us better than by mimicking every motion that we made. Some biscuit was given them, which they pretended to eat, but on our looking aside were observed to spit it out. They wished much to take us to their huts; but, the day being much advanced, without our having made any progress, we were obliged to decline their invitation; and as soon as the boat was reloaded, we took leave of these friendly Indians, whose voices we heard until a turn of the river hid their persons from our view. About two miles higher, at King's River, Lieutenant Oxley landed and recognised his former tracks, which were now much overgrown and nearly effaced; the marks of the axe were, however, sufficiently evident for us to follow them for half a mile along the banks of the river, when we re-imbarked, and continued our course upwards.

The river now became much narrower, not being more than seventy or eighty yards wide; four miles higher up we landed, and joined Mr Cunningham, who was botanizing in the Lady Nelson's boat: this gentleman had overtaken us about an hour before, and passed on to look for a convenient place to encamp for the night; but for want of a better situation, was obliged to land in a brush, the banks of which were so thickly lined with trees and climbing plants, that we should have passed it if the station had not been indicated to us by his boat made fast to the landing place.

Some rain fell during the night, but this inconvenience was trifling compared to the discordant screams of a bird which had roosted over our fires, and which the people called the cat-bird. The *trichillia* and the *ficus*, before noticed, are abundant on these banks, and are all intricately connected with each other by climbing plants, which grow to an incredible size, and hang down in rich clusters from the summit to the root of the tree, tending considerably to beautify the richness of the scene.

The woods included every tree of the soil and climate, excepting a white and straight stemmed *eucalyptus*, which is common at Hunter's River, and there called the Flooded Gum; it is used and reckoned valuable for spars, but the few specimens that I have seen of it have been very brittle and bad. Some of these trees were observed by us to be from fifty to sixty feet high, perfectly straight, and without a fork for forty feet.

The next morning our boats, in company, proceeded for two miles farther up; in this space we crossed four falls, the last of which, running with great rapidity, occasioned some difficulty and trouble in passing over it: a little above this fall our exploration terminated, and we stopped to examine the timber. Several cedar-trees, (*cedrelea toona*) of large growth, were observed; one of which, being measured, was found to be ten feet in diameter at the base.

The upper part of the river is studded with islets covered with the *casuarina paludosa*, which is abundant in the swamps and low grounds at Port Jackson, where the colonists call it the 'Swamp Oak.' The river appeared to be subject to inundations, for marks of floods were visible in all parts, and some considerably beyond the banks.

On our return we landed at a high rocky head on the north bank, from which a tract of open country appeared to recede. From hence Brown's Bluff bore S. 32º W. This Bluff is a remarkable hill, and is distinctly seen from the coast: its position was fixed by Mr Oxley on his last journey, who passing within a few miles, rode to its summit to gain a view of the country, which he described as very extensive and beautiful, and as having abundantly repaid him for his labour.

As we had before passed through the Loudon Branch, we now followed the main stream, and, on our way, landed on the south bank, upon a piece of open forest land, abundantly clothed with luxuriant grass and moderate-sized timber. The water here began to taste brackish, but it was quite fresh about a quarter of a mile higher up, above a spit of rocks which nearly crosses the channel, leaving a passage of ten feet water, over which there is a trifling fall. About three-quarters of a mile lower down, we landed on the north bank, on Rawdon Island, on the edge of the swamp seen near our tent in the Loudon Branch.

We also landed at Black-man Point, and had an interview with twenty-five natives; amongst whom we recognised several that had visited us at the anchorage, and who appeared delighted and happy at meeting us again: after spending half an hour with them we re-embarked, and arrived on board by sunset.

Between this and the 20th our time was busily spent in laying down and making further observations upon the soundings of the port and bar. And on the 21st, at highwater, having completed our object, we left the harbour; in steering over the bar found eleven feet water at about thirty-five yards from the sunken rocks. The Lady Nelson, in following, kept more over towards the north side of the channel and, being near the edge of the sand rollers, had but nine feet.

On reaching the offing Lieutenant Oxley embarked in the Lady Nelson, to return to Port Jackson, and soon afterwards the two vessels parted company.

In consequence of the report made by Lieutenant Oxley to the Governor, upon the result of the expedition, an establishment has been since formed at this harbour; which, at present, is used only as a penal settlement: hitherto, no settlers have been permitted to take their grants at Port Macquarie; but, when this is allowed, it will, from the superiority of its climate, and the great extent of fine country in the interior, become a very important and valuable dependency of the colony of New South Wales.

Narrative of a Survey of the Intertropical and Western Coasts of Australia, Performed between the Years 1818 and 1822 (1827)

———

JOHN LORT STOKES
(1812–85)

British naval surveyor. Stokes served on the Beagle *for eighteen years from 1825, becoming its commander in 1841. During that time, the* Beagle *undertook marine surveys in South America (1826–32), the world voyage recorded by Charles Darwin (1833–36), and surveys of Australian waters (1837–43). Stokes made the following 'discovery', which he named after his former shipmate, in September 1839. He later commanded the* Acheron *while it surveyed the New Zealand and New South Wales coasts (1847–51).*

EXPLORING 'A NEW OPENING'

September 9 — Before the veil of darkness was quite removed, we could faintly distinguish the mouth of the opening; and the sight at daylight was most cheering. A wide bay appearing between two white cliffy heads, and stretching away within to a great distance, presented itself to our view. Far to the southward, between the heads, rose a small table-topped hill. As we pulled in towards the eastern entrance point, the river-like appearance began to wear off, more land making its appearance towards the head of the opening. On reaching this point Mr Forsyth and myself climbed up the cliff, whilst the breakfast was cooking. From the summit we had a good view of the bay, and were delighted to find large openings in the south-east and south-west corners of it. The table hill before mentioned, stood on the point between them. To see the eastern part of it, however, it was necessary to cross the opposite point, where some talc slate, pieces of which measured four inches in length, was found imbedded in quartz. The point was called in consequence, Talc Head. The other rocks near it were of a fine-grained sandstone: — a new feature in the geology of this part of the continent, which afforded us an appropriate opportunity of convincing an old shipmate and friend, that he still lived in our memory; and we accordingly named this sheet of water Port Darwin. A few small bamboos grew on this head; the other trees were chiefly white gums. I climbed to the top of one of them, and obtained thence a view of another opening in the eastern part of the harbour. It now being low water, an extensive shoal was discovered, reaching from abreast of Talc Head to the point separating the S.E. and S.W. openings, an extent of nearly five miles. This somewhat diminished the value of our discovery, as it limited the capabilities of the bay as a harbour.

We now proceeded to explore the north-eastern and largest opening, distant six miles from our station. A large islet and a reef left the entrance only a mile wide. Expanding again, it formed two arms, one running south, the other E.S.E., between small groups of singular isolated haycock-shaped hills, about 250 feet high. Following the latter, being the largest, we found that it soon curved round, taking a southerly direction. A bank free from mangroves occurring in this bend, we availed ourselves of it, as the day was closing in, to secure some early stars for latitude and longitude. The intense pleasure afforded by traversing water that had never before been divided by any keel, in some measure compensated us for the annoyance from the musquitoes and sand-flies, that took the opportunity of assailing us while in the defenceless state of quiet necessary in making observations. Pushing out into the middle of the stream, and each wielding a beater, our tiny enemies were soon shaken off, and borne back to the shore by a refreshing N.W. breeze.

We found it necessary to keep a sharp look out here for the alligators, as they swarmed in dangerous numbers.

The scarcity of fish, and the shallowness of the water did not hold out much hope that the arm we were tracing would prove of great extent; still many speculations were hazarded on the termination of it. The temperature in the night was down to 78°, and the dew sufficiently heavy to wet the boat's awning through. Anxious to know how far this piece of water was to carry us into the untrodden wilds of Australia, we moved off with the first streak of dawn. Ten miles in a S. by E. direction brought us to where the width and depth was not sufficient to induce us to proceed further. Besides, as we were then only fifteen miles from a bend of the upper part of the Adelaide, which must receive the drainage of all that part of the country, it seemed improbable that any other large river existed in the neighbourhood. Six miles from our furthest, which was about thirty miles from the entrance, we passed a small island. The banks on either side of the inlet were, as usual, a thick grove of mangroves, except in one spot, a mile lower down, where we landed on our return for observations. This we found to be a low cliffy projection of slate formation, whilst scattered over the face of the few miles of country, which we are able to explore, were small bits of quartz; large blocks also of which protruded occasionally through a light kind of mould.

The country was a most thirsty looking level, the low brushwood on which cracked and snapped as we walked through it, with a brittle dryness that testified how perfectly parched up was everything. A single spark would instantly have wrapped the whole face of the country in one sheet of fire. Slight blasts of heated withering air, as if from an oven, would occasionally strike the face as we walked along; sometimes they were loaded with those peculiar and most agreeable odours that arise from different kinds of gums. Still the white eucalyptus and the palm, wore in comparison with the other vegetation, an extraordinary green appearance, derived probably from the nightly copious falls of dew, which is the only moisture this part of the continent receives during the present season. The birds we observed were common to other parts of the continent, being a few screaming cockatoos, parrots, and quails, and near the water a small white egret. There was nothing of interest to recall our memories to this first visit to a new part of Australia, save a very large ant's nest, measuring twenty feet in height. This object is always the first that presents itself whenever my thoughts wander to that locality.

As the boat was not provisioned for the time it would take to explore all the openings we had discovered, and as the capabilities of Port Darwin were sufficiently great to require the presence of the ship, I determined on returning immediately to Shoal Bay.

During the time we were absent, some of our people who had been on shore, received a visit from a party of natives, who evinced the most friendly disposition. This verifies what I have before observed, as to the remarkable differences of character that exist between many Australian tribes, though living in the immediate neighbourhood of each other; for, it will be remembered, that at no great distance we had experienced a very different reception.

Those people amounted in number, with their families, to twenty-seven, and came down to our party without any symptoms of hesitation. Both men and women were finer than those we had seen in Adam Bay. The tallest male measured five feet eleven, which is three inches less than a native Flinders measured in the Gulf of Carpentaria. The teeth of these people were *all perfect,* an additional proof that the ceremony of knocking them out, like others practised in Australia, is very partially diffused. The rite of circumcision, for instance, is only performed at King's Sound, on the west side of the Gulf of Carpentaria, and near the head of the Australian bight on the south. Mr Eyre, who discovered the existence of the rite on the last mentioned part of the continent, infers that the natives of the places I have mentioned must have had some communication with each other through the interior; but it is possible that at a distant period of time, circumcision may have been very generally practised, and that having become gradually disused, the custom is now only preserved at two or three points, widely separated from each other. I do not advance this as a theory, but simply as a suggestion, as there is some difficulty in supposing communication to have taken place across the continent.

Some light may be thrown on the migration of the aboriginal inhabitants of Australia, by tracing the parts of the coast on which canoes are in use. It has already been mentioned, that we had not seen any westward of Clarence Strait, neither were they in use in the bottom of the Gulf of Carpentaria, nor on the south coast. By the assistance of these and similar facts, we may hereafter be enabled to discover the exact direction in which the streams of population have flowed over the continent. But I am not prepared to agree entirely with Mr Eyre when he concludes, as I have stated, from the fact of the rite of circumcision having been found on the south and north-west coasts, and on the Gulf of Carpentaria, that there exists any peculiar connection between the tribes inhabiting those several points. This enterprising traveller moreover thinks that the idea he has started goes far towards refuting the theory of an inland sea, another presumption against which he maintains to be the hot winds that blow from the interior. I confess that the theory of an inland sea has long since vanished from my mind, though I base my opinion on reasons different from those of Mr Eyre. The intercourse between natives of opposite sides of the continent, (though it is certainly possible) has never been established, and while it remains hypothetical, cannot be adduced to overthrow another hypothesis. The existence of hot winds also blowing from the interior is not conclusive, as we had, when in the Gulf of Carpentaria, very cold winds coming from the same direction. We know, however, that the temperature of winds depends much on the nature of the soil over which they sweep, for instance, in a cold clayey soil, the radiation of heat is very rapid.

Before quitting this subject it may be as well to mention that my own impression, which the most recent information bears out, is that instead of an inland sea, there is in the centre of Australia a vast desert, the head of which, near Lake Torrens, is not more than three hundred feet above the level of the sea. The coast being surrounded by hilly ranges, the great falls of rain that must occasionally occur in the interior, may convert a vast extent of the central and lowest portion, towards the north side of the continent, into a great morass, or lake, which, from the northerly dip, must discharge its waters slowly into the Gulf of Carpentaria, without possessing sufficient stability to mark either its bed or boundaries.

To return to the party of natives which has given rise to this digression. They had clearly never seen a white person before; for they stepped up to one man of fair complexion, who had his trowsers turned up over his knees, and began rubbing his skin to see whether it was painted. They came fearlessly to our party, as they were collecting shells at the extremity of a long flat. One of the officers, who happened to be very thirsty, placed such confidence in their friendly manner, that he allowed them to conduct him alone to a small well near the beach, but the water was too salt to be drank. The force of habit is astonishing: natives drink this brackish fluid and find it very refreshing. The small quantity that suffices them is also surprising, though they will drink enormously when they can get it.

Their mode of procuring this necessary element is singular, and they exhibit in this particular much ingenuity and great fertility of resources. They are never harassed with the idea of being without any; which not only distresses but adds to the horror of thirst with the European explorer, who has not experienced the constant watchfulness of Providence, and does not know that he may collect from the leaves, with a sponge, on some mornings, as much as a pint of water. This has, however, been done, even on the south coast, where the dews are not so copious as on the north-west. The natives themselves are never at a loss for that indeed precious article, water. They sometimes procure it by digging up the lateral roots of the small gum-tree, a dusty and fatiguing operation: they break them off in short bits, and set them up to drain into a piece of bark or a large shell. By tapping also the knotty excrescences of trees they find the fluid, which they suck out. Many of these modes of obtaining water are of course known to experienced bushmen, like Mr Eyre, whose deeply interesting narrative of his hardships and perils has already enlisted the sympathy of the public.

Discoveries in Australia (1846)

2

THE EAST

WILLIAM CLARK

(dates unknown)

Supercargo. Clark was on board the Sydney Cove, *which was carrying rum and other goods between Calcutta and Sydney, when it was beached on an island in Bass Strait, subsequently known as Preservation Island, in February 1797. He and sixteen other crew members set off for Port Jackson in a long-boat, but the latter was itself wrecked near Point Hicks. The party then began the long walk around the coast towards their destination, sometimes helped by Aborigines, at other times hindered by them. Only Clark and two of his companions survived the arduous journey, the longest made overland in Australia by Europeans to that time. Two boats were sent to Preservation Island to rescue the remaining men from the ship, but one was lost at sea while returning to Sydney.*

'HOSPITABLE NATIVES'

11th [April 1797] — Walked 8 miles and came to a river, where we met fourteen natives, who conducted us to their miserable abodes in the wood adjoining to a large lagoon, and kindly treated us with mussels, for which unexpected civility we made them some presents. These people seem better acquainted with the laws of hospitality than any of their countrymen whom we had yet seen, for to their benevolent treat was added an invitation to remain with them for the night. They did not, however, lodge us in their nominal huts, but after we were seated around our resting-place they brought their women and children to see us, and certainly, to judge from the attention with which they surveyed

[39]

us, we afforded them no small share of entertainment. As far as we could understand, these natives were of a different tribe from those we had seen, and were then at war with them. They possessed a liberality to which the others were strangers, and freely gave us a part of the little they had, which the others were so far from doing that they would have deprived us of the last article in our possession had they not been overawed by the sight of arms, against which they knew not how to defend themselves. We endeavoured to make our entertainers sensible by signs how rudely their neighbours had behaved to us; to compensate for which both the old and the young were anxious to give us part of their shellfish.

12th — Met with another party of the natives who did not attempt to molest us. Walked 16 miles over rising ground and along the sea-side, where we found a dead skate, which, though a little tainted, would not have been unacceptable to an epicure with our appetite.

13th — Came to a large river, where we met with a few natives, who appeared very timorous at seeing us; but in a short time we came to a better understanding, and they kindly carried us over in their canoes. This was not accomplished without several duckings, for their rude little vehicles formed of bark, tied at both ends with twigs, and not exceeding 8 feet in length, by 2 in breadth, are precarious vessels for one unacquainted with them to embark in, though the natives, of whom they will carry three or four, paddle about in them with the greatest facility and security. After crossing the river, and receiving a few small fish at parting, we walked 10 miles.

14th — Met with no obstruction during a walk of 18 miles.

15th — We were joined by our last friends, who ferried us over a very large river in their canoes. Whether this meeting was the effect of chance or one of their fishing excursions, or that perceiving we should find it difficult they had come to our assistance, we could not determine; but had it not been for their aid we must have been detained here for some time in making a raft. The greatest part of the wood of the country being very heavy will not swim, unless it has been felled for some time and exposed to the sun, a fact which we had already been taught by miserable experience. Having walked 9 miles after crossing the river, we rested for the night, and boiled a few shellfish we had picked up by the way like good œconomists, making them serve for both dinner and supper, for our little evening's cookery formed the only meal we could daily afford ourselves, unless we ventured to eat a few wild plants which we sometimes picked up.

16th — Having walked about 12 miles we once more met with our friends, who, a third time, conveyed us over a large river at a shallow part, which they pointed out. On the banks of this river we remained for the night. Our poor unfortunate companions, worn out by want and excessive fatigue, now began to drop behind very fast. At this place we were under the painful necessity of leaving nine of our fellow-sufferers behind, they being totally unable to proceed further; but we flattered ourselves they would be able to come up with us in a day or two, as we now often stopt some time with the natives when we found them kind to us, or loitered about the rocks to pick up shellfish or collect herbs.

F. M. Bladen (ed.), *Historical Record of New South Wales*, vol. III (1895)

———

JOHN PRICE

(*c.* 1779– ?)

Servant and explorer. During the 1790s a number of Irish convicts became convinced of the existence of a 'New World', a colony of White people, about 300 kilometres south-west of Sydney, and planned to escape there to lives of relative luxury. In order to show them that their belief was wrong, Governor John Hunter sent two small parties out on foot into the area in 1798, with former convict and 'wild white man', John Wilson, as guide. Records on each occasion were kept by another participant, John Price, who had come to New South Wales as a free servant to Hunter. Sadly, but not surprisingly, no traces were found of what the governor called the convicts' 'fancied paradise'. This is Price's account of the first expedition, which travelled as far as the Wollondilly River.

'JOURNEY INTO THE INTERIOR OF THE COUNTRY, NEW SOUTH WALES'

January 24th, 1798 — Course, S.S.W. Left Mount Hunter for about 12 miles, till we fell in with the Nepean River, where the rocks run so steep it was with great difficulty we crost them; the rest of the ground run very scrubby. We saw nothing strange except a few rock kangaroos with long black brush tails, and two pheasants, which we could not get a shot at. Distance, 18 miles.

January 25th — Course, S.S.W. The country runs very open; good black soil. We saw a great many kangaroos and emews, and we fell in with a party of natives which gave a very good account of the place we were in search of; that there was a great deal of corn and potatoes, and that the people were very friendly. We hearkened to their advice; we altered our course according to their directions. One of them promised that he would take us to a party of natives which had been there; but he not coming according to his promise, we proceeded on our journey as he had directed us. In the course of this day we found a great deal of salt. Distance, 6 miles.

January 26th — Course, W.S.W. The ground run very rockey and brushey, so that we could scarce pass. We crossed one small river, the banks of which were so rockey and steep that we could scarce pass it. We saw no signs of any natives about it, but we saw several sorts of dung of different animals, one of which Wilson called a whom-batt, which is an animal about 20 inches high, with short legs and a thick body forwards, with a large head, round ears, and very small eyes; is very fat, and has much the appearance of a badger. There is another animal which the natives call a cullawine, which much resembles the stoths in America. Here I shot a bird about the size of a pheasant, but the tail of it very much resembles a peacock, with two large long feathers, which are white, orange, and lead colour, and black at the ends; its body betwixt a brown and green; brown under his neck and black upon his head; black legs and very long claws. Distance, 16 miles.

January 27th — Course, W.S.W. The ground still runs very rockey and scrubby for about 6 miles, then we came to a fine open country, but very mountanious; we crosst one small river, where we saw plenty of coal and limestone, and the banks of the river on the other side runs very steep, and a very high mountain, and within about 2 miles of the top runs very scrubby, intermixed with many vines, and particularly at the very top; and on the other side we saw a very fine meadow flat country, with many kangaroos and emews. The timber runs very thick and short, and scarce ten trees an acre. Distance, 16 miles.

January 28th — Course, W.S.W. The land runs much the same, the timber thin, with a good many stringey-bark trees; and a little further we saw a number of meadows and 100 acres of land without a tree upon it. Here we saw a party of natives. Wilson run and caught one of them, a girl, thinking to learn something from them, but her language was so different from that one which we had with us that we could not understand her. We kept her all night, but she cried and fretted so much that the next morning we gave her a tomahawk and sent her to the rest of the natives, which were covered with large skins, which reached down to their heels. Here we came to the top of a fine hill in the middle of the day, and took a view of the country. We saw nothing very promising. The land seemed open; few trees. We saw to the southward a few high mountains, but good land towards them. To the westward we saw a brook down the country, which we supposed to be a river, which seemed to run N.W. from S.E. The land seemed very high to the southward, but still an open country. Distance, 20 miles.

January 29th — Course, W.S.W. We steered our course for about 4 miles, but the country did not turn out to our expectation, for we here fell in with the heads of creeks which seemed to run towards the river which we saw from the hill before mentioned. The ground run rockey and scrubby, and we saw falls of water in the heads of the creeks — one about 40 feet high, and two more about 20 feet high. Here we altered our course to the north for about 12 miles, thinking to cut off the heads of the creeks, but we fell in with more, so we came to the resolution of steering our former course, W.S.W., but finding the country to run rockey and scrubby. Here we saw another sort of timber; the leaves are lighter than a powder blue; the tree is low, much like an apple-tree, the bark much like a mahogany. We here saw in the creeks many pheasants and rock kangaroos, likewise dung of animals as large as horse-dung, but could not see any of them. We had nothing to eat for two days but one rat about the size of a small kitten. I myself was very sick, and wished myself at home again; the other man was sick like me, for he had hurt his leg and was not able to walk. Wilson was well and hearty. Distance, 24 miles.

January 30th — Course, W.S.W. The country still rockey and scrubby. We fell in with the head of a river very near as large as the Hawkesbury River, which seemed to run from N.W. to S.E. The banks were so steep we could not get down them. The other side seemed open, but the banks very steep. Wilson proposed making a canoe; but the other man and myself were so faint and tired, having nothing to eat but two small birds each, we were afraid to venture on the other side of the river, for fear we should not be able to procure anything to subsist on; likewise our shoes was gone and our feet were very much bruised with the rocks, so that we asked Wilson to return. Distance, 16 miles.

February 1st — Course, S.E. b. E. About 7 miles walk we fell in with many meadows, with scarce any trees upon them for near 200 acres together; the hills also very thin of timber and very light; the ground good, except on the tops of the hills, which was stoney. We were very weak; we could not get anything to eat but a few small birds. We fell in with two birds which Wilson said he had never seen before in the country, and we was fortunate enough to shoot the cock and hen in one of the meadows. They appear to be something like a cockatoo, intermixed with a green, white, and lead colour, the cock with a scarlet head. Distance, 20 miles.

February 2nd — Course, E.N.E. The country still runs very fine; full of large meadows and some thousands of acres of land without any timber upon it, except here and there one tree, and some very large lakes of water some 3 miles long, but saw no birds of any kind about them. This day we had a view from a high hill, which made us better judges of the country, which was rockey and scrubby; 'twas clear and open land from S. to S.W. The land appeared high and good, and to the S.W. we saw two large ridges of mountains, with two heads with the appearance of the entrance of a river between them, which we supposed to be the seacoast. Here we found that the country which appeared low and dark was that which is rockey and scrubby, and that which appeared light and hilly is the most easy to travel in, being the forest. We saw to the northward and westward many hills of those which appeared rockey, but to all appearance more open to the northward. In the latter part of the day, after we had got over the first ridge of mountains, we fell in with a vast number of kangaroos. Here we were fortunate again, for Wilson killed one of them, which was a great refreshment to us. The next morning, about sunrise, I myself heard two guns fire, which sounded to the S.E. I was not certain that it was a gun untill Wilson said, 'Do you hear that gun fire?' I said I did. I then took up my gun and fired again, but we could get no answer, altho' we fired five different times. We here come to a resolution of returning, for Wilson here came to a part of the country which he knew, and a very barren one, for we could not get anything to eat but a few roots and grubbs, and they very scarce. Indeed I thought that we must all have perished with hunger, which certainly would have been the case had it not been for the indefatigable zeal of Wilson to supply us with as much as would support life; for we travelled six days successively over hills and vallies full of rocks, and no appearance of any animals or birds of any size, so that we had no hopes of ever reaching back again, being so weak that Roe and myself were scarce able to travel; but on the sixth day we got through the rocks, and made the forest land about 10 miles from Prospect, which very much enlivened our spirits, for we were all but starved, and were obliged to cut up all our cloathing to cover our feet, which was cut with the rocks. Enlivened as we were at getting good ground to travel on, and being cheered up by Wilson, who said we should soon make Prospect, we then proceeded on our journey with all the spirit and strength we were master of, and to our great joy we reached the desired place a little before sundown. Distance, 16 miles.

F. M. Bladen (ed.), *Historical Records of New South Wales*, vol. III (1895)

————

GEORGE CALEY
(1770–1829)

English naturalist and explorer. For years the Blue Mountains prevented the westward expansion of European settlement in New South Wales. Various attempts to cross them, made by William Dawes (1789), Francis Barrallier (1802, twice), George Caley (1804), and others, failed. In November 1802, well before his own unsuccessful expedition, the 'eccentric and morose' Caley, who spent ten years in the colony from 1800, made these comments in a letter to his employer, Joseph Banks.

SOME THOUGHTS ON THE BLUE MOUNTAINS

I have of late been in that part of the country called the Blue Mountains, where I have met with several new plants. My principal tracts and observations I shall communicate to you by the first opportunity. Though these hills by being seen a long way off, and by the accounts of the few that have visited them, are in general considered as impassable, yet I cannot rank them as such. On gaining the summit of some of the hills that are seen at a great distance, I have found forest land of a good quality, then met with rocky ground covered with thickets, large trees, and interspersed with deep rocky valleys, but have not as yet found a hill that overlooked the first or commanded a prospect into the interior (except Mt Hunter), which has as good a view to the westward as to the eastward.

These ranges of hills seem to me to begin at a considerable distance to the northward and run in the form of a crescent to Cape Howe, and from there it is not improbable but a similar range may run to Wilson's Promontory in Bass's Straits, or the sea, as between these two places is a low and level tract of land; yet in passing over these hills, I am of opinion, will not only be attended with difficulty, but great hazard. For

instance, should a party go out in fine weather and travel a considerable distance, and then wet weather to come on, a stop would be put
to travelling further. Remaining still consumes the provisions. If wet
weather continues, hunger will force a retreat. Many of the valleys will
be flooded. In travelling through the thickets will be as hard as being
up to the neck in water, and in consequence will destroy their clothing, necessaries, &c. But yet again a party conducted under an intelligent and frugal person, provided the weather happens favourable,
might gain the object of the pursuit.

The Gov. has been at some pains seemingly, to know something
more of the country. He lately sent out Mr Barrallier, who was
equipped with six or seven men, two natives, and two horses. They
took their departure from Richmond Hill, and were out 12 or 13 days.
I believe his object was to penetrate into the country westward. On his
return I was informed that he had discovered a new river, lime-stone
in great abundance, iron almost pure, and had been 50 miles or better
in a westerly direction; but of all this I have doubts, for I have every
reason to believe he has been no farther than myself, and I have not
been scarcely half the above distance. The minerals I have not seen, but
it is probable they may fall into your hands, whereby the truth will at
once be ascertained.

The same gentleman is upon the eve of setting off again with a larger party and instead of horses he takes two bullocks. He seeks this time
of fixing stations from which a regular supply is to be forwarded. By
what I already know of travelling in this country gives me to suspect
that this journey will not accomplish the design. However, trial will
decide. I am so vain as to think that with another man besides myself,
and a horse, that I can go further than what this party will, provided
the weather is favourable. I have often lamented that being bred a
horseman has been all lost in forwarding a pursuit in natural history,
but at length I am undeceived, for as a traveller in this country it has
given me an advantage over all others. When Mr Barrallier returned I
perceived his loss for the want of the like.

I am just upon the point of setting off on a journey, and should have
been out at this time, only I am in want of a few articles from the Gov.
If the weather is good I shall be out three weeks. I have seen high land
which is about 45 miles south from Prospect Hill. To the eastward of
this I suspect Hawkesbury River will be found, and from hence I
imagine its source is not far distant. From this place I mean to proceed
to the sea shore, which must also be near at hand. If I found out its
source in the time I reckon, I shall proceed to the SSW if the land is

favourable. If not I shall try a west course. I should have been several journies before this season had I had a horse.

Reflections on the Colony of New South Wales, ed. J.E.B. Currey (1966)

———

GREGORY BLAXLAND
(1778–1853)

English-born settler. In 1813, Blaxland, William Lawson, William Charles Wentworth, and four convicts found a possible route across the Blue Mountains, although they did not actually cross the main range. Here Blaxland describes the last few days of the party's outward journey, which ended at a sugar-loaf hill later named Mount Blaxland.

FINDING A WAY ACROSS THE BLUE MOUNTAINS

Friday, May 28th, 1813 —They got ready about Nine O'Clock and proceeded about 5 Miles and three quarters — not being able to find Water they did not encamp until five O'Clock when they Encamped on the edge of the precipice and discovered to their great satisfaction what they had considered sandy and barren land below the Mountains to be forest land — covered with trees and good grass — in the Evening they got their horses down the Mountain when they again tasted grass for the first time since they left the forest land on the other side of the Mountains, — they were getting into miserable condition, they found Water about two Miles below the foot of the Mountain, the second camp of Natives moved before them about three Miles they passed some timber fit for building in this days track. —

Bearing of their Course North a quarter of a Mile — West South West a quarter of a Mile — North North West half a Mile — West North West a quarter of a Mile — North West a Mile — North West by North a quarter of a Mile — West half a Mile — North North West a quarter of a Mile — North three quarters of a Mile — North West half a Mile — North a quarter of a Mile —

Saturday, May 29th, 1813 — They Fetched up the horses and began to descend the Mountain at 7 O'Clock through a pass in the rocks about thirty feet wide they had discovered the day before when the Want of Water made them more alert — going down they were forced to unload the Horses part of the way and carry their loads themselves as they Could but just keep their footing without a load here a road for a Cart might be easily made by cutting a trench slanting along the side of the Mountain in the earth which lays against it and which at this place joins the earth on the top, they computed this pass to be about twenty Miles North West in a straight line from the place where they ascended the mountain — they reached the foot about Nine O'Clock and proceeded about 2 Miles — Most of the way through open Meadow land Clear of trees covered with grass two and three feet high, they encamped on the bank of a fine stream of water to rest themselves and to refresh their Horses the Natives moved before them as the day before — the timber appeared rotten and not a sort for building, the dogs killed a Kangaroo which was very acceptable, they having lived on Salt Meat since they got the last.

Bearing of their Course, North East half a mile — North North West two Miles. —

Sunday, May 30th, 1813 — They rested this day, Shot a Kangaroo one Hundred and Seventy-five Yards distance with my rifle — they found the Climate very different from either the top of the Mountains or the settlement on the other side where when they left it the winter had not set in nor any frost made its appearance — here this Night the frost covered the ground very thick and froze the leg of a Kangaroo quite through and from the dead appearance of the grass which turned brown and looked like sand at a distance the frost must have been very very severe for some time past they saw the track of the Emue at several places near this Camp. —

Monday, May 31st, 1813 — They loaded their Horses at Nine O'Clock and proceeded through the forest land remarkably well watered about 6 Miles saw several Kangaroo's went through many open Meadows clear of trees covered with high good grass crossed two fine Streams of Water — this day they came on some Native's fires which they had left the day before they appeared to have been very busy sharpening their spears from the shavings and pieces of sharp stones they had left behind they appear on this side of the Mountains to have no huts nor to bark or climb the trees like the natives on the other side the only remains of food they had left round their fireplaces — was the flower of the Honey suckle tree which grows like a bottle brush and are very full of Honey which they had sucked out they encamped by the side of a very fine stream of water a short distance from a high Hill in the shape of a Sugar loaf they left their Camp in the afternoon and ascended to its top which terminated their Journey — from which place they saw forest land all around them sufficient to feed the Stock of the colony, in their opinions for the next thirty Years, — they descended and returned to their Camp the timber still appeared unfit for building the stones at the bottom of the rivers was very fine large grained dark coloured granite the stones all appeared a kind of a granite quite different from the stones of the Mountains or any stones they had before seen in the Colony, this day they Computed they had travelled rather more than fifty six Miles through the Mountains in brush and scrubby brush land which they had walked over three times and six Miles in forest land on the other side Computing the Mountain to be half a Mile down where they descended Mr Blaxland and one Man nearly lost the party by going after a Kangaroo too far —

Bearing of their Course South West three Miles — West two Miles — North West a quarter of a Mile — North North East a quarter of a Mile — South South West a quarter of a mile. —

A Journal of a Tour of Discovery Across the Blue Mountains, New South Wales, in the Year 1813 (1823)

GEORGE EVANS

(1780–1852)

English-born surveyor and explorer. Using Blaxland, Lawson, and Went-worth's route across the Blue Mountains, Evans, then assistant-surveyor in Van Diemen's Land, crossed the main range in late 1813 and continued inland, reaching a point on the Macquarie River some 70 kilometres beyond the site of present-day Bathurst. As a result of Evans's glowing reports of the land that he found, Macquarie authorised the construction of the first road across the Blue Mountains. It was completed in 1815.

'A BEAUTIFUL COUNTRY'

Saturday, 4th [December 1813] — My Progress is through an exceeding good Track of Country; it is the handsomest I have yet seen with gentle rising hills and dales well watered; the distant hills, which are about 5 Miles South, appear as Grounds laid out divided into fields by edges, there are few Trees on them and the Grass quite green; I still keep the river, and at times I walk a few Miles South or North as seems to me most requisite. The Dogs killed a Kangaroo and the river supplies us *with abundance of Fish.*

Sunday, 5th — The Night was very wet; we were uncomfortable having no means to shelter ourselves from it, as the trees will not bark; it has rained most of the day; about 4 o'Clock a violent Thunder Storm came on; since, the Clouds seem to disperce, wind blowing fresh from the West;

We remained near the River as it is Sunday. The Horses are getting fat but am Sorry to observe their backs are sore; the Saddles should have been lined; straw stuffing is too hard to render it easy we put our Blankets under them; I walked out this Evening some Miles; I cannot speak too highly of the Country, indeed I am now at a loss what to say as it exceeds my expectations and daily gets better. We are on an Allowance of Bread having lost so much by the bad Weather on the Mountains, we require little pork in this part, a Kangaroo can be procured at any time, there are also Emu's, we killed some Ducks this day.

Monday, 6th — The Night was very Bad; I was greatly afraid the weather would continue so; this Morning had a better appearance; the river now forms large ponds; at the Space of about a Mile I came on a fine Plain of rich Land, the handsomest Country I ever saw; it surpasseth Port Dalrymple; this place is worth speaking of as good and beautiful; the Track of clear land occupies about a Mile on each side of the River; I have named it after the Lieut. Governor, 'O'Connell Plains,' on which we saw a number of wild Geese but too shy to let us near them; the Timber around is thinly scattered, I do not suppose there are more than ten Gum Trees on an Acre, their Bark is amazing thick at least 2 Inches; At 3 o'Clock I stopped at the commencement of a Plain still more pleasing and very Extensive; I cannot see the termination of it North of me; the soil is exceeding rich and produces the finest grass intermixed with variety of herbs; the hills have the look of a park and Grounds laid out; I am at a loss for Language to describe the Country; I named this part *'Macquarie Plains.'* I have walked till I am quite fatigued being so anxious to look about me; there is Game in abundance; if we want a Fish it is caught immediately; they seem to bite at any time; had I brought a quantity of salt we could cure some 100 lbs of them, I am quite astonished at the number the Men catch every Evening, the Dogs thrive on them; I shall bring one home with me to shew you. Distance, 6 miles.

Tuesday, 7th — I proceeded over the Plains following the Water, which I now name the *'Fish River'*; at about 4 Miles I was brought up by a stream nearly as large from the Southward, and terminates the Plains; I imagine I shall be necessitated to travel up it some distance to find a Ford, I determined upon doing so, and traced it about 2 Miles when we stopped to secure ourselves from an approaching Thunder Storm that came on most severe and threatens a wet Night. Distance (Over Plains 4, up river 1¾), 5¾ Miles.

Wednesday, 8th — We are in Spirits from the good appearance of the Morning, we hope it will be fine, as neither of us have been thoroughly dry these last 3 days and Nights; I see no signs of a Ford at present, therefore am obliged to continue tracing up the Stream; at 2 Miles begins a Plain of rich Land which I call '*Mitchell Plains.*' Observing from a hill the course of the water springs from the S.E., I made up my mind to contrive a Bridge to convey our Luggage over, it was done in the following manner; by driving two forked logs into the Mud as far in the water as we dare venture, and by laying a piece of wood in the Forks, form a Gallows, a party swam across and did the same on the other side; we then fell Trees as large as all six of us could carry, and rolled them down the bank; as soon as one end was carried into the water the stream sent it round, and the ropes secured round the end prevented it being carried too far; we lifted two of these up, which reached from one Gallows to the other, and two from each bank to a Gallows, over which we passed our necessaries; and swam the Horses, first conveying to the other side a Rope that held them, otherwise the force of the water would have carried them a great distance as it did the Men who swam across; I was much pleased at our exertions which took some hours and enabled us to reach the junction of the rivers by sun sett; The Country is beautiful no Mountains to be seen, there are high hills at great distances, but can observe them green to their tops.

I named the last run of Water 'Campbell River.' [...] Distance up river, 4¼ Miles.

Thursday, 9th — I have called the Main Stream '*Macquarie River.*' At 2½ Miles commences a most extensive Plain, the hills around are fine indeed; it requires a clever person to describe this Country properly, I never saw any thing equal to it; the soil is good; I think the lower parts of the Plains are overflowed at times, but do not see marks to any height; the small Trees on the lower banks of the River stand straight, not laying down as you see them on the banks of the river and Creeks at Hawkesbury. The Grass here might be mowed it is so thick and long, particularly on the flat lands. Distance, 8¼ Miles.

Friday, 10th — Yesterdays trace led me much North of West; today it is South of it. The extent of the Plain following the River is 11 Miles and about 2 wide on each side, the whole excellent good land, and the best Grass I have seen in any part of New South Wales; the hills are also covered with fine pasture, the Trees being so far apart must be an acquisition to its Growth; it is in general the sweetest in an open Country.

At the termination of the Plain is a very handsome Mount; I named it '*Mount Pleasant*' from the Prospect it commands to the N.E. The River now winds itself round the Points of Forest hills nearly the same as described some days since.

Emues are numerous; the Dogs will not give chase; I imagine they are bad ones; we have not been able to get a shot at any of the Geese, altho' plentiful, they are so shy; but frequently shoot Ducks. Nothing astonishes me more than the amazing large Fish that are caught; one is now brought me that weighs at least *15 lb*, they are all the same species. I call the Plains last passed over '*Bathurst Plains*' [...]. Distance, 7¼ Miles.

Saturday, 11th — The fine pasture continues but there is a great alteration in the look of the Country; finding the River leads me among hills; the points of them end with rocky Bluffs near the water; at about 4 Miles I was brought too by one of them, which appears to be the termination of a Range of high hills from the South, and is the only Mass of Rocks I have met with since leaving the Blue Mountains, but bears a different aspect being covered with Pines; I determined upon halting a few hours that I may be enabled to look about me; I ascended a Peak and find the River turns about N.W. around the points of stupendous green hills, to the South, and S.W., I cannot discern their end, the tops of the distant ones shew themselves for a great extent; on the North side of the River is also a Ridge of Pasture hills that range Westward, to the East appears the fine Country I came over. I am pleased to find the large hills are covered with Grass nor can I discern any rocky ranges with Pines except the one I am on; they have a very romantic appearance so very different from any other part; the largest of them is about 4 feet in circumference. I am fearful of bad Travelling for a few Miles; it is not so inconvenient to ourselves as the Horses that have such sore backs. The North side looks well, but cannot cross the Water; I found a pass for the Horses and went forward, it is not quite so bad Travelling as I expected; there are many Rocks but the pasture is good. Distance, 6¼ Miles.

Sunday, 12th — We stop this day, I took a walk for a few Miles to the S.W. and find it a fine country for Pasture, being steep healthy hills thickly covered with grass; Water in almost every Valley.

Monday, 13th — The Hills are still steep and not quite so fine as those we have passed, they are rather rough with Rocks, yet the pasture is good; the Gums are much larger and intermixed with the Box Tree; the soil is of a stiffer nature, having pieces of Alabaster rock among it;

the higher Lands in general throughout have a great deal about them, that on the surface is quite white in some places, and of a Yellow cast in others; I do not know what to make of the River, its course seems so irregular, the direction to day has been from S.W. to N.E.; the hills are so very high and close, that from any one of them its run cannot be distinguished; I have hopes of coming to their end, and be able to judge what part the river leads to. […] Distance, 6¾ Miles.

Tuesday, 14th — The Country is much the same for about 2 Miles; the hills then get steeper and not so good, indeed it is the worst part I have been over since leaving the Blue Mountains; this place resembles the hill about Mount Hunter at the Cow Pastures. I hope we shall soon be through these high lands being bad travelling, and am afraid we shall soon feel the want of Shoes; the River still winds much and forms some very curious bends. […] Killed a Kangaroo and two Ducks. Distance, 7 Miles.

Wednesday, 15th — Our Road is very rugged and the hills increase in size, but covered with fine Grass; I was upon a very high one but cannot determine their end; from the S. to W. they are stupenduous, the only open Country to be observed is from N.W. to E. these hills surpass any grazing track on the East side of the Mountains; in the Valleys the Grass is long and thick, which makes it fatiguing to pass over them; I begin to think of returning; the Dogs not being good there is no certainty of obtaining Skins for our feet, the grass has cut our shoes to pieces. *Pampoosers* ware out in a few hours, particularly when wet with the Morning Dew. […] Distance, 7 Miles.

Thursday, 16th — I made up my mind to return in the Morning, seeing no hopes of approaching the end of the high Range of Hills; I would most willingly proceed farther, but the Horses backs being so bad; nor can you have an Idea of the situation we are in with respect to our feet; with patching and mending we may manage to reach home. I am now *98½ measured Miles* from the limitation of Mr Blaxland's excurtion; most part of the distance is through a finer Country than I can describe, not being able for want of Language to dwell on the subject, or explain its real and good appearance with Pen and Ink, but assure you there is no deception in it. I feel satisfied within myself and am happy I can meet your Excellency to say I have done my utmost in endeavouring to accomplish your wish, and that I have succeeded in passing over a Beautiful Country, and make no doubt but that to the Westward of these hills there may be a part equal to it; also beg leave to say I shall be happy and ready to go on at any future time to attempt a Journey to the Western coast, which I think this river leads to; it is a rapid Stream in the

Winter Seasons, is of great width there being two Banks. The Hollow, which I imagine from the hills to be its course, bears North of West. I conceive it strange we have not fell in with the Natives; they are near about us as we find late traces of them; I think they are watching us, but are afraid and keep at some distance. [...] Distance, 6 miles.

Friday, 17th — One of the Men being sick prevented our returning; therefore went with a party a few Miles farther, and returned in the Evening; the high lands are as before described, the corners are particularly good; what I name corners are spaces of Ground of 3 or 400 Acres with grass growing within them that you can scarce walk through; the ground is strong and good with ponds of water which lead to the River; but when within a ¼ of a Mile or so of it the course becomes a Rocky gully, and so steep between the hills, that no person would suspect such places were up them: — it is one Month this day since we crossed the Nepean [...].

Historical Records of Australia, series 1, vol. VIII (1916)

———

JOHN OXLEY
(1785?–1828)

Naval officer, surveyor, and explorer. English-born Oxley had had some experience of Australian coastal survey work before his appointment in 1812 as surveyor-general of New South Wales. He is best known for two expeditions into the interior of the colony, conducted in 1817 and 1818, for both of which George Evans was his second-in-command. During the first, Oxley attempted to trace the course of the Lachlan River, which Evans had 'discovered' in 1815. After following the river for two months Oxley's party was unable to continue because of marshes, so they headed north and then returned to Bathurst along the Macquarie River. In this letter to Governor Lachlan Macquarie, Oxley outlines the fate of the second expedition, the original aim of which was to follow the Macquarie River.

'SURVEYOR-GENERAL OXLEY TO GOVERNOR MACQUARIE'

Port Stephens, 1st Novr., 1818.

Sir,

I have the honor to inform Your Excellency that I arrived at this Port to-day; and Circumstances rendering it necessary that Mr Evans should proceed to Newcastle, I embrace the opportunity to make to Your Excellency a brief Report of the Route pursued by the Western Expedition entrusted to my Direction.

My letter dated the 22d June last will have made Your Excellency acquainted with the sanguine hopes I entertained from the appearance of the river that its termination would be either in interior waters or coastways. When I wrote that letter to your Excellency, I certainly did not anticipate the possibility that a very few days further travelling would lead us to its termination as an accessible river.

On the 29th June, having traced its course without the smallest diminution or addition, about 70 miles further to the N.N.W. there being a slight fresh in the river, it overflowed its banks; and although we were at the distance of near three miles from it, the country was so perfectly level that the waters soon spread over the ground on which we were. We had been for some days before travelling over such very low ground, that the people in the boats finding the country flooded proceeded slowly, a circumstance which enabled me to send them directions to return to the station we had quitted in the morning, where the ground was a little more elevated. This spot being by no means secure, it was arranged that the horses with the provisions should return to the last high land we had quitted, a distance of 16 Miles; and as it appeared to me that the body of water in the river was too important to be much affected by the mere overflowing of its waters, I determined to take the large boat, and in her to endeavour to discover their point of discharge.

On the 2d July I proceeded in the boat down the river and in the course of the day went near 30 miles on a N.N.W. course, for ten of which there had been strictly speaking no land, as the flood made the surrounding country a perfect sea: the banks of the river were heavily timbered; and many large spaces within our view, covered with the common reed, were also encircled with large trees. On the 3d, the main channel of the river was much contracted, but very deep, the banks being under water from a foot to 18 inches; the stream continued for about 20 miles on the same course as yesterday, when we lost sight of land and trees, the channel of the river winding through reeds, among which the water was about three feet deep, the current having the same direction as the river. It continued in this manner for near four miles more; when, without any previous change in the breadth, depth and rapidity of the stream, and when I was sanguine in my expectations of soon entering the long sought for lake, it all at once eluded our further pursuit by spreading on all points from N.W. to

N.E. over the plain of reeds which surrounded us, the river decreasing in depth from upwards of 20 feet to less than five feet, and flowing over a bottom of tenacious blue mud, and the current still running with nearly the same rapidity as when the water was confined within the banks of the river. This point of junction with interior waters, or where the Macquarie ceased to have the form of a river, is in latitude 30° 45' S. and longitude 147° 10' E.

To assert positively that we were on the margin of the lake or sea, into which this great body of water is discharged, might reasonably be deemed a conclusion that has nothing but conjecture for its basis; but if an opinion may be hazarded from actual appearances, which our subsequent route tended more strongly to confirm, I feel confident that we were in the immediate vicinity of an inland sea, most probably a shoal one, and gradually decreasing or being filled up by the immense depositions from the waters flowing into it from the higher lands, which, on this singular *Continent*, seem not to extend beyond a few hundred miles from the sea coast, as, westward of these bounding ranges (which from the observations I have been enabled to make, appear to me to run parallel to the direction of the coast), there is not a single hill or other eminence discoverable on this apparently boundless space, those isolated points excepted, on which we remained until the 20th July, the rock and stones, composing which, are a distinct species from those found on the above ranges.

I trust Your Excellency will believe that, fully impressed with the great importance of the question as to the interior formation of this great Country, I was anxiously solicitous to remove all ground for further conjecture by the most careful observations on the nature of the country; which, though it sufficiently proved to me that the interior was covered with water, yet I felt it my duty to leave no measure untried which could in any way tend to a direct elucidation of the fact.

It was physically impracticable to gain the edges of these waters by making a detour round the flooded portion of the country on the S.W. side of the river, as we proved it to be a barren wet marsh, over-run with a species of polygonum, and not offering a single dry spot to which our course might be directed; and that there was no probability of finding any in that direction, I had a certain knowledge from the observations made during the former Expedition.

To circle the flooded country to the N.E. yet remained to be tried. On the 7th July I returned to the tents, which I found pitched on the high land before mentioned, and from whence we could see mountains at the distance of 80 miles to the eastward, the country between being a perfect level. Mr Evans was sent forward to explore the country to the N.E. that being the point, on which I purposed to set forward.

On the 18th July, Mr Evans returned having been prevented from continuing on a N.E. course beyond two days journey by waters running north-easterly through high reeds, and which were most probably those of the Macquarie River, as during his absence it had swelled so considerably as entirely to surround us, coming within a few yards of the tent. Mr Evans afterwards proceeded more easterly; and, at a distance of 50 miles from the Macquarie River, crossed another much wider but not so deep, running to the North. Advancing still more easterly, he went nearly to the base of the mountains seen from the tent; and returning by a more southerly route, found the country somewhat dryer, but not in the least more elevated.

The discretionary instructions, with which Your Excellency was pleased to furnish me, leaving me at liberty as to the course to be pursued by the Expedition on its return to Port Jackson, I determined to attempt making the sea-coast on an easterly course, first proceeding along the base of the high range before mentioned, which I still indulged hopes might lead me to the margin of these or any other interior waters, which this portion of New South Wales might contain, and embracing a low line of coast on which many small openings remained unexamined, at the same time that the knowledge obtained of the country we should encircle might materially tend to the advantage of the Colony in the event of any communication with the interior being discovered.

We quitted this station on the 20th July, being in latitude 30° 18' S. and longitude 147° 31' E. on our route for the coast, and on the 8th August arrived at the lofty range of mountains to which our course had been directed. From the highest point of this range we had the most extended prospect; From the South by the West to North it was one vast level, resembling the ocean in extent, but yet without water being discerned, the range of high land extending to the N.E. by N., elevated points of which were distinguished upwards of 120 miles.

From this point, in conformity to the resolution I had made on quitting the Macquarie River, I pursued a N.E. course; but after encountering numerous difficulties, from the country being an entire marsh, interspersed with quick sands, until the 20th August, when finding I was surrounded by bogs, I was reluctantly compelled to take a more easterly course, having practically proved that the country could not be traversed on any point deviating from the main range of hills which bound the interior, although partial dry portions of level alluvial land extend from their base westerly to a distance, which I estimate to exceed 150 miles before it is gradually lost in the waters, which I am clearly convinced cover the interior.

The alteration in our course more easterly soon brought us into a very different description of country, forming a remarkable contrast to that which has so long occupied us. Numerous fine streams running northerly watered a rich and beautiful country, through which we passed until the 7th September, when we crossed the meridian of Sydney, as also the most elevated known land in New South Wales, being then in latitude 31° 03' S. We were afterwards considerably embarrassed and impeded by very lofty mountains. On the 20th September, we gained the summit of the most elevated mountain in this extensive range, and from it we were gratified with a view of the ocean at a distance of 50 miles, the country beneath us being formed into an immense triangular valley, the base of which extended along the coast from the *Three Brothers* on the south to high land north of *Smoky Cape*. We had the further gratification to find that we were near the source of a very large stream running to the sea. On descending the mountain, we followed the course of this river, increased by many accessions, until the 8th October, when we arrived on the beach near the entrance of the port which received it, having passed over since the 18th July a tract of country near 500 miles in extent from west to east.

This inlet is situated in latitude 31° 23' 30" S. and longitude 152° 50' 18" East, and had been previously noticed by Captain Flinders, but from the distance at which he was necessarily obliged to keep from the coast, he did not discover that it had a navigable entrance; of course our most anxious attention was directed to this important point, and although the want of a boat rendered the examination as to the depth of water in the channel incomplete, yet there appeared to be at low water at least 3 fathoms with a safe though narrow entrance between the *sand rollers* on either hand. Having ascertained thus far, and that by its means the fine country on the banks and in the neighbourhood of the river might be of future service to the Colony, I took the liberty to name it Port Macquarie, in honour of Your Excellency, as the original promoter of the Expedition.

On the 12th October, we quitted Port Macquarie on our course for Sydney; and although no Charts can be more accurate in their out-line and principal points than those of Captain Flinders, we soon experienced how little the best Marine Charts can be depended upon to shew all the inlets and openings upon an extensive line of coast; the distance, his ship was generally at from that portion of the coast we had to travel over, did not allow him to perceive openings which, though doubtless of little consequence to shipping, yet presented the most serious difficulties to travellers by land, and of which, if they had been laid down in the Chart, I should have hesitated to have attempted the passage without assistance from the sea-ward: as it is, we are indebted for our preservation, and that of the horses, to the providential discovery of a small boat on the beach, which the men with the most chearful alacrity carried upwards of 90 miles on their shoulders, thereby enabling us to overcome obstacles otherwise insurmountable.

Until within these few days, I hoped to have had the satisfaction to report the return of the Expedition without accident to any individual composing it; but such is the ferocious treachery of the Natives along the Coast to the Northward that our utmost circumspection could not save us from having one man (William Blake) severely wounded by them; but by the skilful care bestowed upon him by Dr Harris (who accompanied the Expedition as a volunteer, and to whom, upon this occasion, and throughout the whole course of it, we are indebted for much valuable assistance), I trust his recovery is no longer doubtful.

The general merits of Mr Evans are so well known to your Excellency, that it will be sufficient to observe that, by his zealous attention to every point that could facilitate the progress of the Expedition, he has endeavoured to deserve a continuance of your Excellency's approbation.

Mr Charles Frazier, the Colonial Botanist, has added near 700 new specimens to the already extended Catalogue of Australian plants, besides many seeds, &c. and in the Collection and Preservation he has indefatigably endeavoured to obtain your Excellency's approval of his services.

I confidently hope that the Journal of the Expedition will amply evince to your Excellency the exemplary and praiseworthy conduct of the men employed on it; and I feel the sincerest pleasure in earnestly soliciting for them Your Excellency's favourable consideration.

Respectfully hoping, that on a Perusal and Inspection of the Journals and Charts of the Expedition, that the course I have pursued in the execution of Your Excellency's Instructions will be honoured by your approbation,

I beg leave to subscribe myself,
with the greatest respect, Sir, &c.,
JOHN OXLEY,
Surveyor-General

Historical Records of Australia, series 1, vol. X (1917)

HAMILTON HUME
(1797–1873)

and

WILLIAM HOVELL
(1786–1875)

Explorers, who were born in Australia and England respectively. In October 1824 they left Hovell's station at Gunning, near present-day Yass, heading for Western Port. During their journey, they came across numerous rivers, including one which they named the Hume (later renamed the Murray), and lands suitable for grazing and agriculture. In December they reached Corio Bay in Port Phillip, which they mistook for Western Port, because of a miscalculation made by Hovell. They returned to Gunning by a similar route, arriving back there in January 1825. Hovell discovered his mistake when he was sent to Western Port by sea with another party in 1826. He and Hume later squabbled over various matters relating to the expedition.

'A FINE RIVER'

Tuesday, November 16 — Soon after sunrise they re-commence their journey, and having proceeded three miles and half S. (the land gradually sloping as they advanced), arrive suddenly on the banks of a fine river. This was named 'The Hume.'

This beautiful stream is found to be not less than eighty yards in breadth, apparently of considerable depth; the current about three miles an hour; the water, for so considerable a current, clear.

The river itself is serpentine, the banks clothed with verdure to the water's edge; their general height various, but seldom either more or less than eight or nine feet, inclined, or precipitous, as they happen, by the bendings of the stream, to be more or less exposed to the action of the current. On each side of the river is a perpetual succession of lagoons, extending generally in length from one to two miles, and about a quarter of a mile in breadth. These, which are situate alternately on each side of the river, within those elbows or projections which are formed by its windings, often for miles together, preclude any approach to its banks.

Each of these lagoons was furnished with an inlet from the river, and an outlet into it; the former invariably at its higher or eastern, and the latter at its lower or western extremity.

The form of the lagoons is most frequently a crescent; the line of their course being at first divergent from, but ultimately convergent to, the stream. The spaces between the lagoons and the river — sometimes of more than a mile in breadth — are, however, irregular, as well in form as in size. These interspaces partly consist of swamps and unsound ground, which even when dry, although seemingly passable by man, are impassable, or at least unsafe, for cattle. In general these spots are thickly wooded (the trees consisting principally of the blue gum, mostly of a large growth), are overgrown with vines of various descriptions, and the fern, the peppermint, the flax-plant, and currajong. The fern, the currajong, and the flax, flourish here in abundance; and the peppermint plant, (which they had not seen in any other part of the Colony) seems to surpass, both in odour and taste, the species that is generally produced in our gardens. From the flax plant the natives, as they afterwards discovered, make their fishing lines, and the nets which they use for carrying their travelling gear and provisions.

Unable to devise any means of crossing the river, and in the hope of discovering some practicable ford, they now commence their progress (to the westward) down the stream; proceed three miles and a half, and then halt. At half past two they resume their route, but are soon compelled, from the continual succession of lagoon and swamp, to retire to some higher land, about two miles from the river. Here they travel (nearly in the same direction) about three miles, when they again, at four o'clock, encounter the river, at the foot of a conical hill; where they remain for the night. This hill is similar in form to those which have already been noticed. The internal composition, however, appears to be different, consisting (as it should seem from the specimens of it produced, and which were all derived from nearly the summit of the hill) of proportions; 1st, of rag-stone; 2dly, of quartz-mica; 3dly, of an extraordinary specimen of granite, consisting chiefly of quartz; these were found in different parts of the hill: the rag-stone, and the quartz-mica, a few feet from each other, and the granite in a spot somewhat lower down.

From the summit of this hill, there is a fine view of the river, which appearing and disappearing, in its perpetual windings, is visible to the westward about seven or eight miles; and excepting this addition, the view here is the same, or at least consists of nearly the same objects, changed more or less in appearance, by change in point of sight, as that from Battery-mount. At a short distance beyond the furthest spot where the river is visible, there is another conical hill, but one of the sides of which (apparently as if a portion of it had been cut away) is perpendicular and flat, like a wall. Beyond this remarkable object, not a hill is to be seen, and the country between the points S.W. and N.W. up to the barrier collateral ranges, is one continuous flat, studded with trees, gradually but constantly sloping in the direction of the opening between those ranges. This opening, which bore due west from Battery-mount, now bears W.N.W.

A large clear space in this immense forest (bearing W.N.W. distant about fifteen miles), they name 'Fennel's Plains,' after the late Lieut. Fennel. Smoke, supposed to be that of the natives' fires is seen, but at a less distance, in the same direction. Eastwardly are the bluff extremities of several collateral ranges, which proceeding from the main, or N. and S. range, in a winding course, advance various distances, into the low or flat country.

The extremities of none of these ranges appear to be nearer than seven miles, and some of them considerably more distant.

The main range is not here visible, being, most probably, concealed by the tortuous collateral branches.

W. Bland (ed.), *Journey of Discovery to Port Phillip, New South Wales* (1831)

––––––

ALLAN CUNNINGHAM

(1791–1839)

English botanist and explorer. On Joseph Banks's recommendation, Cunningham became a travelling collector for Kew Gardens. After two years in Brazil, he arrived in Sydney in 1816. He accompanied John Oxley on the latter's first expedition (1817), then took part in Phillip Parker King's surveys of the Australian coasts (1818–22). Cunningham found a way across the Liverpool Range (Pandora's Pass) in 1823, and explored the Liverpool Plains in 1825. He is, however, most famous for 'discovering' the Darling Downs, in what is now south-eastern Queensland, in 1827. As he recounts here, he was much impressed by the nature of the land there. The following year he explored from Moreton Bay on the coast to the Darling Downs.

He left for England in 1831, but returned to New South Wales in 1837. Cunningham, who also spent periods botanising in New Zealand, died in Sydney from consumption in 1839.

'A SUPERIOR COUNTRY'

It was my full intention to have continued my course in the direction of the meridian, at least to the parallel of 27°, before I made the least easting towards the coast-line; this design, however, the existing circumstances of the country we had penetrated compelled me to abandon; for the great debility to which the whole of my horses were reduced, by the labours of the journey through a line of country parched up by the drought, at once obliged me to pursue a more eastern course; in which direction, upon gaining the higher lands, I could alone expect to meet with a better pasture than that on which they had for some time subsisted.

On our new course to the northward and eastward, we had to struggle through a desert waste for many miles, before we gained a more undulated surface to the eastward of 151°, when the country through which we journeyed for about thirty miles, presented a succession of thinly wooded stony hills, or low ridges of sandstone rock, separated from each other by narrow valleys, in which my half-famished horses met with but scanty subsistence. At length, on the 5th of June, having gained an elevation of about nine hundred feet above the bed of Dumaresq's River, we reached the confines of a superior country. It was exceedingly cheering to my people, after they had traversed a waste oftentimes of the most forbiddingly arid character, for a space, more or less, of eighty miles, and had borne, with no ordinary patience, a degree of privation to which I had well nigh sacrificed the weaker of my horses — to observe, from a ridge which lay in our course, that they were within a day's march of open downs of unknown extent, which stretched, easterly, to the base of a lofty range of mountains, distant, apparently, about twenty-five miles. On the 6th and following day, we travelled throughout the whole extent of these plains, to the foot of the mountains extending along their eastern side, and the following is the substance of my observations on their extent, soil, and capability.

These extensive tracts of clear pastoral country, which were subsequently named Darling Downs, in honour of his Excellency the Governor, are situated in, or about, the mean parallel of 28° S., along which they stretch east, eighteen statute miles to the meridian of

152°. Deep ponds, supported by streams from the highlands, immediately to the eastward, extend along their central lower flats; and these, when united, in a wet season, become an auxiliary to Condamine's River — a stream which winds its course along their south-western margin. The downs, we remarked, varied in breadth in different parts of their lengthened surface: at their western extremity they appeared not to exceed a mile and a half, whilst towards their eastern limits, their width might be estimated at three miles. The lower grounds, thus permanently watered, present flats, which furnish an almost inexhaustible range of cattle pasture at all seasons of the year — the grasses and herbage generally exhibiting, in the depth of winter, an extraordinary luxuriance of growth. From these central grounds, rise downs of rich, black and dry soil, and very ample surface; and as they furnish an abundance of grass, and are conveniently watered, yet perfectly beyond the reach of those floods, which take place on the flats in a season of rains, they constitute a valuable and sound sheep pasture. We soon reached the base of some hills, connected laterally with that stupendous chain of mountains, the bold outline of which we had beheld with so much interest during the three preceding days. These hills we found clothed, from their foot upwards, with an underwood of the densest description, in the midst of which, and especially on the ridges, appeared a pine, which I immediately discovered to be the same species as that observed in 1824, on the Brisbane River. Encamping, I ascended a remarkable square-topped mount, which formed the western termination of one of these ridges; and from its summit had a very extensive view of the country lying between north and south, towards the west. At N. and N.N.W. we observed a succession of heavily-timbered ridges, extending laterally from the more elevated chain of mountains immediately to the east, which evidently forms the main dividing range in this part of the country; whilst from north-west to west, and thence to south, within a range of twenty miles, a most beautifully diversified landscape, made up of hill and dale, woodland, and plain, appeared before us.

The Journal of the Royal Geographical Society of London, vol. II (1832)

3

THE SOUTH

CHARLES STURT

(1795–1865)

English soldier, explorer, and public servant. At the time of his arrival in Sydney, as an army captain, in 1827, colonists were puzzling over the 'riddle of the rivers'. What were the courses of the colony's west-flowing rivers? Did they end up, as many people believed, in an inland sea? Sturt helped to solve these questions. On his first expedition (1828–29), he examined the Macquarie River, found the Darling River, and explored part of the Castlereagh River. On his second (1829–30), he travelled along the Murrumbidgee, then entered the Murray River and followed it to its mouth on the south coast. He identified the Darling's junction with the Murray on the way, as he writes here, then returned along the rivers. In 1838, while overlanding cattle to Adelaide, Sturt explored the rest of the Murray River.

THREE CHEERS FOR THE DARLING

We were again roused to action by the boat suddenly striking upon a shoal, which reached from one side of the river to the other. To jump out and push her into deeper water was but the work of a moment with the men, and it was just as she floated again that our attention was withdrawn to a new and beautiful stream, coming apparently from the north. The great body of the natives having posted themselves on the narrow tongue of land formed by the two rivers, the bold savage who had so unhesitatingly interfered on our account, was still in hot dispute with them, and I really feared his generous warmth would have brought down upon him the vengeance of the tribes. I hesitated, therefore, whether or not to go to his assistance. It appeared, however, both to M'Leay and myself, that the tone of the natives had moderated, and the old and young men having listened to the remonstrances of our friend, the middle-aged warriors were alone holding out against him. A party of about seventy blacks were upon the right bank of the newly discovered river, and I thought that by landing among them, we should make a diversion in favour of our late guest; and in this I succeeded. If even they had still meditated violence, they would have to swim a good broad junction, and that, probably, would cool them, or we at least should have the advantage of position. I therefore, ran the boat ashore, and landed with M'Leay amidst the smaller party of natives, wholly unarmed, and having directed the men to keep at a little distance from the bank. Fortunately, what I anticipated was brought about by the stratagem to which I had had recourse. The blacks no sooner observed that we had landed, than curiosity took place of anger. All wrangling ceased, and they came swimming over to us like a parcel of seals. Thus, in less than a quarter of an hour from the moment when it appeared that all human intervention was at an end, and we were on the point of commencing a bloody fray, which, independently of its own disastrous consequences, would have blasted the success of the expedition, we were peacefully surrounded by the hundreds who had so lately threatened us with destruction; nor was until after we had returned to the boat, and had surveyed the multitude upon the sloping bank above us, that we became fully aware of the extent of our danger, and of the almost miraculous intervention of Providence in our favour. There could not have been less than six hundred natives upon that blackened sward. But this was not the only occasion upon which the merciful superintendance of that Providence to which we had humbly committed ourselves, was strikingly manifested. If these pages fail to convey entertainment or information, sufficient may at least be gleaned from them to furnish matter for serious reflection; but to those who have been placed in situations of danger where human ingenuity availed them not, and where human foresight was baffled, I feel persuaded that these remarks are unnecessary.

It was my first care to call for our friend, and to express to him, as well as I could, how much we stood indebted to him, at the same time that I made him a suitable present; but to the chiefs of the tribes, I positively refused all gifts, notwithstanding their earnest solicitations. We next prepared to examine the new river, and turning the boat's head towards it, endeavoured to pull up the stream. Our larboard oars touched the right bank, and the current was too strong for us to conquer it with a pair only; we were, therefore, obliged to put a second upon her, a movement that excited the astonishment and admiration of the natives. One old woman seemed in absolute extacy, to whom M'Leay threw an old tin kettle, in recompense for the amusement she afforded us.

As soon as we got above the entrance of the new river, we found easier pulling, and proceeded up it for some miles, accompanied by the once more noisy multitude. The river preserved a breadth of one hundred yards, and a depth of rather more than twelve feet. Its banks were sloping and grassy, and were overhung by trees of magnificent size. Indeed, its appearance was so different from the water-worn banks of the sister stream, that the men exclaimed, on entering it, that we had got into an English river. Its appearance certainly almost justified the expression; for the greenness of its banks was as new to us as the size of its timber. Its waters, though sweet, were turbid, and had a taste of vegetable decay, as well as a slight tinge of green. Our progress was watched by the natives with evident anxiety. They kept abreast of us, and talked incessantly. At length, however, our course was checked by a net that stretched right across the stream. I say *checked,* because it would have been unfair to have passed over it with the chance of disappointing the numbers who apparently depended on it for subsistence that day. The moment was one of intense interest to me. As the men rested upon their oars, awaiting my further orders, a crowd of thoughts rushed upon me. The various conjectures I had formed of the course and importance of the Darling passed across my mind. Were they indeed realized? An irresistible conviction impressed me that we were now sailing on the bosom of that very stream from whose banks I had been twice forced to retire. I directed the Union Jack to be hoisted, and giving way to our satisfaction, we all stood up in the boat, and gave three distinct cheers. It was an English feeling, an ebullition, an overflow, which I am ready to admit that our circumstances and situation will alone excuse. The eye of every native had been fixed upon that noble flag, at all times a beautiful object, and to them a novel one, as it waved over us in the heart of a desert. They had, until that moment been particularly loquacious, but the sight of that flag and the sound of our voices hushed the tumult, and while they were still lost in astonishment, the boat's head was speedily turned, the sail was sheeted home, both wind and current were in our favour, and we vanished from them with a rapidity that surprised even ourselves, and which precluded every hope of the most adventurous among them to keep up with us.

Two Expeditions into the Interior of Southern Australia, During the Years 1828, 1829, 1830, and 1831, vol. II (1833)

GEORGE AUGUSTUS ROBINSON

(1788–1886)

Protector of Aborigines. In 1829, Robinson, who had arrived in Hobart Town from England in 1824, was appointed by Lieutenant-Governor George Arthur to work with the Van Diemen's Land Aborigines. For the next few years he travelled extensively around the island, initially making contact with Aborigines, later persuading them to live in captivity. As this 1830 journal entry suggests, Robinson incidentally became involved in some exploration during his travels. After running the Aboriginal settlement on Flinders Island (1835–39), he worked as chief protector of Aborigines in the Port Phillip district (1839–49). Robinson left Australia in 1852, spending the remainder of his life in England and on the European continent.

SOUTHERN VAN DIEMEN'S LAND

13 March — At 6 am got breakfast. Fair weather, the atmosphere clear and a gentle pleasant breeze. Found my strength renewed, the fever dissipated. Proceeded to reach the high mountain. Came to another lagoon sunk in the mountain and with a perpendicular cliff rising as before to a considerable height above the base on which I stood: its waters appearing black I called it the Black Lagoon. Then to two other lagoons one of them still deeper, the other about a hundred feet below the surface. In the waters of the second were to be seen small islands and from the shore ran out points with white sandy beaches. The aborigine Tom called them 'boat harbours' and said he would take his farm on one of the islands. Reached the highest part of the mountain. The morning was serene. These mountains, named in Evans' map 'high ridge of white-topped mountains', consist of white quartz which at a distance is frequently mistaken for snow. Saw a large white mountain kangaroo on the top of the mountain. The range is by far the highest land in that part of the country and, I may venture to say, in any of the south part of the island. My object in ascending this mountain was to view the country adjacent, which at this time was unexplored and of which very little was known, and to ascertain if there was any tribes of aborigines in that part and, if I could, discover whether they had a track to the settled districts. The high round mountain named in Evans' map rises up from this ridge of mountains. This range of mountains I named Arthur's range and the round mountain Mount Frederick. Had a very extensive view of the country around. Could see the Peak of Teneriffe. The country to the north-east appeared open marshes with gentle rising hills. An extensive marsh about a mile in width ran along the part of the north-east end of the mountain in a direction north-west by west in a direction of Macquarie Harbour. Could perceive several lakes of fresh water at a distance. These marshes I named Southern Marshes; they intersect each other at the north-east end of the range of mountains.

Proceeded to descend the mountain. The two men as before was hurrying away when I sent after McKay and asked him if he was not ashamed of his conduct and told him of his behaviour on crossing the ravine. I told him he was with me to give assistance. He said if he was to fall down he had no person to help him up, he had no assistance. Indeed I had found him to be a headstrong sort of man from the outset. These sort of men do great injury to an undertaking of this kind. I referred him to my saying that I would not require him or any other man to do what I would not do myself. Purposing to travel through the marsh which took a direction north-west by west, I sent McGeary forward to bring up the rest of the party. Reached the bottom and crossed the river, and after travelling about ten miles stopped for the night in a thick forest on its banks. The day had been fine and the marshes were very good travelling. Saw not the least sign or appearance of natives, or of any white man ever being in this part of the country. The natives that accompanied me assured me there was no natives ever went inland, but I was anxious to be satisfied. Passed another high mountain near to this range, which I named Mount Maria.

N. J. B. Plomley (ed.), *Friendly Mission: The Tasmanian Journals and Papers of George Augustus Robinson, 1829–1834* (1966)

———

ROBERT LAWRENCE

(1808–33)

Botanist. After completing his education in England, Robert followed his father, the wealthy English merchant William Effingham Lawrence, to Van Diemen's Land in 1825. Described as 'a young man of scientific bent', he began collecting for, and corresponding with, the British botanist and director of Kew Gardens, William Jackson Hooker, in 1830. Lawrence died prematurely in October 1833, being 'carried off in a fit of apoplexy' at Formosa, his father's property on the Lake River, where he was overseer. A few months previously he had made this trip, the details of which he recorded for Hooker.

'NOTES ON AN EXCURSION UP THE WESTERN MOUNTAINS'

[15 January] — None of the gentlemen who had engaged to accompany me on my expedition to the Lakes and along the Western range of mountains having arrived, with the exception of Mr Curson, we started with three men at about 6 o'clock a.m. carrying with us about a weeks stock of flour, tea & sugar &c — We had walked nearly six miles before we discovered that we had forgotten our shot. The circumstances of sending a man back for it detained us nearly six hours. During the time we were obliged to wait, the mountain tops became enveloped in clouds and there was every appearance of approaching bad weather. At length we had a pretty heavy fall of rain, accompanied by a squall, and by the time the man had returned with the shot, all was clear again and promised favourably. On his return we proceeded upwards, and reached about half way up the flat topped mountain, where we halted for the night. Our tent was a very portable one, consisting of two strong, coarse sheets sewn together and stretched over such a frame as we could most conveniently construct from the sticks of Prostanthera lasianthos and other shrubs around us. Met with nothing very remarkable to day.

The base of this mountain, to one third of its entire height is composed of White Sand-stone (free-stone) of excellent quality as a building stone; hence, at a future period, we may reckon upon having substantial buildings at Formosa in place of the miserable wooden ones which at present exist there. Though indeed that time must be far off as it is intended to build in pise at present. I had not time to ramble much in this neighbourhood, to seek the minerals which normally associate with this rock; as my principal object was to attain high elevation for the purpose of obtaining specimens of the plants proper to them.

We made a very large fire in the evening in order that those at home might see to what height we had ascended —

[16 January] — The rill which afforded us water, also afforded two or three uncommon Musci, among them Lyellia crispa Dawsonia Polytrichoides and an acquatic moss of peculiar aspect which was unfortunately not in flower.

After collecting the above mentioned varieties we continued our ascent, which became more precipitous as we advanced. In the course of the Day we arrived at the summit of the Flat-topped (I have forgotten how to spell if I ever knew) mountain, after having climbed up places, from which when I looked downwards I felt considerable nervousness though my friend Mr Curson, whose small figure gave him an advantage, mounted up them with apparently the ease of a kangaroo — (Macropus minor?)

We passed during the morning usual alpine plants, such of which as were in flower or fruit I collected. Among them were Drymophila cynocarpa, several species of Pultenaea, Lomatia polymorpha, Leucopogon sp. Hakea sp., Orites sp. &c &c

Mr Curson took two men to hunt while I remained at a place which we had fixed upon as an encampment with one man —

Mr Curson after about two hours absence returned without any game. I collected about the neighbourhood of the tent two species of Richea and an Eucalyptus, together with several other things —

The country here presents a rügged, and romantic appearance, being constituted of small wet flats or plains over which are scattered projecting columns of Basalt, and hemispherical masses of a species of moss, resembling beautiful green cushions; and occasional masses of rock, calling to mind the appearance of ruined Castles.

After our tent was erected I sent two men out again to hunt. During their absence a severe storm came on and they returned unsuccessful. It was exceedingly cold so much so that the mens Kangaroo skin Caps and pouches were quite stiffened. Snowing all night —

[17 January] — We found that during the night there had been a fall of several inches of snow. The sun however when rising promised us a fine day. After looking around us a little, and admiring the extensive panoramic scene beneath us, I started accompanied by Mr Curson and two men to hunt — We were out several hours, but owing to the dogs having lamed themselves in ascending the mountain, and to the ground being very stony we were again unsuccessful. We saw many Kangaroo of both the Forest kind and the Brush. We observed excrement of the Hyhena (Didelphis cynocephalus, vel Thylacinus cyanocephalus) but saw very few traces of quadrupeds, except those named above. Of Birds, there are but few, the most remarkable of

which I have been accustomed to call the Mountain Bird, from the circumstances of always having found in such situations. Its scientific name I do not know but it appears to belong to the Ord. Pici of Blumenloch. Our collection of specimens and seeds of Plants was satisfactory this morning, Richea, a new (to me) small Pultenaea, a trailing Exocarpus, and a trailing aphyllus shrub were among the most prominent.

Returning to the tent, when after having rested a short time, we packed up and proceeded due South towards the Lakes; the Mountains running east and west. These mountains being purely Basaltic there is nothing to interest the mineralogist. After having walked about three miles, we saw a considerable number of Kangaroo. I therefore halted, that we might have the advantage of the evening and the next morning for hunting in the neighbourhood —

The country here is mainly a repetition of small plains, and low stony hills. The Plains having grasses and alpine plants upon them, but evidently being subject to lie under water during the winter season, indeed there is water on, or running through every one of them at this season — The hills bear several Eucalypts of deformed aspect arising from exposure to the winds, which are high and frequent. Tasmannia fragrans, and several Hakeas & Orites appear here. The hunters were unsuccessful though numbers of fine Forester (a larger kind of Kangaroo. I believe not the Macropus giganteus, however) were seen by them. The Dogs would not run though they were half starved —

[18 January] — Two of the men went out to hunt at the dawn of day, one of whom returned to breakfast, the other having lost himself — After waiting for him for several hours we fired some shots, by which we succeeded in leading him to us. No Game. — We were occupied some time in arranging the specimens of Plants and other things, when we had done which we proceeded towards the Lakes; at the first and smallest of which after about two hours walking we arrived. Found a Veronica which I had never seen before with deeply divided leaves — As we were walking through some underwood a Kangaroo started before me which I shot. The next or middle Lake was soon in sight. Here we heard the noise of Dogs, which we attributed to a party of Blacks hunting. — As we were walking along a plain leading to Lake Arthur we discovered a herd of as we thought wild cattle, but on shooting one of them, we found it to be branded with the letters J.J. Shortly afterwards we were surprised to see a flock of sheep. — Arrived at the largest of Arthurs Lakes, called I believe Lake Arthur. In the evening shot a Duck —

[19 January] — This morning we took about 18 lbs of meat from the Bullock killed yesterday. As we were sitting down to breakfast three men appeared, who turned out to be the overseer and stock keepers belonging to a Mr Jones of Jericho, the proprietor of the Cattle and Sheep we had seen, and who had only settled in this neighbourhood about a week before. This was satisfactory as it enabled me to explain to them what I had done. The Overseer was very civil and invited me to his hut. Found Bellendena montana in flower and an Epacris new to me. We remained about the Lake the whole of the day. Found several rare plants and one quite new to me, of the order Compositae. I shot two Ducks from behind some tea-trees (Leptospermum sp.)

The scenery about Arthur's Lakes is less picturesque than it is generally reported to be, though it must be confessed that the largest of the three is a fine sheet of water. The most eastward or smallest is not more than a mile in length, is surrounded by marshes and the south western end is very reedy. The middle Lake is about two or three miles in length. But the only one worth seeing is the largest one, being twenty or thirty miles in circumference. The eastern shore is shallow for a long way in and reminds a little of a seashore from the rocks being worn by the no doubt rolling waves in windy weather, and from the collection of a sand bank inland — I am not aware that there are any fish in this large piece of water save Eels. — Waterfowl abound; two or three kinds of Ducks, Swans, and Divers. The Ornithorynchus paradoxus is plentiful here.

[20 January] — About 11 o'clock after having aired and packed up our specimens &c we made our way to the westward of north towards the Peaks; two conical eminences, about 500 ft above the top of the flat-topped mountain — Collected seeds of the Cyder tree (Eucalyptus sp.) — I shot two Kangaroo in the course of the morning. — Collected specimens of a few uncommon plants. — In the afternoon we reached the foot of the highest Peak where we erected our tent near a plentiful supply of water. — Wind blew cold from the eastward. —

[21 January] — Arranged the specimens collected yesterday previous to ascending the Peaks — In our ramble up the Peak we fell in with Gaultheria hispida, and a new plant in Decandria (Perhaps a Baeckia) — Also a good deal of Lomatia polymorpha. The wind blew very strong & in less than an hour the Thermometer fell 10°. Abundance of Usnea sphacelata? here — If what I have been accustomed to call U. sphacelata is this new one, its distribution is universal over this island from the lowest to the highest altitudes I have visited. As we approached the top it became very precipitous, and the wind being exceedingly

high I became too nervous to be able to ascend further though I made several attempts. — Mr Curson, however, and my gardener went to the top. Very cold indeed all day.

[22 January] — A considerable fall of snow during the night —

Having packed up our traps, we prepared to descend. From the Flat-topped mountain we observed the gully, which appeared to take the desired direction and we determind upon following it to the bottom, where it appeared to constitute the creek which bounds the western side of Mr J. Archer's estate, adjoining my father's upper sheep-run. We found here a hairy moss (Trichostomum?) of which I collected a number of specimens, but they were unfortunately not in flower. A number of very beautiful ravine-plants were passed as we proceeded downwards. The lower Third of this mountain appears to be composed of free-stone; we passed perpendicular and (by the action of water) excavated rocks of it I dare say an hundred feet in height. Fine specimens of Prostanthera lasianthos

From this place we pushed on very hard for the purpose of endeavouring if possible to reach Formosa. We arrived at the level ground at the foot of the mountains, just as it was darkening, and reached Formosa at about 11 o'clock at night, after a walk of about thirty miles, over a rugged country, with considerable weight upon our backs —

I should have enumerated the principal plants seen on this excursion as far as I could, had I not sent you specimens of them.

T. E. Burns & J. R. Skemp, *Van Diemen's Land Correspondents* (1961)

———

JOHN LHOTSKY
(1795?–1865?)

Naturalist, born in Lemberg (Lwów), to Czech parents. Lhotsky had qualified as a doctor of medicine in Europe and spent some 18 months undertaking botanical and zoological research in South America, before he arrived in Sydney in 1832. With some government assistance, he explored the Monaro district of New South Wales in 1834, as a result of which he wrote A Journey from Sydney to the Australian Alps (1835). Some suggestion of his eccentricities can be found in the work's opening paragraphs, reproduced here. He later worked and travelled in Van Diemen's Land, before departing for England in 1838.

DR LHOTSKY TAKES AN AERIAL BATH

After a labour which I may call immense, in order to compress into a narrow compass, and that at the least possible expense, the requisites of a long Journey, I started from Sydney on the 10th of January, 1834. I had with me a cart with one horse, and four men; it matters not whether they were called free or assigned: as long as an assigned servant conducts himself properly, I treat him as a free one, and I should wish to possess the discretion, as often as I should deem it expedient, of acting *vice versa.* — I left behind me all Bills of Exchange, Courts, Summonses, Attorneys, Editors of Newspapers, Gaols and such like, and exulted in the feeling, that abandoning all these delights of ultra-civilized society, I should once again enjoy for some time, a freedom nearly approaching the state of nature. I left Sydney at 10 A.M., and determined to stop for dinner with my party in the bush opposite Grose Farm, as the heat was excessive, and as I was desirous of habituating my half-wild horse, and town-fashioned servants by degrees, to the change of life we were about to commence. We were all in the best possible spirits — At 3 P.M. the heat reached its highest degree, and there were only a few fine cirrho clouds standing in the zenith, at an immense altitude, in the perfectly clear and serene firmament, while a rather fresh N.E. breeze was blowing intermittingly.

My health which did not suffer during an 18 months residence in the hottest parts of the Brazils, had been much impaired since my arrival in New South Wales, and though I cannot call the climate of Sydney unhealthy, yet the sudden transitions of Australian temperature, and the predominance of Southerly Gales, charged as they are with incredible quantities of the dust of our unpaved and unwatered streets, injure the lungs of the inhabitants more than might be believed. This day, however, I was induced to attempt a remedy, which under the necessary precautions and restrictions, may be adopted by persons similarly circumstanced. I bared the upper part of my body, and in that state walked for half an hour in the currents of air among the trees. The effect was excessively beneficial, and I felt the muscles of my thorax so much invigorated, that I repeated the experiment during my journey with the most beneficial result. To physicians at home, this ærial bath has been long known, and it would appear besides, that the slender clothing of tropical nations, rests on a deeper diatetical foundation, than is generally supposed. I stopped the first night at J. Solomon's inn, on the Liverpool Road, where the accommodation as in many other Country inns of the Colony, was not to be complained of. From this place, George's River is distant in a straight line, about 6 miles; Botany, 19; Banks Town, 19; these distances however, do not accord exactly with those given in our latest map, viz: — that published by Captain Sturt; but we rest assured that these, and other errors of that map will be corrected in the shortly expected publication by Major Mitchell, whose application, and exertions as a Surveyor, are so well known to the whole Colony. At 9 P.M., I observed lightning to the N.N.W., although the horizon was clear and the air chilly and bracing. Scarcely a day passes without this phenomenon being observed in the Northern parts of the Colony. Neither heat nor cold, wind or calm, rain or drought, seems to effect the excretion of electric matter, which should therefore appear to be exceedingly copious in our skies. At Sydney I have observed lightning in different, and almost opposite directions.

A Journey from Sydney to the Australian Alps (1835)

———

LAURIE DUGGAN

(1949–)

Australian poet. Duggan focuses on the Victorian region of Gippsland, the land of his forebears, in his award-winning epic documentary poem, The Ash Range *(1987). The work, which draws on various sources, including diaries, letters, and newspapers, has been described by the expatriate poet Peter Porter as a 'paean to the land'. In this section from it we hear the voices of several explorers who ventured towards the area, including John Lhotsky.*

FROM 'MAPS'

Passed through a chain of clear downs to some very extensive ones, where we met a tribe of natives, who fled at our approach, however, we soon, by tokens of kindness, offering them biscuits etc. together with the assistance of a domesticated native of our party,

Mark Currie 4/6/1823

induced them to come nearer and nearer, till by
degrees we ultimately became good friends; but on
no account would they touch or approach our horses,
of which they were from the first much more
frightened than of ourselves. We learned that the
clear country before us was called Monaroo.

Extensive plains
    gently undulating
        destitute of timber
extend, with interruption
    to Maniroon Plains
        south of Lake George,
large portions
    occupied in grazing.

James
Atkinson
1826

The silence and
solitude that reign in these wide spreading untenanted
wastes, are indescribable.

No traces of the works or
even the existence of man are here to be met with,
except perhaps the ashes of a fire on the banks of
some river.

From the contemplation of this vacancy
and solitude the mind recoils with weariness.

*

Near Mr Rose's station is a lofty table-mountain,
forming the commencement of a mountainous range,
extending in a south-west direction,

George
Bennett
1834

named 'Bugong',
from the circumstance of multitudes of small moths
congregating at certain months of the year about
masses of granite. November, December and January
the native blacks assemble to collect the Bugong; the
bodies of these insects contain a quantity of oil, and
they are sought after as a luscious and fattening
food.

12th of December, at dawn, accompanied by
a stock-keeper and some of the blacks, I commenced
my excursion.

The view from the second summit of
Bugong was open to the southward.

Beyond the two counties,
     Murray & St Vincent,
Mitchell's map blankens,
         bare below the 36th parallel;
   lines of rivers,
    valley sources of the Deua, Queanbeyan,
      Shoalhaven and Murrumbidgee
        unmarked;
    sole outcrops Orungal, Mt Murray, The Twins;
   then no lines to trace but Meridians
   as Lhotsky moves south from Lake George
   towards a mountain no-one is sure he discovered.
           *

3 March. Noons rest — 3 Miles further a brook   **John**
1 Mile further Ossian's Seat.   **Lhotsky**
Camped in Byron's Valley.   **1834**

4 March. Right up a high range, 1½ Miles.
Then 2 Miles W.S.W., an other heavy hill,
from the Top the stream — Valley of Snowy River
visible ~~towards E.S.E.~~ in a radius from W to E.
The Snowy turns by a succession of bendings
from ~~from~~ W.S.W. to a Westerly, & then N. Easterly,
and then Easterly direction.

— a world of mountains
30 Miles a Mamellon
beyond which is Omeo (?)

11th March   reached Chalmers' forest,
   an escarped Mountain covered
        with lofty timber
main Alps visible to N.W, runing
     from E.S.E. to W.N.W.
        20 Miles distant.
               Proceeding farther
a Panorama of mountains.

12th March.   From Didik, the pass to Omeo lies W.
Snowy River runs here S.
    Traversed several transversal Yokes

Descended again towards Snowy River, which is very sinuous.
Ascended (almost dead from fatigue)
Dunom Burmongi
— arrived and stopped at Pass Britannia

22 March.   we saw
mountains topped with snow, then
fine cattle land.
Bidda a waterrun of 400 roads breth
& 7 Miles long,
all luxuriant Alpine meadows.

Ascended the seaside range
saw the sea at a distance of 25 to 35 miles
a low scrubby forest intervening

**George
McKillop
1835**

a splendid country,
watered by numerous rivers,
forming one of considerable magnitude
debouching between Ram Head and Cape Howe.

Four years later
Baylis and Wilkinson
moved in on Buchan and Gelantipy.

The Ash Range (1987)

———

RICHARD WHATELY

(1787–1863)

Anglican archbishop of Dublin from 1831 until his death, and vocal opponent of transportation during the 1830s. Whately is considered to have been responsible for writing a fictitious work entitled Account of an Expedition to the Interior of New Holland, *supposedly an authentic report edited by a Lady Mary Fox, which was first published in 1837. The explorers involved leave Bathurst in August 1835 and travel to inland Australia, where they find a 'civilized' nation of between three and four million people of European, mostly English, descent. The nation, remarkably,*

has had no contact with other 'civilized' people for almost three centuries.
The book opens with this description of the explorers' outward journey.

A 'WONDERFUL DISCOVERY'

Our readers will, no doubt, be interested by the few particulars we have
been able to collect of the late wonderful discovery, in the interior of
New Holland, of a civilized nation of European origin, which had, in
so remarkable a manner, been kept separate hitherto from the rest of
the civilized world.

Mr Hopkins Sibthorpe, who planned and conducted this singularly
fortunate enterprise, was accompanied, it appears, in the expedition by
another settler, Mr William Jones, and Messrs Thomas and Robert
Smith (brothers), of the navy; who, together with Wilkins, a sailor,
hired as their servant, constituted the whole party.

It was in the early part of August 1835 that these adventurous
explorers took their departure from the settlement at Bathurst: this, as
our readers are aware, is the last month of the winter of that hemi-
sphere; though, from the greater mildness of the climate, it may be
considered as spring. This season was chosen as the most suitable for
an expedition in such a country as New Holland; in which, not only
the heat of summer and autumn is often very oppressive, but also the
scarcity of water is one of the most formidable impediments: and, on
this occasion, a plentiful supply of water being essential, not only with
a view to their personal wants, but also to the accomplishment of the
peculiar plan they had resolved on trying, it was thought best to take
an early advantage of the effects of the winter's rains.

Their plan was no other than to construct a canoe, to enable them
to proceed in a direction in which farther progress had hitherto been
precluded by a vast expanse of marshy lake. This, as our readers are
probably aware, from the published narratives of former expeditions,
is, in moist seasons, a sort of Mere, or shallow water, encumbered with
aquatic plants; but in times of great drought is, for a considerable
extent, dry, or consisting of mud rather than water; constituting a sort
of swampy plain, so choked up with a rank vegetation of reeds and
flags as to present an almost insuperable obstacle to the traveller.

In the present expedition, accordingly, it was determined to choose
a time when there might be a sufficiency of water to enable the adventurous explorers to proceed in a canoe; and they accordingly carried
with them one or two horses (which they proposed afterwards to turn
loose) — the iron-work, and as much as was thought necessary of the

frame of a canoe, which they proposed to put together and complete on their arrival on the margin of the lake. And as it was impossible to carry with them a sufficient store of provisions for the whole of their contemplated voyage, they boldly resolved to trust in great measure to their guns and fishing-tackle, providing only a sufficiency of salt to preserve such game and fish as they might procure in their way.

The details of the expedition, curious and highly interesting as they are in themselves, we are compelled to omit, lest they should occupy the space wanted for a far more valuable and important portion of the narrative. It will be sufficient, therefore, to say, omitting particulars, that they were enabled to put their design in execution; and having constructed a kind of light flat-bottomed boat, of poles covered with bark (of the kind the natives use for their canoes), and fitted up with a slight awning, to afford shelter from the sun and the dews, they embarked on the above-mentioned shallow lake, and proceeded in a north-west direction; sometimes rowing, assisted occasionally by a sail, and oftener pushing themselves on with poles through the tangled aquatic plants which grew on the muddy bottom.

Their progress was at first tediously slow; but they were at no loss for provision, as the waters abounded with fish and wildfowl, of which they continued to obtain a sufficient supply throughout the voyage. After two days of troublesome navigation they found the water became deeper, and gained a sight of some elevated land towards the west, which they reached on the evening of the third day: they here found the lake not terminated, but confined within narrow limits by hills, for the most part of a rocky, sterile, and uninviting character: at length it became a broad river, flowing in a northerly direction, and serving evidently as a drain to the great expanse of lake they had passed. This gave them hopes of reaching (which was their great object) some large navigable river, which they might follow to the sea: they proceeded, therefore, though with considerable delay and difficulty from shoals and rapids, till, after more than two days' navigation, the high ground receded, and they found themselves entering on another great expanse of water, so extensive that, in pursuing their adventurous course nearly in the same direction, they were, for the greater part of one day, out of sight of land.

They now arrived at another course of rocky hills, of considerable elevation, through which the waters found an exit by a narrow gorge: through this they proceeded in a direction northwards for a considerable distance, when they found the river again expanding itself at intervals into a chain of lakes, smaller but deeper than those they had passed, and surrounded by a much more agreeable country, which continued to improve as they advanced. They landed in several places, and in one instance came in contact with a party of natives, who were of a less savage aspect than those in the vicinity of our settlements, and showed no signs of hostility, and much less of alarm and astonishment than had been expected. From this circumstance, and also from steel knives being in the possession of two or three of them, on which they appeared to set great value, it was conjectured that they must, in their wanderings, have, at some time or other, approached our settlements: their language, however, was perfectly unintelligible to Mr Jones, though he had a considerable acquaintance with that of the natives near Sydney.

Some days after, as they continued their progress, they fell in with another party of natives, who excited still more wonder and speculation in our travellers, from their having among them ornaments evidently fashioned from the tusks of boars; these (as it was understood from the signs they made, in answer to the questions put to them by the same means) they described themselves as having hunted with their dogs, and speared. But all doubt was removed the next day, by the travellers actually obtaining a sight of a wild hog in the woods, and afterwards of a herd of wild cattle, which they distinctly saw with their glasses: these animals being well known not to be indigenous in New Holland, afforded strong indications of the vicinity of some European settlement; though, as they felt certain of being far distant from the coast, they were utterly lost in conjecture.

After proceeding in the manner above described, through a long chain of lakes connected by the river which they were continuing to navigate, through a country continually improving in beauty and fertility, and presenting a strong contrast to the dreary rocks and marshes they had left behind, they were at length surprised and gratified, on entering a lake somewhat more extensive than the last, to see several fishing-boats, the men in which they ascertained by their glasses to be decently clothed, and white men. They ventured to approach and to hail them; and, to their unspeakable surprise and delight, they received an answer in English: the English was, indeed, not precisely similar to their own, but not differing so much from it as many of our provincial dialects; and in a short time the two parties were tolerably intelligible to each other.

We are compelled to pass over the interesting detail of the meeting, which was equally gratifying and surprising to both the parties; of the eager curiosity of their mutual inquiries; and of the hospitable invitation given, and, as may be supposed, joyfully accepted by the travellers. Accompanying their hosts in one of the fishing-boats, they found before them, on turning the point of a wooded promontory which had intercepted their view, a rich and partially cultivated country, interspersed with cheerful-looking villages, having much of an English air of comfort; though the whole was in a far ruder condition than much of what they saw afterwards, as the point they had reached was the extreme skirt of a comparatively recent settlement.

The reception they met with was most friendly and every way refreshing, after an anxious and toilsome journey of above a month. They found themselves, on the second day after their arrival in the colony, the guests of the chief magistrate of a neat town of considerable size, where they were surrounded by visitors from all parts, eager to obtain and to afford information, and overwhelming them with pressing invitations.

Lady Mary Fox (ed.), *Account of an Expedition to the Interior of New Holland* (1837)

———

THOMAS LIVINGSTONE MITCHELL

(1792–1855)

Scottish-born soldier and surveyor. Major Mitchell, who had previously served in the Peninsular War, was surveyor-general of New South Wales from 1828 until his death. He left Parramatta in March 1835 with the aim of finding out whether, as his rival Charles Sturt believed, the Darling flowed into the Murray River. Mitchell traced the Darling River for almost 500 kilometres, but turned back in July after the violent episode that he describes here, without having reached the Murray. His other major expeditions saw him explore around the Gwydir and Burwon Rivers (1831–32), 'discover' the present-day Victorian Western District, which he named Australia Felix (1836), and unsuccessfully attempt to find an inland route from Sydney to the Gulf of Carpentaria (1845–46).

CONFLICT WITH ABORIGINES

July 11 — Soon after sunrise this morning, some natives, I think twelve or thirteen in number, were seen approaching our tents at a kind of run, carrying spears and green boughs. As soon as they arrived within a short distance, three came forward, stuck their spears in the ground, and seemed to beckon me to approach; but as I was advancing towards them, they violently shook their boughs at me, and having set them on fire, dashed them to the ground, calling out 'Nangry,' (sit down). I accordingly obeyed the mandate; but seeing that they stood, and continued their unfriendly gestures, I arose and called to my party, on which the natives immediately turned, and ran away.

I took forward some men, huzzaing after them for a short distance, and we fired one shot over their heads, as they ran stumbling to the other side of an intervening clear flat, towards the tribe, who were assembling, as lookers-on. There they made a fire, and seeming disposed to stop, I ordered four men with muskets to advance and make them quit that spot; but the men had scarcely left the camp when the natives withdrew, and joined the tribe beyond, amid much laughter and noise. These were some natives who had, the day before, arrived from the south-east, having joined the fishing tribe, while they were at our present camp. These men of the south-east, had a remarkable peculiarity of countenance, occasioned by high cheek-bones, and compressed noses. We imagined we had met their bravado very successfully, for soon after they had been chased from our camp, part of them crossed the country to the eastward, as if returning whence they came. They passed us at no great distance, but did not venture to make further demonstrations with burning boughs. At one o'clock, the tribe, for which the messenger had been sent, as I concluded, the day before, appeared on a small clear hill to the south-west of our camp, coming apparently from the very quarter where I wished to go. They soon came up to our tents without ceremony, led on by the same old thief, who had followed us down the river, and who seemed to have been the instigator of all this mischief. As he had been already detected by us, and was aware, that he was a marked man, it appeared that he had coloured his head and beard black, by way of disguise. This was a very remarkable personage, his features decidedly Jewish, having a thin aquiline nose, and a very piercing eye, as intent on mischief, as if it had belonged to Satan himself. I received the strangers, who appeared to be a stupid harmless-looking set, as civilly as I could, giving to one, who appeared to be their chief, a nail. I soon afterwards entered my tent, and they went northward towards the river, motioning that they were going for food, but that they would return and sleep near us. I became now apprehensive, that the party could not be safely separated under such circumstances, and when I ascertained, as I did just then, that a small stream joined the Darling from the west, and that a range was visible in the same direction beyond it, I discontinued the preparations I had been making for exploring the river further with pack animals, and determined to return. The identity of this river with that which had been seen to enter the Murray, now admitted of little doubt, and the continuation of the survey to that point, was scarcely an object worth the peril likely to attend it. I had traced its course upwards of 300 miles, through a country which did not supply a single stream, all the torrents which might descend from the sharp and naked hills, being absorbed by the thirsty earth. Over the whole of this extensive region, there grew but little grass, and few trees available for any useful purpose, except varieties of acacia, a tree so peculiar to these desert interior regions, and which there seemed to be nourished only by the dews of night.

Scarce an hour had elapsed, after I had communicated my deter-mination to the party, when a shot was heard on the river. This was soon followed by several others, which were more plainly audible, because the wind was fortunately from the north-west; and as five of the bullock-drivers and two men, sent for water, were at that time there, and also the tribe of king Peter, it was evident that a collision had taken place between them. The arrival of the other tribe, who still lingered on our right front, made this appear like a preconcerted attack; and two of the tribe again came forward, just as the shots were echoing along the river, to ask for fire and something to eat. Their apparent indifference to the sound of musquetry was curious, and as they had not yet communicated with those to whom they were visitors, I believed they were really ignorant then of what was going on. The river extended along our front from west to north-east, at an average distance of three-quarters of a mile; and this tribe was now about that distance to the eastward of the scene of action: soft and hollow ground, thickly set with polygonum, intervened. I had previously sent a man to amuse and turn back their messenger, when I saw him going towards the fishing tribe; and now this strange tribe having arrived, as I concluded, hungry and expecting the fish, seemed disappointed, and came to ask food from us. I was most anxious to know, what was going on at the river, where all our horses and cattle were seen running about, but the defence of our camp required all my attention. As soon as the firing was heard, several men rushed forward as volunteers to support the party on the river, and take them more ammunition. Those, whose services I accepted, were William Woods, Charles King, and John Johnston (the blacksmith), who all ran through the polygonum bushes with a speed, that seemed to astonish, even the two natives, still sitting before our camp. In the mean time we made every possible preparation for defence. Robert Whiting, who was very ill and weak, crawled to a wheel; and he said that though unable to stand, he had yet strength enough to load and fire. The shots at the river seemed renewed almost as soon as the reinforcement left us, but we were obliged to remain in ignorance of the nature and result of the attack, for at least an hour, after the firing had ceased. At length a man was seen emerging from the scrub near the river bank, whose slow progress almost exhausted our patience, until, as he drew near, we saw that he was wounded and bleeding. This was Joseph Jones, who had been sent for water, and who, although much hurt, brought a pot and a tea-kettle full, driving the sheep before him, according to custom. It now turned out, that the tea-kettle which Jones carried, had been the sole cause of the quarrel. As he was ascending the river bank with the water, Thomas Jones (the sailor) being stationed on the bank, covering the other with his pistol, as was usual and necessary on this journey; king Peter, who had come along the bank with several other natives, met him when half way up, and smilingly took hold of the pot, as if meaning to assist him in carrying it up; but on reaching the top of the bank, he, in the same jocose way, held it fast, until a gin said something to him, upon which he relinquished the pot and seized the kettle with his left hand, and at the same time grasping his waddy or club in his right, he immediately struck Joseph Jones senseless to the ground, by a violent blow on the forehead. On seeing this, the sailor Jones fired, and wounded, in the thigh or groin, king Peter, who thereupon dropped his club, reeled over the bank, swam across the river, and scrambled up the opposite side. This delay gave Jones time to reload for defence against the tribe, who were now advancing towards him. One man who stood covered by a tree, quivered his spear ready to throw, and Jones on firing at him, missed him. His next shot was discharged amongst the mob, and most unfortunately wounded the gin already mentioned; who, with a child fastened to her back, slid down the bank, and lay, apparently dying, with her legs in the water. Just at this time the supports arrived, which the fellow behind the tree observing, passed from it to the river, and was swimming across, when Charles King shot him in the breast, and he immediately went down. These people swim differently from

Europeans; generally back foremost, and nearly upright, as if treading the water. On the arrival of our three men from the camp, the rest of the tribe took to the river, and were fired at in crossing, but without much or any effect. The party next proceeded along the river bank towards the bullock-drivers, who were then at work stript and defenceless, endeavouring to raise a bullock bogged in the muddy bank. The tribe, on the other side, appeared to know this, as they were seen hastening also in that direction, so that the timely aid, afforded by the three men from the camp, probably saved the lives of several of the party. When the men returned up the river, they perceived, that the body of the gin had been taken across and dragged up the opposite bank. The whole party had then to proceed to the higher part of the river in order to collect the cattle, and thus they approached the place, where the newly-arrived tribe were crossing to join the others. Near this spot, the men next endeavoured to raise a bullock, which had got fixed in the bank, and while Robert Muirhead accidentally stooped to lift the animal, two spears were thrown at him from an adjoining scrub with such force, that one was broken in two, and the other entered three inches deep in a tree beside him. He escaped both, only by accidentally stooping at the moment. Such were the particulars, collected from the men after their return, from this affray.

The spears appeared to have been thrown by some members of the fishing tribe, who had been seen with those newly arrived natives from my camp, and who had probably by this time, heard of what had taken place lower down the river. Thus the covetous disposition of these people drew us at length (notwithstanding all my gifts and endeavours to be on friendly terms), into a state of warfare.

We met frequently with instances of natives, receiving from us all they could want on one day, yet approaching us on the next, with the most unequivocal demonstrations of enmity and hostility. Indeed, it seemed impossible, in any manner, to conciliate these people, when united in a body. We wanted nothing, asked for nothing; on the contrary, we gave them presents of articles the most desirable to them; and yet they beset us as keenly and with as little remorse as wild beasts seek their prey. It was a consolation, however, under such unpleasant circumstances, to have men on whose courage, at least, I could depend, for numbers might now be expected to come against us; and it was necessary that we should be prepared to meet them in whatever force they appeared. On the return of the men in the evening, they reported, that, notwithstanding all their exertions, the bullock could not be got up from the mud.

Seven men were accordingly sent to the spot that afternoon, and as they did not succeed, it became necessary to send a party to the river in the morning. This was also proper, I considered, in order to cover our retreat, for by first scouring the river bank, no natives could remain along it to discover, that our journey was not, as they would naturally suppose, continued downwards.

A death-like silence now prevailed along the banks of the river, no far-heard voices of natives at their fires broke, as before, the stillness of the night — while a painful sympathy for the child bereft of its parent, and anticipations of the probable consequences to us, cast a melancholy gloom over the scene. The waning moon at length arose, and I was anxiously occupied with the observations, which were most important at this point of my journey, when a mournful song, strongly expressive of the wailing of women, came from beyond the Darling, on the fitful breeze which still blew from the north-west. It was then that I regretted most bitterly the inconsiderate conduct of some of the men. I was, indeed, liable to pay dear for geographical discovery, when my honour and character were delivered over to convicts, on whom, although I might confide as to courage, I could not always rely for humanity. The necessity for detaching the men in charge of the cattle, had, however, satisfied me that we could not proceed without repeated conflicts, and it remained now to be ascertained, whether greater security would be the result of this first exhibition of our power.

Three Expeditions into the Interior of Eastern Australia (second edition, 1839, first published 1838)

———

ANONYMOUS

The following lines were published in the Sydney Gazette *on 10 March 1836, as Thomas Livingstone Mitchell was setting off on his third expedition. The main purpose of this was to determine once and for all the course of the Darling River. As it turned out, this was also the trip on which Mitchell 'discovered' Australia Felix, and his party killed at least seven Aborigines near Mount Dispersion.*

'LINES
TO T. L. MITCHELL, ESQ, M.R.G.S. & F.G.S.
ON HIS LEAVING SYDNEY FOR THE INTERIOR
ON AN EXPEDITION OF DISCOVERY'

I

Again the 'Australian wilderness' thou piercest,
Though with a scanty band; —
Again, thou goest forth to meet the fiercest
Creatures of the Land.

II

What is thine aim in leaving human faces,
And busy-stirring life?
To follow nature in her wildest traces,
Of harmony, or strife.

III

To traverse plains, where never foot of mortal
Perchance before has trod; —
To gaze, as through some unpermitted portal,
On Nature, and her God.

IV

To watch the thronging stars, — earth's changing bosom,
Her life restoring waters; —
To claim for science many a lovely blossom,
The Forest's unknown Daughters.

V

To do, as though hast done before us bringing
Scenes of no common worth; —
To send thine eager thoughts, like wild birds, winging,
Through Heaven and Earth.

VI

Each rock in Greece for ever stands repeating
Some high and worthy name;

So shall Australian mounts, as life is fleeting
Preserve thy hard-earned Fame.
    4th March, 1836

Sydney Gazette, 10 March 1836

JOSEPH HAWDON

(1813–71)

English-born pioneer and overlander. In 1836, with John Gardiner and John Hepburn, he brought the first cattle overland from New South Wales to Port Phillip, where he settled. Hawdon and Charles Bonney 'helped to fill in the map' in 1838, when they drove cattle from Howlong, not far from present-day Albury, to Adelaide, following the course of the Murray River. This glimpse of their journey is taken from Hawdon's journal, which was not published in book form until 1952. After running sheep and cattle properties in Victoria, Hawdon migrated to New Zealand in 1858.

DROVING ALONG THE MURRAY

March 12th — After having proceeded a few miles we found the river running up against the perpendicular outer bank, consisting of limestone, and had some difficulty to find a pass through which to get the drays out of the valley. From this point I steered due west all day, through thick brush of Eucalyptus bushes about ten feet high, the land consisting of loose sand. At sunset we opened on plains, sprinkled with tufts of grass. I discovered a fine lake of fresh water, about thirty miles in circumference, and on its margin we encamped. Kangaroos appeared to be rather numerous here. The Blacks were encamped further along the Lake, and from the noise they made, we knew they must have noticed our arrival. It was a beautiful moonlight night, and I strolled out along the edge of the lake to shoot some ducks which were seen on the water in thousands. On discharging our guns, the echo of the report rolled along the water magnificently; one would have supposed that a hundred shots had been fired at the same moment. As the reports died away the lake became perfectly alive with the myriads of live fowl in motion on its surface screaming and cackling with alarm at the novel sound.

Gradually the flapping of their wings and the splashes as they alighted in the water ceased, and they again settled upon the Lake in solemn stillness. The wild, sweet, musical note of the swans was heard over our heads, as they returned to rest upon the bosom of the Lake, after feeding during the day amongst the reeds on the river. As we lay enjoying this delightful scene, we could now and then catch the distant noises of a tribe of Natives as they were disputing, with much emotion about this our extraordinary inroad upon their territory. The native name for this fine Lake is 'Nookamka', but in virtue of my privilege as its first European discoverer, I named it Lake Bonney, after my friend and fellow traveller, Mr M. C. Bonney, whose company contributed so much to the pleasure of my expedition.

March 13th — At daybreak two of our men went back to the place where we depastured the stock yesterday, to bring up a heifer that had been left behind, and after galloping the whole way there and back, they rejoined us about noon. They told me that, on arriving at the place, they found the Blacks approaching the heifer with their spears, with the intention, as was supposed, of killing her; but no sooner did they catch sight of the men galloping up the hill towards them than they took to their heels and soon disappeared.

On the edge of Lake Bonney I collected a quantity of nitre. The water has rather a sweet taste, but not unpleasantly so. After a good deal of ceremony the Natives were induced to approach our tent, accompanied by their women and children. I counted in all one hundred and sixty-three. They informed me that most of their men were gone to a fight, at a Lake to the northward; amongst these who were left to protect the women and children, there were not more than thirty able men. They afforded us a good deal of amusement during our halt. Our dogs did not like to see so much familiarity between us and the Blacks, but although they did not interfere so long as the Natives kept a respectful distance, yet whenever one of the tribe laid his hands upon a single article belonging to us, one or other of our canine friends would be sure to catch him by the heels; and when the fellow, on recovering himself, lifted up his spear and in his rage endeavoured to kill the dog, two or three of his companions would promptly interfere, and hold his arms until his passion had cooled down. On the plains around this Lake, the grass is rather more plentiful though still very thinly scattered.

March 14th — Travelled fourteen miles on top of the outer bank of the river. This bank is about three hundred feet high, its sides generally perpendicular; the formation is of soft cream-coloured limestone and clay, the river running in the valley below, wending about alternately against these natural walls, dividing the valley, as it were, into so many small farms. I think the tide must, some centuries ago, have run up this far; for in some places I saw large heaps of very old oyster-shells; in a cave overhanging the valley, there was a heap of these shells, evidently left there at some distant period by the Natives. During the journey I saw, every day, when on the river, similar heaps of fresh water muscle-shells, which are daily piled there by the present generation of Blacks. Whilst riding down in the valley, during the day, in search of a pass through which to bring the Cattle down to water and feed, I tasted the water in many of the holes and found it perfectly salt. Three Blacks passed me on their way to acquaint the next tribe of our approach. They carried a small net full of muscles slung across their shoulders on a spear. As they passed me, trotting along their native path, they saluted me with a laugh and their native 'Menera': We are friends. The language of these tribes is different from that of the tribes near the junction of the Murrumbidgee, and the people are of a much milder and more friendly disposition. Encamping on the top of the outer bank, my men found a pass, and got the stock down to the river to water, and to feed on such herbage as the valley produces.

March 15th — Performed fifteen miles. The country did not vary, the valley and banks of the Murray still exhibiting the same singular scenery. The ground on the top of the outer bank was composed of sandhills, difficult for the drays to surmount. In the evening the ambassadors came to us, bringing with them three old men. One of the latter described to me the course of the river, by drawing his finger on the sand; and also imitated the sea rolling on the beach. On the previous day we had been obliged to leave behind us a fine large Cow, quite exhausted from travelling so far without rest; I now pointed her out to one of the Blacks, and requested him to take care of her until the white men should return to take her away. Parrots now appeared more numerous, Rosellas and others, similar to those on the Eastern coast. The only bird here that is not common on the other side of the Continent is the Crested Pigeon.

March 16th — Travelled over a country of the same description. The sand being heavy for our drays, we descended through a pass into the valley, and proceeded on the firm surface of the flooded flats, but the river running up against the north bank, the dray was obliged to reascend through a steep rocky pass to the top of the outer bank. I found, when in the valley, a great quantity of crystallized lime, or gypsum. It was in masses of some tons weight. We procured also a great number of singular sea shells and fossils embedded in the bank. The natives who were with us at the time, told me they burn these shells in the fire, and then make them into a plaster with which they painted themselves white when going to fight or hold a Karobbory. On the 11th March, I saw some caps made of this plaster. Their shape was that of a scull, and inside was network made of twine. I suppose they were worn by the Natives during their funeral services. I saw them inside a rough round house made of the limbs of trees, rather neatly thatched with reeds. Within this building someone appeared to have been buried. In each burial ground there were about thirty graves, each of which was surmounted with a pile of sticks; those in which there had been recent interments were surrounded by an oval footpath evidently kept with much care and in neat order. While I was examining these burial-grounds, the Blacks kept aloof, looking very solemn, but without uttering a word, and manifestly disapproving of my curiosity. It is rather singular that they should make better houses for the dead than for the living, the latter being composed merely of sheets of bark. Whilst the drays were ploughing through the sand I ascended a high sand-ridge to select a pass for them, when the delightful sight of a high range to the W.S.W. broke upon my view. This of course is what may be considered the sea-coast range, indicating to us a speedy and safe termination to our journey, and giving promise of that better sort of country of which high land is always a mark.

The Journal of a Journey from New South Wales to Adelaide: Performed in 1838 (1952)

―――

WILLIAM LIGHT
(1786–1839)

Soldier and surveyor. Light was born in Kuala Kedah, Malaya, educated in England, and served in both the British navy and army. Taking up his position as South Australia's first surveyor-general in 1836, he chose the site for Adelaide, and began surveys of it and other parts of the new British province. He was, however, hampered by insufficient staff and equipment. Resigning in 1838, after being instructed to undertake temporary surveys for the sake of speed, Light subsequently became the main partner in a private surveying firm. At the request of the South Australian Company, he travelled to the Lynedoch (later Lyndoch) Valley in January 1839, which he had previously visited and named. By then his health was failing. He died from tuberculosis in October 1839.

'DIARY OF A JOURNEY TO LYNEDOCH VALLEY, JANUARY 1839'

Tuesday, 8 January, 1839 — Light breezes and very fine. Left Adelaide at 11 a.m. on one of Hadden's horses, our company consisting of Mr MacLaren [*sic*], Mann, Finniss, Sam Stephens, Mr Randel [*sic*] and myself with a bullock dray, six bullocks, and cart with four — at 5.30 p.m. arrived at Fisher's station in the mountains, a very pretty little valley. Cloudy and threatening a change. At midnight hard rain with thunder.

Wednesday, 9 January — In a.m. thunder and heavy rain all the early part. At 8 a.m. we started. Handcock and Charles Fisher in company came over the hills and descended into the plains about 6 miles from the Para. At 11.30 we arrived at the river and remained until half past 2 p.m.; then rode with Mr MacLaren, Finniss and Randal [*sic*] to examine the other branch. We found this a more respectable stream having plenty of water and it appears to me that it is watered by those streams we saw last year running from the mountains. At 5 p.m. we returned to the Para and dined and slept at the old place.

Thursday, 10 January — Mounted at 7.15 and came to Angas Valley which we saw last year: from this we rode to Lynedoch Valley, here we discovered some fresh water in a spring forming two nice ponds of some depth (and fish in them). Mr MacLaren here determined on a special survey at once. We took some biscuits and cold lamb carried in our pockets and refreshed ourselves with a little brandy and water and then returned to find our tent and cars which had been ordered to move a few miles to the northward, after a very tiresome ride — having been above ten hours on horse back. We found our tent on the bank of the Para about four miles north of the last encampment. We were all much fatigued, but myself in particular being unwell. The country here is very fine, generally hilly but fine sheepwalks. (This river is of more value than people imagine.)

Friday, 11 January — Started at 8.10 a.m. for a northerly direction and traversed over a range of high ground for about five miles then came into a plain of some extent and halted for a part of our party to examine further for fresh water which was found in a rocky basin about three miles further (N.E.). This water is not good having a slight brackishness. We remained at this camp for the purpose of resting the horses that the exploring party might have them less tired next day.

The greater portion of this country is covered with kangaroo grass and its general appearance open with here and there some patches of wood. It's undulating and the soil much the same as the rest. At night some heavy showers with thunder and lightning. (Light and var., at times very hot.)

Saturday, 12 January — Early part some very heavy showers with thunder and lightning. At 7.15 a.m. our party started. I remained behind being too weak to accompany them. At 9 a.m. squalls of rain at times. At 11 fresh breezes and very fine weather. At noon very hot wind, veered round to S.W. at 2 p.m. At 4 ditto weather. Several strong gusts of wind at times and very warm, the flies horribly troublesome. At 5.30 our party returned. Very fine all night. (Fresh breezes N.E., cold air.)

Sunday, 13 January — Left our camp at 9 a.m. and returned to the Para which we reached at 1.15 p.m. Very fine weather and pleasant travelling. We halted here the rest of the day. Having before heard of a dead body being buried under an old tree here we examined the spot and found it. There is a mystery in this affair as it has been kept a secret. The skull is large and the flesh almost entirely gone, part of his dress remained, his trousers of corduroy seemed good as far as the knees, under that much torn, his shirt on one part containing much coagulated blood. The body was covered over again and some of his clothes packed up to be conveyed to Adelaide. (Light breezes westerly.)

Monday, 14 January — Light breezes and hazy at 6.15 a.m. Mr McLaren and Randal left for Adelaide at 6.30. Finniss went also with one of the bullock cars. At 8 I went to survey, at 9 felt very unwell. At 4.05 p.m. returned to the tent quite exhausted. Blowing very strong from the W.S.W. and one of most disagreeable winds I have ever felt; it was hot and cold, cuttingly cold at times and generally oppressively hot. Very unwell all day. At 8 p.m. more moderate but still disagreeable. Blowing very strong all night with some heavy showers.

Tuesday, 15 January — Strong breezes squally at 6 a.m. heavy rain, at 7 cleared up with fresh breezes and squally looking weather. At 7.30 went out to survey. Fresh breezes and squally. At 10.30 while working near the tent we returned for a time — during a squall the tent suffered so much we were obliged to strike and repair, then moved it over to the southern bank for more shelter. At noon strong gales and squally. At 2 p.m. went out again to survey the trending of the river, got on some little distance and left off in consequence of a mistake made by Wellman's leaving his post — at 4.10 returned to the tent. I laid down very worn and soon after fell asleep for nearly half an hour. Woke very unwell with shivering and symptoms of fever. At 7 p.m. more moderate but wild looking weather. Moderate and cloudy all night. (S.W.)

Wednesday, 16 January — Moderate breezes and cloudy. Dark clouds in the N.N.W. and unsettled looking weather. At 8.15 a.m. started for Lynedoch Vale and arrived at the pond at 12.15 p.m. Very fine cool day. At 1.15 p.m. I had my dinner and very soon after felt extremely unwell. This afternoon our men amused themselves by catching a vast number of billet fish, and as we found the water in the ponds much too sweet to be pleasant Penton turned to and dug a well about three feet deep and got very good water. My asthma very troublesome. At 8 p.m. very cold, during night exceedingly cold. (West. Cold wind all day, at times blowing fresh.)

Thursday, 17 January — Very fine cold day, remained at the camp. At 11.30 heard a shot up the valley and soon after saw Finniss, Handcock and Charles Fisher coming. We did not work this day. The men went — some shooting, others fishing — and our well was deepened and widened. At night very fine but very cold winds. (Var.)

Friday, 18 January — Very fine morning. I went out at 9 a.m. to look at the boundaries of the 15,000 acres. Went up Angas hill and afterwards to the mountains. Fine cool morning at first, latterly extremely warm. On our return to the camp found Mr Ormsby sent by the Governor to give over the special survey, but orders had been given by Mr McLaren not to do anything more than mark the boundaries of 15,000 acres — nothing more can be done. Extremely hot all afternoon, at night fine. (Var.)

Saturday, 19 January — Very fine weather. At 7.25 went out with Finniss and Ormsby and marked out the boundaries. Fisher and Handcock left us. At noon returned to our camp, very hot disagreeable weather. P.m. one of the most horrible, disagreeable days I ever felt, the head exceedingly oppressive and the flies most annoying. At 4 weather looking like a change. The air all the afternoon most oppressive; at 8 p.m. very warm with appearance of thunder and rain. At 9 a few drops of rain, at 10 cooler, moderate and cloudy all night. (Var.)

Sunday, 20 January — Early light breezes, cloudy and cool. At 8.20 a.m. we broke up the camp and Finniss, Ormsby and myself proceeded to find a road over the mountains to Fisher's station, but after riding about 8 or 9 miles and coming to the Para we found the river impassable, and after trying many places we were at last obliged to return to the old pass where we arrived at 1 p.m.; and at 1.40 the bullock cars and our men arrived. The weather during the forenoon generally rather pleasant. At 2 p.m. very hot. At 3 p.m. Ormsby left us. At night, fine and cool. (N.W. Westerly.)

Monday, 21 January — Started at 6.40 a.m. Dark, cloudy. At 9.45 arrived at the first river. Several squalls of rain during the way, at 10.40 the bullock cars arrived. Lunched on preserved soup and Bouilli and carrots. At 12 started for Adelaide where we arrived at 3.10 p.m. Fine cool weather all the afternoon. Crossed the Pass at 9.35 [?]. From the Para stopped to feed at a quarter to one. Started... (Westerly.)

William Light's Brief Journal and Australian Diaries, introduction and notes by David Elder (1984)

———

ANGUS McMILLAN
(1810–65)

Explorer and pastoralist. Born on the Isle of Skye, he migrated to New South Wales in 1838. As a result of some of the exploration outlined in this memorandum, McMillan can be considered to be the first European to 'discover' Gippsland, which he named Caledonia Australis, in present-day Victoria. That honour, however, somewhat erroneously, went at the time to Count Strzelecki, who arrived there after McMillan, and named the area after Governor George Gipps. McMillan, who remained in the district, died in 1865 after an accident that occurred while he was cutting alpine tracks.

'CALEDONIA AUSTRALIS'

Start from Maneroo — On the 20th of May 1839, I left Currawang, a station of James McFarlane, Esq., J.P., of the Maneroo district, having heard from the natives of that district that a fine country existed near the sea-coast, to the south-west of Maneroo.

Accompanied by one Black only I was accompanied in my expedition by Jemmy Gibber, the chief of the Maneroo tribe. After five days' journey towards the south-west, I obtained a view of the sea from the top of a mountain, near a hill known as the Haystack, in the Buchan district, and also of the low country towards Wilson's Promontory.

On the sixth day after leaving Currawang the blackfellow who accompanied me became so frightened of the Warrigals, or wild blacks, that he tried to leave me, and refused to proceed any further towards the new country. We pressed on until the evening when we camped, and about twelve o'clock at night I woke up, and found Jemmy Gibber in the act of raising his waddy or club to strike me, as he fancied that, if he succeeded in killing me, he would then be able to get back to Maneroo. I presented a pistol at him, and he begged me not to shoot him, and excused himself by saying that he had dreamt that another blackfellow was taking away his gin, and that he did not mean to kill me.

Omeo — Next morning we started for Omeo, where we arrived after four days' journey over very broken country. There were three settlers at Omeo at this time, viz., Pender, McFarlane, and Hyland.

Numbla-Munjee — On the 16th September 1839 I formed a cattle station at a place called Numbla-Munjee, on the River Tambo, 50 miles to the south of Omeo, for Lachlan Macalister, Esq., J.P. A Mr Buckley had, previous to my arrival here, formed a station ten miles higher up the River Tambo from Numbla-Munjee.

On the 26th of December 1839 I formed a party, consisting of Mr Cameron, Mr Matthew Macalister, Edward Bath, a stockman, and myself, with the view of proceeding towards and exploring the low country I had formerly obtained a view of from the mountain in the Buchan district alluded to in my first trip from Maneroo. After travelling for three days over a hilly and broken country, one of our horses met with a serious accident, tumbling down the side of one of the steep ranges, and staked itself in four or five places. In consequence of this accident we were compelled to return to Numbla-Munjee.

On the 11th of January 1840, the same party as before, with the addition of two Omeo blacks — Cobbon Johnny and Boy Friday — started once more with the same object in view, namely, that of reaching the new country to the south-west, and, if possible, to penetrate as far as Corner Inlet, where I was led to believe there existed an excellent harbour.

Meet with the Aborigines — After a fearful journey of four days, over some of the worst description of country I ever saw, we succeeded in crossing the coast range leading down into the low country. This day we were met by a tribe of the wild blacks who came up quite close to us, and stared at us while on horseback, but the moment I dismounted they commenced yelling out, and took to their heels, running away as fast as possible; and from the astonishment displayed at the circumstance of my dismounting from the horse, I fancied they took both man and horse to constitute one animal.

Lake Victoria — On Wednesday, the 15th of January, our little party encamped on the River Tambo, running towards the sea in a south-easterly direction. On the morning of the 16th we started down the Tambo, in order, if possible, to get a sight of a lake we had previously seen when descending the ranges to the low country and which I was certain must be in our immediate vicinity. The country passed through to-day consisted of open forest, well grassed, the timber consisting chiefly of red and white gum, box, he-and she-oak, and occasionally wattle. At six p.m. we made the lake, to which I gave the name of Lake Victoria. From the appearance of this beautiful sheet of water, I should say that it is fully 20 miles in length and about 8 miles in width. On the north side of this lake the country consists of beautiful open forest, and the grass was up to our stirrup-irons as we rode along, and was absolutely swarming with kangaroos and emus. The lake was covered with wild ducks, swans, and pelicans. We used some of the lake water for tea, but found it quite brackish. We remained on the margin of the lake all night. The River Tambo was about one mile north-east of our camp. The River Tambo, where we first made it, appears to be very deep and from 20 to 30 yards wide. The water is brackish for the distance of about five miles from its mouth, where it empties itself into Lake Victoria.

Nicholson River — On the 17th January, started from the camp, and proceeded in a south-westerly direction. At ten a.m. came upon another river, to which I gave the name of the Nicholson, after Dr Nicholson, of Sydney. This river seemed to be quite as large as the Tambo, and as deep. Finding we were not able to cross it in the low country, we made for the ranges, where, after encountering great difficulties, we succeeded in crossing it — but not until sun-down — high up in the ranges, and encamped for the night. This evening we found that, from the great heat of the weather, our small supply of meat had been quite destroyed. We were, however, fortunate enough to obtain some wild ducks, upon which we made an excellent supper.

River Mitchell — *18th January* — Started again upon our usual course (south-west), and, after travelling about seven miles, came upon a large river, which I named the Mitchell, after Sir Thomas Mitchell, Surveyor-General of New South Wales.

Clifton's Morass — We followed this river up until we came to a large morass, to which I gave the name of Clifton's Morass, from the circumstances of my having nearly lost in it, from its boggy nature, my favourite horse Clifton.

General View of Country from a Hill — Having crossed this morass, we again proceeded on our journey for three miles, when we came once more upon the Mitchell River higher up, and encamped for the night, the country improving at every step. In the evening I ascended a hill near the camp, from the top of which I obtained a good view of the low country still before us, of the high mountains to the north-west, and the lakes stretching towards the sea-coast in a south and south-easterly direction; and, from the general view of the country as I then stood, it put me more in mind of the scenery of Scotland than any other country I had hitherto seen, and therefore I named it at the moment 'Caledonia Australis.'

On the morning of the 19th January we crossed the Mitchell, and proceeded in a south-south-west course, through fine open forest of the she-oak and red and white gum, for about sixteen miles, and encamped upon a chain of ponds in the evening.

20th January — We proceeded in a south-west course, and at ten a.m. came upon the border of a large lake, which I believed to be a continuation of the same lake we had been previously encamped upon.

The Aborigines — While at dinner on the banks of the lake a tribe of blacks were walking quietly up to where we were encamped, but as soon as they saw us on horseback they left their rugs and spears and ran away. They never would make friends with us upon any occasion.

The River Avon — *21st January* — Started upon our usual course (south-west), and, after travelling about four miles, came upon a river flowing through a fine country of fine, open forest, with high banks, to which I gave the name of the Avon. We followed this river up all day, and crossed it about twenty miles from the foot of the mountains. It appears to be a mountain stream, generally not very deep, and runs over a bed of shingle. The country around and beyond the place where we crossed the Avon consists of beautiful, rich, open plains, and appeared, as far as I could judge at the time, to extend as far as the mountains. We encamped upon these plains for the night. From our encampment we had a splendid view of the mountains, the highest of which I named Mount Wellington, and also I named several others, which appear in the Government maps (published) of Gippsland.

22nd January — Left the encampment on the plains, and proceeded on our usual course of south-west, and travelled over a beautiful country, consisting of fine, open plains, intersected by occasional narrow belts of open forest, extending as far as the lakes to the eastward and stretching away west and north-west as far as the foot of the mountains.

Macalister River — After travelling about ten miles we encamped in the evening on a large stream, which I named the Macalister. This river appears deep and rapid, and is about 40 yards wide. Here we saw an immense number of fires of the natives.

23rd January — Started early in the morning, and tried to cross the river, but could not succeed, and followed the River Macalister down to its junction with another very large river called the La Trobe, which river is bounded on both sides by large morasses.

Meet with Aborigines — In the morass to north-east of the river we saw some 100 natives, who, upon our approach, burnt their camps and took to the scrub. We managed to overtake one old man that could not walk, to whom I gave a knife and a pair of trousers, and endeavoured by every means in our power to open a communication with the other blacks, but without success. It was amusing to see the old man. After having shaken hands with us all, he thought it necessary to go through the same form with the horses, and shook the bridles very heartily. The only ornaments he wore were three hands of men and women, beautifully dried and preserved. We were busy all the evening endeavouring to cut a bark canoe, but did not succeed.

On the morning of the 24th January, the provisions having become very short, and as some of the party were unwilling to prosecute the journey upon small allowance, I determined upon returning to the station and bringing down stock to the district. We then returned to Numbla-Munjee, which place we made in seven days from the 24th, and were the last two days without any provisions at all.

I may add that I was the first person who discovered Gippsland, and when I started to explore that district I had no guide but my pocket compass and a chart of Captain Flinders. We had not even a tent, but used to camp out and make rough gunyahs wherever we remained for the night.

On the 27th March 1840, Count Strzelecki and party left our station at Numbla-Munjee for Caledonia Australis. He was supplied with some provisions and a camp kettle, and Mr Matthew Macalister, who was one of my party in January of the same year, accompanied them one day's journey, and, after explaining the situation and nature of the country, about the different crossing-places, left them upon my tracks on the coast range leading to Gippsland, and which tracks Charley, the Sydney blackfellow, who accompanied Count Strzelecki, said he could easily follow.

On my return to Numbla-Munjee on the 31st January, after having discovered the country of Gippsland as far as the La Trobe River, I proceeded immediately to Maneroo, and reported my discovery to Mr

Macalister, who did not publish my report at the time. I had also written another letter to a friend of mine in Sydney, containing a description of my expedition; at the same time I wrote to Mr Macalister, but it unfortunately miscarried. In October 1840 I arrived in Gippsland with 500 head of cattle, and formed a station on the Avon River, after having been six weeks engaged in clearing a road over the mountains.

After four attempts I succeeded in discovering the present shipping place at Port Albert, and marked a road from thence to Numbla-Munjee, a distance of 130 miles.

After having brought stock into the district, and formed the station in about the month of November 1840, the aborigines attacked the station, drove the men from the hut, and took everything from them, compelling them to retreat back upon Numbla-Munjee.

On the 22nd December 1840, I again came down and took possession of the station, when the natives made a second attack.

Thomas Francis Bride (ed.), *Letters from Victorian Pioneers* (1969 edition, first published 1898)

———

PAUL EDMUND DE STRZELECKI

(1791–1873)

Scientist and explorer. Strzelecki was born in Prussian-controlled Poland to an untitled family, but later adopted the title 'Count' while living in England. After travelling in America, the Pacific Islands, and New Zealand, he reached New South Wales in 1839. In early 1840 he explored in the Australian Alps, where he named Mount Kosciusko, Australia's highest mountain. (Whether he climbed the actual peak, or a nearby one, has since been the subject of some debate.) Strzelecki and his party continued through Gippsland (originally Gipps' Land), which he also named, and eventually, in a pathetic state, reached Western Port around the end of March. He also conducted geological surveys in Van Diemen's Land, before leaving Sydney for England in 1843. His Physical Description of New South Wales and Van Diemen's Land *(1845) is said to have 'laid the basis of Australian palaeontology'.*

THE NAMING OF MOUNT KOSCIUSKO

The country which farther on stretches itself to lat. 37°, and which is limited to N. and S. by the Mane's and Ajuk Ranges, offers from its extent, and from having the highest protuberances of New South Wales, a wider and more interesting field to investigation and comment. On entering it from the Mane's Range through Mount Aiken, every feature of that division seems to bear the stamp of foreign grandeur. The broken country to the westward, in which the Tingella Creek takes its rise; to the eastward the dividing range, here called the Australian Alps, with its stupendous peaks and domes; and in front the beautiful valley which the Murray so bountifully waters; unite to form attractions for the explorer of no ordinary kind. I followed the windings of that valley for about 70 miles to the foot of the highest protuberance of the Australian Alps, which it was my object to ascend and examine. The steepness of the numberless ridges, intersected by gullies and torrents, rendered this ascent a matter of no small difficulty, which was not a little increased by the weight of the instruments, which for safety I carried on my back. Once on the crest of the range, the remainder of the ascent to its highest pinnacle was accomplished with comparative ease. On the 15th February, about noon, I found myself on an elevation of 6,510 feet above the level of the sea, seated on perpetual snow, a lucid sky above me, and below an uninterrupted view over more than 7,000 square miles. This pinnacle, rocky and naked, predominant over several others, elevations of the same mountain, was, and always will be, chosen for an important point of trigonometrical survey; clear and standing by itself, it affords a most advantageous position for overlooking the intricacies of the mountain country around. The eye wanders to the Three Brothers, or Tintern, thence to the sources of the Dumut and the Murrumbidgee, discovers with ease the windings of the Murray, the course of the dividing range, the summits of Mounts Aberdeen and Buller, and is seduced even beyond the required limits of a survey. The particular configuration of this eminence struck me so forcibly, by the similarity it bears to a tumulus elevated in Krakow over the tomb of the patriot Kosciusko, that, although in a foreign country, on foreign ground, but amongst a free people, who appreciate freedom and its votaries, I could not refrain from giving it the name of Mount Kosciusko. It is from the view of the adjacent country which I obtained from Mount Kosciusko that the source of the Murray was ascertained, its tributaries traced, the direction of my farther progress to the south and further survey decided upon. My steps were consequently retraced to Cowrang Creek, along which I wound my way till near its source. Here the squatters' stations ceased, and the tracks of man were at an end. The track, now first trodden by me, passing through subordinate, rocky and dry ranges, brought me unexpectedly on the so-called Lake Omeo, and will perhaps serve to open future communication between the Murray and the extensive Omeo country. I found Lake Omeo, like Lake George and Lake Bathurst, preserving only the basin shape of a lake, with scanty water, and rich pasture. Amongst the eminences of its interesting neighbourhood I ascended in the course of my geognostic explorations, I chose Mount Tombo, predominant on an extensive tract of country, as a point to connect the links of the survey; both this point and the position of Omeo were fixed on the chart by trigonometrical longitude and latitude observations. What is marked out, however, as the source of the Mita-Mita, the splendid tributary to the Murray, the delineation of its valleys, that of the Mount Ajuk Range, the formidable barrier which separates the tributaries of the Murray from those of the Ovens River, were rather sketched than surveyed.

British Parliamentary Papers, House of Commons, vol. 17 (1841)

———

EDWARD JOHN EYRE
(1815–1901)

English-born explorer and governor. In 1841, Eyre, who already had experience as an overlander and as an explorer in Australia, became the first European to cross the area now known as the Nullarbor Plain. He, a European overseer named John Baxter, and three Aborigines left Fowler's Bay in February of that year. In April, two of the Aborigines killed Baxter and fled with some of the party's stores. Eyre and the other Aborigine, Wylie, finally reached Albany in July, having been helped for a period by French whalers near present-day Esperance. After serving as resident magistrate and protector of Aborigines at Moorundie in South Australia from 1841, Eyre left Australia in late 1844. His subsequent career as an administrator took him to New Zealand, the West Indies, the Leeward Islands, and Jamaica.

'OVERSEER BEGINS TO DESPOND'

March 28 — At daylight we moved on, every one walking, even the youngest boy could not ride now, as the horses were so weak and jaded. Soon after leaving the camp, one of them laid down, although the weight upon his back was very light; we were consequently obliged to distribute the few things he carried among the others, and let him follow loose. Our route lay along the beach, as the dense scrub inland prevented us from following any other course; we had, therefore, to go far out of our way, tracing round every point, and following along every bay, whilst the sea-weed frequently obstructed our path, and drove us again to the loose sands, above high water mark, causing extra fatigue to our unfortunate horses. At other times we were forced to go between these banks of sea-weed and the sea, into the sea itself, on which occasions it required our utmost vigilance to prevent the wretched horses from drinking the salt water, which would inevitably have destroyed them. In order to prevent this we were obliged to walk ourselves in the water, on the sea-side of them, one of the party being in advance, leading one horse, another being behind to keep up the rear, and the other three being at intervals along the outside of the line, to keep them from stopping for an instant until the danger was past.

We had scarcely advanced six miles from our last night's camp when the little Timor pony I had purchased at Port Lincoln broke down completely; for some time it had been weak, and we were obliged to drive it loose, but it was now unable to proceed further, and we were compelled to abandon it to a miserable and certain death, that by pushing on, we might use every exertion in our power to relieve the others, though scarcely daring to hope that we could save even one of them. It was, indeed, a fearful and heart-rending scene to behold the noble animals which had served us so long and so faithfully, suffering the extremity of thirst and hunger, without having it in our power to relieve them. Five days of misery had passed over their heads since the last water had been left, and one hundred and twelve miles of country had been traversed without the possibility of procuring food for them, other than the dry and sapless remains of last year's grass, and this but rarely to be met with. No rains had fallen to refresh them, and they were reduced to a most pitiable condition, still they travelled onwards, with a spirit and endurance truly surprising. Whenever we halted, they followed us about like dogs wherever we went, appearing to look to us only for aid, and exhibiting that confidence in us which I trust we all reposed in the Almighty, for most truly did we feel, that in His mercy and protection alone our safety could now ever be hoped for.

About ten o'clock the tide became too high for us to keep the beach, and we were compelled to halt for some hours. Our horses were nearly all exhausted, and I dreaded that when we next moved on many of them would be unable to proceed far, and that, one by one, they would all perish, overcome by sufferings which those, who have not witnessed such scenes, can have no conception of. We should then have been entirely dependent on our own strength and exertions, nearly midway between Adelaide and King George's Sound, with a fearful country on either side of us, with a very small supply of provisions, and without water.

The position we were in, frequently forced sad forebodings with respect to the future, and though I by no means contemplated with apathy the probable fate that might await us, yet I was never for a moment undecided as to the plan it would be necessary to adopt, in such a desperate extremity — at all hazards, I was determined to proceed onwards.

The country we had already passed through, precluded all hope of our recrossing it without the horses to carry water for us, and without provisions to enable us to endure the dreadful fatigue of forced marches, across the desert. The country before us was, it is true, quite unknown, but it could hardly be worse than that we had traversed, and the chance was that it might be better. We were now pushing on for some sand-hills, marked down in Captain Flinders' chart at about 126½° of east longitude; I did not expect to procure water until we reached these, but I felt sure we should obtain it on our arrival there. After this point was passed, there appeared to be one more long push without any likelihood of procuring water, as the cliffs again became the boundary of the ocean; but beyond Cape Arid, the change in the character and appearance of the country, as described by Flinders, indicated the existence of a better and more practicable line of country than we had yet fallen in with.

My overseer, however, was now unfortunately beginning to take up an opposite opinion, and though he still went through the duty devolving upon him with assiduity and cheerfulness, it was evident that his mind was ill at ease, and that he had many gloomy anticipations of the future. He fancied there were no sand-hills ahead, that we should never reach any water in that direction, and that there was little hope of saving any of the horses. In this latter idea I rather encouraged him than otherwise, deeming it advisable to contemplate the darker side of the picture, and by accustoming ourselves to look forward to being left entirely dependent upon our own strength and efforts, in some measure to prepare ourselves for such an event, should it unfortunately befal us. In conversing with him upon our prospects, and the position we should be in if we lost all our horses, I regretted extremely to find that his mind was continually occupied with thoughts of returning, and that he seemed to think the only chance of saving our lives, would be to push on to the water ourselves, and then endeavour again to return to Fowler's Bay, where we had buried a large quantity of provisions. Still it was a gratification to find that the only European with me, did not altogether give way to despondency, and could even calmly contemplate the prospect before us, considering and reasoning upon the plan it might be best to adopt, in the event of our worst forebodings being realized. In discussing these subjects, I carefully avoiding irritating or alarming him, by a declaration of my own opinions and resolutions, rather agreeing with him than otherwise, at the same time, that I pointed out the certain risk that would attend any attempt to go back to Fowler's Bay, and the probability there was of much less danger attending the effort to advance to King George's Sound. With respect to the native boys, they appeared to think or care but little about the future; they were not sensible of their danger, and having something still to eat and drink, they played and laughed and joked with each other as much as ever.

Whilst waiting for the tide to fall, to enable us to proceed, the overseer dug a hole, and we buried nearly every thing we had with us, saddles, fire-arms, ammunition, provisions; all things were here abandoned except two guns, the keg with the little water we had left, and a very little flour, tea and sugar. I determined to relieve our horses altogether from every weight (trifling as was the weight of all we had), and by pushing, if possible, on to the water, endeavour to save their lives; after which we could return for the things we had abandoned. Our arrangements being completed, we all bathed in the sea, ate a scanty meal, and again moved onwards at half past two o'clock.

The poor horses started better than could have been expected, but it was soon evident that all were fast failing, and many already quite exhausted. At six miles my favourite mare could no longer keep up with the rest, and we were obliged to let her drop behind. Her foal, now six months old, we got away with some difficulty from her, and kept it with the other horses; at four miles further another of the horses failed, and I had him tied up, in the hope that if we reached water during the evening, I might send back and recover him.

Towards dark we all imagined we saw a long point stretching to the S.W. and backed by high sandy looking cones. We hoped that these might be the sand-hills we were pushing for, and our hearts beat high with hope once more. It, however, soon become too dark to discern anything, and at fourteen miles from where we had halted in the morning, we were again obliged by the tide to encamp for the night, as the country behind the shore was densely scrubby, and quite impracticable as a line of route. It was nine o'clock when we halted, and we were all very tired, and our feet somewhat inflamed, from getting so frequently wet with the salt water, whilst endeavouring to keep the horses from it; there was no grass but the coarse wiry kind that bound the sand together, of this the poor animals cropped a little, as a very heavy dew fell, and served to moisten it. As usual, the overseer and myself kept watch upon the horses at night, whilst the natives enjoyed their undisturbed repose. Two of the boys were young, and none of the three had their frame and muscles sufficiently developed to enable them to undergo the fatigue of walking during the day if deprived of their rest at night; still the duty became very hard upon two persons, where it was of constant occurrence, and superadded to the ordinary day's labour.

Journals of Discovery into Central Australia, and Overland from Adelaide to King George's Sound, in the Years 1840–1, vol. 1 (1845)

———

FRANCIS WEBB

(1925–73)

Australian poet. Webb's fourteen-part poem Eyre All Alone, *first published in full in 1961, was inspired by Eyre's epic expedition. At first glance the choice of title seems curious, given that Eyre was accompanied throughout by the Aborigine Wylie, but as the poet himself explains, 'My insistence upon Eyre's aloneness is not an overlooking of Wylie, but comes from my seeing such a journey of discovery as suggestive of another which is common to us all'. The following section, the tenth, represents the poem's climax.*

FROM 'EYRE ALL ALONE'

Banksia

History, wasted and decadent pack-horse
Munching a handful of chaff, dry old national motives,

Shambles skinny and bony into the final push,
Picking up, putting down his heavy tuneless hooves
Girt with rusted iron, so tenderly.

Baxter is dead. Wylie, can you hear the Sound?

I hear large agnostic ribaldries of an ocean.

Evening in muffler creeps towards epic adventure,
To lull the blazing colossi of a blindness.
But suns will rock in my sleep, maul the moth-eaten pockets
Of memory for a few counterfeit coppers
To thump on the counters of stalls in a looted market.

Wylie, what can you see?
                          I see a flower.

Turn the horses loose. Out of earth a power:
Banksia, honeysuckle, forked-lightning-fruit of pain.
Motive pierces the cloud-scrub once again.

Swimming oversea, underfoot, the brawny light
Sings savour of this unique approaching night.
Stolid elation of a single star.
Banksia, carry fire, like the thurifer
Over my sandy tongue-tied barren ground.

Wylie, what do you hear?
                          I hear the Sound.

Socrates and Other Poems (1961)

———

GEOFFREY DUTTON

(1922–   )

*Australian poet and writer. Dutton's many publications include a biography
of Eyre, originally published as* The Hero as Murderer: The Life of Edward

John Eyre *(1967), the title of which alludes to the subject's controversial sup-pression of a native riot in 1865, while governor of Jamaica. Here Dutton describes a terrible night during Eyre's expedition from South Australia to Western Australia.*

THE DEATH OF BAXTER

The horses were hobbled and turned out to feed, and the party set about making break-winds of boughs to form a shelter from the wind. It was the turn of Eyre and Baxter to watch the horses; the first watch was from 6 p.m. to 11 p.m., the second from 11 p.m. to 4 a.m., at which hour the party usually got ready to move off with the first streak of daylight. This night Baxter asked Eyre whether he would like to take the first or the second watch; Eyre was sleepy, and decided to take the first.

They had no supper that evening, having eaten their second precious meal of the day at midday, and as dusk fell Eyre saw Baxter and the three native boys lie down to sleep behind their respective break-winds, about ten or twelve yards apart. The arms and provisions were piled, as usual, under an oilskin between Eyre's break-wind and that of the overseer, except for Eyre's own gun which he always kept in his own sleeping place.

Eyre slowly followed the horses as they rambled through the scrub, feeding tolerably well in the grassy openings, while the night wind blew hard and cold from the south-west and broken clouds scudded across the moon. About half-past ten Eyre began to move the horses back to where he thought the camp must be, although it was hard to find it, as the fires had burnt down. Suddenly he was startled by a flash and then the report of a gun, about a quarter of a mile away. Thinking that Baxter had mistaken the time and, not being able to see him or the horses, was signalling to him, Eyre called out. There was no answer. Leaving the horses, he hurried towards the camp, only to be met about a hundred yards from it by Wylie crying out 'Oh dear, oh dear, have you heard the gun?' Eyre ran on quickly to find Baxter face down on the ground, dressed in nothing but his shirt, a few yards away from where he had been sleeping. Blood was pouring from a wound in the left side of his chest, and he was in the last convulsions of death. The two other native boys, Joey and Yarry, had disappeared, taking with them the two double-barrelled guns and some ammunition, after plundering the small stock of provisions.

Eyre lifted up the body of his faithful overseer, who had been with him on all his journeys since 1834, but the shot had finished him, and he never spoke a word. 'The frightful, the appalling truth now burst upon me, that I was alone in the desert. He who had faithfully served me for many years, who had followed my fortunes in adversity and in prosperity, who had accompanied me in all my wanderings, and whose attachment to me had been his sole inducement to remain with me in this last, and to him alas, fatal journey, was now no more. For an instant, I was almost tempted to wish that it had been my own fate instead of his. The horrors of my situation glared upon me in such startling reality as for an instant almost to paralyse the mind. At the dead hour of night, in the wildest and most inhospitable wastes of Australia, with the fierce wind raging in unison with the scene of violence before me, I was left, with a single native, whose fidelity I could not rely upon, and who for aught I knew might be in league with the other two, who perhaps were even now, lurking about with the view of taking away my life as they had done that of the overseer.'

Eyre quickly looked for his double-barrelled gun, which he had left under an oilskin at the head of his break-wind. It was gone. So was Baxter's gun. There were no other serviceable weapons; the brace of pistols were without cartridges, and the rifle had a ball stuck fast in the breech. Hastily getting some powder and shot for the pistols, he found that the ramrod for the rifle was gone; he discovered it, with some loose cartridges, near where the boys had been sleeping. They had clearly loaded the guns before plundering the stores.

The first thing now was to find the horses, for without them they could not hope to survive. Eyre and Wylie wandered, looking for them, between the dense belts of scrub looming in the moonlight, conscious all the time that the murderers might be stalking them. Eventually they caught the horses, but the animals moved about restlessly for the remainder of the night, which grew intensely cold and frosty, so that Eyre, dressed only in shirt and trousers, suffered torments of the body as well as anguish of the mind. 'Suffering and distress had well nigh overwhelmed me, and life seemed hardly worth the effort necessary to prolong it. Ages can never efface the horrors of this single night … '

Near the body lay the remains of the plundered stores. Joey and Yarry had stolen all the baked bread, some twenty pounds in weight, some mutton, tea and sugar, Baxter's tobacco and pipes, a one-gallon keg of water, some clothes, the two guns, and some other articles. They had left forty pounds of flour, a little tea and sugar, four gallons of water, and the rifle, pistols and ammunition. Trying to clear the jammed rifle, Eyre took the barrel off the stock and held it in the fire to melt out the ball, when suddenly it went off, the ball whizzing close to his head.

Apparently there had been some powder still in the breech; at least he was still alive, and now had a weapon to defend himself with.

By eight o'clock they were ready to go, and there was nothing they could do but leave poor Baxter's body wrapped in a blanket, for it was impossible to dig a grave in the sheets of rock. The desolation of that scene, and the loneliness of the shrouded corpse left a few miles inland from the sheer cliffs of the Southern Ocean with twelve hundred unknown miles to the north, haunted Eyre for the rest of his life. The two living men walked silently westward, Wylie leading a horse and Eyre driving the rest after him, still more than five hundred walking miles from King George's Sound.

The Hero as Murderer (1967)

————

JANE FRANKLIN
(1791–1875)

English traveller and wife of Arctic explorer Sir John Franklin. During her husband's term of office as lieutenant-governor of Van Diemen's Land (1837–43), Lady Franklin helped to promote science, education, convict welfare, and exploration within the colony. An 'indefatigable traveller', she took part in a challenging expedition overland from Hobart to Macquarie Harbour in 1842, which she describes in this letter to her sister. After organising a number of searches, during the 1850s, for her husband's lost Arctic expedition, she devoted the rest of her life to travelling.

'EXCURSION TO MACQUARIE HARBOUR'

Gordon River. V.D. Land,
On Board the 'Breeze',
Expectation Reach,
22nd. April, 1842.

My Dearest Mary,

I have been under the necessity of letting two or three ships for England sail without taking advantage of them, owing to my absence from Hobart Town in a part of the Colony, remote and uninhabited and where communication with the civilized districts can scarcely be kept up. We are on the point of reaching Macquarie Harbour by land, an expedition which we have been contemplating and preparing for at different periods for the last two years, but have never yet been able to effect.

Macquarie Harbour is the only port on the W. coast of V.D.s Land extremely difficult of excess and access by sea, and totally inaccessible by land, the country between it and the civilized (or settled) districts, a distance of about 80 or 90 miles, consisting of impervious forests, rugged mountains, tremendous gullies, impetuous Rivers and torrents, and swamps and morasses. Macquarie Harbour was a penal settlement, or a place to which the prisoners of V.D.s Land were sent for increase of punishment in the time of Colonel Arthur, but was abandoned in the year 1831 chiefly I believe, on account of the difficulty of keeping up the supplies by sea. During the time it was a penal settlement, various attempts were made by the prisoners to escape by land, but they perished in the forests except 2 or 3 who, utterly worn out, gave themselves up as soon as they arrived at a human habitation. There is a shocking story told, and a true one, of 2 men who having first killed and eaten their companions, were watching each other though over-come with sleep, in order to knock him on the head also and make a last repast. This was effected by one of them, and the surviving mad-man, got into the inhabited country, gave himself up and was hanged.

It is through this wild country made barely practicable for us on foot that we have been wandering for the last 3 weeks. We set off in beautiful weather, and in a season of unusually prolonged drought, but had scarcely commenced it, when the rains came on which made the bogs in a shocking state, and flooded all the torrents and rivers. We were confined a week in our tents in a nook under a snowy mountain, and again were impeded by a wide impetuous river which the surveyor had called the Franklin. It was 70 or 80 yards wide, too wide for any fallen trees to cross it, as we had crossed all the others, and where in consequence the pioneering party had constructed a rude kind of raft which they had fastened by a rope across the River. On our arrival the flood had carried away the warp, but the raft remained; on this after the river had subsided a little, two men (prisoners) volunteered to cross, a measure almost of necessity to effect soon as the 'Breeze' which was waiting for us here to take us back by sea, was to leave by order on the 18th and if gone, we should have to make our retreat by land with increased difficulties through the country we had already traversed.

The two men on the raft were whirled round in an eddy as soon as they pushed from the shore and, unable to cross were carried down the river, over some rapids and disappeared to our eyes in a bend of the stream. Sir John declared however he had no doubt of their safety, (they had been Thames and Bridgewater Bargemen) and in half an hour afterwards their voices were heard on the opposite side coo-y-ing, (the universal colonial cry learnt from the natives) and having given us this notice of their existence and safety, they darted deep into the forest on their mission which was to arrest the 'Breeze' in it's departure.

We remained six days on the banks of the Franklin to get up provisions, (salt pork and flour, brown sugar and tea) which as well as our bedding, blankets and tents were all carried in large knapsacks of kangaroo skin, on the backs of the men; and to build a double canoe which with such rude instruments as we had, was hollowed out of pine trees on the banks of the river. This canoe which I named the 'Eleanor Isabella' was taken in two by the raft, and the latter which had floated down to a smooth part of the river moved across by a double warp and blocks obtained from the 'Breeze'. Arrived at our tiny little Schooner (the name of which should be familiar to you, if you have read Mr Macdowell's diatribe upon it and us in his own newspaper) we part from our convict companions about 20 in number and commit ourselves to the Ocean.

Our party consists of Sir John and myself, Mr Bagot, Dr Milligan, as medical attendant and naturalist, Mr David Burn, a settler lately returned from England where he put various articles into the Colonial Magazine on V.D. Land, an Orderly, and my maid, and Mr Calder the Surveyor and the immediate master of the 20 convicts I have mentioned.

The crew of the 'Breeze' consists only of 5 persons, and a stranger to this country (particularly if he was a member of the former Transportation Committee) would take it for granted that 20 stout able-bodied convicts (chosen expressly for this service because they are such) WOULD find it an easy matter to overwhelm the resistance of 13 persons of whom two are women, and, taking possession of the 'Breeze' carry her off as masters and free. No such idea probably entered any of their heads. With the exception of trying whenever they could to get more than their due share of our scanty provisions, and which probably many free men of their rank in life would have done equally at home, in similar circumstances, they have behaved admirably well, and we have all encamped together, at night within a few yards of each other, in open tents, without a guard, and without a firearm amongst us, or a single instrument of defence, against the axes and tomahawks which were continually in their keeping. You may think it was because the Governor was of the party, and that they had all much to *hope* from him even tho' under the circumstances they could have little to *fear* and this is true,

for they all look to indulgence for this service, that is to say some alleviation of sentence, according to law, and were promised it on good
behaviour, but as far as safety is concerned the sense of security would
have been enjoyed, just as much I believe, by any other set of travellers
as ourselves. Our expedition has been a rough one, and perhaps rather
an anxious one, but on this very account it has afforded a very salutary
change to our thoughts long harassed by recent political matters at head
quarters. Sir John was less in want of it than usual, for the removal of
Mr Montagu [Sir John Franklin suspended the colonial secretary, John
Montagu, a critic of the Franklins, in early 1842] had done him a world
of good, and everything is going on even unusually well in our little
political world.

The enclosed papers include all the remaining official papers of
which I have copies, respecting Mr Montagu's affair, including the
humble and supplicatory letter which he wrote at the last to lead Sir
John to revoke his decision (just at the time he was applying to me
through Dr Turnbull) with Sir John's reply. There is not a dissenting
voice in the Colony now I believe, as to the propriety of Sir John's not
yielding to this letter. When Sir John had thus confirmed his decision,
Mr Montague lost not the first opportunity of declaring that he meant
nothing by it.

Your most affectionate sister,

JANE FRANKLIN

Some Private Correspondence of Sir John and Lady Jane Franklin, introduction, notes, and commentary by George Mackaness, part II (1947)

GEORG NEUMAYER

(1826–1909)

*German scientist. Between 1858 and 1864, Neumayer undertook a
magnetic survey of Victoria. In November 1862, during one of his
expeditions, he continued into New South Wales and climbed 'Pinnacle
Hill', Snowy Peak (present-day Mount Townsend), and Mount Kosciusko.
His companions on this occasion included the artist Eugene von Guérard,
who subsequently completed a number of works based on the sketches that he
made at the time. They include the oil painting entitled* North-East View
from the Northern Top of Mount Kosciusko *(1863), a striking image of
certainty, which actually depicts the view from Mount Townsend. (This*

work inspired Imants Tillers's 1988 painting Mount Analogue.) *Edward Brinkmann, Neumayer's assistant, who was separated from the group on this occasion, eventually caught up with the rest of the party near Albury on 6 December, by which stage he was 'in a most deplorable condition'.*

'THE UNFORTUNATE AFFAIR WITH EDWARD'

Thick fog in the valley on the morning of the 18th [November] but sky clear. Preparing everything for the ascent of Mt Kosciusko. Left three horses at Groggan's and took only Tommy with me packed with all the blankets and rations. Crossed the creek till it led us to a bluff commanding a fine view towards Mts Hope, Haystack and Pilot. Descended a steep incline towards the valley of the *Leather Jacket* Creek (3184) where we arrived at 10.30 a.m. temp. of the creek 56°.7; that of the air 84°.5. Left the place and ascended the steep banks of the creek under much difficulty although the horse behaved admirably. Continued ascending till we arrived at the region of dead timber (4663). The weather was quite calm, but the sky very threatening. About this time all of our party except myself felt very ill so that we were obliged to stop here for some time and take some brandy and water, which enabled them better to resist the effects of heat and fatigue. Crossed an extensive flat at 1.46 p.m., then after a continual ascent came to the upper limit of dwarf timber (6254) (*Eucalyptus*), and resolved to pitch our tents. The aneroid ceased to indicate the pressure of air since the last 1000 feet, the little compensation weight being fixed by the case of the instrument. We arrived at this spot at 5 p.m.; it must be mentioned, however, that the ascent would not have taken all this time had we been able to keep up a proper pace, for with the exception of the crossing of the Leather Jacket, the ascent of Mt *Kosciusko* from the Victorian side is an easy one when compared with that of some of the equally high mountains in other parts of the world; but throughout, our progress was retarded partly by the necessity of clearing a path, and the illness of the men. The vegetation near the camping place reminds one very much of that of the Alps except that the strange look of the dwarf gum trees introduces rather a new feature. Inspected the instruments and found, to my great satisfaction that none of them had received any serious injury from the unavoidable knocking about during the ascent. The temp. of the boiling point 200°.27. 9 p.m., few drops of rain but calm and overcast. An immense number of Bogong moths about the camp. By 10 p.m. a strong breeze rose from the North, which continued in puffs nearly throughout the night. The flapping of the tent although very annoying did not seriously interfere with our sound rest. November 19th at 5 a.m. threatening weather, the wind veering rather more to the West; bar 23".960, temp. 54°.9. This place commands a fine view of the *Manroo plains* and *Thredbo river.* Packed some of the magnetic instruments on Tommy and left our camp at 7 a.m. and after crossing some extensive snow fields arrived at what I named the 'Pinnacle Hill', (7038) at 8 a.m. Resolved to make some observations on terrestrial magnetism and placed the theodolite on a hill, composed of granite boulders, the weather, however, becoming unsettled and the wind being still strong from the North, I deferred these observations until my return. The instruments were consequently packed up again and as it evidently would be extremely difficult to take the horse any farther on, I ordered Edward to secure him properly and provide him with food for the time of our absence, and then started for what we supposed, and subsequently found to be, the highest point of Mt Kosciusko. Our path led us across ravines, snow fields and extensive marshes, covered with alpine vegetation, to a little lake at the foot of the highest summit. A few hundred feet higher up and we reached the watershed between the Murray and Snowy Rivers, the one flowing towards the Indian, the other into the Pacific Ocean. Passing over some snow fields of considerable extent, we arrived at the summit (7176) at 11 a.m. temp. 54°.5.

As the wind blew very strong from the North and rain fell occasionally in showers, I gave Edward my maps to put under shelter during the observations, and I hurried them as much as possible in order that we might yet have time to ascend the 'Snowy Peak', another point of Mt Kosciusko, which, from its being thickly covered with snow, has frequently been believed to be its highest point. Descended into a flat and made a short halt for the purpose of taking dinner, during which I learned that my friend M. de Guérard celebrated his 50th birth-day on this very day and we accordingly drank his health. All at once Edward recollected that he had forgotten to bring my maps with him on leaving the last hill; not much importance was attached to this at the time, as I thought it an easy matter to go and fetch them on our return. At 1 p.m. we reached the Snowy Peak (7140), but the wind was so very strong and the granite boulders, of which the summit is composed were so piled up, that I did not think it prudent to take the barometers to the top and accordingly mounted them some 40 ft lower down. Temp. of boiling point 198°.62. M. de Guérard, meanwhile had seated himself on the summit, which affords a beautiful view of the mountainous country of New South Wales and Victoria, as well as the plains of the Murray River, and was taking a sketch of the scenery, when, just as I was completing my observations, he called out that it appeared to him a heavy storm was approaching from the New South Wales side. It was apparent from the barometrical readings that the pressure of air was rapidly decreasing, and on ascending to the top, I became convinced there was no time to be lost and that we must hasten our return to camp as much as possible. Before leaving, I distinctly stated to our whole party that we were 7 miles distant from our camp in a N.N.W. direction, and that our course would therefore have to be S.S.E.

Left the Snowy Peak at 2.25 p.m. When we reached the snow fields at the foot of the summit, I told Edward to run up and fetch the maps he had forgotten and advised him to take our dog Hector with him. He had scarcely quitted our party five minutes when a terrific gale set in from West and the whole top of the mount was enveloped in dense clouds, the rain falling in torrents. Seeing the danger he was exposed to from the state of the weather, of becoming separated from our party, I cried out to him in order to recall him, but, unfortunately, this had the effect only of recalling the dog and thus leaving Edward to his own resources. It was a very difficult task indeed to find our way against wind and weather, but the watershed once crossed, we could scarcely fail to strike the camp, provided only, we maintained ordinary presence of mind. I entertained the hope that perhaps Edward would succeed in making his way to the little lake above mentioned, but as the fog was so dense that we could hardly see each other and had to steer by the compass and the terrain, we ourselves could not make this lake and it was not till about half an hour later, on the weather clearing up for a moment, that we perceived we had passed it. The roaring of the wind was at this time so loud that it was by no means an easy matter to communicate with each other, and thus it happened that another of our party, Weston, dropped off and could not be found. Another difficulty now was to find 'Pinnacle hill', that we might relieve the poor horse and fetch the instruments, and at times the attempt appeared almost hopeless, the more so from the chilly state of the atmosphere, Mr Twynham, now perfectly exhausted, became quite stiff and unable to move. By great good fortune, however, M. de Guérard and myself dragging him between us through fog and mist, hit upon the very spot where horse and instruments had been left in the morning. I had now to pack the horse — by no means an easy task as neither of my companions was able to assist me, and the animal, terrified by the storm had become entangled in the rope by which he was tethered. Luckily, however, I succeeded in accomplishing it much sooner than I expected. After immense difficulties, it being now nearly dark, M. de Guérard and I — Mr Twynham had been lost a short time before — reached the camp by 8 o'clock. We found it in a terrible state, everything wet through and torn. After fastening the horse and putting things a little in order we went back for Mr Twynham, who could hardly be more than half a mile from us, and were fortunate enough to recover him. Had to carry him as he was in a perfectly helpless state. We were now most anxious to light a fire, but as Edward had the match-box with him and we had but few left, it was no easy thing, but after an hour and a half we succeeded in kindling a fire, which was soon blown into a good blaze by the terrific gale now raging, the roaring of the wind interrupted occasionally only by the thunder. Lightning and rain continued the whole evening. By 11 o'clock we had the water in the kettle boiling and our tent roughly fixed again and, could we only have known something of the whereabouts of our companions, would have been tolerably comfortable, notwithstanding the rough state of the weather. My delight can scarcely be imagined when the barking of the dog announced the return of one of our missing men. It was Weston, who said that, attracted by the light of our fire, he had made his last effort to reach the camp.

At 4 a.m. on the 20th, clear morning so that I was able to have a good view of the whole country. Climbed up a rock in order to fix a piece of canvas to serve as a flag, hoping this might perhaps direct Edward to the camp. Resolved to proceed at once in search of him, M. de Guérard volunteering to accompany me, neither of the other two men being in a fit state to do so, and even he, after walking with me for an hour, declared himself unable to proceed any farther. The search was now left to me alone and my first care was to ascertain whether Edward had reached the summit and taken the maps with him; therefore, when crossing the snow field, I looked carefully for his foot-prints, but though I could plainly make out those of the dog, I could discover none of his. On reaching the top, I found my maps untouched and concluded that he had not succeeded in crossing the snowfield or in ascending the summit, and that, in his bewilderment, he had travelled down into the valley of the Snowy River. After depositing some clear and precise directions with respect to the position of our camp, and the time I intended yet to stay on Mt Kosciusko, I turned back and reached the camp at 12 o'clock, in a very depressed state, enhanced by finding that Edward had not returned during my absence. In the afternoon we could do nothing but rest and recover strength, hoping every moment to hear the foot step of our companion, but in vain. The gale was still blowing so hard from N.N.W. that it was impossible to suspend and register the barometer 'Greiner'; and Edward having the only suitable instrument with him, we could not effect any observations, at 7 p.m. just as we had taken supper and it was already dark, our horse, who had been nibbling at some scanty herbage near the spot, made off and could not be found any more. It seems that the poor animal cared to stop no longer where he hardly could get any thing to eat and had to suffer severely from a temperature of 37°.5. Morning of the 21st cold and foggy. Got up at 4 a.m. and started with the intention of tracking the horse but without success. Weston who went in another direction, returned at 7.45 a.m. without having seen a trace of him and it was now quite clear that he had tried to find his way to Groggan's station — no very pleasant prospect for us, being thus left without any means of transport and our stores fast running out. Sent Weston again with strict injunctions to descend towards the station till he found the horse. It was now my opinion that Edward must already have perished or, if he still survived, had taken such a course as to place him beyond all chance of assistance from us; I therefore resolved to return to Groggan's station as soon as Weston should appear with the horse, which we had the satisfaction of seeing at 10 a.m. He had found him near the lower limit of the belt of dead timber; there is no doubt that, had it not been for the hobbles, he would have succeeded in reaching the station. In the course of the forenoon I made some few magnetic observations near the camp. On the track leading towards Groggan's station, the theodolite was fixed on a stone to the East of which there was a mass of granite.

Leaving all the provisions yet in our possession and exact instructions to Edward, should he ever return to the camp, how to follow our track, we packed the horse and started, after having given three cheers for the missing man. While descending I made it a point to blaze all the trees in such a manner, that even a man in a reduced state of body, would be able to follow the track. During all this time we were still in hope that our friend might have gained the station before us, thus rendering our labour useless. Arrived at the Leather jacket again by 4 p.m. Had great difficulty in getting the horse, in its exhausted state, up the Groggan's side of the banks of the creek. The brave animal tried it three times, and on each occasion succeeded in reaching a height of 80 feet, but rolled back again and there remained. There was no other course left but to unpack and carry the things ourselves to the top of the hill. Got to

Groggan's station at last by 7.15 p.m., but heard nothing of our friend. As already mentioned the ascent of the mountain from this side is by no means very fatiguing, if the lay of the spurs be attended to. The geological formation being in some places of a slaty character, causes the track to be slippery and it requires great precaution to bring the horses safely over such spots. Another difficulty is presented in the Dead Timber Belt, which is about half a mile broad and certainly offers some resistance to a speedy progress; on the other hand, the scrub is not so thick as I have seen it in other parts of Victoria, for instance in Gippsland. We took note of another tree, a large stringy-bark, which had recently been struck by lightning, the electric fluid having marked its passage from the summit to the ground in a spiral similar to that described near Mt Hope. In the gullies between the spurs of the mountains, there are small streams, or creeks the temperature of which is in most cases 32°.0; and whenever they spread over the ground it becomes swampy and the vegetation of a mossy character. Strong winds from the N.W. accompanied by rain and dense fog seem to prevail here at times. On the first day the weather was tolerably fair and quite calm, but the sun being scarcely visible through the thick veil covering the sky, indicated the approach of one of these gales. I regretted very much that in consequence of the absence of Edward, who carried the only suitable barometer for such occasions, it was impossible to record the oscillations in the pressure of the air during this N.W. gale, the comparison of which with observations made at the sea-level or in other localities of the mountainous part of the country, would have proved of considerable interest. The force of the wind was, at times, really fearful, so much so that it was thoroughly impossible to make any headway against it and I do not think I shall be far out in estimating it at from 40 to 45 pounds on the square foot. The unfortunate affair with Edward interfered greatly with the scientific objects during my stay on the mount, my time being entirely taken up in looking for him, and the idea continually preying on my mind that he would not be able to make for the settled districts and thus extricate himself from his very perilous position. I was therefore now determined to hurry to Omeo and secure the assistance of the police, for the purpose of instituting another search after the poor fellow.

Results of the Magnetic Survey of the Colony of Victoria (1869)

4

THE NORTH
AND CENTRE

CHARLES STURT

(1795–1869)

English soldier, explorer, and public servant. Sturt aimed to reach the centre of the continent during his third and final major expedition (1844–46). His party, which included, among others, James Poole as second-in-command, Harris Browne as surgeon, and John McDouall Stuart as draughtsman, left Adelaide in August 1844. Their equipment included a boat for the inland sea that Sturt still hoped to find. After travelling along the Murray and Darling Rivers, they were trapped by drought in the Grey Range from January to July 1845. As recorded here, Poole was destined never to return home. Sturt eventually reached the area known as Simpson's Desert, before returning to Adelaide in a greatly weakened state of health.

THE DEATH OF JAMES POOLE

On the other hand I was vexed to find Mr Poole worse. He had put himself into a furious passion and said that he was neglected and the consequence was a relapse, so that I found it necessary to speak to him very seriously on the subject. This was about the end of June, and for a few days he seemed to rally, but about the 3rd of July he became whimsical, wanted all kind of things made for him, and was dissatisfied. He thought he should be better in the underground room we had made than in his tent, so I had a chimney and fireplace made to it, and got him removed into it on the 12th, the day it commenced to rain so that poor man he did not long enjoy it. On the 13th and 14th it rained heavily, or rather a mild steady rain, and sufficient having fallen to justify me in breaking up the Depôt, I directed the home-returning party to prepare for their departure on the morrow that is on the [15th] and had the dray prepared for Mr Poole's reception. In the morning therefore the men mustered, and Mr Poole was carried up from the underground room and lifted into the dray. Poor man! It went to my heart to see him leave me in such a state but I fully anticipated his speedy improvement as he neared Adelaide. He was much affected when I took leave of him, and assured me that his first visit should be to you. I requested Mr Browne to accompany him the first day, and I told him that I would only go a few miles to enable him the easier to rejoin me. I was in truth anxious to know how he would bear the movement of the dray, and to have Mr Browne's opinion of his prospects to the last moment.

Our separation, Dearest, in such a wilderness as this was sufficiently painful without being aggravated by circumstances, and it was believe me with a beating and a bursting heart that I saw the cavalcade move off.

As is generally the case where one has been for a long time stationary at a place, there were a thousand things to delay us. The horses could not be found, the bullocks so long out of yoke could not be managed and I was at last obliged to give up the idea of leaving the Depôt that day. On the 16th, however, I had the teams up at an early hour, and at 7 we turned our backs on a spot, our sojourn upon which carried not one pleasing recollection with it. It was like a reprieve to me to get away from it and to breathe another air.

The rain, however, had made the ground very soft and our still heavily loaded teams sank deep into it, and one of them fairly stuck in a small gully about a quarter of a mile from the Depôt, and we were labouring to disengage it when Mr Browne rejoined me, and I was glad to learn from him that he had left Mr Poole much calmer, and that he had every hope of his reaching Adelaide in safety and in some measure restored to health. I saw, however, that something unusual had occurred, and on telling Mr Browne so he said that Mr Poole had had one of those violent bursts of passion to which he so often gave way, and that he had had occasion to speak to him in rather angry language and to represent to him that he could not expect the men who have heard him go on in so unbecoming a manner, to respect him who had no respect for himself. I was in truth glad that Mr Poole was gone for he was a mischief-maker in every sense of the word, and had really caused ceaseless disturbances in the camp. Yet he had some good points, and he had a claim to my strongest sympathy, and therefore it was that I did every thing to soothe his mind on his return, and to write in his favour. However let that pass I have forgiven and forgotten any annoyance he ever gave me and only to you, Dearest Charlotte, do I thus open my mind.

This first day of our removal from the Depôt we did not get more than four miles but it satisfied me to get away from it.

Intending to go to Lake Torrens as soon as I had established the Depôt on the western creek, I had employed the men whilst idle in measuring the distance to it, and they had some weeks before we broke up completed thirty miles. In the morning I sent on Mr Stuart with Mr Piesse and a party of chainers to continue the measurement whilst I brought the party up, and they had got on to some distance. It was about 8 o'clock and quite dark when we heard the tramp of a horse, and immediately after it Joseph's voice, with whom I had reluctantly parted to wait on Mr Poole. I called to him and on his coming to the tent asked him what brought him back, for I really thought his temporary master had changed his mind and had determined not to proceed on his journey. But judge of my astonishment when he told me that Mr Poole was dead. Mr B. had left him in the morning about 7 and he had expired at 3 almost without a struggle. Joseph informed me that he was leaning on his side and in the act of taking a dose of your favourite medicine, when he exclaimed, 'My God, Joseph, I fear I am dying,' and falling on his back he heaved two or three deep sighs, and was no more. This melancholy event gave me sincere pain, in the thought that a companion should have thus fallen and I blamed myself for having sent him away, but God knows it was an event that I had not foreseen. It put a stop however to all my arrangements, and obliged me to remain stationary for a few days.

On considering the matter over I determined on having Mr Poole's remains interred at the Depôt. It struck me that his funeral obsequies would be a fitting close to our residence at that dreary spot. On the morning of the [17th] I rode with Mr Browne to the place at which the home-returning party had encamped, having previously sent Flood to recall Mr Stuart and the chainers, and a party of men to prepare a grave at the foot of an old banksia tree that stood in the middle of the camp.

On examining Mr Poole's remains, Mr Browne was clearly of opinion that his sudden death was caused by internal haemorrhage, that is by the rupture of some blood vessel internally, most probably in the region of the abdomen. The singular fairness of his countenance indeed indicated that such had been the case. Be that as it may, he had breathed his last in as gloomy a desert as man ever entered.

After directing Joseph to bring the body down to the Depôt with all the men excepting one, to remain as a guard with Tampawang, I rode back, and taking the Depôt in my way to see how the men had got on with their work, I reached the tents about 5 in the afternoon. Early on the following morning Joseph came to tell me that he had executed my orders, and about 9 Mr Stuart came up so that the party being once more assembled we proceeded to the Depôt, and after I had read the Funeral Service over them we lowered Mr Poole's remains, rolled up in a blanket and laid upon his mattress into their last bed. We had not the wood to make a coffin, so I desired that a kind of chamber should be made at the bottom of the grave, which we planked over so that no dirt should fall upon the body and so left him to sleep until that great day when we shall all be summoned before that Judge with whom human craft will have no avail, no quibble of law have any weight.

Narrative of an Expedition into Central Australia, vol. 2 (1849)

——

MARTIN THOMAS

(1943–)

Australian writer. In his 'blend of fact and fiction', The Roan (1994), Thomas writes movingly about a roan-coloured horse that is abandoned half-dead in the desert in 1845, by the explorer Charles Sturt, during the latter's expedition to central Australia. Here we see the Roan after he has spent many years in the outback. The specific date within the extract gives the reader some indication of the direction in which the story is heading.

A SIGNIFICANT MOMENT

Surprisingly, the Roan had left the comfort of the tribe a week back now and wandered, slowly, for that was the only way in which he travelled these days, towards the east. Shuffling through the bush, perhaps half a dozen miles a day, the old stallion had arrived in a place of his past. The great waterhole of Nappapathera seemed to have changed little, the cockatoos rose screeching, and a hundred black swans huddled almost in a group on the far bank from which he stood. Like Charles Sturt had noted, his ears took in the sounds of the 'ventriloquist' dove, but when he looked beyond the trees towards the clearing from whence the sound came, nothing moved. Suddenly the culprit rose, whirring up and away from just yards in front of him.

The steps were more measured, definitely slower, and every mouthful took longer than ever to chew. Teeth that had once sliced through canegrass now avoided anything except the choicest pieces. The desert sand, picked up grain by grain as unwanted baggage on every tuft of grass, just a grain by grain, had assisted ably in the inevitable wearing down of the Roan's teeth. No close examination was needed to see him for what he was — an aged warrior. He still kept the wonderful shod look of his hooves, and it would not have been possible for even an Aborigine to tell that this horse had been unshod for nigh on 16 years. There was a lightening off, too, in that wonderful tawny, red-into-grey colouration, especially the whiteness, quite pronounced now around the mouth. And two eyes that had the spectacle of white-rimmed glasses around their rims. That stocky frame had lightened, its overburden of muscle now appeared a little wasted, and though slight, the straightest, strongest of backs had begun inevitable submission to gravity and an expanding belly. A quiet, even graceful, aged stallion grazing in the most peaceful of settings.

In these past months, a long-ignored feeling had re-emerged and it was this, I suppose, that had brought him here to old territory. The whinnying, neighing was gone, though the sight of anything strange was greeted with a long stare and snort of distrust. The discontentment, the desire for the companionship of his own kind of those early days had returned. Ears would prick in expectation at sounds, and the grizzled head would turn. A sharp crack in the distance, far over the other side of the creek and to the west, had his ears pricked. Another red gum branch falling, as they do so often? This retort had sounded somehow different. Another 'ventriloquist' dove diverted his attention and he moved closer to the source of the cooing. With the experience of almost 22 years behind him, the Roan knew that life had the capacity to repeat itself endlessly in this place and he bent to pluck into his mouth a delicate oatgrass.

I shall tell you the date, for it would be unfair to hide from you the extent of the years that had passed since the Roan's abandonment, and the significance of this moment. Judging by the sun on that Sunday, 21 April 1861, it was around 9 a.m. and Lottie Poole's Roan stood and sniffed the easterly breeze. Of all his senses, that of smell was as strong as in days bygone and the Roan put his head up again, stopped chewing, snorted, stamped his feet, then abruptly pawed the ground in agitation, something that he hadn't been aroused enough to do for many years. Unmistakably, whisper faint, but most certainly there, caught up with the cocktail of smells of the bush, being brushed over and past by the camel-hair soft breeze, was the scent he had sought for a lifetime. There, fixed on the gossamer breath of the Cooper Creek, was the smell of another horse.

Lottie Poole's Roan, moving unrestrainedly towards the source of the smell, was soon to become a silent witness to one of the most tragic moments of Australia's history. In a state of great anticipation, the old Roan stumbled on, breaking into the closest thing he could get to a gallop. He would not have known, but there was a mile to go.

The Roan (1994)

JOHN AINSWORTH HORROCKS

(1818–46)

Pastoralist and explorer. After his arrival in South Australia in 1839, English-born Horrocks established a station on the Hutt River, and undertook some exploring, 'discovering' Mount Horrocks and the Gulnare Plains. In 1846, he led an expedition, whose members included the artist S. T. Gill (as draughtsman), to explore to the north of Port Augusta. The enterprise ended prematurely after the accident that Horrocks describes in this letter, which he dictated before returning to his property, where he died on 23 September. He has the rather odd, given the nature of his demise, claim to fame of having been the first man to have used a camel for exploration in Australia.

ALAS, POOR HORROCKS

Depot Creek.
September 8, 1846.

Mr E. Platts,
Hon. Secretary Northern Expedition.

It is with the greatest regret I have to inform the Committee and my fellow-colonists who subscribed towards the expenses of the expedition of its untimely and unfortunate termination. Having made an excursion, accompanied by Mr Gill, to the table land on the west of Lake Torrens, to ascertain if it were practicable to form a depot in that neighbourhood, and not succeeding in finding either water or grass, I returned to Depot Creek, determined to make an excursion with the camel, as it was impracticable to take horses sufficiently far, from what I saw of the desolate and barren country.

Having ascertained the morning previous to our departure, from the summit of the range behind Depot Creek, the bearings of the high land seen by Messrs Eyre and Darke to be 32 degrees north of west by compass, and the distance I considered about eight miles, I determined to make straight for that land.

With this view I started on the 28th of August, accompanied by Mr Gill and Bernard Kilroy, with provisions sufficient for three weeks and ten gallons of water, the camel being loaded with about 356 lb. Our first day's journey brought us to one of the creeks running from Lake Torrens into the Gulf, distance about ten miles. The last six miles was over red sandhills, partially covered with oaten grass.

The second day's journey we camped on the west side of the table land, distance fifteen miles. The first eight miles over a continuation of sandhills, the last seven miles over a country covered with stones and salsolaceous plants.

The next day we entered a light scrub and very heavy sandhills, fifteen miles.

The day following scrub and very heavy sandhills, and plain all covered with salsolaceous plants.

The day after, having made six miles, we reached a large saltwater lake about ten miles long and five miles broad. The land we were making for we distinctly saw I supposed about twenty-five miles distant. In rounding this lake, which I named Lake Gill, Bernard Kilroy, who was walking ahead of the party, stopped, saying he saw a beautiful bird, which he recommended me to shoot to add to the collection.

My gun being loaded with slugs in one barrel and ball in the other, I stopped the camel to get at the shot belt, which I could not get without his laying down.

Whilst Mr Gill was unfastening it I was screwing the ramrod into the wad over the slugs, standing close alongside of the camel. At this moment the camel gave a lurch to one side, and caught his pack in the cock of my gun, which discharged the barrel I was unloading, the contents of which first took off the middle fingers of my right hand between the second and third joints, and entered my left cheek by my lower jaw, knocking out a row of teeth from my upper jaw.

In this dilemma I was fortunate in having two most excellent companions. We were now sixty-five miles from the depot or any water that we knew of, and all the water remaining was about five gallons. With very great reluctance I consented to Bernard Kilroy's entreaty for him to return back and fetch Mr Theatstone and two horses, as I knew part of the country was inhabited by a fierce lot of natives, as they had attacked Mr Gill and myself on my previous excursion. He said he was not afraid. Therefore he left and reached the Depot the next morning by about 9 o'clock. Having missed the tracks during the night, he could not have walked less than 100 miles from the morning of the accident to the time he reached the Depot, having most bravely accomplished his task.

Mr Gill stopped to nurse me, and his attention and kindness were not to be surpassed. Considering the distance we were away and the uncertainty of Kilroy's reaching the Depot, Mr Gill showed himself to be a brave and steady companion by remaining with me. He has taken several sketches of this country, which will show to those interested how very improbable it is that any stations can be made to the west of Lake Torrens. All the drainage is into fresh water ponds and salt lakes. The ponds are apparently dry in a very few days after rain, and the water which is in them being of a dark red ochreous color, the size of them varying from half an acre to five acres, and when full not more than 6 in. in depth.

The hill we were making for is table topped, with precipitous sides, about seven miles in length. To the N.N.E. are three smaller hills, and continuing on from them is a low land, gradually diminishing in height until it gains the land running from Lake Torrens. I did not find a spot where there was any probability of finding a spring. Grass there is none except a little wild oaten grass, which grows in the sand here and there, and that not sufficient to feed a horse.

It is with extreme sorrow I am obliged to terminate the expedition, as the two that were with me, the camel and myself were in excellent working condition; and had it not been for this accident it was my intention to have followed down this low land running to the N.N.E., and returned by Lake Torrens, a distance of between 300 and 400 miles; and would then have been able to have given a more accurate account, although I am convinced we should not have found one acre of ground to make a station on, judging from the land I have gone over and what I could discern with my eye, there being a sterile sameness throughout.

Had it been earlier in the season and my wounds healed up I should have started again.

On Sunday last I returned to the Depot, horses, myself, and party all completely knocked up.

I remain, yours truly,
J HORROCKS (Signed).

Proceedings of the Royal Geographical Society of Australasia: South Australian Branch, sessions 1904–05, 1905–06, vol. VIII (1906)

———

THOMAS LIVINGSTONE MITCHELL
(1792–1855)

Surveyor-general of New South Wales. Mitchell left Boree, near Orange, in December 1845, hoping to find a route to Port Essington, on the Cobourg Peninsula in the present-day Northern Territory, preferably by discovering and following a northward-flowing river. He believed that he had come across such a river, which he named the Victoria, in September 1846. Soon afterwards, suffering from a lack of supplies, and concerned about possible conflict with Aborigines, he headed back to Sydney, arriving there, ahead of his party, in December 1846. Mitchell was wrong. Edmund Kennedy explored the 'Victoria' in 1847, gave it back its Aboriginal name of Barcoo, and found that it joined the Thomson River to become Cooper's (later Cooper) Creek.

'THE REALIZATION OF MY LONG CHERISHED HOPES'

15th September — As soon as daylight appeared I hastened towards the gap, and ascended a naked rock on the west side of it. I there beheld downs and plains extending westward beyond the reach of vision, bounded on the S.W. by woods and low ranges, and on the N.E. by higher ranges; the whole of these open downs declining to the N.W., in which direction a line of trees marked the course of a river traceable to the remotest verge of the horizon. There I found then, at last, the realization of my long cherished hopes, an interior river falling to the N.W. in the heart of an open country extending also in that direction. Ulloa's delight at the first view of the Pacific could not have surpassed mine on this occasion, nor could the fervour with which he was impressed at the moment have exceeded my sense of gratitude, for being allowed to make such a discovery. From that rock, the scene was so extensive as to leave no room for doubt as to the course of the river, which, thus and there revealed to me alone, seemed like a reward direct from Heaven for perseverance, and as a compensation for the many sacrifices I had made, in order to solve the question as to the interior rivers of Tropical Australia. To an European, the prospect of an open country has a double charm in regions for the most part covered with primæval forests, calling up pleasing reminiscences of the past, brighter prospects for the future — inspiring a sense of freedom, especially when viewed from the back of a good horse: —

A steed! a steed! of matchless speede,
A sword of metal keene —
All else to noble minds is drosse,
All else on earth is meane! — *Old Song.*

I hastened back to my little party (distant a mile and a half from the gap), and immediately made them mount to follow me down the water-course, which, as I had seen from the rock, would lead us into the open country. The little chain of ponds led westward, until the boundless downs appeared through the woods; a scene most refreshing to us, on emerging from so many thick scrubs. Our little river, after crossing much open plain, fell into another coming from E.S.E., and columns of smoke far in the N.W. showed that there was water, by showing there were inhabitants. The grass on these downs was of the richest sort, chiefly *Panicum lævinode*, and I was not sorry to recognise amongst it, *Salsolæ*, and the *Acacia pendula*, amongst the shrubs. As we followed the river downwards, the open downs appeared on the W.N.W. horizon as if interminable. This river, unlike that I had called the Nive, had no sand in its bed, which consisted of firm clay, and contained deep hollows, and the beds of long reaches, then, however, all dry, while abundance of large *unio* shells lay upon the banks, and proved that the drought was not of common occurrence. The general course of the river I found to be about W.N.W. true. We continued to follow it through its windings all day, which I certainly should not have done, but for the sake of water, as our progress downwards was thus much retarded. Towards evening, Corporal Graham discovered water in a small tributary coming from the S.E., while Yuranigh found some also in the main channel, where that tributary fell into it. We encamped on Graham's ponds, as this was called, and turned our horses loose on the wide plain, up to the knees in grass half dry, half green, that they might be the more fit 'for the field to-morrow.' The sky had been lowering all day, and the heat was intense; but during the night, the air was delicious for sleeping in, under heaven's canopy and protection.

16th September — The 'gorgeous curtains of the East' over grandly formed clouds harmonised well with my sentiments on awaking, again to trace, as if I had been the earliest man, the various features of these fine regions of earth. At 7 A.M. the temperature was 63°; and (from observations registered then) the height above the sea has been found to be 1216 feet. Throughout the day we travelled over fine downs and plains covered with the finest grass, having the river on our right. Beyond it, we saw hills, which seemed to be of greater height in proportion as we descended with the river. Some were much broken, and appeared to present precipices on the other side. A broad valley extended westward from between the farthest of these broken ranges, which range seemed to be an offshoot from one further eastward. On examining the river, below the supposed junction of a tributary from the east, I found its character altered, forming ponds amongst brigalow trees. Water was, however, scarce. We fortunately watered our horses about 3 P.M., at the only hole we had seen that day, a small muddy puddle. The *Acacia pendula* formed a belt outside the brigalow, between the river and the open plains, and many birds and plants reminded us of the Darling; the rose cockatoo and crested-pigeon, amongst the former; *Salsolæ* and *solanum* amongst the latter. At length, we saw before us, to the westward, bold precipitous hills, extending also to the southward of west. A thunder storm came over us, and night advancing, we halted without seeing more, for that day, of the interesting country before us, and having only water enough for our own use, the product of the shower. No pond was found for the horses, although we had searched for one, many miles in the bed of the river. Still, the remains of mussel shells on the banks bore testimony that water was seldom so scarce in this river, flowing as it did through the finest and most extensive pastoral region I had ever seen.

17th September — The temperature at seven this morning was 57°; our height above the sea 1112 feet. 'Like the gay birds that' awoke us from 'repose' we were 'content,' but certainly not 'careless of to-morrow's fare;' for unless we found water to-day, 'to-morrow' had found us unable either to proceed or return! Trusting wholly to Providence, however, we went forward, and found a pond in the river bed, not distant more than two miles from where we had slept. In making a cut next through a brigalow scrub, towards where I hoped to hit the river, in a nearly westerly direction, I came out upon open downs, and turned again into a brigalow scrub on my right. After travelling a good many miles, N.W., through this scrub, we arrived on the verge of a plain of dead brigalow; and still pursuing the same course, we came out, at length, upon open downs extending far to the northward. I continued to ride in that direction to a clear hill, and from it I obtained a view of a range of flat-topped hills, that seemed to extend W.N.W.; the most westerly portion of these being the steep-sided mass seen before us yesterday. They now lay far to the northward, and the intervening country was partly low and woody, and partly consisted of the downs we were upon. But where was the river? Yarra trees and other indications of one appeared nearest to us in an easterly direction, at the foot of some well-formed hollows on that side the downs. Towards that point I therefore shaped my course, and there found the river — no longer a chain of dry ponds in brigalow scrub, but a channel shaded by lofty yarra trees, with open grassy banks, and containing long reaches full of water. White cockatoos shrieked above us; ducks floated, or flew about, and columns of smoke began to ascend from the woods before us. This was now, indeed, a river, and I lost no time in following it downwards. The direction was west; then north-west, tolerably straight. Water was abundant in its bed; the breadth was considerable, and the channel was well-marked by bold lofty banks. I remarked the salt-bush of the Bogan plains, growing here, on sand-islands of this river. The grass surpassed any I had ever seen in the colony in quality and abundance. The slow flying pelican appeared over our heads, and we came to a long broad reach covered with ducks, where the channel had all the appearance of a river of the first magnitude. The old mussle shells (*unio*) lay in heaps, like cart-loads, all along the banks, but still we saw none of the natives. Flames, however, arose from the woods beyond the opposite bank, at once in many directions, as if by magic, as we advanced. At 3 P.M. Fahrenheit's thermometer in the shade stood at 90°. Towards evening, we saw part of the bed dry, and found it continuously so, as night came on. The sun had set, while I still anxiously explored the dry recesses of the channel in search of water, without much hopes of success, when a wild yell arose from the woods back from the channel, which assured us that water was near. Towards that quarter we turned, and Yuranigh soon found a fine pond in a small ana-branch, upon which we immediately halted, and took up our abode there for the night. It may seem strange that so small a number could act thus unmolested by the native tribes, but our safety consisted chiefly in the rapidity of our movements, and their terror of strangers wholly unknown, perhaps unheard of, arriving on the backs of huge animals, or centaurs whose tramp they had only heard at nightfall. Like Burns's 'Auld Nick,'

> — rustling through the boortrees comin'
>   Wi' eerie sough!

our passage was too rapid to admit of any design for attack or annoyance being concocted, much less, carried into effect; next night we hoped to sleep thirty miles off, where our coming would be equally unexpected by natives. Latitude, 24° 34' 30" S.

Journal of an Expedition into the Interior of Tropical Australia (1848)

———

LUDWIG LEICHHARDT
(1813–48?)

Prussian-born naturalist and explorer. Leichhardt, who was educated at the universities of Berlin and Göttingen, arrived in Sydney in 1842. After leading an overland expedition from the Moreton Bay district to Port Essington (1844–45), he was hailed as a hero, as he reports in this letter to his brother-in-law, given awards by geographical societies in London and Paris, and pardoned for being a Prussian military deserter. Leichhardt subsequently planned to travel from the Darling Downs across the north to the west coast of the continent, and then south to the Swan River settlement.

His first attempt, made in 1846–47, was unsuccessful. During a second attempt, he and his party of six others disappeared, having last been seen on the Darling Downs in April 1848. At least nine major searches conducted between 1852 and 1938 failed to discover Leichhardt's fate.

LEICHHARDT RETURNS FROM THE DEAD — ONCE

Sydney, 18th April, 1846

My dear brother-in-law,

Sir Evan Mackenzie (baronet) is returning to England, and intends to go to Germany a few weeks after he arrives Home, to show his young wife the beauties of our Fatherland. I'm taking this opportunity of sending you a few lines, which amount to a short continuation of my journal. In my last letter, written on board the schooner *Heroine*, and posted to William — or rather, to John Nicholson — I told you something of the progress of my journey from Moreton Bay to Port Essington. I arrived at Sydney in the beginning of April, and no king could have been welcomed with greater gladness and deeper interest by a whole people than I was myself. As it had long been presumed that I had either died or been killed by the blacks, my good friend Mr Lynd had written my funeral dirge, of which I'm sending you a copy in English. The poem is a very good one. Mr Nathan, a musician who set Byron's *Hebrew Melodies* to music in England, wrote the music for the dirge. My name was on everybody's lips, for everybody was mourning for the poor unfortunate wanderer through the wilds of Australia; and none but a few went so far as to blame him for the *foolhardiness* of the venture. When nearly everybody had been affected by this prevailing mood of sympathy, sorrow and pity, I popped up out of my grave, successful in my undertaking, and my pockets full of fine discoveries and reports of new country mostly better than anybody had expected. An intelligent tobacconist, a man named *Aldis*, who is generally liked, had been one of my most friendly and generous supporters in the days when I was getting ready to start on my journey, and he was the first person I met when I stepped ashore. As soon as he recognised me — and it took him some time — he began to shout so excitedly that I didn't know what to make of it. On the way to Lynd's house he kept on calling out to everyone in the street, 'This is Leichhardt! the man we buried long ago! the man we've been singing about! He's come from Port Essington and he's beaten the bush!' and I began to think that the whole town was catching the excitement and going mad. My friend didn't recognise me at first, as I look much stronger and heavier than before the journey — but when he did, there was no end to his rejoicing. Congratulations on the success of my journey came pouring in from all directions and from all classes; and you can just imagine how I enjoyed the surprise of this unexpected public response. I had been sure that some of the better informed people would readily acknowledge my contribution towards the exploration of the interior of Australia; but even in this regard, I had reason to be prepared to hear narrow-minded and grudging remarks about the outsider, the fellow of non-British origin. Yet not a single envious word has been spoken, and everybody, even Sir Thomas Mitchell's family, is giving me my due. Groups were promptly formed to raise enough money for a fitting reward for my services; and letters of thanks and generous contributions have been coming in from all sides and from the very confines of the colony. — Like Mr Lynd, who wrote my funeral dirge, a young man named Silvester has written a song of rejoicing, which I'm also sending you. Once again Mr Nathan is the composer, but the music has not yet been published. During the last three weeks everybody who could possibly manage it has come, either to pay his respects in person, or to meet me at functions to which I am invited almost every day. The flattering treatment and special attention that I am receiving everywhere, however, will not be enough to make me so vain as to lose sight of what remains to be done in the light of what I have done, any more than my slender means deterred me from carrying out my [former] plan.

I'm hoping to set out on a new journey at the end of October, which, though longer, will be more interesting than the last. I hope to be on my way back from Swan River in two years' time. What I have in mind is to go up to the Tropics, to make my way thence right across to the West coast of Australia in 22° or 23° of [South] latitude, and then to follow the coast southwards to Swan River. In Lat. 23° 30' [S.] I crossed a river which, though not flowing, held ample supplies of water. I now want to follow this river upstream, hoping that its head-waters will lead me either to those of the Burdekin or to those of the rivers draining to the Gulf of Carpentaria, roughly in Lat. 22° or 23° [S.]. I want to proceed towards Cambridge Gulf across the plateau which presumably sheds these north-flowing waters, and then to swing southwards and make for Swan River, keeping 150 to 200 English miles from the coast. I've written to India for camels, and shall at least try to get the two that are already in the colony.

On my last journey I used to hear mother's and father's parting words ringing in my ears: 'The Lord will never forsake you, son'. And now, even in my success, and in my dreams about my projected journey, I'm still hearing them. The simple words not only calm stirrings of apprehension and revive my courage. They also remind me that I owe my success in a dangerous undertaking to the care and protection of our benign Heavenly Father.

Capt. Perry (the Deputy Surveyor General) is busily engaged in the systematic and elegant reduction of my maps, and it's quite exciting to see how the country I traversed shows up in the undescribed interior of Australia. —

I've translated Ronge's *Protest* into English and intend to publish it. I'm hoping that it will have considerable effect, as everybody is afraid that the Roman Catholic Church is working to gain the upper hand in Australia. Ireland probably sends out most of the immigrants, and, as most of the Irish are Catholics, it's likely that Catholics predominate in number already. I see little difference between Ronge and Luther; but I think it astute of him to keep the word 'catholic' in the name of his sect instead of just going over to lutheranism by himself. Don't neglect to keep me well informed on the course of things in our beloved Germany; and may I suggest that you jot down a few lines every day and so keep a kind of journal going? I'm concerned about your children. Your eldest boy would suit me admirably, supposing that I'll have learnt how to be more at peace with myself in two years' time. Let him go his own way, and see whether or not he develops an interest in botany and natural history. Unfortunately the teachers of natural history in the high schools are mostly such prim and dry sticks that, instead of quickening the seeds of interest and helping them to strike, they kill them dead and turn the boys and girls right against nature-study. If I'm successful on my new journey I may be in a position to do something really worth while for you all. So good-bye, my dear brother-in-law and sister. Give my regards to all our relations and friends — particularly to my dear mother, from

Your affectionate brother-in-law and brother,
Ludwig.

The Letters of F. W. Ludwig Leichhardt, vol. III (1968)

A.B. PATERSON

(1864–1941)

Australian poet. As a result of writing the words of the famous song 'Waltzing Matilda' and ballads such as 'The Man from Snowy River', 'Banjo' Paterson is considered to be the 'chief folk-poet of Australia'. He had this to say about the idea of another search for Leichhardt, proposed decades after the explorer's disappearance in 1848.

'THE LOST LEICHHARDT'

'An English scientific society is fitting out a pioneering party to search for traces of the lost explorer Leichhardt.'

Another search for Leichhardt's tomb,
Though fifty years have fled
Since Leichhardt vanished in the gloom,
Our one Illustrious Dead!

But daring men from Britain's shore,
The fearless bull-dog breed,
Renew the fearful task once more
Determined to succeed.

Rash men, that know not what they seek,
Will find their courage tried.
For things have changed on Cooper's Creek
Since Ludwig Leichhardt died.

Along where Leichhardt journeyed slow
And toiled and strayed in vain;
These rash excursionists must go
Per Queensland Railway Train.

But on those deserts lone and drear
The fierce Australian black
Will say, 'You show it pint o' beer,
It show you Leichhardt's track!'

And loud from every squatter's door
Each pioneering swell
Will hear the wild pianos roar
The strains of 'Daisy Bell'.

The watchers in the forests vast
Will see, at fall of night,
Commercial Travellers bounding past
And darting out of sight.

About their path a fearful fate
Will hover always near.
A dreadful scourge that lies in wait —
The Longreach Horehound Beer!

And then, to crown this tale of guilt,
They'll find some scurvy knave,
Regardless of their quest, has built
A pub on Leichhardt's grave!

*   *   *

Ah yes! Those British pioneers
Had best at home abide,
For things have changed in fifty years
Since Ludwig Leichhardt died.

R. F. Brissenden & Philip Grundy, *The Oxford Book of Australian Light Verse*
(1991)

———

PATRICK WHITE

(1912–90)

Australian writer. White, who was mainly educated in England, served as an intelligence officer with the Royal Air Force in the Middle East and Greece during the Second World War, before returning permanently to Australia in 1948. He won the Nobel Prize for Literature in 1973. His numerous novels include Voss *(1957), which tells the story of a tragic attempt to cross the Australian continent in the mid-1840s, made by the eponymous main character, who is considered by critics to be the 'most celeb-rated fictional representation' of Ludwig Leichhardt. This extract is taken from the final chapter of the book. Richard Meale's opera* Voss, *with lib-retto by David Malouf, which premièred in 1986, is based on White's novel.*

VARIOUS VIEWS OF VOSS

Then Colonel Hebden took a hand. He could still have been holding the lady by an elbow. He said:

'You know, Judd, Miss Trevelyan was a friend of Mr Voss.'

'Ah,' smiled the aged, gummy man. 'Voss.'

He looked at the ground, but presently spoke again.

'Voss left his mark on the country,' he said.

'How?' asked Miss Trevelyan, cautiously.

'Well, the trees, of course. He was cutting his initials in the trees. He was a queer beggar, Voss. The blacks talk about him to this day. He is still there — that is the honest opinion of many of them — he is there in the country, and always will be.'

'How?' repeated Miss Trevelyan. Her voice was that of a man. She dared anyone.

Judd was feeling his way with his hands.

'Well, you see, if you live and suffer long enough in a place, you do not leave it altogether. Your spirit is still there.'

'Like a god, in fact,' said Colonel Hebden, but laughed to show his scepticism.

Judd looked up, out of the distance.

'Voss? No. He was never God, though he liked to think that he was. Sometimes, when he forgot, he was a man.'

He hesitated, and fumbled.

'He was more than a man,' Judd continued, with the gratified air of one who had found that for which he had been looking. 'He was a Christian, such as I understand it.'

Miss Trevelyan was holding a handkerchief to her lips, as though her life-blood might gush out.

'Not according to my interpretation of the word,' the Colonel inter-rupted, remorselessly, 'not by what I have heard.'

'Poor fellow,' sighed old Sanderson, again unhappy. 'He was somewhat twisted. But is dead and gone.'

Now that he was launched, Judd was determined to pursue his wavering way.

'He would wash the sores of the men. He would sit all night with them when they were sick, and clean up their filth with his own hands.

I cried, I tell you, after he was dead. There was none of us could believe it when we saw the spear, hanging from his side, and shaking.'

'The spear?'

Colonel Hebden behaved almost as though he himself were mortally wounded.

'But this is an addition to the story,' protested old Mr Sanderson, who also was greatly perturbed. 'You did not mention the spear, Judd. You never suggested you were present at the death of Voss, simply that you mutinied, and moved off with those who chose to follow you. If we understood you rightly.'

'It was me who closed his eyes,' said Judd.

In the same instant that the Colonel and Mr Sanderson looked across at each other, Miss Trevelyan succeeded in drawing a shroud about herself.

Finally, the old grazier put an arm round the convict's shoulders, and said:

'I think you are tired and confused, eh, Judd? Let me take you back to your lodgings.'

'I am tired,' echoed Judd.

Mr Sanderson was glad to get him away, and into a hired brougham that was waiting.

Colonel Hebden became aware that the woman was still standing at his side, and that he must recognize the fact. So he turned to her awkwardly at last, and said:

'Your saint is canonized.'

'I am content.'

'On the evidence of a poor madman?'

'I am content.'

'Do not tell me any longer that you respect the truth.'

She was digging at the tough roots of grass with the ferrule of her parasol.

'All truths are particoloured. Except the greatest truth of all.'

'Your Voss was particoloured. I grant you that. A perfect magpie!'

Looking at the monstrous ants at the roots of the grass, Miss Trevelyan replied:

'Whether Judd is an impostor, or a madman, or simply a poor creature who has suffered too much, I am convinced that Voss had in him a little of Christ, like other men. If he was composed of evil along with the good, he struggled with that evil. And failed.'

Voss (1960 edition, first published 1957)

JANIS BALODIS

(1950–)

Playwright. Balodis was born in Tully, Queensland, to parents who had migrated from Latvia after the Second World War. His works include a play about post-war immigrant experiences, Too Young for Ghosts *(1985), in which he 'parallels the story of the early explorer, Ludwig Leichhardt and his blundering, often lunatic wanderings in the North Queensland bush, with the arrival of a group of desperate displaced persons from the camps of war-ravaged Europe'. This scene is taken from the first of the play's two parts.*

SCENE TWO

North Queensland, 1845. The explorers' camp. Day.
LEICHHARDT *takes a bearing with a sextant. He wears a coolie's hat.*
MURPHY *stands beside him with a book, pen and ink.* LEICHHARDT *reads the sextant, hands it to* MURPHY *and prepares to write. He checks the previous entry.* LEICHHARDT *speaks with a German accent. In the camp,* GILBERT *crushes some leaves and bark which he puts in a billy.*

LEICHHARDT: Ach! What is this?
 [*Re-reading the sextant*] You have not fiddled this?
MURPHY: No, sir, Doctor Leichhardt.
LEICHHARDT: Then something is not right or we have gone backwards from yesterday. Impossible, no? With the sun over the same shoulder, it is so easy to say north, south, east and west. But north from where, or east to where, that is a little more difficult. Ja?
MURPHY: [*hopefully*] Can't you take another reading?
LEICHHARDT: Not today. We know we are here so we cannot be lost.
MURPHY: Yeah, but where is here?
LEICHHARDT: We will see tomorrow.
 [LEICHHARDT *takes the book, pen and ink and goes up to the camp.* MURPHY *tries to read the sextant.*]
GILBERT: This morning as we crested that ridge, I thought I could smell the sea on the breeze. From the north-west.
LEICHHARDT: Sometimes I think I can smell my mother's back garden and fresh bread baking in the oven. But that is in Austria and my mother has been dead for some years.

GILBERT: I am suggesting we could be nearer to the Gulf than you think.

LEICHHARDT: In Austria we have a saying, 'Take your eyes in your hand and your nose will show you.' You think we should follow your nose? [GILBERT *says nothing*] Quite so.

[*taking an axe and going off singing into the trees*]

> Don't ask me, friend, why I rushed away
> And left you with a heart that's full of pain.
> Don't ask me why, why I said, 'I love you',
> That's one thing now that I can't understand.

[*There is the sound of chopping, off.*]

MURPHY: [*showing* GILBERT *the sextant*] Can you read where we are, Mr Gilbert?

GILBERT: No, Johnny.

MURPHY: We're truly lost, then.

GILBERT: There's a line of marked trees all the way back to the Darling Downs waiting to be joined up like dots in a child's drawing.

MURPHY: It's a big country — bigger'an I can think — but I seen a lot of it in the past eight months. An' I'd like to see a whole lot more, so dyin' in the middle of nowhere ain't part of me plans. If we was to go home now, I'd be goin' home a man.

[*There is the sharp crack of a branch breaking.* MURPHY *jumps for his gun.*]

Halt. Who goes there?

PHILLIPS: [*off*] The Queen of Sheba, who yer bloody think? Put that gun down, you feeble-minded idiot afore you shoot someone.

[PHILLIPS *enters.*]

MURPHY: Sorry, Phillips.

PHILLIPS: Yer more damn skittish than an unbroken filly. Where's the gallant leader?

GILBERT: Carving his inspirational message into yet another tree.

PHILLIPS: 'L eighteen forty five'? Wonder who he reckons will be readin' 'em after we're gone. Last year it was 'L eighteen forty four', next year it'll be L eighteen forty six.

GILBERT: That's progress. What's the big hurry?

PHILLIPS: Blacks' camp, Mr Gilbert, about a mile away. Could mean nosh. He'll be wantin' to know.

GILBERT: If you want to be sure of a fair share you better be getting there before Doctor Leichhardt. You go too, Johnny.

MURPHY: Ain't you comin', Mr Gilbert.

GILBERT: I've work to do. I'll stay and inform the good doctor when he's done attackin' that tree.

PHILLIPS: Com'n, boyo, me arse is eatin' me trousers.

MURPHY: I'll bring some back for you, Mr Gilbert.

GILBERT: Thank you, Johnny.

[MURPHY *and* PHILLIPS *go.*]

PHILLIPS: Mind where you're pointin' that damn thing.

[RUTH *enters opposite* GILBERT. *She stops and looks briefly, then turns to go.* GILBERT *turns in time to see her leaving. He stares.* LEICHHARDT *comes down into the camp. He carries the axe and mops his brow. He drinks from the billy.*]

LEICHHARDT: Good tea. Like consommé. Probably quite medicinal. [*He spits out some leaves and drinks some more.*]

GILBERT: Yes. Should be good for the bowels. It was a tanning mixture for my bird skins.

LEICHHARDT: Delicious! You must make some more. It will help sustain us on the road ahead.

GILBERT: Just now I thought I saw someone.

LEICHHARDT: Yes. It is me.

GILBERT: No. Before.

LEICHHARDT: So. Who was it?

GILBERT: I didn't see.

LEICHHARDT: [*gloating*] Who did you think you saw when you didn't see?

[*Pause.*]

It is your language.

[*He laughs.*]

GILBERT: Perhaps it was a native.

LEICHHARDT: Perhaps you are seeing viney-viney like the blacks.

GILBERT: We are the viney-viney to the blacks. I think they are right in believing that spirits roam this land.

LEICHHARDT: Perhaps you could collect them instead of birds. Spirit is lighter. The rate you are collecting, my trees will be devoided of life and your boxes will break the backs of the oxen before we reach Port Essington.

GILBERT: If we reach there.

LEICHHARDT: I will. Even if it kills me.

[*He laughs and drains the billy.*]

Excellent brew, Mr Gilbert.

[*Cooees are heard off.*]

KARL: [*off*] Hello!

GILBERT: It's the others. They found a native's camp.

LEICHHARDT: Ah ha! You see! Just like the promised land, food lying on the ground.

GILBERT: Hardly manna from heaven.

LEICHHARDT: Depends on how you look. I will go see.

GILBERT: About a mile that way.

[*Hardly bothering to look,* LEICHHARDT *goes.*]

LEICHHARDT: Ja. Ja. My nose will show me.

[GILBERT *is left in the camp alone.*]

Too Young For Ghosts (1991 edition, first published 1985)

———

CHARLES AUGUSTUS FITZROY
(1796–1858)

British colonial administrator. While governor of New South Wales, FitzRoy gave these instructions for the exploration of the Cape York Peninsula to Edmund Kennedy, assistant surveyor, in April 1848. The expedition itself became a tragedy, with ten of its thirteen members perishing. One of the survivors was a man named Jackey Jackey.

INSTRUCTIONS TO KENNEDY

1st. It having been judged expedient that an Expedition should be undertaken for the purpose of further exploring the Northern portion of New South Wales, namely from Rockingham Bay in Latitude 18° South and Longitude 146° East, to Cape York in Latitude 10,30 and Longitude 142.40, and of the Country between the Head of the Gulf of Carpentaria and the Rivers lately discovered by Sir Thomas Mitchell; And Whereas I have reason to repose confidence in your zeal and prudence from the satisfactory manner in which you conducted the Mission from which you have recently returned, I do hereby constitute and appoint you to command and to take charge of the said Expedition, and direct that in the prosecution of this service you be guided by the following general instructions.

2nd. After landing your party and equipment at Rockingham Bay, you will carefully organize the party who are placed under your orders and make all necessary arrangements for your journey.

3rd. Your first object will be to proceed by the most practicable route to the bottom of Princess Charlotte's Bay, and thence up the Eastern side of the Peninsula to Cape York. You will then return down the Western side of the Peninsula to the mouth of the Water Plaets in Latitude 15° 10' South and Longitude 141° East, which is supposed by Leichhardt to be the embouchure of his River Mitchell.

4th. Having reached this point, you will trace the River up and satisfy yourself of its identity with the above River, by reaching, in about Latitude 16° 27' and Longitude 142° 51', its junction with the River Lynd.

5th. Should, however, this not prove to be the case, you will endeavour to reach the junction of the above River, and there deposit in a conspicuous place some notice of your visit, and then proceed in a West South West direction to Leichhardt's River 'Yapper' (the Flinders of Captain Stokes).

6th. It being considered an important part of your journey to ascertain the character of the Country where the 'Yapper' takes its rise, you will endeavour to ascertain this with all possible care, particularly the height of the land above the Sea or above that part of the River where the Tide ceases to flow.

7th. You will then proceed to the South East to intersect the Country situated between the head of the 'Yapper' and the Belyando or other Rivers discovered by Sir Thomas Mitchell, and then return by the most practicable route to the Settled Districts of the Colony.

8th. During the progress of the Expedition, whether outwards or homewards, you will use your discretion in deviating from its main object, for the purpose of examining any new feature of importance in the Country or River of magnitude that may be fallen in with; but, in doing so, care must be taken that no risk is incurred by the detention of the party beyond the time for which your supplies are calculated to last.

9th. That you appoint some one of the party accompanying you, whom you deem best qualified for the purpose, to take the Command of the Expedition in the event of any accident happening to you; upon such Person, the execution of these instructions will in such case devolve, and with the details of which you will therefore take an early opportunity of making him acquainted.

10th. That you be also accompanied by Mr R. S. Wall who will act as Naturalist, and Mr Caron, who will act as Botanist to the Expedition.

11th. That your Party, exclusive of yourself and the two Gentlemen already mentioned, be composed of the persons you have selected for that purpose.

12th. It is to be clearly understood that in the execution of these instructions you are not required to compromise the safety of the party placed under your orders. One of the greatest dangers, to which Expeditions such as this upon which you are to proceed, arises usually from the want of provisions; you will, therefore, use every possible economy in the distribution of those with which you are supplied, and carefully avoid any manner of waste.

13th. You are to keep a Journal, in which shall be given a detailed account of all your proceedings with such observations, as you may deem important or interesting. The general face and geological structure of the Country through which you pass, and the nature of its productions, animal, vegetable, and mineral, are to be carefully noted; together with the character of the climate, as to heat, cold, moisture, winds, rain, etc.; a Register being kept of the temperature by Fahrenheit's Thermometer as observed at two or three periods of the day, and of the atmospheric pressure shewn by the Barometer whenever circumstances will permit. The height of any mountain you may ascend and the direction, velocity, breadth, and depth of any Rivers or Streams, you may discover, are also to be carefully given.

14th. That you note in your Journal the description and numbers of the people you may meet, their means of subsistence, their character, and disposition, the nature of their amusements, their diseases and remedies, their objects of worship, religious ceremonies; and adding a vocabulary of any words of their language you may learn.

15th. That, in your intercourse with the Aboriginal Inhabitants, you are to endeavour by every possible means to conciliate their good will, from which the most important assistance may be derived; and, in the event of any hostile demonstration on their part, the utmost forbearance is to be shewn by all persons composing the Expedition; nor is the use of fire arms or force of any kind to be resorted to unless the safety of the party should absolutely require it.

16th. You will of course afford every facility to Messrs Wall and Caron in the prosecution of their researches, and for preserving and conveying the collections they may be enabled to make of animals, plants, Roots and Seeds.

17th. Specimens of every kind obtained during the Expedition are to be considered the property of the Public, and lists are to be made of them from time to time as they are collected, setting forth the places where they have been found, and any facts that may tend to elucidate their natural history and character. On the return of the Expedition, all such Specimens of the animal and mineral world, with the corresponding lists, are to be placed in the Australian Museum, and the vegetable productions in the Botanical Garden.

18th. That you avail yourself of every opportunity which may occur for informing me of the progress of the Expedition.

19th. That, on your return, you cause all the Journals or other written Documents belonging to and curiosities collected by the several individuals comprising the Expedition, to be carefully Sealed up with your own Seal and kept in that State, until you shall have made your report to me in writing of the result of the Expedition. You will also, as soon as possible after your return, furnish me with a copy of your Journal, accompanied by a Chart of your discoveries, exhibiting your route after leaving the Settled Districts in going and returning.

The originals are to be carefully preserved of all observations whether of Celestial or Terrestrial objects, as also the original calculations made upon the Spot.

20th. It does not seem to me necessary to give you any precise instructions as to the nature of the observations to be taken for the purpose of ascertaining your daily position on the Earth's surface. If provided with any instrument which can be used for taking the transits and moon-culminating stars, you will of course as often as possible make and record these valuable observations.

In your meteorological Journal, you will insert as often as possible the dip and variation of the Needle, and note all the phenomena, Magnetic or electrical, which may present themselves, Meteors, Luminaries, appearances in the heavens and falling Stars wherever they may occur in unusual numbers. In your Meteorological Journal, the State of the wet bulb of the Thermometer should always be inserted.

Historical Records of Australia, series 1, vol. XXVI (1925)

———

JACKEY JACKEY

(? –1854)

Aboriginal guide. Jackey Jackey was a member of Edmund Kennedy's Cape York Peninsula expedition, which set out from Rockingham Bay in May

1848. After the party of thirteen was weakened by sickness, exhaustion, and a shortage of supplies, Kennedy left eight men at Weymouth Bay in November, and went on with Jackey Jackey and three others, intending to seek help from a supply ship waiting at Cape York. In late December, Jackey Jackey, who was subsequently much praised for his actions, alone reached the ship, where he told this truly 'woeful tale'. In addition, only two of the men at Weymouth Bay survived, their six companions starving to death, and no trace was ever found of the three who were last seen near Shelburne Bay.

JACKEY JACKEY'S STATEMENT

I started with Mr Kennedy from Weymouth Bay for Cape York, on the 13th November, 1848, accompanied by Costigan, Dunn, and Luff, leaving eight men at the camp, at Weymouth Bay. We went on till we came to a river which empties itself into Weymouth Bay. A little further north we crossed the river; next morning a lot of natives camped on the other side of the river. Mr Kennedy and the rest of us went on a very high hill and came to a flat on the other side and camped there; I went on a good way next day; a horse fell down a creek; the flour we took with us lasted three days; we had much trouble in getting the horse out of the creek; we went on, and came out, and camped on the ridges; we had no water. Next morning went on and Luff was taken ill with a very bad knee; we left him behind, and Dunn went back again and brought him on; Luff was riding a horse named Fiddler; then we went on and camped at a little creek; the flour being out this day we commenced eating horse-flesh, which Carron gave us when we left Weymouth Bay; as we went on we came on a small river, and saw no blacks there; as we proceeded we gathered nondas, and lived upon them and the meat; we stopped at a little creek and it came on raining, and Costigan shot himself; in putting his saddle under the tarpaulin, a string caught the trigger and the ball went in under the right arm and came out at his back under the shoulder; we went on this morning all of us, and stopped at another creek in the evening, and the next morning we killed a horse named Browney, smoked him that night and went on next day, taking as much of the horse as we could with us, and went on about a mile and then turned back again to where we killed the horse, because Costigan was very bad and in much pain; we went back again because there was no water; then Mr Kennedy and I had dinner there, and went on in the afternoon leaving Dunn, Costigan, and Luff at the creek. This was at Pudding-pan Hill, near Shelburne Bay. Mr Kennedy called it Pudding-pan Hill. We left some horse meat with the three men at Pudding-pan Hill, and carried some with us on a pack horse. Mr Kennedy wanted to make great haste when he left this place, in order to get the doctor to go down to the men that were ill. This was about three weeks after leaving Weymouth Bay. One horse was left with the three men at Pudding-pan Hill, and we (Kennedy and myself) took with us three horses. The three men were to remain there until Mr Kennedy and myself had gone to and returned from Cape York for them. Mr Kennedy told Luff and Dunn when he left them if Costigan died they were to come along the beach till they saw the ship, and then to fire a gun; he told them he would not be long away, so it was not likely they would move from there for some time. They stopped to take care of the man that was shot, we (me and Mr Kennedy) killed a horse for them before we came away; having left these three men, we camped that night where there was no water; next morning Mr Kennedy and me went on with the four horses, two pack horses, and two saddle horses; one horse got bogged in a swamp. We tried to get him out all day, but could not, we left him there, and camped at another creek. The next day Mr Kennedy and I went on again, and passed up a ridge very scrubby, and had to turn back again, and went along gulleys to get clear of the creek and scrub. Now it rained, and we camped; there were plenty of blacks here, but we did not see them, but plenty of fresh tracks, and camps, and smoke. Next morning we went on and camped at another creek, and on the following morning we continued going on, and camped in the evening close to a scrub; it rained in the night. Next day we went on in the scrub, but could not get through. I cut and cleared away, and it was near sundown before we got through the scrub — there we camped. It was heavy rain next morning, and we went on in the rain, then I changed horses and rode a black colt, to spell the other, and rode him all day, and in the afternoon we got on clear ground, and the horse fell down, me and all; the horse lay upon my right hip. Here Mr Kennedy got off his horse and moved my horse from my thigh; we stopped there that night, and could not get the horse up; we looked to him in the morning and he was dead; we left him there; we had some horse meat left to eat, and went on that day and crossed a little river and camped. The next day we went a good way; Mr Kennedy told me to go up a tree to see a sandy hill somewhere; I went up a tree, and saw a sandy hill a little way down from Port Albany. That day we camped near a swamp; it was a very rainy day. The next morning we went on, and Mr Kennedy told me we should get round to Port Albany in a day; we travelled on all day till twelve o'clock (noon), and then we saw Port

Albany; then he said, 'There is Port Albany, Jackey — a ship is there — you see that island there,' pointing to Albany Island; this was when we were at the mouth of Escape River; we stopped there a little while; all the meat was gone; I tried to get some fish but could not; we went on in the afternoon half a mile along the river side, and met a good lot of blacks, and we camped; the blacks all cried out 'powad powad,' and rubbed their bellies; and we thought they were friendly, and Mr Kennedy gave them fish-hooks all round; every one asked me if I had anything to give away, and I said, no; and Mr Kennedy said, give them your knife, Jackey; this fellow on board was the man I gave the knife to; I am sure of it; I know him well; the black that was shot in the canoe was the most active in urging all the others on to spear Mr Kennedy; I gave the man on board my knife; we went on this day, and I looked behind, and they were getting up their spears, and ran all round the camp which we had left; I told Mr Kennedy that very likely those black fellows would follow us, and he said, 'No, Jackey, those blacks are very friendly;' I said to him 'I know these black fellows well, they too much speak;' we went on some two or three miles and camped; I and Mr Kennedy watched them that night, taking it turns every hour all night; by-and-by I saw the black fellows; it was a moonlight night; and I walked up to Mr Kennedy, and said to him, there is plenty of black fellows now; this was in the middle of the night; Mr Kennedy told me to get my gun ready; the blacks did not know where we slept, as we did not make a fire; we both sat up all night; after this, daylight came, and I fetched the horses and saddled them; then we went on a good way up the river, and then we sat down a little while, and we saw three black fellows coming along our track, and they saw us, and one fellow ran back as hard as he could run, and fetched up plenty more, like a flock of sheep almost; I told Mr Kennedy to put the saddles on the two horses and go on, and the blacks came up, and they followed us all the day; all along it was raining, and I now told him to leave the horses and come on without them, that the horses made too much track. Mr Kennedy was too weak, and would not leave the horses. We went on this day till towards evening, raining hard, and the blacks followed us all the day, some behind, some planted before; in fact, blacks all around following us. Now we went on into a little bit of a scrub, and I told Mr Kennedy to look behind always; sometimes he would do so, and sometimes he would not look behind to look out for the blacks. Then a good many black fellows came behind in the scrub, and threw plenty of spears, and hit Mr Kennedy in the back first. Mr Kennedy said to me, 'Oh! Jackey, Jackey! shoot 'em, shoot 'em.' Then I pulled out my gun and fired, and hit one fellow all over the face with buck shot; he tumbled down, and got up again and again and wheeled right round, and two black-fellows picked him up and carried him away. They went away then a little way, and came back again, throwing spears all around, more than they did before; very large spears. I pulled out the spear at once from Mr Kennedy's back, and cut out the jag with Mr Kennedy's knife; then Mr Kennedy got his gun and snapped, but the gun would not go off. The blacks sneaked all along by the trees, and speared Mr Kennedy again in the right leg, above the knee a little, and I got speared over the eye, and the blacks were now throwing their spears all ways, never giving over, and shortly again speared Mr Kennedy in the right side; there were large jags to the spears, and I cut them out and put them into my pocket. At the same time we got speared, the horses got speared too, and jumped and bucked all about, and got into the swamp. I now told Mr Kennedy to sit down, while I looked after the saddle-bags, which I did; and when I came back again, I saw blacks along with Mr Kennedy; I then asked him if he saw the blacks with him, he was stupid with the spear wounds, and said 'No;' then I asked where was his watch? I saw the blacks taking away watch and hat as I was returning to Mr Kennedy; then I carried Mr Kennedy into the scrub: he said, 'Don't carry me a good way;' then Mr Kennedy looked this way, very bad (Jackey rolling his eyes). I said to him, 'Don't look far away,' as I thought he would be frightened; I asked him often 'Are you well now?' and he said, 'I don't care for the spear wound in my leg, Jackey, but for the other two spear wounds in my side and back,' and said, 'I am bad inside, Jackey.' I told him blackfellow always die when he got spear in there (the back); he said, 'I am out of wind, Jackey;' I asked him, 'Mr Kennedy, are you going to leave me?' and he said, 'Yes, my boy, I am going to leave you;' he said, 'I am very bad, Jackey; you take the books, Jackey, to the captain, but not the big ones, the Governor will give anything for them;' I then tied up the papers: he then said, 'Jackey, give me paper and I will write;' I gave him paper and pencil, and he tried to write, and he then fell back and died, and I caught him as he fell back and held him, and I then turned round myself and cried: I was crying a good while until I got well; that was about an hour, and then I buried him; I digged up the ground with a tomahawk, and covered him over with logs, then grass, and my shirt and trowsers; that night I left him near dark; I would go through the scrub, and the blacks threw spears at me, a good many, and I went back again into the scrub; then I went down the creek which runs into Escape River, and I walked along the

water in the creek very easy, with my head only above water, to avoid
the blacks, and get out of their way; in this way I went half a mile; then
I got out of the creek, and got clear of them, and walked on all night
nearly, and slept in the bush without a fire; I went on next morning,
and felt very bad, and I spelled for two days; I lived upon nothing but
salt water; next day I went on and camped one mile away from where
I left, and ate one of the pandanus fruits; next morning I went on two
miles, and sat down there, and I wanted to spell a little there, and go
on; but when I tried to get up, I could not, but fell down again very
tired and cramped, and I spelled here two days; then I went on again
one mile, and got nothing to eat but one nonda; and I went on that
day and camped, and on again next morning, about half a mile, and
sat down where there was good water, and remained all day. On the
following morning, I went a good way, went round a great swamp and
mangroves, and got a good way by sundown; the next morning I went
and saw a very large track of blackfellows; I went clear of the track and
of swamp or sandy ground; then I came to a very large river, and a large
lagoon; plenty of alligators in the lagoon, about ten miles from Port
Albany. I now got into the ridges by sundown, and went up a tree and
saw Albany Island; then next morning at four o'clock, I went on as
hard as I could go all the way down, over fine clear ground, fine iron
bark timber, and plenty of good grass; I went on round the point (this
was towards Cape York, north of Albany Island) and went on and
followed a creek down, and went on top of the hill, and saw Cape York;
I knew it was Cape York, because the sand did not go on further; I sat
down then a good while; I said to myself this is Port Albany, I believe
inside somewhere; Mr Kennedy also told me that the ship was inside,
close up to the main land; I went on a little way, and saw the ship and
boat; I met close up here two black gins and a good many piccaninies;
one said to me 'powad, powad;' then I asked her for eggs, she gave me
turtle's eggs, and I gave her a burning glass; she pointed to the ship
which I had seen before; I was very frightened of seeing the black men
all along here, and when I was on the rock cooeying, and murry murry
glad when the boat came for me.

John MacGillivray, *Narrative of the Voyage of H.M.S. Rattlesnake*, vol. II
(1852)

ERNEST FAVENC

(1845–1908)

English-born explorer, journalist, and historian. Having acquired bush skills while working on properties in north Queensland, Favenc explored between Blackall and Darwin (1878–79), in the vicinity of the south-west coast of the Gulf of Carpentaria (1883), and in north-west Western Australia (1888). He also wrote a number of books, fictitious and otherwise, about exploration. In this piece from his best-known work, The History of Australian Exploration *(1888), he recounts the story of Augustus Charles Gregory's 1855–56 expedition across northern Australia.*

'AN EXTENSIVE EXPEDITION'

In 1855, public interest was once more excited in the mysterious disappearance of Leichhardt; this brought forward the question of further exploration in the interior, and some generous offers were made by private individuals to provide money for the outfit of a party. The English Government, however, working through New South Wales, took the matter in hand and furnished the necessary funds.

The command was given to A. C. Gregory, who had with him the celebrated botanist, Dr Mueller, and his brother H. C. Gregory. Mr Elsey, surgeon and naturalist, Mr Baines, artist, and the requisite number of men made the party up to a total of eighteen. Their live stock consisted of horses and sheep.

The plan of the expedition was to proceed north to the Victoria River, which from the report of Captain Stokes was then considered an important stream, and probably a means of easily gaining the interior.

On the 18th July, 1855, they left Sydney for Moreton Bay, in the barque *Monarch*, attended by the schooner *Tom Tough*. At Moreton Bay they took on board the remainder of the party, with fifty horses and two hundred sheep, and after some accidents caused by the *Monarch* running on a reef, reached Point Pearce at the mouth of the Victoria River, on the 24th September. Here the horses were landed, much weakened by their voyage, and Gregory, Dr Mueller, and seven men proceeded to the upper part of the Victoria overland, leaving the schooner to work her way up the river with the sheep on board. The land party first made the Macadam Range, so named by Stokes, thence they went to the Fitzmaurice River, where their horses were attacked by alligators and three of them severely wounded; and on the 10th of October they reached the Victoria, and rejoined the remainder of the party. Unfortunately, troubles had now set in, the schooner was aground on a bank eight miles below the camp, and having sprung a leak a considerable quantity of stores were damaged; the sheep, too, had been foolishly kept penned up on board, and so many had died that when finally landed the number was reduced to about forty. All this considerably weakened Gregory's resources.

An attempt to ascend the river in an india-rubber boat was a failure, the craft not being adapted to surmount the obstacles encountered in the shape of rocky bars. On the 24th of November, Gregory, with his brother, Dr Mueller, and Wilson, followed the Victoria to the south, on horseback. The party reached latitude 16½ south, finding the tributary sources of the river to flow from fine open plains, and level forest country, all well grassed. From this point they returned to camp.

On the 3rd January, 1856, another start was made, with a much larger party, consisting of eight men and thirty horses. On reaching their old point below the 16th parallel, a depôt camp was formed, and accompanied by Dr Mueller, his brother, and one man, Gregory advanced south. The head of the Victoria was found sooner than expected, and crossing the watershed, and following down some small creeks running south through the tableland, they reached a grassy plain in which these watercourses were lost; beyond, the country was sandy and barren. A westerly course was then kept, and on the 15th the head of a creek was reached, which turning at first northerly, afterwards kept a distinct S.W. course for about three hundred miles. The country passed through for a large portion of the upper part was good available pastoral land, but as the lower part of the creek was reached a more desert formation took its place, and at last the creek terminated in extensive salt lakes. Beyond this point no continuation of the channel could be found, and Gregory too easily recognised the aspect of the desert country that had baffled him before. The creek was named Sturt's Creek, and a prominent hill, parallel with the lowest salt lake was called Mount Mueller. The party then retraced their steps; the water on which they depended in Sturt's Creek drying up so rapidly as to render more extended exploration very hazardous. They rejoined their companions at the depôt camp on the Victoria, and making a detour to the eastward, followed down the Wickham, a considerable tributary of the Victoria, to its junction with that river.

Arrangements were now made for the homeward journey by way of the Gulf of Carpentaria; the *Tom Tough* having been repaired and caulked, started for Timor, to obtain more provisions, and then return and meet the party at a rendezvous appointed on the Albert River. The land party consisted of the leader and his brother, Dr Mueller, Elsey and three men. They started on the 21st June.

Following up an eastern tributary of the Victoria, they crossed on to a creek running into the Roper, which was called the Elsey, and on this creek a camp was found, which suggested the idea that it had been occupied by whites. It consisted of the framework of a substantial-looking hut, of a different shape to that usually made by the natives; but no marked trees were found, nor anything more seen to confirm the supposition. Thence the party followed down the Roper for some distance, and then crossing the head waters of the Limmen Bight River, skirted the Gulf at some considerable way south of Leichhardt's track, crossing the same rivers that he did, only higher up on their courses. They struck the Nicholson far above where it had been so named by Leichhardt, and following it down reached the rendezvous at the Albert River (which is the outlet of the Nicholson), but the schooner had not arrived.

Gregory determined not to wait, but to proceed home overland. He buried a note at the foot of a marked tree for the information of the schooner people when they should arrive, and on the 3rd September started. Two days' journey from the true Albert, they reached a stream which Leichhardt had erroneously taken for that river, and many of the errors in his map may be traced as being due to this cause.

This also has led to a good deal of confusion about the Plains of Promise so much vaunted by Captain Stokes, Leichhardt mistaking the level country on the river that bears his name for the spot. Gregory, who rightly identified the place, professes great disappointment with them compared to what he had been led to expect. Since then many conflicting opinions have been given as to their value. Settlement, however, as it generally does, decided the question; they have been found to be very suitable for cattle, but quite unadapted for sheep-breeding. Stokes gave them a taking name, which probably led to a false estimate being entertained, as the country is in no way superior to the district to the eastward.

On the morning Gregory left the Leichhardt his party was attacked by the blacks, who were, however, easily repulsed, the leading native being shot in the short struggle. The Flinders was crossed on the 9th of September, but Gregory did not think that it gave promise of draining a very large extent of country. Instead, therefore, of following it up, and thereby lessening his journey, and discovering the beautiful pastoral downs that this most important river flows through, he wandered away to the north, and followed up the Gilbert River, thus duplicating, only further to the south, the eccentric course of Leichhardt. The divided watershed was crossed on the basaltic plateau at the head of the Burdekin, and this stream was traced to the Suttor junction, where Leichhardt first struck it. They travelled on up the Suttor, and also up the Belyando, connecting with Major Mitchell's track. Their course then lay through the country traversed by Leichhardt on both his expeditions, watered by the Mackenzie and the Comet, and on the 22nd November the party reached a station on the Dawson owned by Messrs Fitz and Connor.

This successful conclusion to such an extensive expedition as he had undertaken, stamped Gregory as possessing the highest qualifications for an explorer. His travels embraced journeys extending over a distance of nearly five thousand miles, and he was absent in all sixteen months. His equipment certainly was of the very best, but a series of unfortunate accidents, which could not have been prevented, left him nearly as short as some of his brother explorers had been. One thing about this journey of Gregory's has always been regretted — the short and scanty record which he published, it being little more than a list of dates, and the distances daily travelled. However we may lament this reticence from a man of Gregory's ability and reputation, it is a pity that his example in this respect had not been followed by some of the explorers of the last two decades.

The History of Australian Exploration from 1788 to 1888 (1888)

———

WILLIAM JOHN WILLS
(1834–61)

English-born surveyor and explorer. Wills was promoted to second-in-command during the Victorian Exploring Expedition, led by the inexperienced Robert O'Hara Burke, which set off from Melbourne amid much fanfare in August 1860. Leaving their Cooper's Creek base in December, Burke, Wills, John King, and Charles Gray reached the edge of the Gulf of Carpentaria in February 1861, achieving their goal of making the first crossing of Australia from south to north, ahead of their South Australian rivals. Gray died on the return to Cooper's Creek, but the others got there on 21 April, only to discover that the base had been abandoned that day. After a failed attempt to reach Mount Hopeless, and a period wandering in the desert, Burke and Wills died from malnutrition and exhaustion around the end of June. King, however, survived, and was found, living with Aborigines, by A. W. Howitt's search party in September. Wills's journals and letter were subsequently edited by his father and published under the rather bizarre title of A Successful Exploration through the Interior *(1863).*

THE LAST ENTRY IN WILLS'S JOURNAL

Friday, 29th June, 1861 — Clear cold night, slight breeze from the east, day beautifully warm and pleasant. Mr Burke suffers greatly from the cold and is getting extremely weak; he and King start to-morrow up the creek to look for the blacks; it is the only chance we have of being saved from starvation. I am weaker than ever, although I have a good appetite and relish the nardoo much; but it seems to give us no nutriment, and the birds here are so shy as not to be got at. Even if we got a good supply of fish, I doubt whether we could do much work on them and the nardoo alone. Nothing now but the greatest good luck can save any of us; and as for myself I may live four or five days if the weather continues warm. My pulse is at forty-eight, and very weak, and my legs and arms are nearly skin and bone. I can only look out, like Mr Micawber, 'for *something to turn* up;' starvation on nardoo is by no means very unpleasant, but for the weakness one feels, and the utter inability to move one's self; for as far as appetite is concerned, it gives the greatest satisfaction. Certainly fat and sugar would be more to one's taste; in fact those seem to me to be the great stand-by for one in this extraordinary continent: not that I mean to depreciate the farinaceous food; but the want of sugar and fat in all substances obtainable here is so great that they become almost valueless to us as articles of food, without the addition of something else.

A Successful Exploration through the Interior of Australia, ed. William Wills (1863)

CATHERINE MARTIN

CATHERINE MARTIN
(1847–1937)

Writer. Catherine Martin (née Mackay), who migrated from Scotland to South Australia with her family in 1855, is best known for her first novel, An Australian Girl *(1890). Her other writings include a long narrative poem about the Burke and Wills expedition, entitled* The Explorers. *It opens with an account of the party's departure from Melbourne, which was in reality an over-the-top occasion.*

FROM 'THE EXPLORERS'

The sound of many voices fills the air,
A festal look people and city wear;
And all around, the tread of hurrying feet
Rings ceaselessly along each throngëd street.
The sun is shining from a cloudless sky,
Glad expectation beams in every eye,
And now and then a burst of laughter loud
Breaks through the hum of small talk in the crowd.
Towards one spot in haste it seems to tend,
In one quick moving stream the masses blend.
Then one who joined the crowd with searching gaze,
Seemed to regard the scene with deep amaze;
He was a stooped grey man in bush costume,
Guiltless of gloves, or studs, or rare perfume;
Bronzed was his face with an Australian sun,
And as he went he turned to speak to one
Who walked beside him: 'Say, friend, I pray,
Why are the people crowding all this way?'
This one answered — 'In what distant spot
Hast thou been living, that thou knowest not
Of the great Expedition now sent forth
To explore our mighty isle from south to north?'
The Bushman's eyes lit with a twinkling gleam,
'Within the Bush life passes like a dream
In strange oblivion of the wondrous strides
The world at large is making. He who bides

[159]

Through many years within the drowsy shade
Of lonely haunts, will find the great world fade
In mem'ry's tablets, till such far-off hum,
And scraps of information, as may come
Through newspapers, and rumours unto him,
From its unceasing whirl, will seem as dim
And vague, as the faint lines trac'd by a hand
Long, long returned to dust.
          Unto this land
I came from England, fifteen years ago.
The Yarra passed as now, with even flow,
From Baw Baw's shady heights; Macedon's brow
Was dark with the same trees that shade it now;
But in the place of this great stately town,
(This city, rather), gleaming like a crown,
Superbly fair, for these far Southern lands,
Set by the mighty ocean, by the hands
Of sturdy toil, with its grand streets and squares,
And round it, many a home that proudly wears
The aspect of great wealth, there were rude huts
And tents, and where we walk were gaping ruts,
Over which rumbled laden bullock-drays,
Instead of landaus, with sleek prancing greys;
And where soft knuckled dandies lisp and drawl,
And would-be exquisites, at snail's pace crawl,
With eye-glass fixed, in idiotic stare,
And locks front parted with stupendous care,
Who think the tasks of life have been well done
When they a ballet-dancer's smiles have won;
Whose fittest duties are to guard the pets
Ladies call poodles, from life's jars and frets,
And to proclaim a luckless tailor's skill
When sallying forth, (unfit to think or till,)
In Dent's best kids, to keep their hands from harm, —
There stalked the digger with his brawny arm,
The hardy pioneer, who, with his axe,
Hew'd trees as quickly as the fire melts wax.
In place of dainty Dames, in silk and lace,
Who flirt in drawing-rooms, with well-bred grace,
Whose weightiest care is, how to dress the hair,
And wear a shawl with a becoming air;

Whose fate the milliner holds in her hands
When she decides on puffs, or rigid bands;
Whose version of a man's chief aim and end,
Is purring flattery, with a courtly bend —
You then might see helpmates in word and truth,
Who staggered not at work, hard and uncouth;
The foremost article of whose homely creed
Was not, that God gave hands in very deed,
To serve them as soft-jewelled toys through life,
But to do battle in the daily strife
Of a prosaic, and hard-working world,
Instead of jingling tunes, ribboned and curl'd.
Truly the change is great, but greater still
The tireless energy, unflinching will
That wrought such changes, in so short a time.
I have liv'd ere now in many a clime — '

Here, as the garrulous and stooped old man
Spoke with uplifted hand, a youth who ran
With unthinking haste, push'd him aside
And stopped his speech. The people ran, and cried,
And jostled onward, in a mighty throng
Unto the verdant glades, where the glad song
Of birds is heard the livelong summer day;
Where from the turmoil of the dusty way,
And the loud grating noises of the street,
A wearied soul might find a quiet retreat,
Till wand'ring in the gum-tree's lengthened shade,
The feverish discords of life might fade
From the tired heart, while, softly as the kiss
Prest by fond lips, that fear to break the peace
Of a dear sleeper, the warm slumbrous breeze
Strays dreamily amid the stately trees.
But none of this unnumbered multitude
Have sought the leafy Park for solitude;
Yet all the discord, and the jarring strife
That mar the highest purposes of life,
Were in that hour forgotten, laid aside,
In gazing on the men, who in the pride
Of strength and manhood, were to seek this day
A perilous, all unknown, and toilsome way

Through this great land, unto the far-off shore,
Where foot of man had never trod before,
Through unknown dangers and unrecked-of pain.
It was no narrow question of mere gain
Which prompted this great scheme. But from the first
Lone pioneers that gained our land, none durst
Attempt to pierce the trackless realms that lay,
Enwrapped in mystery, from day to day; —
If fertile regions, or vast deserts bare,
Bleached by the great fierce sun's insatiate glare;
If watered vales and meads, or plains of sand,
Formed the interior of our new-found land —
These were the questions men were wont to ask,
In vague conjecture. Now the arduous task
Of solving them was to be carried out,
Points long disputed placed beyond a doubt;
To men of science and of busy trade,
To the Philanthropists, who long had made
Humanity's great cause their weightiest care —
To all the enterprise great int'rests bare.

But see! Among the crowd one rises now,
Earnestly speaking, with uncovered brow.
His voice is broken with emotion deep —
'Ay, they are pledged, through every change to keep
The memory of this day, within their heart,
Whate'er privations yet may be their part;
Howe'er the expedition yet may end,
As through unknown realms their way they wend,
The enthusiasm of this mighty crowd,
The ringing echoes of their plaudits loud,
The mighty cheer — the tremulous God-speed,
Will urge them to success, through pain and need,
Until the goal of all their hopes is won,
And the great work on which they are bent is done.'
Thus spake the Leader, then upon their way
Through the vast crowd, the Explorers passed away.
Now, pressing to the front, the old man went,
And on the passing train his keen gaze bent,
And said aloud — 'A score in all but three
Of men, and thirty camels; if on me

Rested the weighty burden of command,
I should have chosen a much smaller band.
Ah, I can see, Robert O'Hara Burke,
That ere success is thine, thou hast thy work
To do. And those same camels — friend, dost think,'
(This to one near, for bushmen do not shrink
From strangers — nor stand much on etiquette,
Nor let formalities their souls much fret,)
'Those animals should be so much esteemed?
From what I've always seen of them, they seemed
(Away from the Bedouin's skilful hand,
And the accustomed routes o'er burning sand)
To be most obstinate.'
           'There I agree
With you,' the stranger said. 'Aye, I foresee
No little trouble to be laid in store
For our Explorers by the brutes. The lore
Of Eastern lands has thrown a marvellous haze
Around them, so that when one fain would gaze,
And judge them with impartial eyes, a train
Of childish, crude beliefs rises again
From memory's mystic realms, and we perceive
Them, not as they are, but as we believe
They ought to be. But, notwithstanding this,
I feel sure our Explorers will not miss
The aim in view. There is my young friend Wills —
His presence in the expedition fills
Me with confidence. I daresay you deem
My judgment over fond, and that I seem
To overrate his worth. Ah, if you knew
How courageous and brave, how leal and true,
How modest, yet determined — but I know
When I speak of him, that my words will grow,
Despite myself, too warm, I would that all
Who start were like him! I don't wish to pall
The general joy, with auguries of dark ill,
Not play the raven, 'mid glad birds — but still
Incompetence and self-will have ofttimes been
The ruin of great purposes, and I ween
Such fatal qualities are not wanting here.'

The crowd surged onward, and now loud and clear
The last cheer floated to the sunny skies:
And thousands gazed, with eager, wistful eyes
On the retreating forms, that slowly wound
Out from the city, while each clamorous sound
Quietly died away, as out of sight
The Explorers passed. Then in the fading light
Of that first evening, lit their first camp fire.
While sitting round one said: — ' 'Ere we retire
(That I believe is the genteelest phrase)
On the long nights, we might recite some lays
And stories of the Bush as a pastime.'
To which all were agreed; of these in rime
A few are here set down.

The Explorers and Other Poems (1874)

———

BARRY OAKLEY

(1931–)

Short-story writer, novelist, and literary editor of the Australian *from 1988.
Oakley, who was born and educated in Melbourne, focuses on the dying days
of the Burke and Wills expedition in his story 'O'Hara 1861', which was
published in* Southerly *magazine in 1959. His O'Hara, modelled on Robert
O'Hara Burke, is a somewhat demented character.*

FROM 'O'HARA 1861'

O'Hara, his eyes heavy, lifted his massive head from its rags to gaze
back into his sleep as it receded from him, like a stately, unattainable
four-master. A curse on my empty belly and throbbing legs, he
thought, his breath rancid through his itching beard; a curse on this
whole bloody business of groan and struggle for life, on this stinking
shelter and fatal lagoon; no way for a white man to live or to die. The
sunlight outside told him it was midday, but the inner man was his real
chronometer; its chafing and blistered spirit said that rescue or death
was not very far away. Even at this late hour his two companions in
suffering were still sleeping the limp sleep of exhaustion; they huddled

together as corpses do, bony and dishevelled, as though someone had just disinterred them. Wills, in fact, seemed to be trying to bite at the earth, and a brown translucent discharge linked him to it.

So O'Hara for a time was alone, and had to bear on his own shoulders their triune misery; he envied the others their oblivion but let them sleep on, while he indulged in the rare pleasure of privacy. Here we are, he thought, by a lagoon of Cooper's Creek, hundreds of miles from what's mapped and known; an oasis in the gibber plain that tossed all round them in petrified rollers.

The precious water glittered over to him through the coolabahs' foliage, and spiked his eye and belly with its promise of fish they couldn't catch, and of birds they could rarely bring down. The wurley's opening made a crude eternal triangle of it all, the sight, the hope, the weariness; and roughly at its apex part of a camel's haunch was suspended — poor Rajah was drying in the sun, and with him their last hopes of progress. A strange end for a vaudeville camel, thought O'Hara: to be pushed on to the stage to the oohs and aahs of a colonial audience; to be sold to an expedition into the interior, trained, petted, then ridden till his ribs stuck out like a whaleboat's frame; and finally eaten.

But just so with us as well, O'Hara thought. We leave to a thousand hurrahs, cheered every foot of the way out of Melbourne — speeches, toasts, hats and shouts hanging in the air — a holiday tour through the colony, hands wrung, backs patted — then over the Murray and out of the theatre, civilization's behind us with its gasbag and bugles, and you soon discover what a man's made of.

O'Hara's thoughts in these last few days of final fatigue and sudden stop, after the frantic weeks of rushing to and from the Gulf, usually fell away to this subject; little else seemed to interest him. Why couldn't he get men to follow his directions? The need to know the answer was like a hunger that weakened his peace of mind. He was an irascible, impulsive man, he knew; if a man wouldn't go his way he would row with him. They'd hardly left Victorian soil when he fell out with Landells the camel-master because the fellow insisted they carry rum; but O'Hara knew what he wanted the rum for — mutiny and desertion, number one.

Lying back on his rags, staring at the rustling canopy that was so ineffective against the needle breezes of a winter's night, O'Hara agreed that after all he was leader, and some of the pretty words they said about him at the farewell dinner must be true. But what if all the fellows who'd cleared off had their own little get-together in Melbourne?

Quite an impressive collection of bastards they'd make, especially if they joined forces with the men who'd opposed his appointment as leader. He remembered the letter in the *Argus*: 'Mr O'Hara's attire is really extraordinary considering his high position with the Castlemaine Police. I have seen him myself, parading his men on a charger and conducting an inspection while he himself was dressed in no more than old check trousers, a rough monkey jacket, with a battered wideawake over his face.' To hell with his knockers. Wasn't this the free-and-easy colonies?

'I know the real bloody reason,' he said aloud, a ragged Lazarus vivified by the intensity of his feeling. 'It's because I'm an Irishman. An Irishman is like a red rag to Johnny Bull. He's all right if he's kept in his place.'

Now King was stirring. As he was the fittest he had to sleep with his feet in the wurley entrance, where they stuck up on clear moonlit nights, like the ears of a pantomime rabbit. He was now mainly responsible for gathering their food, so in a sense their three lives depended more on his legs than all O'Hara's plans and orders. It was a symbol in a way of the constitution of things; for O'Hara as a soldier had travelled widely, had smelt the odours of overripe royalty at Schonbrunn where he was a hussar, and had seen the barricades go up in Vienna in 1848; the John Kings were coming to power.

'How are you this morning, Mr O'Hara?' said King with his usual feckless cheerfulness, the defence of the ordinary man thrown into the society of his betters.

'Alive but not kicking, John,' replied his leader, who found King's badinage a relief from the morose silence of Wills.

'Look, sir — what a show our friend puts on when he's waking!'

'He's done it every morning I've been with him, strange fellow. I've never seen such goings-on in a human before. The first time we were together I thought he'd gone mad.'

O'Hara watched with a paternal eye as his second-in-command grimaced, ground his teeth and clenched his fists, as though holding on to something in the womb of his sleep; with his puffed belly and lank emaciated limbs, he resembled a homunculus, not fully formed, unready yet for birth.

'It's all right, me boy,' said O'Hara tolerantly, 'just easy now, easy.'

'A nightmare, we take it, Mr Wills?' said King brightly.

Wills's eyes now were open over their heavy sagging pouches, but his body was still.

'The nightmare commences when one wakes up.' O'Hara winked at King. 'A cheerful fellow, upon my soul,' he said. How strange Wills looked, with his round face's periphery of beard and rags.

Wills spoke vacantly. 'I dreamed we were saved' — ('Ah!' interposed O'Hara, raising a shanked forearm) — 'We struggled to a railway, and paid our fares back to Melbourne, where they threw us a big dinner. However now my head aches and my legs hurt. I presume I speak for all.'

O'Hara didn't care for the wryness that had lately entered Wills's comments; he interpreted it as weakness, lack of hope; but King saved him answering: 'If they take as long to get the rails to 'ere as they did to put down the track to Sandridge, then we've a long wait ahead.' King would never have ventured such a remark a few weeks before, but his new responsibility had given him confidence.

Wills ignored this pleasantry. 'Malnutrition affects souls as well as bodies,' he said. 'My sleep's a pale thing, almost half-conscious. I'd like to be able to record its changing character in some way.'

Poor Wills, thought O'Hara; so precise, proper and conscientious, the genuine English article. I'll wager he's never kissed anyone but his mother. O'Hara prided himself on being hot-blooded. 'I have the genuine rich Irish running in me veins,' he would often say, thumping himself and laughing his hearty extrovert's laugh.

'Well, my scientific young Joseph,' he said, 'interpret Pharaoh's dream for him.'

O'Hara, a storyteller to his cracked fingernails, held up his hand for silence. 'I was staggering down Great Bourke Street in my present rags, feeling dreadful, and Rajah dropping dung on the pavement. I had to be at the Theatre Royal in time for my act. I just made it, hurried in past the bar and saddling paddock, and seemed to regain all my strength as I strode on to the stage. The audience was hushed while I explained to them how to build a native shelter. The secret, ladies and gentlemen, I said to them, lies in the splicing of the boughs at the top. But lo!' (at this O'Hara's voice became muted with mystery, and his other hand rose) 'they'd all disappeared, and now natives were crouching behind the empty seats. Suddenly they all stood up, showing the white skeletons they'd painted on their glistening bodies. Then spears started flying at me from all directions. I rushed into the shelter while trying to get my pistol out of its holster, but it was stuck, so I started yelling out for the manager. At last my gun came out, but the shots became the honks of the lagoon frogs, and lo and behold, I was awake, sweating in unholy terror.'

But Wills was unmoved by such oratory. 'It's superstitious to give any meaning to dreams. I dreamed we were saved, you that we were attacked. Who's right?'

'But it was all so clear, so true, it was uncanny.' In the silence that followed, King decided to get up. He rolled on to his stomach, then using his hands and knees, and groaning a little, managed at length to get to his feet. The others watched, quiet save for an occasional word of encouragement, almost as though it were a camel they were coaxing: 'Easy John, easy, lad.' 'Grab the bough at your shoulder.' 'Don't move till you get your balance.'

'I'll be right, gents,' King said, 'it's just the dizziness more than any-thing, as though you were up the top of a tree.'

'It's nothing to what you look like, lad,' O'Hara answered. 'Why, you've nearly lost your trousers — lucky there's no ladies present. Here, put some twine round the cloth on your legs. You'll be grateful for its warmth later.'

'Right, sir. And if you'll just pass me the bag, I'll be off on my rounds.'

Southerly, vol. 20, no. 3 (1959)

ALAN MOOREHEAD

(1910–83)

Journalist and writer. Moorehead, who was born and educated in Melbourne, worked for the Melbourne Herald *(1930–36), before joining the London* Daily Express *(1936–46). He made his name reporting from the Middle East during the Second World War. After the war, he lived and wrote in Italy. His many books include* Mediterranean Front *(1941),* A Year of Battle *(1943),* The End in Africa *(1943),* Gallipoli *(1956), and* The Fatal Impact *(1966). The following pages are taken from his account of the Burke and Wills expedition,* Cooper's Creek *(1963).*

FOLLOWING BURKE'S ROUTE

It is still quite possible today to retrace Burke's march to the Gulf, camping where he camped, and seeing more or less the same things he saw.

In Victoria the land has been fairly heavily settled, but the old Cobb's Coach route (now a highway) still leads out from Royal Park in Melbourne to Castlemaine and Bendigo; and at Swan Hill one can drive along the Murray river-bank to the junction with the Darling. In the fruit-growing district of Mildura one sees the skeletons of Captain Cadell's old paddle-steamers breaking up on the bank, but some of them are still prodded into action.

The Darling is a narrow, muddy stream, with dun-coloured earthen banks shaded by eucalypts, but it has managed to keep some of the wildness and remoteness it had a hundred years ago. Here at last one catches a glimpse of the kangaroo bounding away through the scrub, and the flocks of parrots are almost as plentiful as they ever were. Kinchega station, which used to cover a million and a quarter acres in Wright's time, still exists, but Menindie is now a railway junction and the centre of a water conservation scheme. Bulldozers roar by throwing up new earthworks between the lakes, and there is not a camel to be seen. But the outpost atmosphere persists. The local people will show you 'Burke's room' in Paine's old pub on the river bank, and out at Pamamaroo Creek the expedition's camping site is easily recognizable from Ludwig Becker's drawings. On the lake nearby regattas of black swans and pelicans sail about, and in the evening the slender grey herons arrive. They stand motionless on the banks of the creek and stab for fish, and they are closely overlooked by flocks of cormorants that perch like black bobbins in the trees above. When the fishing is good these cormorants swoop together on to the water and drive the herons away — a scene Becker must have watched a hundred times. By day the flies are troublesome and it is very hot, but in this clean dry air the traveller is filled with energy, and he wants to go on across the great desolate plains stretching away to the north — to go on and on through Mootwingee and Torowoto and Bulloo until he reaches the Cooper, four hundred miles away.

If he goes up in the late spring (as Burke did) he will see the wild-flowers in bloom on the red soil, and especially great fields of Paterson's Curse, which is a weed presumably imported by a Mr Paterson and which Burke did not see. All this country is so flat that the Barrier Range (minus Piesse's Knob — it has been demolished by the Broken Hill miners) is seen from a very long way off, and even the sparse lines of trees in the dry creeks look like forests on the horizon. But at Mootwingee the plain really does break up, and it is a delight to go into these gullies that Wills found so gloomy, and to slither down the flaking rock into the still water of the pools. In these rough hills the kangaroos and emus seem to be larger and tamer than they were on the open plain, and the parrots have a brighter colour in the softer light. Tourists have been here and with their guns have taken pot-shots at the native carvings on the rocks, and have cut their initials among the stencilled hands in the overhanging caves: those hands that probably signified a meeting-place, the fingers representing tracks leading into a central junction. However, the damage is not yet complete, and although there are no longer any blacks to hold corroborees now, the somewhat eerie spirit of the place persists.

Beyond Mootwingee one is in the country where Wright's party wandered and died, and it is indeed very deserty, but cattle manage to survive even where there is no grass, only bushes, and the waterholes have become the sites of station homesteads.

Some of these places have tennis courts lit by electric light (it being too hot to play by day), swimming-pools and lawns and lemon groves (no danger of scurvy today), and the cattle are rounded up by cowboys in Volkswagens. The station owner in his aircraft will make the journey from Cooper's Creek to the Darling in a single afternoon.

A new kind of fauna lives on these great fenced plains, the domestic animals gone wild: a lone white cat lopes across the track, miles from anywhere, and homestead dogs that have mated with dingoes bound away at the approach of a car. They keep glancing backward as they run, since they are sheep-killers and are always shot at. Then there are scrub cattle, so lean and bony nobody bothers to brand them any more, and the brumbies, the wild horses which are rounded up from time to time to be slaughtered and sold in the cities as cats' meat.

Near Torowoto (a name now forgotten), a plaque has been set up on a cairn, and it indicates the place where Sturt spent that long furnace-like summer in 1845, unable to go forward or to go back. Following on along the track one comes next to an eight-foot netted dog-fence which marks the border of New South Wales and Queensland (neither state wants the others' dogs), and one passes through at Warri Gate, which is somewhat to the west of Burke's route. Then the plain again disintegrates into hard stony ravines and gullies; this was the place where the expedition had to make its last long waterless march to the Cooper. It is fearful country to walk on or even ride over; the ground is covered with sharp dark brown stones known as gibbers, which are as hard as iron and brutal to the feet.

And now the desert takes a stronger hold. The trees grow spines instead of leaves, their bark peels away like paper, and except for a few desiccated bushes every green thing on the ground has been defeated by the sun. The first approach to the Cooper is through a series of low ridges which, in the distance, look like long flat-topped hills, then there is another gibber plain, and finally you reach the blessed shade of the creek itself. On that muddy, grey-green water — and sometimes the billabongs are half a mile long and as much as sixty feet deep — life begins again; the incessant passage of the birds, the little turtle thrusting up his doubting snout, the scamper of rabbits on the bank. The site of the depot lies a few miles downstream from the Napper Merrie homestead, and it is a moving thing to see there the original tree with the word 'DIG' still discernible, to build your campfire under its branches and to spread your bedroll on the ground where the stockade used to stand before it was carried away by floods. Except that a cairn with a plaque has been erected on the bank, nothing has changed. The boomerang shape of the waterhole that curves round the site is the same as it always was, and Brahe and his men must have gazed a thousand times (with what boredom) at a great eucalypt on the opposite bank, which is a favourite roost for the corellas. Apart from the Napper Merrie homestead there are no human beings for many miles around, and in the midday heat and again at night the silence is complete. The nights are remarkable. Once the evening commotion of birds is over and the theatrical light of the sunset has faded, the dark sky, studded with enormous stars, descends from the great height it had by day, and there is a kind of joy in just lying there on one's camp-bed, cool and relaxed and safe in the midst of so much unvisited space. As a rule the night is very still, and thus seems timeless while it lasts; and perhaps — one dreams a good deal on the Cooper — there might be something in all this to reconcile the mind with death. But then the dawn comes up with a sunburst of coloured searchlights, the first fly settles on the sleeper's nose, and he struggles back to life again.

One fancies one might be prepared to wait patiently for a long time in this solitary and beautiful place. Little by little, as the days pass, a rhythm takes command, and one can tell the time without looking at a watch by many different signs: the seven o'clock breeze ruffling the waterhole, the midday flight of lilac kingfishers coming down the creek, the evening appearance of the rabbits. The light is so clear that every passing bird makes a precise moving shadow on the ground, and the smallest ants arrest the eye as though seen through a microscope. Soon it becomes apparent that the chief effects here are not of harmony but of contrast; the cool night succeeding the overpowering day, the scarlet dragon-fly that is made doubly brilliant by the drab background of the bush, the cacophony of parrots in silence. One's thirst is so great that a cool drink of water really does taste — as Wills said — like sparkling wine.

And yet there is a certain menace on the Cooper. It remains basically inimical to man, it rejects him, the climate is too arid and too hard. The cattlemen here contract sores and swollen gums which they call Barcoo Rot (Barcoo being the other name for the Cooper), and it is that same vitamin deficiency that killed Ludwig Becker and the others. Sometimes, too, the men shake violently in a spasm of nerves, a condition known as the 'Dry Horrors', but this usually only besets those who spend their vacations in prolonged bouts of drunkenness, and whose craving in these dry wastes becomes ungovernable. A week or two in the pubs in the south generally puts them right, and they can continue for another six months or so without a drink. Burke was clearly wise to leave the camels' rum behind at Menindie.

But perhaps the really undermining thing about the Cooper is the inertia that overtakes one there. It is not the soporific torpor of the tropics, but rather a feeling of deep physical exhaustion, a fatalistic passivity in the mind; one longs to take refuge in a slow, safe, uneventful routine, and it is not long before the demands of civilization drop away. One lives upon the bare minimum of effort, one accepts discomforts, and to gaze on and on into the campfire, to do nothing, to say nothing, to succumb to solitariness, becomes at last the only bearable existence. This is a condition which is admirable for hermits but may have done as much as anything else to destroy the expedition.

Burke's grave is in a lonely place about fifteen miles down the creek from the depot. You reach it by making a wide detour over the stones on the south bank, and then, doubling back to the creek, you come on a splendid waterhole with steep sandy sides. About fifty yards back from the bank there is a big coolibah tree, and it was under this tree that Burke died. Nothing except a small memorial cairn distinguishes the place from anywhere else on this part of the Cooper, and yet it is much more evocative of his death — the scribbling of the last note about King, the sinking back with the revolver in his hand — than the grandiose distance-peering statue in Melbourne. Burke's death became him very well, and one supposes that at the end it was not grand horizons that he perceived, nor glory, nor even probably did he feel resentment, but rather the humility of exhaustion, the acceptance of defeat, and perhaps too, great affection for King.

All this part of the Cooper is embraced by the Innamincka station, some 10,000 square miles in extent (including the 200 square miles the blacks were to have had), and there is a homestead on the creek close to the spot where King was found. But the little township that sprang up after Burke's time has collapsed through want of trade and all that remains of it now are a few ruined buildings and a thousand empty beer bottles glittering in the sun. Northwards on the expedition's route lies Sturt's Stony Desert, and here, at a place called King's Lookout, you can survey that unearthly prismatic landscape which is really closer to an abstract pattern than to anything recognizable in nature. According to the time of day the sandhills that stretch away on every side are vermilion, scarlet, rose-red or orange, but always the colour is of a startling intensity. Sometimes the ridges are dotted with grey and green bushes, and a bare rock breaks through to the surface, and so the general appearance is of a formal Japanese garden, always with the bright pale blue sky beyond. One finds a track through this gay maze by keeping to the salt pans that lie between the ridges, and at the end of the day you finally come out into the open plain again. Here a number of homesteads have been abandoned in the last half-century — the droughts were too long and the loneliness too abrasive — but still the artesian bores gush out on to the dry ground. The water comes up through an L-shaped metal pipe, hissing and steaming, and it is hot enough to boil an egg, hot enough to make your billy of tea. It cools off as it runs away, and in a sandstorm you will see the strange wraiths of cattle looming through the gloom at the places where they know they can drink. The bones of dead animals lie everywhere.

There is only one township in this desolation, Birdsville, and since it lies between Sturt's Stony Desert and the Simpson Desert where virtually nothing grows, it is perfectly placed to take the full brunt of these sandstorms no matter from what quarter the wind blows, and it may blow for days on end until the grit lines your very stomach and red-rimmed eyes can stand no more. But invariably the 'blow' subsides at last into a dead calm, and one wakes to a morning of such sparkling freshness and clarity that Burke, in these latitudes, must have been much encouraged to go on.

Beyond Birdsville the country gradually improves as the rainfall increases; grass finds a hold on the blown sand, the creeks are more frequent, and now once again there are flights of birds and groups of kangaroos. One does well to watch the kangaroos, since they will not survive much longer except in the remote parts of Australia. Like the wild horses, they are being shot for pets' food, and something like a million of them are destroyed every year.

The invasion of civilization here is, indeed, very strange, very ruthless and very haphazard. Some of the new towns, with their banks and

shops and petrol pumps, have a bright suburban look, but at their outskirts there is sure to be a collection of iron shanties of appalling
squalor, to which the few remaining blacks have been banished. These
places swarm with rats; broken bottles and rusting cans are strewn
about among the wreckage of old trucks and cars. But then in a few
minutes you are out on the wide plain again, and the half-caste drover,
whom yesterday you saw sprawling drunken in the pub, now rides by
with his mob of cattle, graceful, handsome and erect, absolutely in
command of his world.

And so the traveller continues on to the north, following Eyre's
Creek which becomes the Georgina and finally the Burke, until eventually he comes to the town of Djarra, and here rocky hills rise up on
the horizon, the first real hills he has seen since leaving Victoria, a
thousand miles away. The scrub now thickens and extends back from
the banks of the creeks, with a stronger, greener shade, and after the
hardness of the centre this is a great relief. The anthills now begin, at
first quite small, only two or three feet high, but they occur in colonies
of many thousands and they make the ground look as though it is
covered with sawn-off tree trunks. Beyond Cloncurry they grow bigger
and bigger until they are six foot or more in height, and they are
sculpted in the shapes of turreted castles, pinnacles and jagged
mountain ranges. In the creeks here there are avenues of lovely ghost-
gums and paperbarks, everything grows larger and more luxuriantly,
and the birds one sees are bush turkeys and great elegant storks, and
cranes like the brolga and the jabiru. Now at last one is nearing the
coast, and on the Flinders River the air grows soft, heavy and humid
— the first true breath of the tropics. There is a rumble of thunder in
the air, and if one is caught here by the wet season (as Burke was), the
rain is incessant and the tracks become impassable for weeks or even
months at a time.

Burke's last camp on the Byno River can be found very easily, and
King's report is perfectly true: the water is salt, the rocks and sandbanks
vanish and reappear with the rising and falling of the tide, and there
are even sluggish jellyfish floating in the stream. It is a pretty place and
yet somehow oppressive — perhaps because of the crocodiles lurking
under the gently-moving tide, perhaps because of the woolly air and
the leaden, tropical glare of the sun. The silence here is heavy and
claustrophobic.

Burke and his companions can hardly have had much sense of
achievement in this uneventful place, and one wishes very much that
they had somehow got through to the sea and had had their moment

of triumph there before turning back to that fatal depot on the Cooper. After all, another day would have made no difference.

But this seems to have been a story of predestined anticlimax, and it is a little sad to reflect that had Burke and Wills succeeded in getting back to the depot in time we would take much less interest in them than we do. Without the tragedy on the Cooper they would have remained rather minor figures, but with it they were lifted to another and a higher plane, one might even say a state of grace. And that perhaps was more important for them than the conquest of the ghastly blank.

Cooper's Creek (1985 edition, first published 1963)

———

WILLIAM LANDSBOROUGH
(1825–86)

Explorer. Landsborough migrated in 1841 from Scotland to Australia, where he became an 'expert bushman'. In 1861, he was appointed to lead one of the search parties for Burke and Wills; others were led by A. W. Howitt, John McKinlay, and Frederick Walker. Leaving from the Gulf of Carpentaria, Landsborough conducted his search, then continued to Melbourne, thereby making the first crossing of the continent from north to south. En route he wrote this letter, outlining his progress. Landsborough's reports of good pastoral country created much interest in the Gulf country.

LANDSBOROUGH WRITES TO THE ROYAL SOCIETY OF VICTORIA

Bunnawaunah, Darling River, June 2, 1862.
Sir, — I have the honour to inform you that the exploring party under my command arrived here yesterday, in safety, and in good health. From the Gulf of Carpentaria we came, in search of Burke's party, without difficulty, to Gregory's route from Queensland to South Australia, to a point within 280 miles of the point marked first depôt, on Burke's route, on the map which shows the routes of different explorers.

Our route from the Gulf of Carpentaria, Mr Gregory's route to South Australia, and the routes of other explorers, demonstrate the fact that sheep, cattle, and horses can be taken at a small cost, and in the finest condition, from South Australia, Victoria, New South Wales, and the inland districts of Queensland, to stock the country near the Gulf of Carpentaria, or for exportation to India or elsewhere.

The road we came was so easy, from the richness of the pasturage and the abundance of water, that a foal, named Flinders, from his having been foaled on the Flinders River, followed his mother most bravely from the time he was a few hours old until he reached here. When we were on Gregory's route to South Australia, and for some time previously, we took many opportunities of asking the blacks respecting the explorers they had seen. This we were enabled to do, as Jemmy, the native police trooper, could speak their language. We learned from them that they had seen during the last ten moons explorers to the eastward, but that they had seen none with larger animals than horses.

I am sorry to have to inform you that our familiarity at last led to our having a hostile collision with them on the Barcoo River, near where the blacks treacherously tried to take Mr Gregory's party by surprise during the night. They tried to take us at night by surprise. If they had succeeded they would no doubt have overpowered us; but it was during Jemmy's watch, and as he always kept his watch well, he awoke us when they were within a few yards of our fire, and we fortunately succeeded in driving them away. Next morning (very early) two of them came near our camp. At my request Jemmy warned them to leave us, for we had now a most hostile feeling towards them. Instead of their showing the least symptom of leaving us, they got their companions (who were in ambush, heavily armed with clubs and throwing-sticks) to join them. Under these circumstances, we fired on them. In doing so, and in following them up to where the horses were feeding, one was shot, and another slightly wounded in the leg.

I had very little assistance from Walker's previous discoveries, as he had left instructions that, while his chart and journal were in Captain Norman's charge, no one should be allowed to take notes from them. I tried to follow Mr Walker's tracks to the Flinders River, where he reported he had left the tracks of Burke's party. After tracing Mr Walker's tracks for four days with considerable difficulty, we reached plains near the Leichardt River, where so much rain had fallen on the rich soft soil that it was impossible to trace them further.

From the Leichardt River we travelled over well watered country to the Flinders River; then travelled up that river, through fine rich pastoral country, to about lat. 20 deg. 40 min.; from there we reached Bowen Downs in a few miles. The creeks and the river that water that country I knew previously to a certain point down the river, but beyond this point I did not know where the river flowed. On this expedition I followed it down to near its junction with the Barcoo River (formerly known as the Victoria and as the Cooper), and discovered that it was the Thomson River. After leaving the well-watered country of Bowen Downs, with the assistance of one of the blacks of that locality, we came through a fine rich country to the Barcoo River; then, without following the river further, or searching ahead for water, we went across to the Warrego River, without the horses being at any time longer than a day and part of a night without water. The country is, therefore, I have no doubt, on the whole, well watered.

From the Warrego River we tried to go to the south-eastward, but, from not knowing the country, we had to return, owing to the want of water. On this occasion, although the weather was cold, the horses suffered very much. We travelled almost incessantly, day and night. In going from and returning to water, the horses were without it for seventy-two hours. In returning, we found water in a creek in which we had found no water at the place we crossed it in our outward route. If I had had plenty of rations, I probably would have searched with one of the aborigines for water before taking the whole of the horses on a journey of that kind. Afterwards, we followed the river down to near Kennedy's No. 19 Camp, to the station of Messrs Williams, where we met with a most hospitable reception, and learned for the first time the melancholy fate of Messrs Burke and Wills. Sold some expedition supplies, which we thought we would not require any more, and bought rations to take us here.

Following the Flinders River up from the Gulf of Carpentaria took us for a long distance in a more southerly than easterly direction, then in a more easterly than southerly direction. About twenty miles below where we left the Flinders River, we saw horse tracks, which were probably made by Mr Walker's party, when on his route from the Nogoa River to the depôt at the Gulf of Carpentaria. Where we saw the tracks of Walker's party the channel was about 120 yards wide, with a sandy bed and a shallow stream flowing along the surface; lower down and higher up the river we saw the fresh tracks of a steer or cow, and on Bowen Downs saw similar tracks. We had so little meat that we would have tried hard to have found the beast to kill it for provisions, if I had not thought, from seeing the tracks of a dray in the same locality, that we were near a station.

The point where we reached the Barcoo River, in lat. 24 deg. 37 min., is nearly south from where we left the Flinders River.

Several times in the course of our journey from the Gulf of Carpentaria, Gleeson, Jemmy, and Fisherman, were unwell. This was owing, I have no doubt, in a great measure, if not altogether, to the rations I issued being insufficient. Our usual ration was a pint of flour, in bad condition, and barely half a pound of spoiled meat per day, without tea or sugar. The annexed list of rations will show that the quantity obtained on starting would not admit of my issuing a larger supply. The remainder of us, viz., Mr Bourne, Jackey, and myself, did not lose our health on this meagre fare.

After reaching the Warrego River, Jemmy unfortunately lay so near the fire on a frosty night, that his shirt caught fire and burned him severely; so much so, that he exhibited great pluck in continuing his journey here.

Last night I learned from the newspapers that Mr Howitt had received instructions to wait for us at the depôt at Cooper's Creek. If I had known that there was to be a depôt there I would have gladly gone to it from the Thomson River. Now I intend proceeding down the river to Menindie, where I purpose, if necessary, to take the most advisable mode to let Mr Howitt know of our return from the Gulf of Carpentaria.

I might have sent a letter off yesterday to the neighbouring station if I had only known that the postman had been delayed from starting until this morning. There is a camel on this run, which I will endeavour to get and take to Menindie.

Mr Bourne, who is an experienced bushman, has read this letter, and thinks I have not given too favourable an account of the country along our route from the Gulf of Carpentaria.

When I reach town I will make a return of the money I received of Messrs Williams for the expedition stores, a copy of my journal, and a sketch showing our route.

I have the honour to be Sir,
Your obedient servant,
W. LANDSBOROUGH,
Commander of the Victorian and Queensland
Exploring Expedition from Brisbane.
To Hon. Sec. Exploration Committee of Royal Society Victoria.

List of provisions received at the depôt, Gulf of Carpentaria, on the 8th February, 1862: —

40 lb. peas.
96 lb. salt beef.

40 lb. rice.

268 lb. damaged beef, jerked.

27 lb. do. bacon.

650 do. flour.

10 lb. broken biscuits.

18 lb. tobacco.

Left from previous expedition to south-west.

90 lb. flour.

40 lb. sugar.

These provisions were all our party, consisting of six, had up to the 21st May, the date of our arrival at the station of Messrs Williams, on the Warrego.

Journal of Landsborough's Expedition from Carpentaria in Search of Burke and Wills (1862)

———

JOHN McDOUALL STUART

(1815–66)

Scottish-born explorer. Stuart, who arrived in South Australia in 1839, was a draughtsman with Charles Sturt's expeditions to central Australia (1844–46). In 1858 he explored an area near Lake Torrens and Lake Gairdner. In 1859 he searched for a permanent route to the north, travelling to an area beyond Lake Eyre, which he surveyed on another trip later that year. In 1860 Stuart first attempted to cross the continent from south to north; he visited what he considered to be the centre of Australia, climbed nearby Central Mount Sturt (later Stuart), and reached as far north as Attack Creek. His second failed attempt, funded by the South Australian government and conducted in competition with the Burke and Wills expedition, took place in the first half of 1861. His third attempt, made in 1861–62, was successful. Burke and Wills had beaten him, but died on their return trip. The overland telegraph line was built along Stuart's successful route.

THE SEA

Thursday, July 24 [1862] — Thring's Creek entering the Marsh. Started twenty minutes to 8 o'clock, course north. I have taken this course in order to make the sea-coast as soon as possible, which I suppose to be distant about eight and a-half miles; by this I hope to avoid the marsh. I shall travel along the beach to the north of the Adelaide. I did not inform any of the party, except Thring and Auld, that I was so near to the sea, as I wished to give them a surprise on reaching it. Proceeded through a light soil, slightly elevated, with a little ironstone on the surface, the volcanic rock cropping out occasionally, also some flats of black alluvial soil. The timber much smaller approaching scrub, showing that we are nearing the sea. At eight and a-half miles came up in a broad valley of black alluvial soil, covered with long grass; from this I can hear the wash of the sea on the other side of the valley, which is rather more than a-quarter of a mile wide, is growing a line of thick heavy bushes, very dense, showing that to be the boundary of the beach. Crossed the valley and entered the scrub, which was a complete network of vines. Stopped the horses to clear a way, whilst I advanced a few yards on to the beach, and was gratified and delighted to behold the water of the Indian Ocean in Van Diemen's Gulf, before the party with the horses knew anything of its proximity. Thring, who rode in advance of me, called out 'The Sea!' which so took them all by surprise, and were so astonished, that he had to repeat the call before they fully understood what was meant. Hearing which they immediately gave three lóng and hearty cheers. The beach is covered with a soft blue mud; it being ebb tide, I could see some distance, found it would be impossible for me to take the horses along it; I therefore kept them where I had halted them, and allowed half the party to come on to the beach and gratify themselves by a sight of the sea, while the other half remained to watch the horses until their return. I dipped my feet, and washed my face and hands in the sea, as I promised the late Governor Sir Richard MacDonnell I would do if I reached it. The mud has nearly covered all the shells; we got a few, however. I could see no sea-weed. There is a point of land some distance off, bearing 70°. After all the party had had some time on the beach, at which they were much pleased and gratified, they collected a few shells; I returned to the valley, where I had my initials cut on a large tree (J.M.D.S.), as I intended putting my flag up at the mouth of the Adelaide. Proceeded on a course of 302° along the valley; at one and a-half miles, coming upon a small creek, with running water, and the valley being covered with beautiful green grass, I have camped to give the horses the benefit of it. Thus have I, through the instrumentality of Divine Providence, been led to accomplish the great object of the expedition, and take the whole party through as witnesses to the fact, and through one of the finest countries man would wish to pass — good to the coast, and with a stream of running water within half-a-mile of the sea. From Newcastle Water to the sea-beach, the main body of the horses have been only one night without water, and then got it within the next day. If this country is settled, it will be one of the finest colonies under the Crown, suitable for the growth of any and everything — what a splendid country for producing cotton! Judging from the number of the pathways from the water to the beach, across the valley, the natives must be very numerous; we have not seen any, although we have passed many of their recent tracks and encampments. The cabbage and fan-palm trees have been very plentiful during to-day's journey down to this valley. This creek I named Charles's Creek, after the eldest son of John Chambers, Esq.; it is one by which some large bodies of springs discharge their surplus water into Van Diemen's Gulf; its banks are of soft mud, and boggy. Wind south. Lat. 12° 13'30".

J. M'Douall Stuart's Explorations across the Continent of Australia, 1861–62 (1863)

————

ARCHIBALD JOHN RICHARDSON

(1837–1900)

Scottish-born surveyor. In 1864, Richardson was appointed by the Queensland government to accompany Frank and Alexander Jardine on their expedition to overland cattle, and to explore the country on the way, to the new settlement of Somerset, on the northern tip of the Cape York Peninsula. Here Richardson describes the first week's progress after the party finally left Carpentaria Downs station, not far from present-day Einasleigh, with 250 cattle, on 11 October 1864. Following months of difficulties, the group reached Somerset, with 'a remnant of their stock', in March 1865.

'MASSES OF ROCK'

11th — Our party numbered ten persons, 36 horses, both pack and saddle, and three tents, as well as provisions, estimated to last us, with care, four months. We travelled about 19 miles, our general course being N.W. by N.: the first four miles of our journey being over basaltic flats, timbered with box and apple-gum; the remainder ridges, both sandy and stony, tolerably well grassed, and timbered with iron-bark. Encamped near the river in latitude 18° 23' 59".

About a mile up the river from this camp it is joined by a large creek from the south-east, and 5 miles beyond its mouth the river is shut in by a long rocky range trending south-west. The river is here about 250 yards wide, and its bed filled with huge masses of granite and basalt, its banks sloping and rocky. Water good and plentiful, but not running.

12th — Shifted our camp one mile to the N.N.E. to the bank of a small lagoon, within a quarter of a mile of the river. The horses enjoyed good grass, fresh and green, for the rest of the day.

Box, barringtonia, flooded gum, and pandanus were the prevailing varieties found here.

13th — Travelled about 10 miles N.N.W., 5 miles sandy ridges, timbered chiefly with box-trees of small girth; the remaining distance the ridges became stony. Seven miles from camp we passed a fine reach of water in the river, which is there about 500 yards wide and filled with masses of basalt. Some prominent peaks rise from broken country to the east; to the westward the rocky range, before mentioned, continues to run nearly parallel with the river, having a steep rocky bluff nearly opposite our camp. I have named this Startwell Bluff. Encamped on the bank of the river, which is here broad and shallow; its bed is filled with melaleuca, and some excellent water in rocky holes. Grass very dry.

14th — Travelled about 11 miles north-west; irregular ridges, very rocky and difficult for the horses and cattle, quartz, basalt, and a rock full of large leaflets of mica. Across the river the country is mountainous and broken, and on this side the grass has been recently burned by the natives. The river-bed is broad, shallow, and more sandy, and is joined by a deep, sandy, dry creek, 80 yards wide, coming from E.N.E., its banks steep and lined with immense melaleuca-trees. We encamped on its north bank near the river, and found water in the creek by digging. Noticed blood-wood and the Leichhardt-tree and ironbark.

15th — Travelled to-day about 8 miles N.W. by N.; at first ironbark forest and sandy ridges, basalt cropping up in places; afterwards basalt became more plentiful, and made travelling difficult. The river-bank was intersected by deep gullies, and at 4 miles from last camp its bed narrowed to 150 yards, one deep sandy channel, banks lined with melaleuca. At about 7 miles from last camp we were compelled to leave the river, whose bed is there filled with masses of rock, it is also shut in on both sides by abrupt rocky ranges. We then crossed a low basaltic ridge and flat, and encamped near a large swamp, on its western side, not deep. I ascended the range to the north of our camp, and had a capital view of the surrounding country. The rocky range before mentioned, of which Startwell Bluff is a prominent point, from thence makes a great bend to the west, and then north, running into the river a mile or two to the north of our present camp. The country enclosed by the range and river appears to be level. To the east I saw nothing but rocky ranges quite near us, but to the S.E. by W. my view extended for at least 25 miles, enabling me to note the bearing of a prominent peak at that distance (Carl's Peak).

Latitude 18° 2' 7". The mean of a north and south observation.

16th — Travelled to-day about 11 miles, our general course being N.N.W., passing through a gap in the range about 2½ miles to the north-east of our camp. The remaining part of our journey was difficult travelling; basaltic flats and ridges openly timbered, and all the grass burnt. We encamped on the eastern bank of a creek which took its rise near the range. The creek is connected with the river by a channel near our present camp; it was named Parallel Creek by Mr A. Jardine, on his previous exploration-trip down this river, although from this point it becomes an ana-branch. We enjoy fine strong breezes from the eastward, with fine clear weather. The thermometer reading 73° at sunrise this morning.

The Journal of the Royal Geographical Society, vol. 36 (1866)

———

ANNE ROBERTSON

(1937–)

Librarian. Robertson was field librarian at the New South Wales Library when she wrote this article about Caroline Creaghe for the Sydney Morning Herald in 1976. The library had recently acquired Creaghe's diary, upon which the piece is based. Creaghe took part in Ernest Favenc's expedition through northern Australia in 1883, thereby qualifying as one of Australia's few female explorers.

'THE LITTLE EXPLORER'

'My dearest Papa,' wrote Emily Caroline Creaghe from Telegraph Station, Katherine, south of Port Darwin on July 12, 1883, 'we have arrived safely so far at last, and hope to get to the end of our journey (Port Darwin) in a few weeks' time.'

'I suppose you received Harry's telegram from Powell's Creek in May, telling you of our safe arrival there,' she continued.

'Our horses were so knocked up at that stage, having had such hard work and several long stages without water, that Harry and I were obliged to come on here with five of the worst horses, and Mr Favenc went out with nine others to finish the exploring of the McArthur River … You will be glad to hear that I was not in the slightest degree unwell the whole way … .'

Well might she boast, for Emily Caroline, then aged 22, and for at least part of the journey pregnant, had travelled on horseback across Northern Australia for almost six months.

She was the only woman in Ernest Favenc's exploring party of four; the first white woman, she claimed, ever to be seen in that remote region; and surely one of few women of that century entitled to be called, as her husband Harry half-teasingly described her, The Little Explorer.

Why did she do it? Her diary, a small, battered, brown volume, kept meticulously from December 23, 1882, until September 5, 1883, recorded the miles travelled each day, the heat, flies, exhaustion, thirst, sandy blight, and encounters with Aborigines.

But it never actually makes her motivation clear, though a love of high-spirited adventure must have been one reason.

Or perhaps she simply wished not to be parted from Harry, her husband of only 13 months.

Caroline's achievements were the more remarkable in that she had no previous experience of the hardships of the outback.

As a young girl, she had led a sheltered life, typical of the Victorian era, as the daughter of Major George Cayley Robinson, a retired officer of the British Army in India.

But once her husband had agreed to accompany Favenc on his exploring trip, to report on the country of the Northern Territory (then part of South Australia) for the South Australian Government, Caroline joyfully became a member of the party.

She recorded in her diary: '11th April, 1883. To my intense delight and astonishment … dear old Harry (is) to take me away to Port

Darwin with the exploring party. After all my loneliness, to be going with them after all. Hurrah! We leave tomorrow.'

The journey had really started on December 23, 1882 when they left Sydney in the vessel Corea, travelling up the Queensland coast to Thursday Island.

'The drinking that goes on in this little place is something tremendous,' Caroline wrote.

Then down the Gulf of Carpentaria to the Flinders Telegraph Station, at the mouth of the Norman River, about 30 miles from Normanton.

But the overland part of the trip began on January 20 when the party left Normanton on horseback.

Caroline soon became conscious of the rarity of women in those parts, even 16 miles from Normanton, when they arrived at the station Magowrah to find a dozen men camped there.

'Being the only female except one in the kitchen, I felt decidedly queer amongst such a number of men.'

But soon she was to have far more serious matters to concern her, for early in the trip occurred its saddest episode.

On January 24, she recorded that one of the party, a Mr Warner, was suffering from a fearful headache, followed a day later by terrible fits.

By the next evening 'Warner is much worse … He is quite unconscious and has been so since 10 am. It is most painful to hear his groans.'

On the following morning, the young man died from the effects of sunstroke — 'a death in a camping party is an awful thing … Harry and I spent a miserable day … by ourselves in camp guarding the body from native dogs.

'They have just sewn up his body in his blanket in the midst of a heavy thunderstorm, while some of the others are digging the grave. The poor fellow was quite young, strong, tall and healthy three days ago … they finished the grave at 2 am and so poor Warner was buried in the dead of night.'

This was to be the only death in the exploring party, though there were many times in the course of the journey when the small group was to suffer distress from the intense heat.

But there were pleasant interludes as well. On January 30, after they left Gregory Downs, she wrote of their camping place by the Gregory River:

' … such a pretty river with palm trees and pandanas growing on either side. The water is as clear as crystal running over pebbles … '

That day they covered 20 miles. But as day followed day, the flies and the heat and the need to find water were hard on both horses and humans.

On March 31, Mrs Creaghe was writing in her diary:

'Since I last wrote, I have been blind in one eye and nearly so in the other but am now better. This Gulf Sandy Blight is perfect agony. Ernie was bitten by a red spotted black spider on Wednesday night and since then has suffered frightfully.

'This morning and afternoon he has been frantic with pain. It bit him on the nape of the neck and it swelled down his shoulder and both that and his head is dreadful. The first night he was bad nearly all night, improving next morning and then getting worse.

'Yesterday he had no bad attack until 5 in the afternoon when it was more severe than ever until he went to sleep after two doses of laudanum at 10 o'clock ... '

The sun brought severe thirst, and some of their worst privations involved shortage of water and the search for it.

By April 23 — 'Tonight for tea we were all on an allowance of a pannikin of water each ... (we carried our two water bags full on purpose). The bags hold four and two quarts, so till tomorrow sometime during the day we have to make that do.

'We none of us ate any salt meat or anything that would tend to give us a thirst.'

The next day they went until 2 pm without any water; the horses had been almost 24 hours without it. Relief this time came when they reached a lagoon — 'We are now camped by the side of a large beautiful lagoon which Mr Favenc has named "The Caroline" after me.'

For most of the journey hunger was not as severe as thirst, though the food was monotonous and scarcely appetising.

Towards the end of January, Caroline noted that their diet consisted of 'nasty dirty, hairy, dried salt beef, dark brown sugar (half dust) and hard, dry damper.' There were some tinned meats, but 'the jolting has made them uneatable.' Sometimes they ate anchovy paste, or rice and tinned fruit, but the most unusual meal was duck — garnished.

On April 17, Caroline recorded that Mr Crawford had shot two fine black ducks which she curried that evening for breakfast the following day. In the next breath, she noted in passing the dreadful flies, which nearly drive the party to distraction.

The following morning, the party 'got up before daylight and left camp at half past eight. We had the curry for breakfast... and I accused

Mr Crawford of leaving the quills in the ducks instead of plucking them clean.

'Later, however, when it was broad daylight, when I went to empty the remains of the curry out of the billy, I discovered the supposed quills to be thousands of flies which had evidently blown off the long grass as I was making it in the semi-darkness. The men, after discovering that they had had a meal of flies, were all ill.'

On April 16 she recorded riding across a plain 'and then through 17 or 18 miles of thickly wooded plain country with coarse grass about four or five feet high. Picked and ate a quantity of native black currants, small black fruit growing on high bushes.

'They are very sweet but not much taste, and rather sickening to eat too many.

'After unpacking a pack horse and unsaddling mine I washed out some of Harry's soiled clothes, which was hard work as he got them so very dirty.

'All along the way today we saw signs of the Blacks viz holes in trees out of which they have got possums and sugarbags (native honey). Did not stop for dinner. Seven hours in the saddle. NW course.'

Caroline tried to observe every aspect of life on the journey, but, she was particularly interested in the Aborigines, and always carefully recorded signs of their tracks or camps, their appearance and behaviour.

One of the most alarming sights she saw, significant of the savagery of those days, was at Lorne Hill, a property not far from the Gregory River, where there were '40 pairs of blacks' ears nailed round the walls, collected during raiding parties after losses of many cattle speared by the blacks.'

No less savage was the method of 'bringing in a new wild black gin.' At Carl Creek the usual procedure was 'to put a rope round her neck and drag her along from horseback, the gin on foot.' She was then chained to a tree a few yards from the house, not to be loosed until thought to be tamed.

The exploring party watched closely for signs of Aborigines as they moved through the outback. On April 16, they came upon a native wet weather camp, which Caroline described in detail in her diary, remarking on its humpies made of coarse grass, bound roughly together with strips of bark, built in a semi-circle.

A few days later, they reached a branch of the River Nicholson, and were sleeping every night with double-barrelled breech-loaders outside the bed, for fear of native attack.

By April 21, the number of freshly made black footprints in the sand had grown steadily, as had signs of the Aborigines' fires, and Caroline was well aware that they were in the depths of dangerous country. They rode all day with revolvers in their hands, in case of ambush.

But when at last, early in May, the party actually came face-to-face with Aborigines, there was no trouble. The natives had never seen a white man before, and showed no fear at all when Favenc pulled his revolver.

'There were seven men and nine gins and some piccaninnies,' wrote Caroline. 'The gins bolted at our appearance and we saw nothing of them. One poor little baby was left by the mother in her fright and it was toddling about crying ... The blacks wear no clothes of any sort, and one of them had a carpet snake, which he had killed, tied round his waist ready to cook for his supper ... All the men amongst these blacks are circumcised.'

The natives were fascinated by the sight of a white woman; they had apparently believed that all whites were men. Later in the journey, when the worst privations were over and she was staying at a telegraph station, Caroline was told that most of the natives there had decamped after seeing her — they thought she was a devil devil.

Another group, never having set eyes on a white woman before, had 'put out their hands and felt my head and arms, evidently to see if I were real.'

The water shortage was a recurring problem for the exploring party.

There were limits to the amount of fresh supplies they could carry and 14 hours a day in the saddle was thirsty work.

By May 4, 1883, there was no damper left and no water to make any.

The horses were nearly mad from thirst after travelling up to 30 miles a day.

The party had nothing to eat for almost 24 hours, and only a mouthful of water each in the middle of the day — the last drops.

There was no rice or meat, only anchovy paste and a little preserved milk, neither of which they would touch, for fear of increasing their thirst.

They even kept smooth stones in their mouths to moisten the lips.

Caroline wrote: 'We were getting almost hopeless, when the horses were getting worse and worse, having been 50 hours without water, when Harry who had been again for the 5th or 6th time to see if timber ahead was a creek, galloped back and told us if we held the horses, not allowing them to rush, there was enough water in a hole for us and them. How thankful we were to be sure.

'I immediately went on and did have a good drink of muddy water. I enjoyed it, however, as much as the clearest, and thought my poor little "Gipsey" would never stop drinking.

'She and all the horses were perfectly mad and it was no use trying to keep them back; they smelt the water from a distance and several of them came headlong into the hole and drank until they could scarcely move.'

On May 13 she wrote in her diary: 'We had a terrible day from 6 o'clock in the morning till 11 at night. We left last night's camp at 8 a.m. and after about two hours riding out on to open "downs" country ground full of small holes and very hard on the horses; not a tree to be seen at times anywhere around the horizon. A cold wind was blowing all day. We stopped at 1 for lunch in the middle of the plain.

'Crawford chased a turkey but did not succeed in getting a shot at it much to our disgust not having had meat except at one meal, since this day fortnight, we were longing for some game...

'At last just after 10 pm we got to a place where some herbs were growing but no grass to speak of so we camped not knowing how much further we might have to go before we got anything better. I was off my poor mare in a second and lit a fire as quickly as I could with my numbed fingers.

'The billy was soon boiling with a little of the remaining water from the bags and we had a "feed" of damper with a little anchovy, but could not spare water for potatoes. We did not put up tents but just lay down in our clothes under a tree and needed no rocking to send us off to sleep immediately.

'This morning before we got on to the plain we got some native oranges, but they were over ripe unfortunately so they had no taste in them. They were about the size of a small cultivated orange and when ripe are green.'

By mid-May, the party had reached Powell's Creek.

'At half past seven pm, to our delight, we came all of a sudden on to the telegraph line, and our joy was unbounded,' wrote Caroline.

Civilisation, if it could be called that, at last, and the adventurous part of the journey was over. What had it achieved ? Favenc had obtained for the South Australian Government a fair idea of the nature of the land and the location of water in the remote regions of Northern Australia.

And Emily Caroline Creaghe had proved her mettle!

One of the charms of her diary is its femininity. Interspersed with detailed and accurate descriptions of scenery, vegetation, natives and the search for water is a glimpse of the Little Explorer patching her riding-habit under a large shady tree on the banks of a creek in the depths of the north.

'I was patching my riding habit all the afternoon under a large shady tree on the banks of the creek and it would have been pleasant if the flies had not been so troublesome. I had my veil on all the time, but they still managed to get in somehow.

'It is almost impossible to remain five minutes during the day without a covering over the face. The poor horses have great holes under their eyes where the flies have been eating them.'

There are snatches of hymns, copied into the back pages of the journal — 'If we only just could simply understand that our life is safe with Jesus — in his hand.'

There are lists of purchases, including 'stuff for baby's dresses,' 'bibs,' 'baby's medicine,' 'cot and crib' presumably made when her exploring days were over; (with true Victorian modesty, she never refers to her pregnancy in her diary).

There are prescriptions for the treatment of dysentery and neuralgia, and recipes for 'aunties cakes' and guava jelly and damper; and a knitting pattern for a baby's shawl, 'Slip 1, make 1, knit 22.'

'A "paper yabber" came over from the Katherine,' she wrote in the diary under July 7, when they were staying at Springvale with Mrs Giles 'to tell us the Murrays would be here for dinner tomorrow.

'A Paper Yabber is what the blacks call a letter. The whites employ the blacks as messengers and very delightful ones they are. They have a stick in which a slit is made and the letter placed in it.

'In wet or fine weather, the letter is taken every care of, and if going a long distance in rainy weather the black sleeps over it to keep it dry, and when travelling it is wrapped in tea-tree or paper bark. The black is repaid for bringing in the letter with a fig of tobacco which completely satisfies him.'

Emily Caroline Creaghe was left a widow with two young sons in 1886.

Writing to a newspaper later, the explorer David Lindsay described the strange circumstances of Captain Creaghe's death:

'Captain Creaghe was killed on Hodgson Downs station in remarkable circumstances. While he was breaking in a young mare he was wearing a ring, an heirloom, about which there was attached a tradition that he who lost it would meet with a violent death. In the struggle with the mare, Creaghe who had become thin through fever, lost the ring. He then related the prophecy, saying "I suspect that mare will be the death of me." Next day she dashed into a tree and Creaghe was killed.'

She married again in 1889, and spent the next 20 years as Mrs Joseph Barnett on a cattle station near Rockhampton.

In 1899, she was aboard the S.S. Perthshire with five of her children when that vessel was adrift with a broken shaft for seven weeks in the Tasman Sea.

But of that experience, and the rest of her life until she died in 1944 aged 84, no diaries remain to tell the tale.

Sydney Morning Herald (13, 14, 20 May 1976)

CHARLES WINNECKE

(1856–1902)

South Australian explorer and botanist. Winnecke led the Horn Scientific Expedition to Central Australia (1894), which was organised and equipped by the mining magnate, William Horn. The party included the Melbourne University scientist, Walter Baldwin Spencer, who edited the four-volume report covering the expedition's zoological, geological, botanical, and anthropological findings. Winnecke also published the journal of the expedition.

'SUMMARY OF JOURNAL'

The expedition left Oodnadatta, the terminus of the Great Northern Railway, on the 5th of May, 1894. Apart from Mr Horn and myself, the party then consisted of four scientists, who represented the Universities of Sydney, Melbourne, and Adelaide, and collectively the interests of anthropology, biology, botany, geology, ethnology, meteorology, palæontology, and petrology; two naturalists and collectors; four camel-drivers, a cook, and a black boy. We set out with twenty-three camels (twelve pack, nine riding, and two buggy camels) and two horses. The time at our disposal was limited to three months, the University professors not being able to be away for a longer period from the institutions with which they are associated.

Travelling northward, near the transcontinental telegraph line, we arrived at the Goyder river on the 14th of May. Meantime we obtained an additional camel at Charlotte Waters. The journeying till the Goyder was reached had to be done by easy stages, the distance covered averaging but seventeen miles a day. This was caused by the low condition of the camels, which made anything like rapid movement utterly impossible. The country traversed up to this point comprised chiefly stony undulating plains, woefully arid and desolate, and, except for a few salsolaceous plants, completely devoid of vegetation. Not long before we passed through it this part of South Australia had been visited by a heavy rainfall; consequently we had expected to find it admirably suited to scientific examination, but almost the contrary proved to be the case. A succession of dry seasons previously had resulted in a great scarcity of animal and vegetable life, and our collections suffered accordingly.

From the Goyder a five days' excursion to the west was made by a detachment of the party. This section was absent from the main caravan for five days, travelling during that time a distance of 145 miles. Numerous tent-shaped hills and ranges were discovered and correctly mapped. About fifty miles of the country covered consisted of mulga scrub (*Acacia aneura*), which was well grassed, the remainder being red sandridges densely overgrown with porcupine. In places where the latter had been burnt by the natives good feed was plentiful, indicating that the whole of this country could be made available for stock. Only one small sand soakage water was found throughout the whole of the trip, which terminated at Engoordina, on the Finke river. Here the two branches of the expedition re-united. Meanwhile the camel buggy had been found to be somewhat of an impediment. It had therefore been left at Crown Point, twenty miles south of Engoordina, and pack-saddles had been made for the draught camels. From Engoordina the whole expedition proceeded to Idracowra, passing *en route* through a detached range of table-top hills. These and all the other noteworthy natural features were mapped in detail. From Idracowra an excursion was made to Chambers Pillar, and photographs of this unique natural monument were obtained. Mr Horn left the party at Idracowra on the 23rd May. Upon his departure I conducted the expedition towards Henbury, following the course of the Finke river. The river flats extending for a short distance on either side of this, the largest Central Australian watercourse, were found to be splendidly grassed; otherwise the country revealed itself as barren sandridges clothed with porcupine grass, the prevailing timber being mulga and casuarina or desert oak, with river gums in the watercourses. We arrived at Henbury on the 27th of May, and were joined by a couple of Government prospectors from Alice Springs, who brought two additional camels, thus increasing the camel-train to twenty-six. From sixteen miles south of Henbury the change in the nature of the country was most noticeable. Magnificently-grassed flats were in strong evidence, with but an occasional extent of barren sandridges. Hills more or less conspicuous were also observed. These characteristics continued until we reached the James Ranges in lat. 24° 20', long. 133° 1' E. Hitherto we had been travelling in a general N.N.W. direction. On entering the James Ranges this was changed to a westerly route. The plains between these heights must be considered to be among the very best pastoral country in South Australia. Growing in rich profusion were seen splendid grasses, including the Mitchell grass of Queensland, interspersed with salt-bush and cotton-bush of the best quality. Here also we found an abundance of water. The ranges, whose constitution is sandstone and quartzite, are of a very rugged character, and are densely timbered with acacia. Their elevation is from 700ft to 800ft above the plains, and 2,500ft above sea level. In lat. 24° 17' S., long. 132° 55' E. we finally left the Finke river, which in this region is a running stream, and continued on a westerly course along the valleys of the James Range near its southern limit. Crossing the Palmer river, the most important tributary of the Finke, we reached Tempe Downs on the 2nd of June.

I formed a depôt camp at a small waterhole in the Petermann Creek, six miles to the south of Tempe Downs. Here Mr Cowle, with nine additional horses, joined the expedition. The Petermann is the dividing line between the Levi and James ranges, which have characteristics in common, the main difference being that the former is of very limited extent. On the 7th of June we continued our journey towards Gill's Range, still going westward, and still passing through magnificently-grassed country. Various deposits of fossils were examined in the James, Levi, and Gill's ranges, and numerous specimens procured for the petrological collection. Gill's Range is similar in its principal aspects to the Levi Range. We inspected the various 'permanent waters' on its south side — springs of no magnitude, but furnishing an abundant supply. The well-grassed country does not extend beyond a mile to the south of the range, sandhills then appearing as far as the vision can reach. From Reedy Creek, in lat. 24° 17' 49" S., long. 131° 38' E., some of the party, under Mr Cowle's guidance, visited Ayers Rock and Mount Olga. The main body still pursued a westerly course over the same fertile plains already described. The Gill's Range terminates in long.

131° 35' E. Low sandstone ridges then occur, and these extend to the west and beyond Laurie's Creek. This creek was reached on the 13th of June, and a short halt was made in order to examine the fossiliferous deposits in its vicinity. Some perfect specimens of rare fossils were obtained. Altering our course now to a northerly direction, over continuous sandridges, we came into view of several imposing mountains of the Macdonnell Ranges. At Glen Edith we found the Tarn of Auber, a reputed 'permanent water,' to be dry, proving the unfavorable nature of this season. On the 16th of June we arrived at Deering Creek, and once more were in well-watered country. The Macdonnell Ranges were now immediately to the north of us, and we pursued our journey in an easterly direction towards Mereenie Bluff.

On the 19th of June we entered a remarkable valley, which was subsequently found to extend, between wall-like ranges, for over 100 miles to the eastward; I have named it Mereenie Valley. The Mereenie Escarpment on the south side of this immense pass is a noteworthy feature of this part of the Macdonnell Ranges. It extends in an unbroken line for twenty miles, and recurs at short intervals for many miles farther to the eastward. In lat. 23° 34' 23" S. and long. 132° 5' E. we again took a northerly course and visited several mountains on the northern confines of the ranges. A most unusual geological feature was here noted. The Macdonnell Ranges in these parts consist of apparently isolated mountains joined by low ridges and interspersed with well-grassed plains. The waters, however, are limited in number and of small extent. Here, for the first time since leaving Oodnadatta, metalliferous rocks were found, and the prospectors diligently examined various localities.

On the 24th June we again turned towards the east, reaching Glen Helen on the 26th. Here the detachment under Mr Cowle rejoined the main party. Mount Sonder and other mountains were correctly charted and their exact heights determined. On the 30th of June we arrived at the Finke Gorge, in the Finke river, and from there pursued a southerly course. Leaving the Macdonnell Ranges and crossing the Missionaries Plain we reached Hermannsburg Mission Station on the 2nd of July. An extended stay was made at this place for the purpose of examining the Finke river, Glen of Palms, and the Krichauff Ranges to the south, the geologist and prospectors meanwhile inspecting the Macdonnell Ranges to the north and eastward as far as the transcontinental telegraph line. On the 9th of July we departed from the mission station, and on the following day, in lat. 23° 59' 50" S., long. 133° 6', the main party took a direct course for Alice Springs. At the same time a contingent of the expedition started for Paisley's and Brinkley's bluffs, afterwards crossing to the north side of the Macdonnell Ranges, passing over finely-grassed plains, and eventually reaching Alice Springs on the 15th of July. Here the other members were already in camp, and here valuable additions were made to the several collections.

The expedition left Alice Springs on its return journey on the 18th of July. The biologist, however, remained for the purpose of prosecuting inquiries arising out of certain zoological discoveries, and the geologist of the expedition, with one of the prospectors, stayed in order to examine the ruby fields and auriferous country on the Hale river to the eastward, both undertaking to rejoin the party ere its arrival at its terminal point. Travelling southward over splendidly-grassed and lightly-timbered country, we crossed the Ooraminna and James ranges, and the overland telegraph line was again struck at the Alice Well on the Hugh river on the 22nd of July. Here the work of the expedition ended, and all haste was made towards Oodnadatta, by way of Crown Point and Charlotte Waters. The party reached Oodnadatta on the 5th of August. It had been absent exactly three months. During that period it travelled 2,200 miles. Over 27,000 square miles of country were correctly mapped in detail. Of this territory 14,000 square miles were of good pastoral country, consisting of loamy soil with abundance of grass and herbaceous bushes; and 13,000 square miles of inferior sandridges and porcupine, which, however, in conjunction with the former country, might be made available for pastoral purposes.

The Johnston, Chandler, Bacon, Newland, James, Levi, Gill's, Ooraminna, Krichauff, Gardiner, Waterhouse, Hart, and almost the whole of the Macdonnell Ranges were examined. Careful astronomical, meteorological, and magnetic observations were taken on every available occasion. In regard to the last mentioned, the magnetic dip, which hitherto has received but little attention in Australia, was carefully observed at regular distances. The elevation above sea level of all important points was ascertained. Several hundred excellent photographs were taken of the most striking natural features of the country passed through, types of natives, &c. Every possible opportunity of studying the habits and customs of the blacks was embraced. Much interesting information concerning them was gathered, and many native curios and relics were acquired. But the aboriginals encountered were singularly few. In the sphere of our travels they have greatly diminished in number during late years, and they are still passing away. Where not long ago they comprised hundreds they will soon be represented by units. For the most part those we saw were of the semi-civilised type who affect the neighborhood of stations. The doom of these has already been sealed. Their indescribably filthy habits and vices are fast hurrying them out of existence.

Unfortunately the expedition made no discovery of mineral wealth in the Macdonnell Ranges; still its work even in this connection is of no mean importance. The value of it is certainly of a negative nature; none the less it is real. In settling the question whether or not gold is present in the region visited an undoubted public service has been rendered. But if the country did not yield up any rich secret to the prospector, the purely scientific results secured are most noteworthy. Large collections were made in many of the departments of science. Botany and zoology, ornithology and conchology, petrology and ethnology, geology and anthropology — not to mention other branches of knowledge — had most enthusiastic votaries in different members of the expedition. Nothing, indeed, could exceed the zeal which was shown in the work of investigation and collection. How great has been the reward of this scientific ardor can be gathered only from a perusal of the reports of the specialists attached to this journal. That fact cannot be too strongly emphasized, and it is equally satisfactory to note that the journey from start to finish was accomplished without a single mishap.

Journal of the Horn Scientific Exploring Expedition, 1894 (1897)

ANONYMOUS

In July 1930, an expedition, led by Fred Blakeley and guided by Lewis Hubert (Harold Bell) Lasseter, left Alice Springs to look for a huge gold reef in central Australia, which Lasseter claimed to have found many years earlier. Finding no sign of it, the rest of the party abandoned the search, but Lasseter, now accompanied by a dingo shooter, Paul Johns, went on with several camels. After the two men fell out, Lasseter continued alone, only to die in the desert. This newspaper article was published in late April 1931, several weeks after the discovery of his body. Although the eccentric, unreliable Lasseter claimed in his diary to have rediscovered the reef while on his own, all subsequent searches for it have been unsuccessful.

'DEATH OF PROSPECTOR'

Adelaide, Tuesday — A message from Alice Springs states that the remains of the prospector, Mr H. L. B. Lasseter, were found in a shallow grave, covered with boughs, by Mr R. Buck, on March 29, at the head of the Shaw River, in the Petermann ranges. Mr Buck had been employed to search for Mr Lasseter as early as the end of February, although little hope was held of finding him alive. The old prospector died of starvation waiting for his connections to arrive with rations. According to a story by the blacks he had lived with them for 16 weeks, and had died some time in January, through becoming too weak to travel.

Evidently Mr Lasseter lost his camels in November, shortly after leaving his partner, Johns, and picked up with a tribe travelling about the Petermann Ranges.

Mr Buck left Hermannsburg mission station on February 24, and travelled west. On March 5 he found some strange camel tracks, but was unable to find the animals. He was overtaken by thunder-storms and bad weather, and one of his camels was poisoned, but he was able to save it. He continued until March 15, although the weather was still bad, and the camels were becoming fractious. He went to Ilbilla, where he found that some of his stores were missing, and then started off in a south-westerly direction. On March 22 he reached Buttaputta and water, after having been on a dry stage for six days. There he learned that a white man had lost his camels and died. He traced the blacks who had been with Mr Lasseter, and questioned them. The only information procurable was that 'white man live with them four moons close up, and him finish two feller moon next time jump up.' Mr Buck buried the body, and then, with the help of the blacks, discovered Mr Lasseter's camps.

The last article the prospector possessed was a camp sheet, which he gave to the blacks for their help. He had broken his revolver so that the aborigines could not use it. At various camps pieces of camp rugs, a broken camera, and a note expressing the dead man's last wish were picked up. About 150 blacks followed Mr Buck about the old camps. Mr Buck returned to Hermannsburg via Ayer's Rock and Basedow Range, and reported the discovery to Mr H. A. Heinrich, who came to the conclusion that death was due to starvation through supplies not going forward as should have been arranged. The blacks said that a claim was pegged by Mr Lasseter, but the camera films and the majority of the papers were destroyed. Those left are in possession of the local police.

Fears were first expressed for the safety of Mr Lasseter at the beginning of this year. It was then learned that at the end of last October Mr Johns, who was Mr Lasseter's prospecting partner, returned to Alice Springs and said that he and Mr Lasseter had quarrelled. He had departed from a camp, leaving Mr Lasseter with two camels and about two months' supply of rations. Mr Johns's story included an account of a dispute in which revolvers were drawn, but he said that he disarmed Mr Lasseter. It was in searching for Mr Lasseter that Messrs W. L. Pittendrigh and S. J. Hamre were lost in Central Australia when their 'plane made a forced landing. They were found on January 10 by an Air Force search party.

Many unfortunate incidents have marred the efforts of goldseekers, inspired by Mr Lasseter's story that in 1893, when he was aged 17 years, he found a colossal reef of gold in the region south-west of Ilbilla. One expedition, of which Mr Lasseter was a member, left Alice Springs last June, but its aeroplane, Golden Quest, crashed. A new engine was installed, but the pilot made a forced landing and had to return. Mr Lasseter, who was a member of the Central Australia Gold Exploration Co., left Alice Springs to seek this reef, which he had not visited since he originally discovered it.

Argus (29 April 1931)

———

ION IDRIESS

(1889–1979)

Australian writer. Idriess served on Gallipoli and in the Middle East with the Australian Imperial Force during the First World War, then travelled extensively throughout Australia and New Guinea, working in various places and at assorted occupations, before becoming a full-time writer in the late 1920s. He was to become a master of faction, decades before the term was invented, his popular works including The Cattle King *(1936),* Flynn of the Inland *(1932), and* Lasseter's Last Ride *(1931). The latter book, from which this chapter is taken, has helped to perpetuate the myth of Lasseter's Reef.*

'LASSETER'S LAST RIDE: ELDORADO FOUND'

Lasseter rode happily away on his last journey. He felt master of the situation now. Disappointing experiences had undermined his faith in modern transport, its boasted speed and surety. As he travelled, he mused on the curious slipping back of the expedition's transport; right back now to camels and man. What memories this land must have, could it only speak! Strange, how he felt part of it! Quite uncanny, this surety that he was of this land and always would be: it had drawn him back again after thirty years. After all, he felt a warm satisfaction in going out alone to find his reef. Alone he had found it first; again he would find it alone. And then — ?

Lasseter gazed up at the clear blue sky. Out of it would come aeroplanes. That was where modern transport would come into its own, when the pathfinders' job was done. Then would come the rush, the opening up of a goldfield, the settlement of a new State. A native, rising Phoenix-like from the land, watched him as he passed.

Each sundown he picked carefully his camping-ground, never camping where natives might creep on him unobserved and unheard. He slept lightly, alert at the rustle of a twig, and he was always awake before dawn. That was the most dangerous time. A hundred miles from Ilbilba he saw the first smoke spiral ascending; another from a distant ridge answered. Myall natives were signalling the lone rider's approach. In late afternoon he watched two crows, flying low, going to water. He would watch for their early morning flight, for they camp near water.

That evening Lasseter hobbled his camels without bells, lit a fire, and ate his solitary meal. A mopoke croaked dismally. As the fire burned down to coals the man became shadowed just out of the glow. Around him settled the desert silence; above, a dome of velvet black blazed with stars. The air was sweet and cool. At stealthy steps behind him Lasseter turned, revolver in hand. A camel grunted restively, answered harshly by its mate. The brutes, without reason, were becoming more bad-tempered day by day. He threw some twigs on the coals and in the light of their blaze spread his blankets and turned in. As the twigs burned down the shape of the sleeper merged with the night.

But Lasseter was stealthily piling up sand alongside his body nearest the fire. He drew one blanket over the body-like mound, then, pushing the other before him, crawled fifty yards into the deepest shadows. He slept well, not caring much even should a shower of spears fly into that mound by the fire. And so he slept on other lonely nights.

Next afternoon, black figures abruptly crested a hill in front. In menacing array they rattled spears, brandished arms, and leaped with a piercing chorus to stamp the ground in savage rhythm.

In readiness for, but dreading a fight, Lasseter kept on, his camels never deviating as they lurched along the foot of the hill. He knew that if he turned aside they would never let him return again. But a fight meant that if he won out the natives would dog him for days, unseen, tireless, deadly enemies. Hopefully, he recognized they were only a hunting party. Had they flaunted the ochred feathers of a fighting party, his position would have been serious indeed. He stared steadily up as he rode along, hand on revolver, watching those poised spears now settled down into the wommeras, ready to fire the instant a spear arm was jerked for the throw. But he passed and jeering voices grew fainter. Looking back, he saw the natives grouped on the hilltop like black statues against the sunset.

Thereafter they watched him daily all the way to Winter's Glen. Twice they rose from the bushes almost within spear throw. Should he find one of their hidden soaks, or unwittingly camp on one of their sacred grounds, there would be a fight.

Though the surface water had dried up, much of the country was beautiful after the rains. Acacia and quandong trees, Mitchell and kangaroo grasses were abundant. Some shrubs were in flower, and grass parrots were noisy among the seeds. While in the sandhills country he rode past one red hill vivid with scarlet flowers. Occasionally, a desert bush was a yellow glory of trailing vines. His fat camels one day waded across a plain knee-deep in luscious grass, and Lasseter dreamed again of a goldfields stampede and artesian water and this country under sheep and wheat. This country was not the desert proper, with its leagues of barren sand, but part of the great 'desert fringe' — desert mainly through lack of water. He yelled like a boy one day at the sight of rabbits. The white-tailed little beasts were as great wanderers as himself. Fancy them making their way right out here! How the desert men must welcome them!

At Winter's Glen he spelled his camels. Later on, he hoped to meet Johns and Johannsen at Lake Christopher, eighty miles west of the Glen. He often wondered how the directors had taken the break-up of the expedition. He had a conviction they would seek him by aeroplane, although they were under no obligation to do so. Lasseter travelled on to the Western Australian border, skirting the edge of the true desert. His heart sang as he recognized landmark after landmark. He had seen no sign of natives since leaving the Glen. Now he suddenly became aware of unseen presences watching and following him. He gazed all around at sombre rocky hills, between which were plains of sand dotted by clumps of desert bush. There was not a sign of native, in person or by 'talk' smoke.

But this sixth sense developed on former trips was sharpening since the desert had again taken Lasseter to its heart. He knew natives were there. One morning he crept from his retreat to light the fire and found men's tracks in the ashes. This was 'another' country, inhabited by a different tribe. Uneasily he wondered what their methods would be. He urged his camels away from that clump of gidgee on ahead. He swore at the camels, jerking the brutes in the direction he wanted them to take. They lifted high their heads and roared out across the desert, slathering the sands with foam. The brutes for some inexplicable reason were becoming almost unmanageable.

Lasseter found his reef. As he gazed upon it, a feeling came over him that he had done his life's work. He sat down by the greenish-white quartz, staring across the hill where the reef outcropped like a yellowish-brown cap, and for two hours never moved. These blobs of dull yellow in this quartz had been the magnet drawing his thoughts for thirty years. This reef, he felt, was his life. He stood erect, with a long sigh, staring at the tallest of the hills, fixing them indelibly in his mind. He would peg the reef, then return to the nearest soak he knew of, more than a day's travel away, then scout out towards Lake Christopher and wait for Johns and Johannsen with supplies. How he wished now that the *Golden Quest* was coming, to hurry back to civilization with the news! He felt that his mates were coming. Taylor had been his best chum; he felt sure Taylor was coming. If the Company could only see him now!

He knapped off some of the stone. His heart beat violently at the sight of the yellow gleaming in the fractured rock. The reef was phenomenally rich: some of the stone was actually held together by threads of gold. Laughing aloud, he held up a gleaming specimen! It thrilled him. How it glistened! That yellow stuff that could make a man a king! Where was Harding now? In the heat of his delight he stared soberly around, sensing that his long-dead surveyor mate was with him. Quietly he filled a bag with specimens.

There was no water near the reef, but the camels carried sufficient to last him out. He hobbled the camels and by sundown had cut the pegs and driven in the datum peg. The rest took much longer. It was two days before he had pegged the reef and recorded the necessary observations. In the letter describing the location he wrote, among other things: 'I am afraid the natives will pull up the pegs after I have gone, for the reef is upon one of their sacred grounds. However, I have written upon the posts and photographed them and will bury the evidences of truth, with a bag of specimens, under the camp-fire ashes.'

In that manner Lasseter usually buried letters, so that members of the party could follow him up. He knew the natives would scratch up anything they believed he had buried. But letters in a tin buried under a camp-fire would be the safest place. The keenest eyes could detect no sign of anything buried underneath a little heap of still-warm ashes.

It had been a hard day and the camels were savage, expecting water. To-morrow they must have it, though the bad-tempered brutes could go without for another day if necessary. Lasseter started off in the afternoon, seeking to make the most of nearly three hours of daylight left. The camels travelled swiftly. The brutes always know when they are travelling back to water. The sun set in a fiery glow that made the Western Australian desert cruelly beautiful. Those rolling leagues of barren sand appeared a sea of softest pink set in a dreadful silence. Lasseter urged his beasts to earth on a clear patch of sand between low hills fringed by desert bush. There was little chance of natives successfully sneaking on him here. As he stooped over the kneeling brutes he spoke to them, 'Ssh! Ssh!' as he began to unload, crooning a quietness to their snarling grunts. He turned to dump a bag of foodstuffs upon the ground. A swishing of the sand, a creaking lurch, wheeled him swiftly. The camels were almost to their feet. As he shouted and ran they were up on their knees, and as he sprang at the rump of the nearest he was flung violently on to the sand and they were away. He sprang up and grabbed a nosepeg. The camel bellowed and swung him high, with a vicious shake of the head that sent Lasseter flying. He jumped up again and raced after them, shrieking, the nosepeg in his hand. A bolting camel travels at an amazing speed. These beasts, gone 'macnoon', covered the ground in giant strides, frothily bellowing. With the terrific shaking the water-tin lid flew loose and sprays of priceless fluid rained out on the desert sand.

Lasseter went 'macnoon', too. He drew his revolver and fired again and again. He fired to kill the camel and save his water — his life. But the camels sped into the distance, disappearing among stunted bush, appearing again on the sands, disappearing and reappearing until they faded like gigantic spiders into the ribboned sunset. They would travel, fifty, eighty, a hundred miles or more without stopping.

Lasseter was alone in the desert without water; with food perhaps for a fortnight. His food! What if the blacks were robbing the only thing now that was his! Anxiously he started back on his tracks. He had a long way to go. His footsteps slowed as in the twilight he saw the bag of food lying on the sand. He stood by the bag and listened. What a silence! Shadows stood straight up out of the sands. Lasseter's heart thumped as he whipped out his revolver and faced those desert men.

Lasseter's Last Ride (1950 edition, first published 1931)

HEDLEY HERBERT FINLAYSON
(1895–1991)

Australian naturalist. Finlayson, honorary curator of mammals at the South Australian museum, took part in what has been dubbed a 'romance of modern zoology' in 1931. At the time, naturalists believed that the plain rat-kangaroo, Caloprymnus, *was extinct, the only known examples being three specimens sent to the British Museum from South Australia by Governor George Grey during the 1840s. Finlayson came to suspect that little creatures known to Aborigines as oolacuntas, of which he had heard, and plain rat-kangaroos might be one and the same. So in December 1931, he and pastoralist Lou Reese set out from the latter's property, Appamunna, to look for oolacuntas in the Lake Eyre basin. They were accompanied by three Wongkuroo people, one of whom, Jimmy, was known as the 'rat boss', because of his ability to catch small mammals, and a Yalliyanda hunter named Butcher. Here Finlayson tells the rest of the story.*

IN SEARCH OF OOLACUNTAS

The plan of campaign had been anxiously debated all the way in from Appamunna. The great open sweep of the country is so immense, that all methods of procedure partook somewhat of hunting for a needle in a haystack. Snaring and trapping were out of the question, shooting was too damaging to skeletons, and the most practicable method (while the horses lasted) seemed to be for the whole party to beat up the country mounted, and gallop anything which was put up.

At this juncture Butcher created a sensation by announcing that he could catch oolacuntas by hand. When questioned, he explained that many years ago when 'big mob jump up alonga Barcoo,' the blacks used to locate the grass nests and then, determining the direction in which the opening lay, would, if the wind were right, sneak up behind and, silently slipping a coolamon or their hands over the top, bag the occupant! Some jealousy existed between Butcher and Jimmy, and Reese and I were inclined to attribute this account to a desire to shine. Moreover, there was a certain Alice-in-Wonderlandish touch about this method of capture by the 'laying on of hands.' So much so, that Reese, on reflection, was constrained to administer a grave rebuke to Butcher, suggesting indeed, that he was a sanguinary liar. But in this we wronged him.

Seldom do the things one keenly desires come easily. But on our very first cast we got a prize. The six of us rode east in the early morning, and on a sand-hill picked up fresh oolacunta tracks crossing to a flat on the far side. We followed them out till we lost them in the gibbers; then we opened out to a half-mile front and rode slowly south, each man scanning every lump and tussock for a possible nest. We had ridden less than half an hour when there came a shrill excited '*Yuchai*' from the horse-boy farthest out, and the chase was on. The prearranged plan was for each of us to take up the galloping in turn, the rat being headed whenever possible and turned in towards the rest of the party who remained in a group. When the first horse showed signs of losing heart, the next man took the first opportunity of replacing him, and so on.

Following the yell, Tommy came heading back down the line towards the sand-hill, but it was only after much straining of eyes that the oolacunta could be distinguished — a mere speck, thirty or forty yards ahead. At that distance it seemed scarcely to touch the ground; it almost floated ahead in an eerie, effortless way that made the thundering horse behind seem, by comparison, like a coal hulk wallowing in a heavy sea.

They were great moments as it came nearer; moments filled with curiosity and excitement, but with a steady undercurrent of relief and satisfaction. It was here!

Caloprymnus bears a strong external resemblance to five or six other related species and from a distance there was little to distinguish that which was approaching from either of two other marsupials known to occur in adjoining tracts. But as it came down the flat towards me, a little pale ghost from the 1840s, all doubt fled. The thing was holding itself very differently from the bettongs. As I watched it through the shimmering heat haze, some sense of the incongruous brought back a vivid memory of a very different scene, two years before, when I had sought the nearest living relative of *Caloprymnus*, above the snow-line on a Tasmanian range.

Imagine a little animal about the bulk of a rabbit, but built like a kangaroo, with long spindly hind legs, tiny forelegs folded tight on its chest, and a tail half as long again as the body but not much thicker than a lead pencil, and you have it in the rough. But its head, short and blunt and wide, is very different from that of any kangaroo or wallaby, and its coat is uniformly coloured a clear pale yellowish ochre — exactly like the great clay-pans and flood plains.

As it came up to us I galloped alongside to keep it under observation as long as possible. Its speed, for such an atom, was wonderful, and its endurance amazing. We had considerable difficulty in heading it with fresh horses. When we finally got it, it had taken the starch out of three mounts and run us twelve miles; all under such adverse conditions of heat and rough going, as to make it almost incredible that so small a frame should be capable of such an immense output of energy. All examples obtained subsequently by this method behaved similarly; they persisted to the very limit of their strength, and quite literally, they paused only to die.

Back at the camp all was jubilation. The afternoon and most of next day were spent in examining, sketching, photographing, measuring, dissecting, and preserving — for luck is not to be trusted. And I wanted to make the very most of the first specimen lest it be also the last. We rode out each day, sometimes to success, sometimes not. In the afternoons we worked on the rats which the 'rat boss' had dug, while the heat under the corkwoods grew ever worse and worse. Even the old hands, reared under the grim old tradition of 'salt beef, damper, and constipation,' who love to hark back to the summers when it really *was* hot, admitted subsequently that it had been bad. I had thought the still days bad, but when the hot winds came I thought again. When the flies and ants and heat and sand could be endured no longer, we left the skinning and spelled. And while we gazed out over the white-hot flats and sandhills, we sipped boiling tea, and had torturing visions of iced Quellthaler in an old-time shady garden.

On the day before we broke camp to start on the long ride to Cordilla and the Innamincka track, Butcher quashed for ever the soft impeachment which Reese had made on his veracity and covered himself with glory.

It was usual for two of the boys to take the horses to water each evening near sundown, and fill the canteens at the hole five miles away. On this afternoon they had been gone no more than half an hour when Butcher rode back into camp alone. With impassive face and in dignified silence, he handed over a bag tied at the mouth. Very cautious investigation showed it to contain a beautiful fully-adult oolacunta and a half-grown joey — both alive and undamaged. Those we had run down were too exhausted to make good life-studies for a camera, but here were fitting subjects at last.

In riding over the country, we had ample confirmation of Butcher's statement about the nest-building habit of *Caloprymnus*. In a fiery land, where a burrowing habit is the chief factor in the survival of most species, the oolacunta clings pathetically to a flimsy shelter of grass and leaves, which it makes in a shallow depression scratched out of the loam. And now, here was a splendid proof of his second claim. The Yalliyanda boy had, while riding with the others, spotted a nest and noted the head of the occupant in the opening, watching the party. He rode on without pause for a quarter of a mile, then, leaving his horse, made a rapid stalk up the wind and grabbed both mother and babe from behind.

The laying on of hands was no myth!

The Red Centre (1935)

ARTHUR GROOM

(1904–53)

Australian conservationist and writer. Groom, whose career included periods as a jackeroo, salesman, and guesthouse manager, helped to found the National Parks Association of Queensland in 1930. A 'remarkable walker' and keen photographer, he travelled extensively in central Australia after the Second World War. In this chapter from his book I Saw a Strange Land *(1950), Groom recalls visiting Lake Amadeus, during a journey that he made to Ayers Rock (Uluru) and the Olgas (Kata Tjuta) in 1947. His main guide was Tiger Tjalkalyiri.*

'AMADEUS — LAKE OF MYSTERY'

Perhaps two or three miles ahead, visible between the trunks of the dark, scattered, desert oaks, the vivid white of water and gleaming beach extended many miles right and left. Perhaps ten or fifteen miles to the west Ernest Giles had sighted Mount Olga, in October 1872, and so impressed had he been by its distant horizon of domes that it led him on towards the lake, where for several days he floundered about in an unsuccessful attempt at crossing. The name of Olga was attributed later to the elusive goal at the suggestion of Baron von Mueller.

Thus, with the spectacular lifting of the cloud masses, higher and higher, Tiger and I ascended a high sandhill in an attempt to sight Mount Olga and Ayers Rock beyond the waters of the lake; but in that direction the clouds were still dark and bunched. To the north-west, and nearly behind, an unmapped hill rose abruptly. It was clear blue against a distant angry black cloud. A patch of roving sunlight topped it in sharp relief. The waters of the lake spread away before us, running into many fingers and bays. Tiger shook his head. 'Last year I bring Ol' Man Thommasin and Misser Borgell across lake — and it properly dry — we cross him easy, thataway —— ' he pointed to the sheet of western water. 'Now, too much water everywhere. This time, we must go long way round — long way, thataway —— ' He pointed away to the south-east where the lake broke up into long placid fingers, framed within mile after mile of clean sandy beach topped by bushes and low trees. The clouds were piling up again in magnificent grandeur over the loneliness of Australia's most mysterious lake; more often parched and dry, radiating the sun's terrific heat of summer, treacherous with salt-pans and bog to wandering animals. I was enjoying a sight of it seldom seen by man.

'Tiger,' I asked, 'which way Ayers Rock?' He was searching in the south-west.

'Can't see him. Too many big cloud; but must be thataway all right.' And he indicated the south-west with a quick drop of his outstretched hand. 'We must go right up to lake now; then we must go round salt-bush country for long time. Maybe tomorrow we see Ayers Rock.'

We moved in to the northern shore of the lake. The desert and its tall, majestic desert oaks, and the frail desert grasses and clumps of spinifex, continued right to the beach, and then ceased abruptly where hardened rock-salt formed a dividing layer between the bed of the lake and the plant-life of the desert. There were many camel tracks along the beach and in the shallows. Although the water was undrinkable they probably fed and existed largely on the juicy saltbush lining the beaches. The sheet of water continued unbroken over the western horizon; but it probably was nowhere more than two or three feet deep, and much of it only a few inches deep. I walked across the crackling salt encrustation, and gingerly to the edge of the water. There was no perceptible movement of wind or wave. The water had a green transparency for some yards out; and from there on it was like a vast sheet of mercury reflecting every cloud in the sky. Two or three days of hot weather would reduce the size of the lake by hundreds of acres.

The camels refused to travel close to the water's edge. We continued slowly through the afternoon, running each salt-pan finger a mile or more to its end, crossing the brown, muddy saltbush flat at its tip, twisting, turning, unloading and reloading as the camels jibbed, stumbled in the mud, and went down. Tiger persuaded and cajoled; Tamalji laughed and shrieked and did little more; Njunowa conveniently disappeared; but by evening we were round the worst of the fingers, and at the base of a great bare, pink sandhill, rippled with wind, where Tiger informed me would be 'properly good camping-place', because 'no more bad lake country now. Tomorrow we all go thataway. *Must* see Ayers Rock soon now. Two more days, and we go *right* up — close. Puttem hand on him properly.'

We made camp at the base of the sandhill; and within a few feet an arm of salt water went out to meet the lake, directly into the west, taking with it the deep-crimson reflection of the sunset; still, silent, incredibly dead, yet beautiful.

I sat on my swag and ate boiled onions and stewed prunes, and a tin of bully-beef. Perhaps thirty feet away, the three boys squatted beside their fire and tore at the remains of the kangaroo, now stinking and dirty. In thanksgiving, they had said Christian grace in their native tongue, and preferred the kangaroo to the tinned meat I had offered them. My last impression of the passing of that day was the sight of the four camels a little to the south-west, dark and shadowy, one after another in silhouette against the dying crimson, moving off in search of trees and bushes they liked.

About midnight the sky clouded over again, and blotted out the millions of brilliant stars that had ruled for a couple of short hours. A sharp shower hissed viciously over the sand before dawn. I could hear it half a mile away. It brought me from my sleeping-bag in time to rebuild the fire. The heavy rain killed the sunrise and heralded another dirty, grey day. In absolute disgust we sat and ate in silence. The boys were thoroughly subdued once again. I was frankly worried. If the bad weather continued another day or so, I would have to abandon the journey and turn eastward. The sky looked hopeless, and particularly bad to westward over the course of the lake. Apparently the vapour rising from the long sheet of water was causing much of the trouble. It made me wonder to what extent an inland sea might influence the climate of Central Australia. I climbed the high sandhill. It was perhaps eighty feet high, pink, almost bare, and several hundred yards long, ending at its western end as a sloping tongue into the lake. The only plants about it, like a fringe of hair round a balding man's head, were low, flowering wattles, and bushes of white heath. A sharp breeze whipped up from the south, the clouds jarred, tufted, and broke with the rapidity of minutes; and then far to the south-west, but very low down, I could see the unmistakable flattened dome of Ayers Rock, Oolra of the natives, pale mauve against the troubled sky beyond, pale mauve above the dark green of desert trees and the dull pink of the sandhills. I shouted to the boys and pointed. They jumped to their feet and called back, and Tamalji's great guffaw set them off; and, within another minute, fat little Njunowa was streaking to eastward for the camels.

I Saw a Strange Land (1950)

—————

BARRY HILL

(1943–)

Australian writer and poet. Previously a teacher, psychologist, and journalist, Hill became a full-time writer in the mid-1970s. His works include fiction, non-fiction, and poetry. Hill's interest in the Aboriginal presence in Australia, displayed in his long narrative poem, Ghosting William Buckley *(1993), is further developed in* The Rock *(1994), a work about travelling, in many different ways, to Uluru. He draws upon his own, Arthur Groom's, and Tiger Tjalkalyiri's travels for this section from* The Rock.

'LAUGHTER AND NECTAR'

Arthur Groom was the lucky one. His timing, as might be expected from a former Spitfire pilot, was fortunate. The year before Tuitt got the road in, Groom managed to journey in by camel, making one of the last 'explorer trips' to the Rock before mass tourism. In his charming book, *I Saw a Strange Land* (1950) he sketches the state of transport in 1947:

> Camels, donkeys and packhorses are now rare. Cars and trucks grind over hundreds of miles of rocky desert, sandy desert or fertile plain; and the average man's vehicle is a heavy truck ready equipped with drums of water and petrol, and food and swag for any long, sudden journey.

Many of the old camel and packhorse mail services are now replaced by Eddie Connellan's little planes, centred at Alice Springs, jumping like grasshoppers in a fortnightly service over distances from a few miles up to hundreds of miles, from station to station, Mission depot, or mining field; and many of the native watchers whose keen eyes once saw the ground mail approaching slowly, hours before its arrival, now attune their ears to the sky, and yell at the faintest distant drone of a powerful engine, 'Hareyplane come up sit down now. Gottem mail-bag for ebbrybody!

Groom was travelling for the adventure itself, he says. But he would also look at the country with a mind to the tourist of the future, and consider the fate of what he thought to be a dying race. 'I might find out what was being done to ease the passing of Australia's primitive man.' Groom's Darwinian philanthropy would have sat easily at Spencer's campfire.

The Aborigines who led him across the country and looked after his camels were hardly examples of 'a dying race'. The opposite, really. There was Tamalji, a young Pitjantjatjara man who spoke no English, whose laughter used to frighten the camels. 'I have never seen or heard any man, black or white', Groom says, 'laugh with such physical power or volume... His laughter rose up and up, until he seemed to reach a crisis where it could continue no longer; and then down from his amazing high guffaw with a long, drawn, dying scream of finality. It was enough to wake all the skeletons of the desert.' The other young man was Njunowa, who was the silent type, amused and watchful and always hungry. Groom detected a deep wildness in him. Both young men were always running off to chase goannas and lizards to eat and 'pappy dawg' for bushtucker and scalps for sale to government men. Then they would come back, out of the blue, to the camel train, where they would once again adjust to the white man's slow and determined progress towards the Rock. It was the unassailable vitality of their companionship that helped Groom through.

Everything depended on an older man, Tiger Tjalkalyiri.

'I'm Tige', he commenced, patting an expanding chest. 'Tjalkalyiri my name. Mr Albrecht send me — take you Ayers Rock — long way. Kings Creek we go too — right up — cross him — I know good place. Last year I take Ol' Man Thommasin an' Misser Borgell from Adelaide, and Metingeri he come, too — lazy beggar, nearly losem everybody.'

It was Tiger who knew the country like the back of his hand. Little could Groom know the important part Tiger would play in years to come, when traditional owners of the country would step forward to reclaim their land. Travelling with Groom, Tiger was content to gesture towards inhabitants all around. When they got to Kings Canyon they could see 'smokes', mostly out in the great native reserve.

'Tiger and Tamalji and Njunowa held urgent conferences and pointed excitedly to the smokes. They were trying to work out the direction of travel of those who had fired them. Tiger explained some of them: "That one — might belong to half-caste feller — maybe — go out with one camella to get puppy-dawg scalp. 'Nother one — thataway." He pointed directly south. "Maybe Ernabella men go back across desert, and walkabout little while in rocky country, spear kangaroo-euro." He then indicated a line of smokes extending for several miles. "Maybe someone come up tonight from Petermann country — maybe we see 'em."'

The excitement was connected to where they were going. They were coming into Tiger's own country. 'Tiger was proud of his childhood country and patted himself on the chest time and time again with closed fist. "This one good country all the time. I live here — runabout — when little boy. Good country altogether. Reedy Creek we call Lilla. Bagotty Spring country we call Wynmurra. All good country. *My* country — go all the way across Lake Amadeus and Oolra and Kattatuta. I take you and show you. Tomorrow — we go cross desert? We take them ol' camella — plenty water canteen — we got good tucker — good! WE go three, maybe four, days, thataway — right up by lake country — right up Ayers Rock, we go!"'

Earlier on Tiger took a long shot at a kangaroo. He was sixty yards off and saw it stumble. Then he took off from his camel and went after it on foot, disappearing into the mulga. Half an hour later he came back, done in. But here was malu, the carcass of which he tossed on the pebbles. He said, 'Got him — he go close up Oolra (Uluru). I been run — and — chase — him — and just about when I close up fall over meself, him fall over first.'

Tiger the knower of the country, Tiger the joker. Both were to make him famous among white men in the years to come. The malu was tucker for days to come. Its furry carcass was thrown into the fire that night; and the half-cooked meat cooked again the next day, and for days afterwards, carried in stinking condition so that it could be cooked again. It was never eaten before Tiger said grace. This was another aspect of the man, at least when he was conducting whitemen through the country. Tiger had been living at the Hermannsburg Mission under the strong pastoral care of Pastor F. W. Albrecht.

Albrecht thought highly of Tiger when he had sent him to work for Groom; and, clearly, Tiger thought well enough of the mission and its food supply to be saying grace even when he was away from the place. One night, when the moon was up and they were in the ranges near the tree which had a big G carved into it — G for Giles, or was it Gosse? — Tiger stood up and sang a hymn. It was a strange night, says Groom, filled with awe for the country and history.

They went Tiger's way around the east end of Lake Amadeus. They encountered bog, mist, an eerie desolation. It had rained, and there was more danger than Tiger expected. All the way, Groom was bursting to get his sight of the Rock, to consolidate his sense of place by seeing as much as he can at the one time. From the Gill Range he thought he had seen it: 'a low faint-blue dome curved a little above the horizon'. Maybe. On the south side of the lake it was a great relief to reach a bare pink sandhill 'where Tiger informed me would be properly good camping place', because 'no more bad lake country now. Tomorrow we all go thataway. *Must* see Ayers Rock soon now. Two more days and we go *right* up — close. Puttem hand on him properly.'

It was days before Groom could put a hand on him properly. The best he could do the next day was climb a sand dune and see the Rock from afar. 'The unmistakable flattened dome, Oolra of the natives, pale mauve against the troubled sky.' On into the dunes. The great red waves that we now know so well from everybody else's travelling! Eventually the Rock is regularly in view. Then not. Hide and seek with the Rock, as you go up and down in the dunes. And then, on one dune summit the great vision beyond the Rock — 'the ethereal blue of many domes splitting the horizon like the temples of an ancient city'.

'Kata Tjuta!' Tiger spoke excitedly.

'Mount Olga!' writes Groom. 'The elusive goal of Ernest Giles, and still seen only by few men.'

The closer Groom gets, the less pragmatic his sense of wonder.

'The boys sent up smoke signals; but no answers came back from the Rock. Its solitude was real, and there were times when I felt I was approaching the immense coloured tomb of a dead age into which I had no right to look. The solitude might have been even more impressive had it not been for the continuous bell-call of a bird which surely had beaten place and distance with its high run of notes and contralto base, ventriloquial, distant yet all about, and invisible. Tiger informed me "That one Bunbunbililila!" and at my attempts at repetition Tamalji threw back his head and laughed aloud.'

(*Panpanpalala*, Pitjantjatjara for bellbird, today.)

Next day, they are within striking distance. And it is as if some dance of nature is taking place to welcome them. 'We got away within the hour,' says Groom with a kind of religious measure, 'our slow approach now accompanied by budgerigars, crows, finches, mulga and ringneck parrots; and a rapid increase of wildflowers on the areas where wandering natives had burnt the spinifex a year or so before, and enriched the sand with ash. One particular bush, about five to six feet high, had golden and green flowers waving up and down in the light wind, remarkably like green parrots in flight. I thought the bush was a type of banksia. Later investigation revealed that it was a type of desert Grevillea. Tamalji and Njunowa left the camels and ran from flower to flower, bending low at each bush, sucking nectar from the flowers, and passing on.'

'I felt', says Groom in awe and in ecstasy, when they finally reached the Rock, 'like an ant at the door of a cathedral.'

The Rock (1994)

5

THE WEST

GEORGE GREY

(1812–98)

British explorer, governor, and politician. The inexperienced Grey, who had previously served in Ireland with the army, led two fiascos of expeditions in north-western Australia between 1837 and 1839. After arriving at Hanover Bay in November 1837, he and his party set off inland the following January, heading for the Swan River settlement (present-day Perth). This expedition, however, was aborted in April, Grey having been speared by Aborigines in February. The second expedition, in 1839, ultimately involved a dreadful forced march over hundreds of kilometres, after Grey's whaleboats were wrecked, and cost the life of one member of the party. Grey's later career, also controversial, included periods as governor of South Australia (1841–45), New Zealand (1845–53, 1861–67), and Cape Colony (1855–59); and as prime minister of New Zealand (1877–79). As Kathleen Fitzpatrick observes, Grey, who made the following 'discoveries' in March 1838, was 'the first explorer to publish descriptions and drawings of Australian aboriginal art'.

ABORIGINAL PAINTINGS

Finding that it would be useless to lose more time in searching for a route through this country, I proceeded to rejoin the party once more; but whilst returning to them, my attention was drawn to the numerous remains of native fires and encampments which we met with, till at last, on looking over some bushes, at the sandstone rocks which were above us, I suddenly saw from one of them a most extraordinary large figure peering down upon me. Upon examination, this proved to be a drawing at the entrance to a cave, which, on entering, I found to contain, besides, many remarkable paintings.

The cave appeared to be a natural hollow in the sandstone rocks; its floor was elevated about five feet from the ground, and numerous flat broken pieces of the same rock, which were scattered about, looked at a distance like steps leading up to the cave, which was thirty-five feet wide at the entrance, and sixteen feet deep; but beyond this, several small branches ran further back. Its height in front was rather more than eight feet, the roof being formed by a solid slab of sandstone, about nine feet thick, and which rapidly inclined towards the back of the cave, which was there not more than five feet high.

On this sloping roof, the principal figure which I have just alluded to, was drawn; in order to produce the greater effect, the rock about it was painted black, and the figure itself coloured with the most vivid red and white. It thus appeared to stand out from the rock; and I was certainly rather surprised at the moment that I first saw this gigantic head and upper part of a body bending over and staring grimly down at me.

It would be impossible to convey in words an adequate idea of this uncouth and savage figure; I shall therefore only give such a succinct account of this and the other paintings as will serve as a sort of description to accompany the annexed plates.

The dimensions of the figure were:

	ft	in.
Length of head and face	2	0
Width of face	0	17
Length from bottom of face to navel	2	6

Its head was encircled by bright red rays, something like the rays which one sees proceeding from the sun, when depicted on the signboard of a public house; inside of this came a broad stripe of very brilliant red, which was coped by lines of white, but both inside and outside of this red space, were narrow stripes of a still deeper red, intended probably to mark its boundaries; the face was painted vividly white, and the eyes black, being however surrounded by red and yellow lines; the body, hands, and arms were outlined in red, — the body being curiously painted with red stripes and bars.

Upon the rock which formed the left hand wall of this cave, and which partly faced you on entering, was a very singular painting, vividly coloured, representing four heads joined together. From the mild expression of the countenances, I imagined them to represent females, and they appeared to be drawn in such a manner, and in such a position, as to look up at the principal figure which I have before described; each had a very remarkable head-dress, coloured with a deep bright blue, and one had a necklace on. Both of the lower figures had a sort of dress, painted with red in the same manner as that of the principal figure, and one of them had a band round her waist. Each of the four faces was marked by a totally distinct expression of countenance, and although none of them had mouths, two, I thought, were otherwise rather good looking. The whole painting was executed on a white ground, and its dimensions were, —

	ft	in.
Total length of painting	3	6¾
Breadth across two upper heads	2	6
Ditto across the two lower ones	3	1½

The next most remarkable drawing in the cave, was an ellipse, three feet in length, and one foot ten inches in breadth: the outside line of this painting was of a deep blue colour, the body of the ellipse being of a bright yellow dotted over with red lines and spots, whilst across it ran two transverse lines of blue. The portion of the painting above described formed the ground, or main part of the picture, and upon this ground was painted a kangaroo in the act of feeding, two stone spear-heads, and two black balls; one of the spear-heads was flying to the kangaroo, and one away from it; so that the whole subject probably constituted a sort of charm by which the luck of an enquirer in killing game could be ascertained.

There was another rather humorous sketch, which represented a native in the act of carrying a kangaroo; the height of the man being three feet. The number of drawings in the cave could not altogether have been less than from fifty to sixty, but the majority of them consisted of men, kangaroos, &c.; the figures being carelessly and badly executed, and having evidently a very different origin to those which I have first described. Another very striking piece of art was exhibited in the little gloomy cavities situated at the back of the main cavern. In these instances some rock at the sides of the cavity had been selected, and the stamp of a hand and arm by some means transferred to it; this outline of the hand and arm was then painted black, and the rock about it white, so that on entering that part of the cave, it appeared as if a human hand and arm were projecting through a crevice admitting light.

After having discovered this cave I returned to the party, and directing them to prepare for moving on, I ordered that as soon as all was ready they should proceed past the cave, so that all would have an opportunity of examining it, and in the mean time I returned in order to make sketches of the principal paintings. The party soon arrived, and when my sketches, and notes, were completed, we retraced a portion of our route of this morning, moving round the sandstone ridge, through one portion of which I saw a sort of pass, which I thought might perhaps afford us a means of egress. I therefore halted the party, and moved up with Corporal Auger to examine it. After proceeding some distance, we found a cave larger than the one seen this morning; of its actual size, however, I have no idea, for being pressed for time I did not attempt to explore it, having merely ascertained that it contained no paintings. I was moving on, when we observed the profile of a human face and head cut out in a sandstone rock which fronted the cave; this rock was so hard, that to have removed such a large portion of it with no better tool than a knife and hatchet made of stone, such as the Australian natives generally possess, would have been a work of very great labour. The head was two feet in length, and sixteen inches in breadth in the broadest part; the depth of the profile increased gradually from the edges where it was nothing, to the centre where it was an inch and a-half; the ear was rather badly placed, but otherwise the whole of the work was good, and far superior to what a savage race could be supposed capable of executing. The only proof of antiquity that it bore about it was that all the edges of the cutting were rounded and perfectly smooth, much more so than they could have been from any other cause than long exposure to atmospheric influences.

After having made a sketch of this head, I returned to the party, and as I had not been able to find a path which would lead us across the sandstone ridge, we continued our course round it, retracing our steps until we reached the stream which had been crossed this morning, and then moved westward, keeping along its southern bank, until we had turned the sandstone range and reached another stream running from the south, which we traced up in the direction of its source, travelling through a series of basaltic valleys of so luxuriant a character that those of the party who were not very tall, travelled, as they themselves expressed it, between two high green walls, over which they could not see; and these green walls were composed of rich grass, which the ponies eat with avidity. On a subsequent occasion when we visited this valley, we had to call to one another in order to ascertain our relative positions, when only a few yards apart; and yet the vegetation was neither rank nor coarse, but as fine a grass as I have ever seen.

We halted for the night in one of these lovely valleys; a clear stream bubbled along within about fifty yards of us, and about a mile beyond, two darkly wooded basaltic hills raised their heads, and between these and the stream, our ponies were feeding in grass higher than themselves. I sat in the fading light, looking at the beautiful scenery around me, which now for the first time gladdened the eyes of Europeans; and I wondered that so fair a land should only be the abode of savage men; and then I thought of the curious paintings we had this day seen, — of the timid character of the natives, — of their anomalous position in so fertile a country, — and wondered how long these things were to be. With so wide a field of conjecture before me, thought naturally thronged on thought, and the night was far advanced ere I laid down to seek repose from the fatigues of the day.

Journals of Two Expeditions of Discovery in North-West and Western Australia, During the Years 1837, 38, and 39, vol. 1 (1841)

———

KEVIN COATE

(?–)

Australian bushwalker. Coate was one of a group of nine men and three women who, in recent times, retraced the route of George Grey's 1838 expedition. They particularly hoped to solve 'a 150-year-old mystery' during their trek.

'QUEST IN WANDJINA LAND'

The bushfire raced across the valley floor, and on the red sandstone cliffs above us trees blazed against a night sky lit by exploding spinifex tussocks. Camped below, I watched flames lick to within 2 metres of my group and hoped no-one would recall the legend of the Aboriginal cave spirit, Djilinja.

Shown in a cave painting discovered by 19th-century explorer George Grey — whose footsteps we were following — she is said to have turned vengeful after her child was burned to death ...

We spent a sleepless night huddled among tumbled rocks, the cliffs lit by an unholy glow, spinifex bursting into sparks and plunging with fiery comet tails into Walker Valley. There were murmurs of concern. Someone mentioned the date — Friday the 13th of May.

I reassured everyone, but I was worried about the wind. If it turned, our only escape route lay across a deep creek and a slick, grey-mud mangrove swamp that was home to a 3 m saltwater crocodile. With 11 tired, mostly middle-aged comrades I didn't need an emergency evacuation.

It was a demoralising start. That evening at Hanover Bay we had disembarked from our charter boat *Wave Spirit* — long since departed for its return to the pearling town of Broome, 400 kilometres south-east — excited about retracing the path of British Lieutenant George Grey, the area's first European explorer, and hoping to solve his 150-year-old mystery. Now we feared for our lives in the face of one of the awesome elemental forces that shape the Kimberley.

Lisbon-born Grey's illustrious career would later include a knighthood, the governorship of South Australia, premiership of New Zealand, and governorship of Cape Colony (South Africa) during the Zulu wars. These successes overshadowed his earlier achievement — in 1838 he explored Australia's harsh but magnificent north-west and discovered the Kimberley's Wandjina cave paintings, considered the most spectacular examples of Aboriginal art in Western Australia.

Grey also made another apparently significant find. On 26 March 1838 he wrote in his journal: *I was moving on when we observed the profile of a human face and head cut out in a sandstone rock ... the ear was rather badly placed, but otherwise the whole of the work was ... far superior to what a savage race could be supposed capable of executing.* Grey, wounded by Aboriginal spears, sketched the carving and continued his journey.

The carving remained lost for 150 years, and some sceptical anthropologists suggested that the injured Grey might have been hallucinating when he saw the image. But Peter Knight, a Perth-based engineer who had compared Grey's journal maps with modern maps and aerial photos, claimed that Grey was lucid when he reported finding the carving. When Peter heard that a quest for the carving was the main objective of our 14-day A[ustralian]G[eographic]-assisted expedition, he and his wife Glen immediately flew from Singapore to join us.

The expedition also included a doctor, a nurse, an academic, a bricklayer, a film-maker, a farmer, a public servant, an import consultant and an office worker; ordinary people ranging in age from 32 to 52, but all keen bushwalkers with interests in botany or ornithology.

We each contributed $450 towards the expedition's $7400 total cost and our only training for the trek had been to walk around our neighbourhoods carrying backpacks weighted with books or birdseed.

So there we were on our first night, huddled in a fiery valley with only the forbidding mangroves and empty coastline at our backs. At first light we saw that the fire had cleared a blackened path between charred, smoking paperbark trees. Our meandering 120 km route would take us southwards over the Macdonald Range, through lowlands and across the rugged Elizabeth and Catherine Range to the headwaters of the Glenelg River. Grey had quit there, forced back by his wounds. We would go on to Pantijan station on the Sale River. With acrid smoke in our nostrils, we broke camp and shrugged into our backpacks.

Moving 4 km south we reached the junction of Greys 87° Creek, a narrow, steep-sided ravine that we unofficially named for its angle to Walker Valley. We breakfasted on porridge and rye bread before hiking through the ravine's fly-infested wattle trees and climbing into the Macdonald Range.

I had been asked to look for flowers of the rare *Grevillea adenotricha*, thought to grow only in this region. There were no photographs on record and some were needed for a new book. I was surprised to literally walk into the plant, with its small, distinctive red flowers, on a rocky hill above Grey's 87° Creek. We took photographs and pressed specimens in our diaries.

Stiff from our first day's march over ankle-turning sandstone rocks and through spiny spinifex clumps and numerous creeks, we reached Lushington Valley. Near a cave with faded Aboriginal paintings we stripped for a swim in a pool given over to ferns and blue waterlilies.

By the third day we had set the pattern for our trip: The billy on before first light at 5 a.m., walk until breakfast at 9 a.m., move on until 11 a.m., lunch and rest until 2.30 p.m., then press on to night camp.

With the sun's heat bouncing off our hats, we spent the day acclimatising to the rigours of the trek. The humidity was in the 80s, the temperature in the mid-30s, and flies tormented us. They rode on our backpacks in seething black masses, rising to swarm in the muggy air and madden us whenever we paused.

We trudged out of the Macdonald Range on the morning of 16 May. A brassy sun beat down as we crossed jumbled sandstone terrain and picked our way south between massive outcrops towards a shimmering horizon of hazy blue smears; the distant Elizabeth and Catherine Range.

'You wouldn't last long up here without water and a calm head,' panted 52-year-old Berkeley Allen as he groped for his water bottle. At the rim of an escarpment we had chanced upon a deserted Aboriginal stoneworking site littered with the debris of spearhead flakes. It overlooked black basalt terrain and a dry watercourse where, during the Wet (November–March), a waterfall rages over the slick volcanic rocks. We stood, awed by the scene beyond — a breathtaking lowland of conical hills, watercourses and grassy plains.

Hamish pointed out that this must have been the spot Grey was referring to when he wrote: *I have seen no land, no scenery to equal it. We were upon the confines of a great volcanic district, clothed with tropical vegetation.*

Within days we became steeped in the magic of this timeless country, with its heady scents of eucalypts and pungent, sun-melted spinifex gum. We woke to birdsong and magnificent dawns and slept with the haunting call of the curlew who, according to Aboriginal myth, was a promiscuous wife whose lover was changed into the moon; grief-stricken, she roams the night calling him.

The Kimberley's austere beauty captivated our minds and spirits, but its rugged terrain was taking its toll on our bodies. Hamish and Rosemary McGlashan's bush medical kit was soon at war with a strain of bacteria that had blossomed in our numerous wounds from the prickly spinifex. My hand, ripped on a barbed pandanus, was also badly inflamed. Most of us had blisters, especially the 'Blisto Kids', Peter and his ever-smiling wife Glen. Bob Goodale, 44, was buckling under his heavy 16 mm camera gear and David Dale, 51, was fighting asthma.

Mike Cusack, 48 (no relation to Michael and Susan Cusack, AG's year in the wilderness couple), was in pain from a fall, but he never held us up and even went off with his rifle to bring down a young scrub bull for much-needed meat. Later we discovered he had broken a rib and cracked three lower vertebrae.

At 9 a.m. on 18 May we reached the Glenelg River. *There burst upon the sight a noble river, running through a beautiful country, and where we saw it, at least three or four miles across, and studded with numerous verdant islands. I have since seen many Australian rivers, but none to equal this either in magnitude or beauty,* wrote Grey.

Where we met the river, 8 km south of Mount Trevor, it was only 50 m wide but running swiftly. With its spectacular sandy beaches and high banks, orange sandstone cliffs, pandanus and magnificent paperbark trees with their showy bottlebrush flowers it was a paradise for birds. A lanky black-necked stork plodded through shallow water, and a flock of stately brolgas eclipsed the sun. While searching for a campsite we flushed from the long grass several rare partridge pigeons, identified by the yellow circle of skin around their eyes. Lee Vernon's bird list grew rapidly as she scribbled furiously in her notebook.

The fish were biting, so that night we feasted on a few black-skinned sooty grunters and a 4 kg barramundi (a bigger one got away — of course). Spiced with lemon pepper and cooked in foil, they were delicious. The next day — surprise! — my compatriots presented me with a damper birthday cake, and a Kimberley-cool (warm) can of beer that my brother-in-law Allan Smith had hidden in his pack.

After traversing 5 km of rugged country, in which we spotted a quoll (native cat) crouched on a rocky outcrop, we found Greys 26 March Cave, which we unofficially named for its date of discovery in 1838. The cave is one of three containing paintings that immortalise the sexual exploits of Dalimen, a Wandjina hero, and his female followers (including Djilinja, reputed to have later turned killer and cannibal).

According to tradition, the Wandjina spirits are preserved by the annual retouching of the ochre paintings by a tribal elder. If this was so, I thought as I crouched in the cave's cool interior, then Dalimen and his women would be feeling a little wan, for there was no sign of recent work on the faded figures. Tragically, in a few more decades they might be bleached out of existence.

As we emerged from the cave a sense of expectancy rose and seemed to crackle between us like electricity. If our map references were correct, somewhere near this cave we would find the head carving — if it existed! The odds against us were daunting. We would be looking for one rock among thousands scattered in perhaps 100 narrow gullies. We had only one clue. 'Grey was wounded,' Peter said. 'He had to be on his horse when he saw the head, so search only those gullies wide enough for a mounted group.'

Excited, we split up. An hour later I returned, dejected, to our rendezvous to find Peter waiting. 'Want to see it now, or after lunch?' he asked.

The head was etched into the centre of a large sandstone boulder. The measurements were right — 40 centimetres long, with a badly placed ear — and despite the passage of time, there was no doubt that it was the formation Grey had sketched. There was, however, no sign that any tool had ever struck the rock. It looked to us as if the head-like shape had been formed by natural, albeit uncanny, erosion. It was

25-year-old Grey's stylised artwork that had puzzled anthropologists for six generations.

It was the 20th of May and our quest was over. I called for three cheers.

Three days' trek south brought us into the Ngarinjin tribal area and to Greys 29 March Cave, known by Aboriginals as Bandidjin, an ancient ceremonial centre. This cave has a controversial figure painted on the roof, thought by 19th-century anthropologists to be a shipwrecked mariner with an ancient oriental or Arab message written in his head-dress.

Erich von Daniken, in his 1973 book *In Search of Ancient Gods*, went further, claiming the figure's round head-dress was a space-helmet and that the figure was clearly an extra-terrestrial. Today we know the cave is an Aboriginal site concerned with yam harvests, and that the marks in the headress are nothing more exotic than lightning symbols and red cockatoo feathers.

Near the cave Lee found a fledgling black grasswren. Fussed over by three adult birds, it was fearless before our cameras, and I believe our photographs are world firsts. Further sightings could add to our scant knowledge — the eggs have yet to be described — of the species.

That night, listening to the curlew's sad song and a dingo's howls, I lay at peace with this ageless land — until a satellite streaked across the sky and jolted me back into the 20th century.

On 25 May we limped out of the bush at Pantijan, 220 km northeast of Derby, to be greeted by cattle-mustering families of the Worrorra, Ngarinyin, and Wunambal people. Relaxing under a mango tree, we drank strong tea and listened to music on a ghetto blaster, incongruous in this dusty, dilapidated station. In a bush lean-to I used a solar-powered telephone to call pilot Dick Robertson in Derby and arrange our transport home. As I hobbled back to my group my feet hurt but, like the others, my spirit soared, elated by the success of an unforgettable adventure.

Australian Geographic, no. 21 (March 1991)

FRANCIS THOMAS GREGORY

(1821–88)

English-born surveyor and explorer. In 1829, Gregory came to the Swan River settlement with his family. He and his brothers Augustus and Henry explored to the north of Perth in 1846. After exploring along the Murchison River in 1857, Frank Gregory, as he was called, led an expedition to the Gascoyne River the following year. He subsequently commanded another expedition in 1861, in the area of the Ashburton, Fortescue, De Grey, and Oakover Rivers, to look for a site for a proposed cotton-growing settlement. Although the latter did not eventuate, new pastoral lands were found.

MOUTH OF THE DE GREY RIVER

26th September — This morning we found the water in the well quite salt, in consequence of the tide having risen during the night; and as our horses required water, it was found desirable to fall back upon some of the fresh pools to form a camp, while a day or two could be devoted to the examination of this fertile and interesting tract of country. We accordingly crossed the channel and proceeded westward for nearly three miles, when we came upon the other branch, which proved eventually to join again several miles below, forming an island containing some 8,000 or 9,000 acres of alluvial flat soil, covered with a quantity of mixed grasses. To this was given the name of Ripon Island. The western channel was found to be over 300 yards wide, and to contain several fine reaches of open water, some fresh and others slightly brackish; they were all teeming with ducks and a great variety of water-fowl. Having selected a suitable spot for a camp, I started with Messrs Brown and Harding to examine the country towards the inlet. At a little more than two miles we crossed the river between two pools of salt water, subject to the influence of the tides, and proceeded northward over an open grassy flat for two miles further, when the grass gave place to samphire and small mangrove bushes, which gradually thickened to dense mangroves, cut up by deep muddy creeks, which put a stop to proceeding further in that direction. Here we observed several remarkable stacks of dead mangroves, evidently piled together by the natives, but for what purpose we could not ascertain, unless to escape upon from the tide when fishing. Having gained firm ground, we made a detour more to the eastward, and at last succeeded in reaching the bank of the river close to the head of the inlet. The tide being at the ebb, I was able to walk over the mud and sand to the mouth of the river, and obtain bearings to Points Larrey and Poissonier, and observe the character of the entrance, from which I formed the opinion that the breakers seen by Captain Stokes when surveying this portion of the coast, and which deterred him from entering the inlet, were nothing more than the sea-rollers meeting a strong ebb tide setting out of the De Grey, possibly backed up by freshes from the interior which would, from a river of this size, occasion a considerable commotion where the tide amounts to twenty feet; at any rate, I could not observe any rocks, and there appeared to be a channel with at least five or six feet of water in it at low tide. For the first mile the river has a breadth of from 400 to 800 yards, and would admit with the tide vessels of twelve or fourteen feet draft of water with perfect safety up as far as Ripon Island, where they could lie completely sheltered in all weathers quite close to the shore, which here has steep banks twenty to thirty feet high; they would however, be left aground at low water, as we did not observe any deep pools in this part of the river. I had only just time to complete my observations when the roaring of the incoming tide warned me that no time was to be lost in returning to the horses, which were nearly a mile higher up the river. Although I ran part of the way, the mud creeks filled up so rapidly, there was some risk of my being cut off from the shore and having to take up a roost on the top of the mangroves until the tide fell; I had time, however, to observe that the head of the tide carried with it thousands of fish of great variety, amongst them a very remarkable one from three to six inches in length, in form resembling a mullet, but with fins like a flying-fish; it is amphibious, landing on the mud and running with the speed of a lizard, and when frightened can jump five or six feet at a bound; I did not, however, succeed in capturing one for a specimen. Swarms of beautiful bright-crimson crabs, about two inches diameter, were to be seen issuing from their holes to welcome the coming flood, on which was borne a great number of sea-fowl, who, it was evident, came in for an abundant feast in the general turmoil. Mounting our horses, that had stood for the last two hours without touching a mouthful of the rank grass around them for want of water, we returned to the camp by a different route, through open grass flats bordering the deep reaches of water that encompass the north-west side of Ripon Island.

Augustus Charles Gregory & Francis Thomas Gregory, *Journals of Australian Explorations* (1884)

JOHN FORREST

(1847–1918)

Australian surveyor, explorer, and politician. Born and educated in Western Australia, John Forrest worked in the survey department in that colony from 1865 to 1890, becoming surveyor-general in 1883. During the first of his three major exploratory expeditions, he searched in 1869 for traces of Ludwig Leichhardt, who had been missing since 1848. The second, towards the end of which he wrote this report, saw him lead a party of men and horses from Perth to Adelaide, the first explorers to cross Western Australia from west to east, between March and August 1870. He made another west–east crossing in 1874, this time from Champion Bay to the overland telegraph line, and then on to Adelaide. John Forrest later became premier of Western Australia (1890–1901), a member of the federal House of Representatives (1901–18), and the first Australian-born person to be raised to the British peerage.

REPORT TO THE COLONIAL SECRETARY

Port Eucla, 7th July, 1870.

Sir, — It is with much pleasure I have the honour to report, for the information of His Excellency the Governor, the safe arrival here of the expedition entrusted to my guidance, as also the meeting of the schooner 'Adur.'

Leaving Esperance Bay on the 9th of May, we travelled in an easterly direction, over plains generally poorly grassed, to Israelite Bay (situated in latitude 33° 36' 51" S., and longitude 123° 48' E.), which we reached on the 18th May, and met the 'Adur,' according to instructions issued to the master. Here we recruited our horses and had them re-shod, put the pack-saddles in good order, packed provisions, &c., and gave the master of the 'Adur' very strict and detailed instructions to proceed to Eucla Harbour, and await my arrival until the 2nd of September, when, if I did not reach there, he was to bury provisions under the Black Beacon and sail for Fremantle, *viâ* Israelite and Esperance Bays. Everything being in readiness, on the 30th of May we left Israelite Bay *en route* for Eucla, carrying with us three months' provisions. Keeping near the coast for sixty miles, having taken a flying trip inland on my way, we reached the sand-patches a little to the west of Point Culver, in latitude 32° 55' 34" S., and longitude 124° 25' E., on the 2nd of June.

On the 3rd went on a flying trip to the N.E., returning on the 4th along the cliffs and Point Culver. I found the country entirely destitute of permanent water, but, after leaving the coast a few miles, to be, in places, beautifully grassed. On the coast near the cliffs it was very rocky, and there was neither feed nor water. Finding there was no chance of permanent water being found, that the only water in the country was in small rocky holes — and those very scarce indeed — and the feed being very bad at Point Culver, I determined, after very mature consideration, to attempt at all hazards to reach the water shown on Mr Eyre's track in longitude 126° 24' E., or 140 miles distant.

In accordance with these arrangements, on the 7th day of June started on our journey, carrying over thirty gallons of water on three of our riding horses, and taking it in turns walking. Travelled about N.E. for four days, which brought us to latitude 32° 11' S., and longitude 125° 37' E., finding, during that time, in rocky holes, sufficient water to give each horse two gallons. On the fifth day we were more fortunate, and were able to give them each two gallons more, and on the sixth day (the 12th June, Sunday) found a large rock hole containing sufficient to give them five gallons each, which placed us in safety, as the water in longitude 126° 24' E. was only thirty-two miles distant. Continuing we reached the water on Tuesday, June 14th, and by observation found it to be in latitude 32° 14' 50" S., and longitude 126° 24' E., the variation of the compass being about 1° 6' easterly.

The country passed over between Point Culver and longitude 126° 24' E., was in many places beautifully grassed, level, without the slightest undulation, about 300 feet above the sea, and not very thickly wood. It improves to the northward, being clearer and more grassy, and the horizon to the north, in every place where I could get an extensive view, was as uniform and well-defined as that of the sea. On the route from Point Culver to longitude 126° 24' E., we were from twenty to twenty-five miles from the sea.

Recruiting ourselves and horses till the 30th, I took a flying trip to the northward. For the first twelve miles from the sea was through a dense and almost impenetrable scrub, when we reached the cliffs, and after ascending them we came into the same description of level country that we travelled over from Point Culver, save that this was more open and grassy, and became still clearer as we proceeded north, until, at our farthest point north, in latitude 31° 33' S., and longitude 126° 33' E., scarcely a tree was visible, and vast plains of grass and saltbush extended as far as the eye could reach in every direction. We found a little water for our horses in rock holes. Returning, we reached camp on June 22nd. On the 23rd we were engaged making preparations for a start for Eucla. In looking round camp, Tommy Windich found the shoulder-blade of a horse and two small pieces of leather belonging to a pack-saddle. The shoulder-blade is no doubt the remains of the horse Mr Eyre was obliged for kill for food at this spot.

On June 24th started for Eucla, carrying, as before, over thirty gallons of water, and walking in turns. On the 25th found on the top of the cliffs a large rock hole, containing sufficient water to give the horses as much as they required, and on the 26th were equally fortunate. From the 26th to the 30th we met with scarcely any water, and our horses appeared very distressed, more so as the weather was very warm. On the evening of the 30th, however, we were again fortunate enough to find a water-hole containing sufficient to give them six gallons each, and were again in safety, Eucla water being only thirty miles distant. On the morning of the 1st day of July we reached the cliffs, or Hampton Range (these cliffs recede from the sea in longitude 126° 12' E., and run along at the average distance of twelve or fifteen miles from the sea until they join it again at Wilson's Bluff, in longitude 129° E. They are very steep and rough, and water may generally be found in rock holes in the gorges. I, however, wished to keep further inland, and therefore did not follow them), and shortly afterwards we beheld the Wilson's Bluff and the Eucla sand-hills. Camped for the night near the Hampton Range, about five miles from Eucla Harbour, and on the 2nd July, on nearing the anchorage, discovered the schooner 'Adur' lying safely at anchor, which proved by no means the least pleasing feature to our little band of weary travellers. Camped on west side of Delisser sand-hills, and found water by digging.

The country passed over between longitude 126° 24' E., as a grazing country, far surpasses anything I have ever seen. There is nothing in the settled portions of Western Australia equal to it, either in extent or quality; but the absence of permanent water is the great drawback, and I do not think water would be procured by sinking, except at great depths, as the country is at least three hundred feet above the sea, and there is nothing to indicate water being within an easy depth from the surface. The country is very level, with scarcely any undulation, and becomes clearer as you proceed northward.

Since leaving Cape Arid I have not seen a gully or water-course of any description — a distance of 400 miles.

The route from longitude 126° 24' E. to Eucla was generally about thirty miles from the sea.

The natives met with appeared friendly and harmless; they are entirely destitute of clothing, and I think not very numerous.

Very little game exists along the route; a few kangaroos were seen, but no emus — an almost certain sign, I believe, of the scarcity of water.

The health of the party has been excellent; and I cannot speak too highly of the manner in which each member of the expedition has conducted himself, under circumstances often of privation and difficulty.

All our horses are also in splendid condition; and when I reflect how great were the sufferings of the only other Europeans who traversed this route, I cannot but thank Almighty God who has guarded and guided us in safety through such a waterless region, without the loss of even a single horse.

I am afraid I shall not be able to get far inland northward, unless we are favoured with rain. We have not had any rain since the end of April, and on that account our difficulties have been far greater than if it had been an ordinary wet season.

I intend despatching the 'Adur' for Fremantle to-morrow. The charter-party has been carried out entirely to my satisfaction. With the assistance of the crew of the 'Adur' I have repainted the Red and Black Beacons. The latter had been blown down; we, however, re-erected it firmly again. I have also erected a flagstaff, thirty feet high, near camp on west side of Delisser sand-hills, with a copper-plate nailed on it, with its position, my name, and that of the colony engraved on it.

We are now within 140 miles from the nearest Adelaide station. I will write to you as soon as I reach there. It will probably be a month from this date.

Trusting that the foregoing brief account of my proceedings, as leader of the expedition entrusted to my guidance, may meet with the approval of his Excellency the Governor,

I have, &c.,
JOHN FORREST,

Leader of Expedition to Eucla and Adelaide.

The Hon. the Colonial Secretary,
Perth, W.A.

Explorations in Australia (1875)

WILLIAM GOSSE

(1842–81)

English-born surveyor and explorer. Gosse, who was educated in Adelaide, joined the South Australian surveyor-general's department in 1859, rising to the position of deputy surveyor-general in 1875. Aiming for Perth, he led a party from Alice Springs in April 1873. Lack of water forced him to turn back in September, without reaching his destination. Although the expedition, which he summarises in this letter to George Woodroofe Goyder, the South Australian surveyor-general, was a failure, the maps from it contributed to the success of John Forrest's west–east crossing the following year.

GOSSE'S CENTRAL AND WESTERN
EXPLORING EXPEDITION

February 1st, 1874

Sir — I have the honor to enclose, for the information of the Honorable the Commissioner of Crown Lands and Immigration, diary and map of my exploration, also to report that leaving the Alice Springs, April 21st, with a party consisting of four white men, three Affghans, and a black boy, I travelled along the telegraph line to latitude 22°28′ S., about forty miles south of Central Mount Stuart.

From this point I followed the Reynolds Range about W.N.W. for forty-five miles; I was then obliged to turn S.W., passing a high bluff, piled by Major Warburton, and on to the western extremity of the MacDonnell Ranges (Giles's Mount Liebig).

Here I was compelled to turn south, crossing Mr Giles's track several times, the eastern arm of his Lake Amadeus, and on to a high hill, east of Mount Olga, which I named Ayers Rock (I have given a full account of this wonderful feature, in my diary). The country to this point is chiefly sandy soil, densely timbered with mulga (a name given to small trees found numerous in the interior of Australia, a species of genus acacia, belonging to the natural order leguminosæ), or stretches of spinifex sandhills. In the vicinity of the lake the sandhills are higher, and very few small patches of mulga, nothing fit for occupation. I found a spring at Ayer's Rock — the first permanent water seen since leaving Alice Springs, but the good country very limited, not more than thirty square miles.

Proceeding west and south-west, I passed nothing worthy of note, until I reached high ranges on the northern boundary of South Australia (the Mann). The waters here, as far as I could judge, had every appearance of being permanent, and the country equal to anything in the north. This strip, about eight miles wide, extends to the boundary of Western Australia, and is well adapted for stock. From here to my furthest point, latitude 26° 32' S., longitude 126° 59' east, the country is poor, getting worse as I advanced, until I got clear of all ranges, and into spinifex and sandhills, and dense mulga flats, destitute of water. I was reluctantly obliged to commence my return on September 22nd, retracing my track to where I first struck the Mann Ranges, then along the south side, the same rich flats still continuing. From here, going east, I made the high range seen from Ayers's Rock, and named the Musgrave. There is a greater extent of good country in these ranges, averaging about twenty miles in width, and 100 long, but the waters getting scarce towards the eastern end. In latitude 26° 9' S., longitude 132° 50' E, I struck the head of a large creek, which turned out to be the Alberga. This is very badly watered, indeed from the east end of the Musgrave Ranges to the telegraph line, there is scarcely a water to be depended upon. This must always be a great drawback to the occupation of the good country. I found upon reaching the telegraph line, that this had been an exceptionally dry season — waters that were considered permanent, having been dry for months. It is impossible to say what alteration a good fall of rain might make, but I do not think a practicable route will ever be found between the lower part of Western Australia, and the telegraph line. I pushed my exploration as far west as I could, and when I commenced my return had barely sufficient stores left to carry party to telegraph line.

I have the honor, &c.,

W. C. GOSSE,

Leader of C. & W. Exploring Expedition.

To the Surveyor-General.

Report and Diary of Mr. W. C. Gosse's Central and Western Exploring Expedition 1873 (1874)

PETER EGERTON WARBURTON

(1813–89)

English soldier and explorer. Warburton, who had previously explored parts of South Australia during his term of office as that colony's commissioner of police (1853–67), left Adelaide in September 1872 in charge of an expedition, financed by Thomas Elder and Walter Hughes, to explore from central Australia to Perth. After leaving Alice Springs in April 1873, Warburton and his men had to battle against harsh country, lack of water, extreme heat, and illness, and were forced to abandon their original goal. Had they not eaten some of their seventeen camels they would have perished. The bedraggled party finally reached Roebourne, in north-west Western Australia, in January 1874, becoming the first explorers to cross Australia from the centre to the west. Warburton made these distasteful comments in London in 1874, in an address to the Royal Geographical Society, which had awarded him its gold medal.

CAMELS

Another subject that perhaps may interest you is to be found in the camels. Most surely no other animal in creation could have carried us across. For hundreds of miles there was not a blade of grass, nothing that any animal, bullock, donkey, horse, could possibly feed upon; nothing but the tops of the bushes which the camels managed to browse. No animal but the camel could have served our turn. I say this with confidence, because every other animal which has been tried has failed, and this is the sixth expedition. These camels are most patient and easily managed, but it is generally requisite to have a master amongst them. There is one master, a bull-camel, who always establishes himself at the head of the party; and so long as he is in good spirits and able to move about, all the younger ones are kept in admirable order; but directly he falls sick, they become exceedingly troublesome. Amongst other misfortunes, we were unlucky enough to have our master-bull eat something that disagreed with him, and we had no medicine to give him except a chance bottle of mustard. It did not do him any good; but before we ourselves were aware that this master-bull was at all sick, the young bulls were all acquainted with it and were jumping about in most lively style. The necessity of having a comptroller, a President over the camels, will be apparent when I tell you that the trick the young ones have is to cut off two or three female camels and run them away as hard as they can; so that we were obliged to knee-halter them and tie them as tight as we could, or else we should have left our bones in the sand, because all our camels would have run away from us in little troops. However, they certainly behaved well to us when we did not give them the opportunity of doing the reverse.

Perhaps you would like to learn, too, what sort of eating they make. Unfortunately, we had to eat seven of them. I daresay when the animal is fat and well fed on oilcake and other things, it cannot be very bad; but when he has been worked to that extent that he is unable to stand, and is shot only because it would be a pity to leave him to rot, his meat is not very good, and it is interlaced with large sheets of parchment. He looks a very large animal, but there is very little meat on him. He is more bone than anything else; and I can assure you that of all the buckets of meat — for the bucket was our cooking-vessel — that we cooked when a camel was killed, never, in any single instance that I can remember, was there one single bubble of grease on the surface. The head is somewhat of a delicacy, and the feet are really very good, for his condition does not affect his feet very much. In our distress, however, we were obliged to eat him, inside and outside too; and his hide is pretty good when you cannot get anything else: but if anybody here has had the boldness to taste the contents of a carpenter's glue-pot, it comes to very much the same thing. We were compelled, by absolute starvation, to eat our last camel all but the hair — clean through from end to end; and after the bones had been lying in the sand for some days, they were broken up to make broth of, and, in the course of a short time, I don't think any of the animal was to be seen. The advantage of the camel is, that he can work until he cannot work any longer, and then you can eat him.

Perhaps one of our greatest misfortunes connected with the camels was, that a good many of them were struck with the land-wind at night in the loins, so that when we got up at three or four o'clock in the morning it was reported that this camel or that camel could not move. Of course every camel we lost was a reduction — and a very considerable one — in the chance of our saving our lives; and, therefore, such an accident would be a thing to be guarded against in future by covering the camels. When it was too late we took the precaution; but many of our camels were dead or ruined before we knew anything at all about it. No Australian bushman ever thinks himself badly off if he has a quart pot, a blanket for himself, a pair of hobbles for his horse, and a little flour, tea, sugar, and tobacco for provisions. Our lives depended on the welfare of the camels, and whenever a camel even looked sick our march was delayed; for, though hunger pressed us on, we were compelled to sit down until that camel got well — then our provisions were consumed to a considerable extent in idleness on our part waiting to restore the camels, because we dared not go on while the camel was ailing. I took six months' provisions with me, but that turned out to be too little, though I do not think I am much to blame for it, because my calculations were based on a certain distance, and I allowed for detentions and digressions; but the detentions were so frequent and great that we ran short of provisions, and at the end we had no flour, no tea, no sugar. The only thing we had was the miserable meat scraped off the bones of a half-dead camel, and put on the bushes and dried in the sun. We had that, and nothing whatever with it. It will, therefore, be readily understood that we did not grow fat or gain much strength. Whilst the camels were tolerably good we were able to travel during the daytime, and therefore, of course, had the use of our eyes and the chance of finding water by running up native tracks; but when the summer began, that is, about September — when our provisions ran short and our camels began to fail — the heat became so excessive that we dared not travel through the day. The camels would have been knocked up in the course of two days, and we would have been left in the desert. We were therefore compelled to travel in the dark, when it was a little cooler, and the consequence was, that we were cut off from our chance of finding water during our march. When we came to our halt for the day the camels were so tired that we were unable to go out and look about us.

Proceedings of the Royal Geographical Society, vol. XIX, 1874–75 (1875)

―――

JULES VERNE
(1828–1905)

French novelist. Warburton's trials and tribulations inspired a particularly melodramatic novel by Verne, entitled Mistress Branican *(1892). An American beauty of Mexican descent, Dolly Branican is married to Captain John Branican, who is lost at sea in 1875. In 1890, at the age of 37, she sets off in search of her long-lost husband, now believed to be being held captive by Aborigines. Her party heads west from Alice Springs in late October, following Warburton's route. A couple of chapters of the book are devoted to extracts from her expedition journal, which are said to reveal her 'ardent soul, her firmness under trial, her unshakable and never-despairing tenacity, even at the moment when the greater part of her companions despaired around her'.*

AN ENTRY FROM DOLLY BRANICAN'S JOURNAL

14th February — Eleven days have passed during which we have had but two hours' rain. We could hardly replenish our kegs after the men had had enough to satisfy their thirst, and the animals had taken enough for their store. Under these circumstances we have reached Emily Spring, which is quite dry. Our camels are exhausted; Jos Meritt does not know what to do to get his camel along. He will not strike it, however, and merely appeals to its feelings. I heard him say, —

'Look here, you poor brute, if you are in pain, at least you have no grief!'

But the poor brute did not seem to understand the distinction.

We will resume our journey more uneasy than we have ever been.

Two camels are sick. They are crawling along, and will not be able to last. The provisions carried by the pack camel have been shifted on to a saddle camel.

Luckily the male camel, ridden by Tom Marix, has kept its strength up to now. Without him, the others, more particularly the females, would disband, and nothing would stop them.

We have found it necessary to leave behind the two which fell sick. To leave them to die of hunger and thirst, a prey to a long agony, would have been more inhuman than to end their misery at a blow.

The caravan journeys on and turns round a sand-hill. There are two reports. Tom Marix returns to rejoin us, and the journey continues.

What is more alarming is that the health of two of our people gives us much uneasiness. They have been seized with fever, and we have dosed them well with sulphate of quinine, with which the medicine-chest is well supplied. But a burning thirst devours them. Our store of water is exhausted, and nothing indicates that we are in the proximity of a spring.

The invalids are on their backs on two camels which their companions lead by the hand. Man cannot be left behind like camels. We must look after them; it is our duty, and we will not fail in it. But this pitiless temperature is gradually devouring them.

Those of us who stand fatigue best, who can bear excessive heat without suffering, are the blacks of our escort.

But though they have less to bear, their discontent increases daily. In vain Tom Marix busies himself in tranquillizing them. The most excited keep apart when we halt, and talk together, and the signs of an approaching revolt are only too evident.

During the 21st, all, with one accord, refused to continue the journey to the north-west, giving as a reason that they were dying of thirst. The reason was only too well founded. For twelve hours there had not been a single drop of water in our kegs. We are reduced to alcoholic drinks, the effect of which is deplorable, as they get into our heads.

I had to personally intervene among these obstinate natives. I had to make them understand that to stop under such conditions was not the way to put an end to their sufferings.

'What we want,' said one of them, 'is to go back.'

'Back? Where to?'

'To Mary Spring.'

'To Mary Spring!' I answered, 'there is no water there, and you know it.'

'If there is no water at Mary Spring,' replied the black, 'we may find it a little further up, near Mount Wilson, in the direction of Sturt Creek.'

I looked at Tom Marix. He went to look at the special map of the Great Sandy Desert. We consulted it. In fact, north of Mary Spring there is a somewhat important watercourse which might not perhaps be entirely dry. But how could the native have known of the existence of this watercourse? I interrogated him on the subject. He hesitated at first, and at last told me Mr Burker had spoken to him about it. It was from him that the proposition of heading for Sturt Creek had come.

I am much annoyed that Len Burker has had the imprudence — was it only imprudence? — to instigate a part of the escort to return towards the east. It will not only lead to delay, but to a serious modification of our route, which will take us a long way from Fitzroy River.

I told him what I thought rather strongly.

'What would you have, Dolly?' he replied. 'Better submit to delays and go a little way round, than to obstinately follow a road where there are no wells.'

'In that case, Mr Burker,' said Zach Fren, sharply, 'you should have spoken to Mrs Branican, and not to the blacks.'

'You are carrying on with the blacks in such a way,' said Tom Marix, 'that I have no control over them. Are you in command of them, Mr Burker or am I?'

'I think that observation is rather unseemly, Tom Marix,' said Len Burker.

'Unseemly or not, it is justified by your proceedings, sir, and you would do well to think over it.'

'I take orders from nobody here but from Mrs Branican — '

'Be it so, Len Burker,' I replied; 'but for the future, if you have any observations to make, I beg you will make them to me and not to others.'

'Mrs Branican,' said Godfrey, 'shall I go on in advance of the caravan in search of a well? I am sure to find one.'

'A well without water!' muttered Len Burker, shrugging his shoulders.

I can easily imagine what Jane must have suffered as she heard this discussion. Her husband's conduct, which was so prejudicial to the good feeling which ought to exist among our people might be the cause of serious difficulty. I had to support Tom Marix in obtaining the consent of the blacks not to persevere in their intention of returning to the rear. We succeeded after considerable difficulty. But they declared that if we did not find water in twenty-four hours, they would return to Mary Spring in order to reach Sturt Creek.

Mistress Branican (1892)

ERNEST GILES

(1835–97)

English-born explorer. After exploring in central Australia in 1872, Giles became obsessed with the idea of crossing the interior from the centre to the west. He tried to do so in 1873–74, but failed. During this expedition one of his men died in, and as a result gave his name to, Gibson's Desert. Giles, who later claimed to be 'the last of the Australian explorers', finally crossed from east to west in 1875, and back again the following year, using camels provided by Thomas Elder. He is better known for his journals, which contain some very purple prose, than for his exploits. This piece, written in 1874, is one of his more restrained pieces of writing.

THE RUINED RAMPART

Friday, 13th March — Thermometer last night 90°, this morning 80°; at two a.m. this morning we heard the slight rumblings of thunder and saw one or two flashes of lighting, which cooled the air a little; there was very fine grass here, and the horses stayed well. At starting we continued on up this creek, which appeared to rise in some low hills to the south, though it wound about so much, that it was only by travelling we found it went more easterly towards a peculiar ridge, upon whose top was a fanciful looking broken wall or rampart with a little pinnacle on one side; the creek came from the low hills near the foot of those higher ones, and when nearly abreast of the little pinnacle we found some water in the creek-bed, which now became very stony; the water was not very good, but the horses drank it with avidity. Above this we soon got some very good water in rocks and sand; I called this queer-looking wall 'The Ruined Rampart.' There was a large quantity of greenish and ammonia-tasting water in some of the rock-holes here, some saltish, others nearly putrid; one or two ducks flew up from these strange ponds. We remained here a couple of hours. There was an overhanging ledge or cave, which gave us good shade, the morning being very hot. We left this singular place, where I believe a good supply of water is always to be obtained, at twelve o'clock, first calling it 'MacBain's Springs,' after James MacBain, Esq., MLA, of Toorak, a subscriber to the fund for my expedition. When we left, the thermometer stood at 102°; in the afternoon it was much hotter. On leaving here we continued to follow up the creek; it took its rise in a mass of broken tablelands, we still having the high walls of the Petermann-Range to the north and very close to us. Our course was now a few degrees to the south of east; in five miles we got over the water-shed and descended the rough bed of another creek running to the eastward; it also had some very queer water in it, being pink, green and blue; there were a few ducks here also, and some good water was obtained by scratching in the sand. I called these 'Harry Hull's Springs,' after my sister's step-son, Mr Harry Hull, jun., of St Kilda; and the creek I named after him also. Following it down it traversed a fine piece of open grassy country, which was very pretty and excellent travelling ground. This was a very park-like piece of scenery. This creek joined another, which we struck in a short distance. The new creek was of enormous size, as far as width is concerned; it came from the lower hills to the south, and ran north, where the main ranges parted to allow its passage. The natives were burning the country some distance down the creek. Where on earth can it go to? No doubt water exists in plenty up at its head, but there was none where we struck it. I called this 'The Hull,' after the Hon. Wm. Hull, of St Kilda, my brother-in-law's father, and a subscriber to the fund for my expedition. The main range now ran on in more disconnected portions than formerly, whose general direction was 25° south of east; we still had a low mass of hills to the south, but they were some miles away. We continued on, travelling under the lea of the main range until night, when we camped without water, having travelled 25 miles from the Ruined Rampart. A few miles before we came to camp we passed a high cone in an isolated range, which formed the eastern part of a valley or pass through which Hull's Creek runs to the north; I called this 'Mount Curdie,' and the range of which it is the highest point, 'Curdie's Range,' after Dr Daniel Curdie, MA, of Camperdown, a subscriber to the fund for my expedition.

Geographic Travels in Central Australia from 1872 to 1874 (1875)

———

RAY ERICKSEN
(1919–)

Australian academic and writer. After serving in the army during the Second World War, Ericksen worked at the University of Melbourne for many years (1947–67, 1969), first as an historian and later as an administrator. He travelled alone, by Land Rover, through the western interior from March to September 1967, partly following in the tracks of Ernest Giles. These reflections are taken from his very personal account of that trip, West of Centre: A Journey of Discovery into the Heartland of Australia *(1972). Ericksen later wrote a prize-winning biography entitled* Ernest Giles: Explorer and Traveller 1835–1897 *(1978).*

'SACRED PLACES'

At the Docker, there is a dramatic breach in the main range. The river emerges through the deep cleft of Livingstone Pass, and on the far side the creeks which form the river are separate. One of them curls from the east along the mountain's foot past a feature which Giles named the Ruined Rampart. It is a hard way of creek bed and high-shouldered plain, through scattered timber and tangled herbage and across steep water channels, dry and rough. I drove and walked far enough to get a close look at this place of caves and bulges, jagged and cratered; but I did not enter it.

I felt a strong sense of unease, as if the place were still peopled and intrusion would be resented. I was too burdened just then with the great sadness of what we have done to those who a short time ago used to celebrate here their rites and ceremonies, who built their mythology on the wonders around them, and peopled the rocks with their spirits; too recently exposed to suburban chit-chat in the camping ground at Ayers Rock, and to the unawareness of mystery in those who sight-see the cathedral home of the Pitjandjara as they might a sterile modern building. We descend on these sacred places like illiterate vandals rampaging through a great library, without respect for what we cannot share and with brash impatience. Later, just a little later, when the untended spirits have gone and the grief of the old men locked in the towns has been stilled, it will matter less if we subject inorganic rock and sand to our quite different scrutiny and use. But not yet. It is still too soon.

A few months earlier, in such a place, I would not have been so inhibited, nor would my recurring vision of our future have been so bleakly pessimistic. These were personal reactions, and it is likely that most other men might follow much the same route as mine and not be troubled. Yet there seemed to be a sufficient connection between my experience in travel and the rather gloomy attitudes I developed to suggest that at least some others might gather similar impressions if they travelled under comparable conditions.

It would be difficult to spend time in some of these regions and not feel growing respect and admiration for a people who had found a way to support life in them; who knew the land in all its harsh reality yet brought it dancing to life in their legends; who built a social system which blended intricate complexity with great simplicity; who balanced terror, cruelty and aggression with gentleness, laughter and wonder as successfully as most human societies have managed to do. To find these regions now unpeopled, and to see the apparent half-life of the lost ones around the white man's places, makes it hard not to feel shame at the blind arrogance with which we assumed that because they were different they were inferior; or guilt and anger at the brutality with which we destroyed them; or grief and despair at the near hopelessness of the present situation.

It would also be difficult to traverse wide areas of untouched country and not fear what we might do to it and not curse the devastation we have wrought in adjacent parts. To travel alone is in itself an act of separation from one's fellows, and the peculiar quality of the bush in these inland regions further encourages one's sense of alienation. The threats that it holds — distance, heat, aridity — are all of a generalised kind. There is no specific menace in the land itself nor in the plants that clothe it nor in the creatures that inhabit it. One can travel without fear; camp at night and know that there is no danger in the life around. And so, because in a strange way gentleness matches harshness, it is easy in these regions to come to appreciate and enjoy their beauty and their strength and their great variety, and to value and respect them for what they are. And because of that it is easy to be drawn into siding with the land against one's fellows in the conflict which we precipitate by our uncaring destruction.

West of Centre (1972)

———

DAVID CARNEGIE

(1871–1900)

British engineer and explorer. After arriving in gold-rush Coolgardie in 1892, Carnegie, the son of the 6th earl of Southesk, worked in various mines for eighteen months, and made two commissioned prospecting expeditions for a pastoral company (1894–95). Since described as a 'thoroughly professional explorer', despite his deplorable treatment of Aborigines, Carnegie then crossed Western Australia from south to north and back in 1896–97, looking for gold and a possible stock route from the Kimberley area to Coolgardie. On completion of his outward journey, in December 1896, Carnegie received gloomy news about the Calvert Scientific Exploring Expedition, led by Larry Wells, as he recalls in this chapter of his book Spinifex and Sand *(1898). Several days earlier, a member of Carnegie's own party, Charlie Stansmore, had accidentally shot himself dead. Although Carnegie survived the rigours of the Australian desert, he also died prematurely, killed by a poisoned arrow in northern Nigeria in 1900.*

'WELLS EXPLORING EXPEDITION'

The first news that we heard was of the disaster that the expedition under Mr L. A. Wells had met with. Two of his party were missing, and it was feared that they had met with some serious mishap. Fortunately Hall's Creek can boast of telegraphic communication with Derby and Wyndham on the coast, and from thence to Perth; so that I lost no time in letting Wells know of our arrival, that we had seen no traces of the lost men, and that we were ready to do whatever he, who knew all particulars of the matter, should think best. When I told Breaden that I had put my camels and party at Wells's disposal, he said at once that he was ready to go, but that in his opinion the camels were not fit to do another week's journey; Godfrey, too, was as ready. Indeed it would have been strange if we, who had so lately come through the desert, and knew its dangers, had not been eager to help the poor fellows in distress, although from the first we were morally certain there could be no hope for them; the only theory compatible with their being still alive, was that they were camped at some water easy of access, and were waiting for relief, keeping themselves from starvation by eating camel-flesh.

For many reasons, that need not be gone into, it was thought best by the promoters of the expedition in Adelaide that we should remain where we were; and, thanking me very heartily for our proffered assistance, they assured me they would be very glad to avail themselves of it should the search-parties already in the field meet with no success. Had we felt any hope whatever of the men being alive we should certainly have started off then and there; since, however, the chances of finding any but dead men were so very infinitesimal, I agreed to wait and to put myself at their command for a given time. It will be as well to give here a short account, as gathered from letters from Wells and others to the newspapers, of the unfortunate expedition.

This expedition, fitted out partly by the Royal Geographical Society, South Australia, and partly by a Mr Calvert, was under command of L. A. Wells, who was surveyor to the Elder Expedition (1891–92). The party, besides the leader, consisted of his cousin, C. F. Wells, G. A. Keartland, G. L. Jones, another white man as cook, two Afghans, and one black-boy, with twenty-five camels. The objects of this expedition were much the same as those of my own, viz., to ascertain the nature of the country still unexplored in the central portions of West Australia, 'hopes being entertained of the possibility of opening up a valuable stock route from the Northern Territory to the West Australian Goldfields, and of discovering much auriferous country' (vide *Adelaide Observer*, June 6, 1896). A collection of the flora and fauna was to be made, as well as a map of the country passed through. The expedition started from Cue, Murchison district, left civilisation at Lake Way, and travelled in a North-Easterly direction from there to Lake Augusta, thence in a Northerly direction past Joanna Springs to the Fitzroy River. Thus their course was almost parallel to our upgoing journey, and some 150 to 200 miles to the westward, nearer the coast. The class of country encountered was similar to that already described by me — that is sand, undulating and in ridges.

A well, since called 'Separation Well,' was found in long. 123° 53', lat. 22° 51'. At this point the expedition split up: Charles Wells and G. L. Jones, with three camels, were to make a flying trip ninety miles to the Westward; then, turning North-East, were to cut the tracks of the main party, who were to travel nearly due North.

The rendezvous was fixed at or near Joanna Springs — which place, however, the leader failed to find (until some months afterwards, when he proved them to have been placed on the chart some eighteen miles too far West by Colonel Warburton in 1873, who in his diary doubts the accuracy of the position assigned to the spring by himself, and remarks, 'What matter in such country as this?'). When the latitude of the spring was reached, about a day and a half was spent in searching to the east and west without result. A native smoke was seen to the eastward, but the leader failed to reach it.

The camels were on the brink of collapse, many had already collapsed, and the leader considered that by further search for the spring he would be bringing almost certain death on the whole party. Therefore, abandoning all collections, and in fact everything except just enough to keep him and his companions alive, he pushed on for the Fitzroy River — travelling by night and camping in the day — a distance of 170 miles. They arrived at the Fitzroy River after the greatest difficulties, with one bucket of water left, and only two camels fit to carry even the lightest packs.

The flying party were daily expected, for the arrangement had been that, failing a meeting at Joanna Springs, both parties were to push on to the Fitzroy. Days passed, however, and no flying party appeared.

Before long fears as to their safety began to grow, and Mr Wells made numerous attempts to return on his tracks. The heat, however, was too much for his camels, and he was unable to penetrate to any distance. Mr Rudall in the meantime, who had been surveying in the

Nor'-West, was despatched by the Western Australian Government to make a search from the West. He had a good base in the Oakover River, and pushed out as far as Separation Well. Nothing, however, came of his gallant efforts, for he was misled, not only by lying natives, but by the tracks of camels and men, which subsequently turned out to be those of prospectors. His journey, however, had many useful results, for he discovered a new creek running out into the desert (Rudall River), and the existence of auriferous country north of the Ophthalmia Range, besides confirming Gregory's account of the country East of the Oakover.

It was not until April, 1897, that Mr Wells found the bodies of his cousin, Charles Wells, and George Jones. From their diaries (so much of them at least as was published) the dreadful tale of suffering can be traced. It appears that on leaving the main party they travelled westward as directed, and started to turn North-East to cut the tracks of the others. Before many miles on the fresh course, however, they for some reason changed their minds and retraced their steps to Separation Well. From this point they started to follow the main party, but before long they seem to have become sick and exhausted, and the camels to show signs of collapse. Later we read that, exhausted from heat, hardship, and thirst, they lay down, each in the scanty shade of a gum tree; that the camels wandered away too far for them to follow; efforts to recover the stragglers only ended in their falling faint to the ground, and so, deserted by their means of transport, without water, without hope, these two poor fellows laid down to die, and added their names to the long roll of brave but unfortunate men whose lives have been claimed by the wild bush of Australia.

What a death! Alone in that vast sea of sand — hundreds of miles from family or friends — alone absolutely! not a sign of life around them — no bird or beast to tell them that life existed for any — no sound to break the stillness of that ghastly wilderness — no green grass or trees to relieve the monotony of the sand — nothing but the eternal spinifex and a few shrunken stems of trees that have been — no shade from the burning sun — above them the clear sky only clouded by death! slow, cruel death, and yet in their stout hearts love and courage! Poor fellows! they died like men, with a message written by dying fingers for those they left to mourn them — a message full of affection, expressing no fear of death, but perfect faith in God. So might all mothers be content to see their sons die — when their time comes.

They had died, it appears, too soon for any aid to have reached them. Even had Mr Wells been able to turn back on his tracks at once on arrival at the Fitzroy, it is doubtful if he could have been in time to give any help to his suffering comrades.

The bodies were taken to Adelaide, where the whole country joined in doing honour to the dead.

Spinifex and Sand (1898)

LOUIS DE ROUGEMONT

(1847–1921)

Swiss-born hoaxer. Controversy raged over de Rougemont's claims, made in The Adventures of Louis de Rougemont: As Told by Himself *(1899), originally serialised in* Wide World Magazine *in 1897–98, that he had lived among Australian Aborigines for some thirty years, after having been shipwrecked. Critics, including genuine explorer David Carnegie, soon exposed de Rougemont as a fraud. He was really Henri Louis Grin, who had lived in much more mundane circumstances in Australia between 1875 and 1897. According to the author of his* Australian Dictionary of Biography *entry, his work is 'essentially the plausible concoction of a colonial Munchausen [sic]'. Barely plausible. This incident, in which de Rougemont's fictitious Aboriginal wife Yamba plays a role, is one of his less dramatic adventures.*

'A FIGHT WITH AN ALLIGATOR'

One day I decided to go and explore one of the islands that studded Cambridge Gulf, in search of a kind of shell mud-fish which I was very partial to. I also wanted to make the acquaintance of the bats or flying foxes I had seen rising in clouds every evening at sunset. I required the skins of these curious creatures for sandals. This would perhaps be a year after my advent among the blacks. As usual, Yamba was my only companion, and we soon reached a likely island. As I could find no suitable place for landing, I turned the canoe up a small creek. From this course, however, my companion strongly dissuaded me. Into the creek, nevertheless, we went, and when I saw it was a hopeless *impasse*, I scrambled ashore and waded through five inches or six inches of mud. The little island was densely covered with luxuriant tropical vegetation, the mangroves coming right down to the water's edge; so that

I had actually to force my way through them to gain the top of the bank. I then entered a very narrow track through the forest, the bush on both sides being so dense as to resemble an impenetrable wall or dense hedge. It is necessary to bear this in mind to realise what followed. I had not gone many yards along this track, when I was horrified to see, right in front of me, an enormous alligator! This great reptile was shuffling along down the path towards me, evidently making for the water, and it not only blocked my advance, but also necessitated my immediate retreat. The moment the brute caught sight of me he stopped, and began snapping his jaws viciously. I confess I was quite nonplussed for the moment as to how best to commence the attack upon this unexpected visitor. It was impossible for me to get round him in any way, on account of the dense bush on either side of the narrow forest track. I decided, however, to make a bold dash for victory, having always in mind the prestige that was so necessary to my existence among the blacks. I therefore walked straight up to the evil-looking monster; then, taking a short run, I leaped high into the air, shot over his head, and landed on his scaly back, at the same time giving a tremendous yell in order to attract Yamba, whom I had left in charge of the boat.

The moment I landed on his back I struck the alligator with all my force with my tomahawk, on what I considered the most vulnerable part of his head. So powerful was my stroke, that I found to my dismay that I could not get the weapon out of his head again. While I was in this extraordinary situation — standing on the back of an enormous alligator, and tugging at my tomahawk, embedded in its head — Yamba came rushing up the path, carrying one of the paddles, which, without a moment's hesitation, she thrust down the alligator's throat as he turned to snap at her. She immediately let go her hold and retreated. The alligator tried to follow her, but the shaft of the paddle caught among some tree trunks and stuck. In this way the monster was prevented from moving his head, either backwards or forwards, and then, drawing my stiletto, I blinded him in both eyes, afterwards finishing him leisurely with my tomahawk, when at length I managed to release it. Yamba was immensely proud of me after this achievement, and when we returned to the mainland she gave her tribesmen a graphic account of my gallantry and bravery. But she always did this. She was my advance agent and bill-poster, so to say. I found in going into a new country that my fame had preceded me; and I must say this was most convenient and useful in obtaining hospitality, concessions, and assistance generally. The part I had played in connection with the death of the two whales had already earned for me the admiration of the blacks — not only in my own tribe, but all over the adjacent country. And after this encounter with the alligator they looked upon me as a very great and powerful personage indeed. We did not bring the dead monster back with us, but next day a number of the blacks went over with their catamarans, and towed the reptile back to the mainland, where it was viewed with open-mouthed amazement by crowds of admiring natives. So great was the estimation in which my prowess was held, that little scraps of the dead alligator were distributed (as relics, presumably) among the tribes throughout the whole of the surrounding country. Singularly enough this last achievement of mine was considered much more commendable than the killing of the whale, for the simple reason that it sometimes happened they caught a whale themselves stranded on the beach; whereas the killing of an alligator with their primitive weapons was a feat never attempted. They chanted praises in my honour at night, and wherever I moved, my performances with the whales and alligator were always the first things to be sung. Nor did I attempt to depreciate my achievements; on the contrary, I exaggerated the facts as much as I possibly could. I described to them how I had fought and killed the whale with my stiletto in spite of the fact that the monster had smashed my boat. I told them that I was not afraid of facing anything single-handed, and I even went so far as to allege that I was good enough to go out against a nation! My whole object was to impress this people with my imaginary greatness, and I constantly made them marvel at my prowess with the bow and arrow. The fact of my being able to bring down a bird on the wing was nothing more nor less than a miracle to them. I was given the name of 'Winnimah' by these people, because my arrows sped like lightning. Six of the alligator's teeth I took for myself, and made them into a circlet which I wore round my head.

The Adventures of Louis de Rougemont: As Told by Himself (1899)

─────

ROBYN DAVIDSON
(1950–)

Australian adventurer. Queensland-born Davidson completed an epic solo trek with four camels, across the western half of the Australian continent, in 1977. Starting at Glen Helen, west of Alice Springs, and ending at Hamelin

*Rock on the Western Australian coast, she covered some 2700 kilometres on
her travels. In this extract from her best-selling account of the trip,* Tracks
(1980), she reflects on her changing relationship with the land.

'CAUSE AND EFFECT'

Throughout the trip I had been gaining an awareness and an understanding of the earth as I learnt how to depend on it. The openness and
emptiness which had at first threatened me were now a comfort which
allowed my sense of freedom and joyful aimlessness to grow. This sense
of space works deep in the Australian collective consciousness. It is
frightening and most of the people huddle around the eastern seaboard
where life is easy and space a graspable concept, but it produces a sense
of potential and possibility nevertheless that may not exist now in any
European country. It will not be long, however, before the land is con-
quered, fenced up and beaten into submission. But here, here it was
free, unspoilt and seemingly indestructible.

And as I walked through that country, I was becoming involved
with it in a most intense and yet not fully conscious way. The motions
and patterns and connections of things became apparent on a gut level.
I didn't just see the animal tracks, I knew them. I didn't just see the
bird, I knew it in relationship to its actions and effects. My
environment began to teach me about itself without my full awareness
of the process. It became an animate being of which I was a part. The
only way I can describe how the process occurred is to give an example:
I would see a beetle's tracks in the sand. What once would have been
merely a pretty visual design with few associations attached, now
became a sign which produced in me instantaneous associations — the
type of beetle, which direction it was going in and why, when it made
the tracks, who its predators were. Having been taught some
rudimentary knowledge of the pattern of things at the beginning of
the trip, I now had enough to provide a structure in which I could
learn to learn. A new plant would appear and I would recognize it
immediately because I could perceive its association with other plants
and animals in the overall pattern, its place. I would recognize and
know the plant without naming it or studying it away from its
environment. What was once a thing that merely existed became
something that everything else acted upon and had a relationship with
and vice versa. In picking up a rock I could no longer simply say, 'This
is a rock,' I could now say, 'This is part of a net,' or closer, 'This, which
everything acts upon, acts.' When this way of thinking became too

ordinary for me, I too became lost in the net and the boundaries of myself stretched out for ever. In the beginning I had known at some level that this could happen. It had frightened me then. I had seen it as a chaotic principle and I fought it tooth and nail. I had given myself the structures of habit and routine with which to fortify myself and these were very necessary at the time. Because if you are fragmented and uncertain it is terrifying to find the boundaries of yourself melt. Survival in a desert, then, requires that you lose this fragmentation, and fast. It is not a mystical experience, or rather, it is dangerous to attach these sorts of words to it. They are too hackneyed and prone to misinterpretation. It is something that happens, that's all. Cause and effect. In different places, survival requires different things, based on the environment. Capacity for survival may be the ability to be changed by environment.

Changing to this view of reality had been a long hard struggle against the old conditioning. Not that it was a conscious battle, rather it was being forced on me and I could either accept it or reject it. In rejecting it I had almost gone over the edge. The person inside whom I had previously relied on for survival had, out here and in a different circumstance, become the enemy. This internal warring had almost sent me around the bend. The intellectual and critical faculties did everything they could think of to keep the boundaries there. They dredged up memory. They became obsessed with time and measurement. But they were having to take second place, because they simply were no longer necessary. The subconscious mind became much more active and important. And this in the form of dreams, feelings. A growing awareness of the character of a particular place, whether it was a good place to be with a calming influence, or whether it gave me the creeps. And this all linked up with the Aboriginal reality, their vision of the world as being something they could never be separate from, which showed in their language. In Pitjantjara and, I suspect, all other Aboriginal languages, there is no word for 'exist'. Everything in the universe is in constant interaction with everything else. You cannot say, this is a rock. You can only say, there sits, leans, stands, falls over, lies down, a rock.

The self did not seem to be an entity living somewhere inside the skull, but a reaction between mind and stimulus. And when the stimulus was non-social, the self had a hard time defining its essence and realizing its dimensions. The self in a desert becomes more and more like the desert. It has to, to survive. It becomes limitless, with its roots more in the subconscious than the conscious — it gets stripped of nonmeaningful habits and becomes more concerned with realities related to survival. But as is its nature, it desperately wants to assimilate and make sense of the information it receives, which in a desert is almost always going to be translated into the language of mysticism.

What I'm trying to say is, when you walk on, sleep on, stand on, defecate on, wallow in, get covered in, and eat the dirt around you, and when there is no one to remind you what society's rules are, and nothing to keep you linked to that society, you had better be prepared for some startling changes. And just as Aborigines seem to be in perfect rapport with themselves and their country, so the embryonic beginnings of that rapport were happening to me. I loved it.

Tracks (1980)

ROBERT DREWE

(1943–   )

Australian writer. There have been a number of contenders for the title of 'the last explorer', ranging from Ernest Giles to Robyn Davidson. My first choice is Drewe's fictitious character.

'THE LAST EXPLORER'

The last explorer wears green pyjamas, embossed with tiny heraldic shields, buttoned up to his chin. A pink coverlet is drawn up to his chest.

From his bed at the end of the ward he can see the Indian Ocean, choppy and blue, outside his window. He never learned to swim. The view of the sea is a favour they have given him, but he does not appreciate it.

Henry Ford also did not like the sea, a point he mentioned during their meeting in Detroit. Hence Ford's concentration on land transport.

The only 'ship' he himself appreciates is the 'ship of the desert' — the camel. The camel is the explorer's best friend, as long as you treat him fairly. You are mad to tease a camel. He can kill you by sitting on you. The chestbone takes the full weight of the camel's body when he squats. The chestbone is the camel's instrument of death.

He addressed the British on camels in 1933. The wireless station was in Hampstead. The publicity woman took him to lunch afterwards. The broadcast the British particularly lapped up was the one on the virtues of camels, especially their sense of humour. Camels like a joke. He told them about the camel which disgorged its entire half-digested meal over him, from head to waist, outside Tennant Creek. And that a camel never opens a gate, he just sits on it.

Miss Teasdale appreciated his camel anecdotes both during the broadcast and over lunch.

Funny, he told her, he'd used a motor for his first expedition in 1923, but after that he used camels. He switched to camels because they were slower. The slowness made them better for mineral surveying. In a motor you might ride right over something interesting without seeing it. Swaying along on a camel you could see a reef, some interesting feature, quite readily.

The wireless station played camel sound-effects from a gramophone record. The camel noises punctuating his talk included bells, bazaar bartering and guttural exclamations in Arabic. Miss Teasdale said the British listening public wouldn't know the difference.

The last explorer's body makes hardly a lump under the covers. Against a pile of pillows his big pale, strong-jawed head seems disembodied. He removes a hand from under the bedclothes to slowly rub his eyes. They overdid the sleeping drug again last night.

It is awkward being here.

He thought he would be out of here within twenty-four hours.

He has twenty-three lines in *Who's Who*. 'Explorer, broadcaster, author, Fellow of the Royal Geographical Society ... ' A life of luck and action encapsulated in a paragraph. He wore a Colt .38 on his belt. He forbade his white men to take their revolvers off their gunbelts. Better safe than sorry.

In London both times he wore a double-breasted suit and his Royal Navy Air Service tie from fighting with the White Russians against the Reds in 1917. He cut a dash.

He was popular with the Fleet Street boys with his demonstration of Aboriginal sign language and how to make fires in Hampstead with sticks. Miss Teasdale kindly arranged the photographic sessions and afterwards they went off to the Dorchester and discussed the desert.

She asked enthusiastic questions about risks and deprivation. An understanding of man's inner resources was not beyond her.

Grace would not face the desert.

Grace desired the coast; it was a mistake. A house facing the sea, looking back towards England, was her wish. She refused to turn her back on the coast.

The house on the hill at Cottesloe was always windy because she had to face the ocean. For five years the sea-breeze howled through the pines and slammed the doors. A small dugite crawled across the lawn from the golf links. While Grace swooned on the buffalo grass he cracked its back like a whip.

Captain Scott-Bowdler was never optimistic about their chances. He couldn't visualise his daughter as a West Australian. Night after night Grace sat on the verandah facing the ocean and writing letters home.

On one expedition he rode camels from Alice Springs to Laverton on a nine-month nickel survey. He had his affinity for the desert and two good men under him. Purposely they travelled slowly and allowed themselves to get three months behind, spinning out their rations with bush tucker. They relied on themselves and their bushcraft. When they finally reached Laverton they circled the town on their camels for two days. They didn't want to come in.

Grace was not sitting on the verandah, she was two months gone on the *Stratheden*. The opal he found for her at Lightning Ridge was on the dresser with her front door key.

There was a shipping list cut from the *West Australian* with the *Stratheden*'s departure time circled. The cutting was yellow by then and the *Stratheden* well and truly berthed and unloaded at Southampton.

It was the old *Oakland* he caught to San Francisco, then the train from Oakland to Detroit via Chicago.

It was true what they said about Henry Ford being as tight as a fish's rectum.

Ford gave him coffee and one fig newton and listened intently to his tale. He said, 'You're a very fine and ambitious young man,' shook his hand again and kept his wallet in his pocket.

So he travelled on to Washington and sold his photographs and story to the National Geographic Society for $150, big money in those days.

The Royal Geographic Society was also generous in spirit. In London they gave a special dinner for him, the youngest man ever to read a paper to the Society, and Captain Scott-Bowdler introduced him to Grace. This was after his first expedition when he crossed the continent from east to west, three thousand miles from Winton, Queensland, to Broome, Western Australia.

For transport he chose a ten-year-old Model-T Ford which cost him £50. Because of the climate and terrain he replaced its wooden wheels with metal ones. He put in a magneto because the coils were dodgy. He met a man in a pub with £4/1/3 and made him an expedition partner. They crossed the desert on £8/13/2 and arrived in Broome ten months later, where he sold the Ford for £100.

His epic trip would surely earn him a fortune from the Ford Company. He travelled to America and gained an audience with the founder. He had a manila folder containing suggestions for advertising and promotion and his fig newton vanished in one eager bite.

Henry Ford was more in awe of his sea trip across the Pacific. He still had the *Titanic* on the brain.

As for the Model-T crossing the Australian desert, east to west, Ford said that was only to be expected. It was a Ford after all.

Recovery from a cerebral haemorrhage is slow at eighty-two, he must be realistic. He has been thinking again that there is something behind his existence. It was obviously planned for him to do things.

In the Depression men were in a mess and had confidence in him. In the thirties he was never busier or more prosperous. He'd return from some expedition or other thinking 'that's that' and next week he'd be out again on the camels from Darwin to Adelaide, from Port Hedland to Melbourne.

For twenty years he led expeditions into the interior on behalf of companies seeking minerals. He surveyed geographical and geological features, made botanical, soil and meteorological readings, assayed deposits, discovered new lakes and rare caves and took photographs by the thousand.

He mapped a lot of country.

Moira Teasdale enjoyed his story about crouching behind a barricade of camel saddles while he fought off hostile blacks. At the Dorchester he ate asparagus and a chicken-and-leek pie and she said it was better than Kipling to listen to him.

The blacks crept up on their camp in their feathered *kadaitcha* boots to spear them. Luckily Tommy the camel boy, camped thirty yards away, spotted them. They got behind the saddles and fought them off all night.

Moira's letter caught up with him in Wyndham. Her face today is a blur but Grace's is clear. Occasionally in dreams they run together. Scott-Bowdler said marrying an Australian was a curious thing. Maybe so, maybe less curious than sitting on a verandah staring at the Indian Ocean.

The explorer's life is an independent one. He never got around to replying. In the desert he attempted three letters but threw them away. Another English woman, what was the point? At the time he was recovering from another snake bite, a gwarder, and not himself. The venom confuses you.

The next night the blacks returned. But I scared them away for good. To be frank, Miss Teasdale, they ran away because in all the ruddy panic I got tangled up in my mosquito net. I stood up like a white ghost and they fled into the spinifex.

I thought you'd enjoy that story.

In the early morning when he is lying there, the only patient awake, the sea shallows are dotted with variously coloured balls or buoys. Against his will he looked, turned away and they were gone. A nurse had no answer to his question. Not for some time did it dawn on him they were women's bathing caps.

Women were bobbing in the waves in the early morning, chatting to each other.

The penny dropped when he saw them walking up the hill from the beach into the pines, most of them elderly and wearing bathing gowns over their swimming costumes. A couple of them still had their bathing caps on.

As soon as his curiosity was satisfied he again lost all interest in the sea.

Unless he is drugged he does not sleep. He lives on air, he hardly moves. He has been made aware of the salivation problem and keeps a handkerchief handy for the dribble.

Strange tastes come into his mouth. Once it was damper, burnt and crunchy. Once it was grilled barramundi. Another time sour-grass. In dreams caused by sleeping pills he sometimes smells camels' breath and feels his nostrils clogged with dust.

A Fleet Street interviewer asked him in 1933 what the desert meant to him. The question stopped him in his tracks. 'Finding your own love,' he remembers replying. Moira touched his sleeve. It still embarrasses him to recall saying it.

He runs his book titles through his mind. There were six books but today he can remember only four, all out of print. They were all most discursive on exploration.

The National Library has all his expeditions' logbooks and the thousands of photographs taken over the years. Sand fell from the spines of his logbooks when he plonked them on the Chief Librarian's desk.

His life and expeditions are now in the hands of the general public.

In his papers for the library he found a social page from a 1924 edition of the London *Daily Telegraph* recording the marriage.

He came up the steps. There were pine cones on the verandah, blown there by the sea breeze. The opal was on the dresser and the shipping list.

He was lucky to be out of it.

He was known for his many lucky escapes. He always knew the right people. He was good in a crisis, the men put their trust in him. He showed the Fleet Street boys how to make fire in Hampstead with sticks. Never tease a camel, he advised the British.

When we got to the town we circled it on our camels. We didn't want to come in.

A young woman approaches his bed. Her skin is sun-tanned, she has a bossy, confident manner.

'Have we done a wee this morning?' she demands.

He stares past her. His face is white as paper.

'Yes,' says the last explorer.

When she is gone he lies back on his pillows with the heavy pulse of the sea and the whine of the sea-breeze in his ears.

A little later he manages to slowly remove the bedclothes. He inches himself out of bed. Supporting himself on the head rail, he carefully stands. He holds on to the head rail of the bed and pushes. The bed moves silently on its coasters.

He manages to turn the bed completely around. With difficulty he climbs back into bed. His pulse is racing. Gradually he relaxes and lies back on his pillows, staring into the far distance. He cannot see out the window. The sea is behind his back, its noise is gone.

Facing the desert, he feels up to laughing.

The Bodysurfers (1983)

Part Two

—

NEW GUINEA

JOHN MacGILLIVRAY

(1821–67)

Scottish-born naturalist. From 1842 onwards, MacGillivray worked mainly in Australia and the south-west Pacific. Voyages in which he participated included those of HMS Fly *(1842–46) and HMS* Herald *(1852–55). He also served on HMS* Rattlesnake *(1846–50), during its survey of areas of the Queensland coast, the southern coast of New Guinea, and the Louisiade Archipelago, under the command of Captain Owen Stanley. MacGillivray's narrative of that voyage, from which this 1849 extract is taken, was published in 1852.*

'WATERING CREEK, LOUISIADE ARCHIPELAGO'

June 26th — Yesterday afternoon the Rattlesnake was removed to the neighbourhood of the proposed watering-place on South-east Island, and anchored in seventeen fathoms, mud, a mile off shore. Soon after daylight I accompanied Captain Stanley and a party in two boats to ascend the neighbouring creek and determine whether a practicable watering-place existed there. For several hundred yards above the entrance we found the channel preserving a nearly uniform width of about fifteen yards, with low muddy shores covered with mangroves, some of which attained the unusual dimensions of 60 to 80 feet in height, with a circumference at the base of 6 to 8 feet. To this succeeded during our upward progress a low bank of red clay backed by rising ground and tangled brush, with very large trees at intervals, and others arching over the stream, their branches nearly touching the water. Gigantic climbers hung down in long festoons passing from branch to branch, and the more aged trunks supported clumps of ferns and parasitical plants. Here and there an areca palm shot up its slender stem surmounted by a cluster of pale-green feathery leaves, or the attention was arrested for a moment by a magnificent pandanus — its trunk raised high above the ground by the enormous supporting root-like shoots, — or some graceful tree-fern with dark widely-spreading foliage exceeding in delicacy the finest lace.

Meanwhile the creek had slightly narrowed, the dead trees in the water became more frequent and troublesome, and the thickets on the banks encroached more and more upon the channel so as not to allow room for the oars to pass, obliging the men to use them as poles. At every turn in the windings of the stream (still too brackish to be fit to drink) some beautiful glimpse of jungle scenery presented itself as we passed upwards — long vistas and stray bursts of sunshine alternating with the gloomy shadows of the surrounding woods. A deep silence pervaded the banks of this water never before visited by civilized man, its monotony broken only by the occasional brief word of command, the splash of the oars, or the shrill notes of some passing flights of parrots. The river, for now it might fairly be called one, retained the same character until we had gone up about a mile, when further progress was stopped by a ridge of rocks stretching across from side to side marking the limits of the tidal influence. Over this the rush of fresh water formed a strong rapid backed by a deep, sluggish, winding stream, draining a large basin-like valley bounded behind by the central ridge of the island, the principal hills of which attain an elevation of from 992 to 1421 feet, and one, Mount Rattlesnake, is 2689 feet in height. At times the body of water discharged here must be immense, judging from the quantity of drift wood and other detritus lodged in the trees twelve feet above the present level of the stream, probably during the inundations of the rainy season. These floods must also spread over the low land on the margin of the river to a considerable distance, the deep red clay there, evidently the washings of the hills, bearing the marks of having been under water. The jungle in places is very dense, but, with the exercise of a little patience and labour, it can be penetrated at almost every point. On rising ground it is often bordered by a thicket of creeping and climbing plants mixed up with bushes and patches of *Hellenia cærulea.* The low wooded hills are covered with tall grass growing on very poor soil — of partially decomposed mica-slate with lumps of quartz.

Narrative of the Voyage of H.M.S. Rattlesnake, vol. 1 (1852)

————

JOHN MORESBY

(1830–1922)

English-born hydrographer and explorer. Moresby came to the Australia station in command of HMS Basilisk in 1871. He conducted important surveys in Torres Strait and along the southern coast of New Guinea between

1872 and 1874, when he returned to England. Moresby made the following 'discoveries' in February 1873. Later that year, at Possession Island, he claimed New Guinea for Britain.

'PORT MORESBY AND FAIRFAX HARBOUR'

At ten o'clock on Friday morning, the 'Basilisk' was off the opening we had found in the reef, henceforth to be known as Basilisk Passage, and from the foretop, whence every reef could be seen, I conned her through the passage into the still waters of Port Moresby to Jane Island, and past it into landlocked many-bayed Fairfax Harbour, where we anchored in five fathoms water. As we broke into these unknown waters I determined that the outer and inner harbours should bear these names of my father, the venerable admiral of the fleet.

Port Moresby, situated where coral and white sand has succeeded the low mangrove-covered coast, lies in latitude 9° 30' south, and longitude 147° 10' east. The entrance is good, and the land, which is covered with many trees, rises gently on either side, to a considerable height. The inner, Fairfax Harbour, is an irregular basin surrounded by round-topped grassy hills, having the Australian gum-tree scattered over them, with rich valleys between. The depth of water is from between seven and four fathoms to within a few yards of the beach. The sides of the hills are well cultivated, and yield abundance of yams and taro.

We must have been a surprising sight to the natives, for they flocked on board in hundreds, eager and curious, chattering like monkeys, as they pointed out to each other the marvels that took their fancy.

Mr Mourilyan and I now began to make a survey of the harbour, and Lieutenant Hayter went away with the galley and a fresh crew to continue our exploration inside the Barrier Reef, for forty miles east of Port Moresby to Hood's Point, where the barrier reef curves in and joins the mainland, forming a *cul-de-sac.*

A singular feature in this hilly country, intersected by deep valleys, is the almost total absence of running water. The soil is very porous, and the streams probably take an underground course till they reach the mangrove swamps, in which the valleys abutting on Fairfax Harbour terminate.

We went to visit one of the hill villages in the afternoon, going quite unarmed, such was our confidence in the people, and climbing a steep hillside sprinkled with gum trees, and covered with granite boulders and quartz, found ourselves overlooking a rich tropical valley, and saw the village on the opposite hillside amongst abundant trees. The thin rocky soil gave place as we began to descend the slope, to rich dark mould, from which grass sprang nearly shoulder high, varied with occasional clumps of splendid hard wood, tropical trees, and groups of the sago palm. Here and there spaces, some three acres in extent, were enclosed by stiff bamboo fences, and produced bananas, yams, and taro in profusion, although no effort seemed to be made to keep the weeds under. The bananas, which were nearly ripe, were tied up in leaves to save them from the flying foxes.

The village consisted of about six houses, built on poles, and looking as if they were marching out from amongst the trees on stilts. The houses, which consisted of one room as usual, were tenanted below, in the space between the poles, by pigs and wretched looking dogs, that kept up an eager fight for the pieces of broken cocoa-nut that had fallen from above to their share. The villagers gave us a few stone clubs and wooden spears in exchange for our bottles and beads, but would not look at our iron-hoop and axes. They were not nearly so much adorned with feathers and shells as their neighbours on the sea-shore, and I fancied their complexion to be of a slightly darker shade. Their only tools for turning up the soil were stone adzes, capable of penetrating for about four inches. We showed the women a looking-glass, and they started back and would not look a second time. I offered my watch to be examined, but no one would touch the possessed-looking thing.

All the valleys we travelled over were covered with rich grass, shoulder high, and had we possessed an army of Irish scythes, and an English market, we might have cut down our fortune. The hills on the north of the harbour are separated from a loftier range behind by extensive grass plains, abounding in water holes, well dotted over with timber, and having a rich black soil.

Nothing could exceed the kindness of the natives, in proof of which I will mention but one fact. Mr Watts, one of our engineers, lost his way the evening before our visit to this village, and when beginning to grow anxious, fell in with a party of natives; far from attempting to take any advantage of his helplessness, they fed him, and took him to their village, making signs that they wished him to sleep there. Finding that he wanted to return to his companions, they offered to guide him, stipulating, however, that he should show himself off in the village first, and permit all the inhabitants to admire his white skin. This he did with a great deal of pleasure, placing himself on a verandah, to be handled and gazed at by scores of beholders.

The large village at the entrance to Port Moresby, which consists of two rows of well-built houses, separated by groves of cocoa-nut trees, was often visited by us. Its inhabitants, numbering perhaps 800 of all ages, were well fed, contented-looking people. The women seemed to busy themselves much in pottery, and moulded clay into large globe-shaped jars, which they baked slowly amongst the embers of wood fires. They use these jars much in their cookery, and I have partaken of a vegetable porridge cooked in them, consisting of mangrove fruit, taro, and yams, with cocoa-nut finely shred over all, and found it excellent. They are skilful in netting bags and fishing-nets, which they do so precisely in our mode that our men often took up their shuttles and went on with the net. These nets are made of the fibre of a small nettle-like plant, and are shaped like our English seine.

On one occasion an incident happened here which surprised us. A number of natives came on board, bringing with them a bundle of rushes, and knotting them together carefully measured the length and breadth of the ship. They evidently wished to preserve a record of the size, for they stowed the rush line away in their canoe with many signs of wonderment.

At most of the villages on this coast we observed that the men liked to hold our hands as we walked through, and that they did not wish us to enter their houses; but if we pressed the point they yielded in this, and awaited us patiently outside. We used sometimes to sit and rest on the verandah or landing-place outside the door of the upper storey, and they would bring us fresh cocoa-nut milk, or some of the sago they had boiled for their meal. These people, and all the light-coloured Malay race of eastern New Guinea, are without bows and arrows. As far as Redscar Bay we saw toy bows amongst the children, but beyond that point the bow ceases altogether, till it reappears on the northern shores, west of Astrolabe Gulf. The houses visited by us all contained spears and stone weapons, some of the latter very well shaped and finished.

Discoveries & Surveys in New Guinea and the D'Entrecasteaux Islands (1876)

J. A. LAWSON

(dates unknown)

Who was Captain J. A. Lawson, the pseudonymous author of the fictional
Wanderings in the Interior of New Guinea, *published in London in 1875?*
Was he, as some would have it, William Edington Armit, leader of the later
disastrous 1883 Argus *expedition to New Guinea? Or was he really Robert*
Henry Armit, naval surveyor and promoter of a New Guinea colonisation
scheme (1875–76), as others have argued? The book itself is a wild affair, full
of extraordinary adventures, including the discovery and naming of Mount
Hercules, said to be 32 783 feet high, that is, almost 4000 feet higher than
Everest. Many people, however, apparently took the work at face value,
including the 1875 reviewer who wrote, 'This is, upon the whole, the most
valuable contribution to the literature of travel that has appeared for years'.
One might have thought that reading the following section alone would have
alerted the suspicions of all but the most absent-minded of readers.

ASCENT AND DESCENT OF MOUNT HERCULES

Sept. 16 — Commenced the ascent soon after four o'clock. Toolo and
Danang, with the two Australians, were left behind, and I took Aboo
only with me. We carried with us a supply of food and water, our arms
and blankets, and a stout staff each. The first part of our way lay
through the forest, but the trees gradually became less thick together,
and at a height of two thousand feet they were very sparsely scattered
about, though there was still plenty of scrubby undergrowth, and a
sufficient quantity of coarse grass to impede our progress. On the
outskirts of the forest many large eagles were seen, one of them
carrying some small animal in its talons. A few lizards were here also,
scared from our path, together with a brown horned snake, about five
feet in length, and a few quails. The latter were met with as high up as
four thousand feet.

The soil, which was not found, except in odd patches, at a greater
height than six thousand feet, was of a stiff nature, but I cannot speak
of its quality. As far as it extended it was covered with grass and
herbage, and a few pines and other trees. Pines of four different kinds
grew on the bare rock, where there was no soil at all, their roots

running into every little fissure and crevice that was capable of affording them a holdfast. Volcanic debris was not very abundant, but still we met with a few blocks of lava and masses of broken rock. Such signs of the vicinity of volcanoes were very rare at a greater height than eight thousand feet, and were not observed at all after twelve thousand feet.

Shortly after sunrise, the sight over the country to the north and north-east was grand in the extreme. In those directions it was a nearly level plain, and we could scan its surface for at least forty miles around. Another large lake lay north, slightly west, about twelve miles; and half-a-dozen streams of water were traceable running in a north-west direction. Near the base of the mountain, and away to the westward, the ground was covered with forests of immense extent, but due north it was a fine savanna, where, through a glass, I could make out many herds of cattle grazing amidst the tall grass. One of the most prominent objects on this plain was a grove of palm trees, growing probably on the margin of a pool or small lake.

Continuing the ascent we soon got above the clouds, and this beautiful panoramic view was lost to sight. It was somewhat curious to look down and perceive a creamy looking white mist below us; and then directing our gaze aloft, to find a similar canopy hanging over our heads. The sun's rays were now shut out, and it was getting very chilly. The atmosphere had a dull, over-cast look, as if a heavy rain was about to set in; in fact, the weather was just such as we have in England on a raw November morning.

By nine o'clock we had ascended fourteen thousand feet, having so far met with no serious difficulty. Even at this great height we found a few species of moss. The last trees (a dwarfed pine or two) were passed at eleven thousand feet; and a little higher the grass ceased. Between ten and fourteen thousand feet the rock was dangerously slippery, owing to a kind of slimy moss that grew upon it. I was compelled to take off my shoes, and Aboo his sandals, in order to maintain a footing. At the height of fifteen thousand feet we came to the first snow, it was two or three inches thick, and frozen very hard, but with the aid of our staves we got over it with comparative ease. Hitherto, though the side of the mountain had been steep, it was not rough, or broken much by cliffs and gullies, but at this point crag rose above crag, with such abruptness, that frequently we had to climb up an almost perpendicular face. In doing so masses of the rock sometimes gave way under our weight, and we received some ugly falls in consequence. By eleven o'clock we were pretty well tired out, and halted for a rest and a little refreshment. While we were eating, Aboo fell asleep, and I was myself so drowsy that it was no easy task to keep my eyes open. As I knew full well, however, that in our present position sleep and death were synonymous, I awoke Aboo at once, and proceeded upward.

The cold now shortly became excessive, and our desire to sleep increased with it. The thermometer fell twelve degrees below freezing-point, my hands were so numb that I could not feel whether I had fingers or not, and the water in our bottle was a mass of ice. Unfortunately we had very little extra clothing, with the exception of our blankets, and consequently we felt the coldness of the atmosphere most acutely. Aboo became quite lethargic, and several times sat down and fell asleep instantly, and so soundly that I was obliged to use rough means to awaken him. But in defiance of all drawbacks we held on our way, walking, and in some places crawling, over frozen snow of unsearchable depth. Nothing was visible but snow of the most dazzling whiteness. Every peak and crag was covered with it, and it hung over the edges of the cliffs in long fleecy masses. Beneath, and above, and on either side, as far as I could see, nothing but snow, arranged in all manner of fantastic patterns, like the frosting on the top of a gigantic bride-cake. Some of the enveloped crags looked like ruined churches and fortresses, and one was remarkably like a bare rampart. My eyes grew weary and pained with wandering over it, and I closed them to obtain ease, but immediately I began to stagger in sleep, and had not the shock of my fall aroused me I should certainly never have seen the foot of Mount Hercules again. Aboo moved along mechanically, like a man in a dream, and if I spoke to him I had to repeat my remark five or six times before he heard or comprehended me.

At length blood began to flow from our noses and ears, and my head ached in a distracting manner. Aboo, also, complained of a headache, and entreated me to let him sit down and rest. With much trouble I restrained him from so doing, for I knew that if we halted sleep could not be resisted. As it was, I saw that our only chance of pre-serving life was to retreat without delay; for we were in a pitiful plight. Our lips and gums, and the skin of our hands and faces, were cracked and bleeding, and our eyes were bloodshot and swollen to an alarming extent. The thermometer had sunk to twenty-two degrees below the freezing-point, and the air was so rarified that we were gasping rather than breathing. Our staves fell from our grasp, and we could not pick them up again, so benumbed were our arms and hands. It was now one o'clock, and the greatest elevation we had attained was twenty-five thousand three hundred and fourteen feet. It took us three hours to descend to the limit of the snow; but after that point was reached we pushed forward more rapidly. As soon as I had recovered the use of my hands sufficiently to hold the flask, I served out a little brandy, which put new life into us. Just before we left the boundary of the snow, three large white eagles were seen; and many black ones as high up as the limit of the trees. We arrived at our camp about half-past seven in the evening thoroughly beat.

Wanderings in the Interior of New Guinea (1875)

———

LUIGI D'ALBERTIS

(1841–1901)

Italian naturalist and explorer. D'Albertis, who had previously travelled widely in Europe, spent time in western New Guinea with Odoardo Beccari in 1872, and explored the Papuan coast and lower Fly River in 1875. Flying both the Italian and New South Wales flags, he entered the Fly River in May 1876, in the Neva, *a launch borrowed from the New South Wales government. After steaming up the river for forty-five days, during which time his looting of villages shocked the boat's engineer, Lawrence Hargrave, D'Albertis turned back. His claim to have travelled 580 miles up the Fly was later questioned. A further trip up the same river in 1877 was a disaster, involving the death of a crew member beaten by D'Albertis and the desertion of others. His two-volume work,* New Guinea: What I Did and What I Saw, *from which this brief piece about the 1876 expedition is taken, was published in English and Italian in 1880.*

'WE BEGIN ANOTHER WEEK BADLY'

June 19th — Another week beginning badly! We have indeed made our way into the interior of the 'Enchanted Castle,' as a Brisbane newspaper once called New Guinea; and for this very reason we must be prepared to face the hardest trials and to call upon all our courage and endurance. The spectre of Hunger rises before us in all its horror. Our provisions, however elastic they have hitherto proved, are almost at an end. Birds have become more scarce; and since we have entered a mountainous country, there are no traces of cassowary or wild pig.

Even the fish are few; and, either because the current is too strong, or because the bed of the river is too full of pebbles, and consequently impoverished, dynamite no longer serves to provide us with food. To keep my people quiet, I talk of the probability of finding gold; but to what extent do they believe me?

If the country continues like this, what can I give them to eat to-morrow? What an incubus this problem — what shall we eat to-morrow? — is to me! Meanwhile the river is becoming narrower and more shallow; the lead is continually in use, yet we cannot avoid shocks against banks of stones, or against trunks of trees, any one of which might be fatal. Even to-day we had the ill-luck to ground three times. After covering seven or eight miles in five hours, we had to come to a standstill while we replenished our fire-wood. While the men were felling timber, I climbed some hills covered with tree-ferns. There are gigantic trees about here, and the forest is almost free from ivy and other small growths. In the little streams at the foot of the hills I found an abundance of quartz pebbles, but no trace of gold as yet. The soil is of red clay, covered with fine begonias and nepenthes.

New Guinea: What I Did and What I Saw, vol. II (1880)

―――――

LAWRENCE HARGRAVE

(1850–1915)

Australian engineer, explorer, and aeronautical pioneer. Born and educated in England, Hargrave arrived in Australia in 1865. He took part in several expeditions to New Guinea during the 1870s, including Luigi D'Albertis's 1876 investigation of the Fly River. His life and experiences in New Guinea inspired Barry Conyngham's opera Fly *(1984). His aeronautical inventions, which included lifting himself off the ground with a box kite in 1894, were recognised by the inclusion of his portrait on one of the Australian twenty dollar notes. Hargrave offered these comments in a letter to the Geographical Society of Australasia in 1883.*

SOME WORDS OF ADVICE

Mr Chairman,

After the interesting paper that has just been delivered a few remarks from one who has actively participated in four New Guinea expeditions may be deemed admissable by you in the form of a note: if this is in order I shall confine my observations to stating the course that I should pursue in my endeavours to find out as much as possible about New Guinea, in, say, 5 years; that is if I were in your leader's place.

I should despatch my 1st Lieutenant with about 20 men to Port Moresby with orders to buy the herd of horses that I believe are nominally owned by Rua Toka, and form a station at Mo-mé-le about 15 miles E.N.E. of Anna-párter on the east branch of the Laróker River; (all native names are phonetically spelt) and there break them into mountain and jungle travelling; giving men and horses daily and constant work, even if they can find nothing to do but pack timber and clear plantations for the Moon-e-ki-é-ler natives; this I feel confident would leave my second in command at the end of three or four months with perhaps six men and twenty horses thoroughly acclimatised, the rest would prefer to return to civilization.

By the way in picking my men in the first instance I should prefer those who were used to the coast districts of Northern Queensland and the Northern Territory. I should send for a consignment of Malays to meet me at Thursday Island, care being taken in their selection to have men conversant with the preparation of Sago which with a sparing allowance of well cooked meat should form the principal diet of the expedition.

With these Malays and a fresh batch of white men I would go to Orangerie Bay and work northward on foot to Mo-mé-le: this would considerably sift *my* party and I should hope to start at once with 25 strong healthy men for Coo-ber-re (the tobacco producing country that lies round the sources of the Fly River.)

I would keep to the eastward of Mount Yule giving the Roar-ro and Mi-var districts a wide berth, and be very wary of dealing with any natives who spoke of or claimed acquaintance with Tap-pé-yan [native name for W. G. Lawes of the London Missionary Society]. If any of my party were unfit to proceed beyond Coo-ber-re I should despatch them by canoe down the Fly River to Go-wer (the district round the mouth of or the lower waters of the Fly) where I believe the London Missionary Society now has some evangelists stationed.

I should pay particular attention to the water system of central New Guinea as from my knowledge of the western bank of the Fly, that river, large as it is, is quite insufficient to drain the district extending to the Outer-nar-ter River and there is an ample basin for another river of larger capacity than the Fly River, between the two, the mouth of which I should expect to find near Frederick Henry Island and probably in Dourga Straits (of course you are aware that the Baxter and that other river near Deliverance Island cannot extend 60 miles from the coast); however, the pearl-shellers are working westward along the coast and will soon settle this point.

I would confine my researches to the S.W. side of the dividing range as it is evident the N.E. slopes are very precipitous and are better attacked from the seaward side.

I should deem the expedition eminently successful if four or five of the party got through to Salwatty with one water-tight case of note-books, a gun and tomahawk each, brown and naked as the day they were born.

Trusting this meagre outline of my ideas on the subject may be of some little use to your leader, let me close it by calling his attention to the importance of insisting that no unboiled water shall be drunk by any of the party, and to the fact that those who perspire most freely will probably retain the best health.

Hargrave Papers

GEORGE ERNEST MORRISON
(1862–1920)

Australian-born adventurer and journalist. A former medical student, Morrison investigated the blackbirding trade in Queensland in 1882, before returning on foot to Melbourne from Normanton in the Gulf of Carpentaria between December 1882 and April 1883, a distance of more than 3220 kilometres. He set out to cross New Guinea in July 1883, not long after William Armit's similar attempt, organised by the Argus, had failed. Morrison's own expedition came to a sticky ending, as he explains in this telegram to the Age, which was sponsoring him. He subsequently received treatment, and completed his medical studies, in Edinburgh. Later in his career, as The Times's *correspondent in China, he was to become known as 'Chinese' Morrison.*

'MORRISON WOUNDED WHEN 100 MILES FROM THE COAST'

Cooktown, 20th November.

I have failed in my attempt to cross the continent of New Guinea, and have returned to Queensland. Our party had to turn back when on the point of success. Pursuing a north-easterly direction from Port Moresby we had, with much labor and difficulty, taken horses over the mountains, and where the diggers turned back from want of grass we, by keeping a different track, got into country splendidly grassed right up to the main watershed. Latterly we had kept bearing to the east to find a place low enough to cross. We had reached the foot of the dividing range, and a day later expected to be across it. For a few hours we were going to camp there. The range ran into a spur at the top, far less steep than many we had previously surmounted. Once across we intended as soon as possible to bend round to the west, and to strike for the great land belt. We could not, however, get on with the natives. They saw the weakness of our party, and took advantage of it. The country was thickly populated, and the natives of each district resorted to every means but open violence to prevent our moving further. Our camp was always more or less surrounded by natives, waiting an opportunity to make a raid. By day and night we had to keep watch, and scarcely a night passed but we had to fire shots to frighten the natives, who were heard in the neighborhood of the tents. The work was most fatiguing, for there were only three of us to share the watch, as we could not trust the black boys. In spite of all our vigilance we had axes and tomahawks stolen, and a native sneaked off in open daylight with one large red blanket. We awoke one morning to find our tea stolen. The natives ultimately regarded our firearms as harmless instruments of noise, and crowds of men were in the habit of coming with spears, clubs and shields, and motioning to us to go back. They would also run with their spears and pretend to discharge them at us. On one occasion a man brought a shield down to our camp, laid it at our feet, signed to us that it would be to our advantage to go back, and immediately ran away. Our only safety lay in conciliating the chiefs by a liberal distribution of gifts. Whenever we were going to shift camp a crowd would come down to oppose our further passage, and I had then to give each of the more surly looking men a present, which pleased them, and before they had lapsed into their bad humor we had dodged through their district. Our party was very weak. The old digger who swore to go with me to death gave in at the end of 15 miles from the start, and only one man could be obtained in his place. This was a worthless half-witted new chum, who became a constant source of danger to us. The two black boys could never be taught to fire a gun. My other man, Lyons, gave unqualified satisfaction, but when he went forward to prospect the track I was never certain but that I might find the camp wrecked on my return. As we got further inland the country became densely populated, and the natives increased in boldness. One came quietly down to where three of us were packing the last horse, picked up a tomahawk and darted for the scrub. I could have shot him easily, but, instead of doing this, one of the party chased him, caught him, punched his head and let him go, though the savage had turned round half-way and flung the tomahawk at his pursuer. We decided next time to use the gun. The opportunity came on the 2nd October. On that day I went out with four natives to cut the track, all the others but the new chum being sick with fever. I gave the natives a valuable scrub knife, which we took turn and turn about in using. As we proceeded with our work the natives increased in number until 4 had become 40, most of them carrying spears. When about three miles from the camp, one of them suddenly seized the knife and bolted with it. This stealing was getting a farce, so I waited until the man had got such a distance that a shot would not inflict much injury, and I then gave him one charge in the back. Everyone declares that I made a mistake in not shooting the man dead, as I might then have effectually frightened the natives and given them an idea of our superior power. As it was they inferred that the worst our arms could do was to inflict but a temporary pain. That afternoon we could hear the news travelling everywhere, and see crowds of men collecting with piles of spears, and intently watching us. In the morning when I loaded up early, intending to shift the camp, warriors with heavy bundles of spears gathered in crowds at some points which we had to pass, until the long grass where they stood fully bristled with spears. Lyons was at this time very ill with fever and could hardly walk. We went on, however, exercising extreme caution till we reached the last rise we had to go up. I was leading the horse some distance ahead of the rest, and was just taking a steep step from the scrub into the long grass at the top when I was struck by two spears, one in the hollow of the right leg and the other in the stomach. The steep step saved me. I pulled the spears out, and fired a shot from my Winchester. I saw no men, though they must have been within four or five yards when I was struck. I had then to lie down, as blood flowed from me freely, and my stomach gave me great pain. When Lyons came up he thought I was mortally injured, for I was lying in a pool of blood, vomiting large quantities of blood, and suffering frightful pain. To save my life he resolved to abandon everything and bring me down to the coast. We were then over 100 miles from Port Moresby, but we could not return by the way we had travelled as we knew the natives were waiting for us. Over 50 spears in bundles were picked up near where I was wounded, showing the attack to have been premeditated but badly planned. Lyons, when packing the horses, could get no help from the new chum, who was paralysed with terror, and in consequence we retreated, leaving our stores behind, and escaped from the natives to nearly perish from starvation. For eight days I had not a morsel to eat, but the change of air healed my wounds, which are now quite well. Lyons, by the exercise of extraordinary courage and endurance, brought us safely into port. The first twenty miles of our return journey was through new and very rough country. For nine days Lyons was entirely without food, and but for his marvellous stamina I should now be rotting in the New Guinea bush.

Age (21 November 1883)

ANONYMOUS

Unidentified member of James Erskine's 1884 expedition to proclaim a British protectorate over south-eastern New Guinea. In this piece from his particularly jaunty account of the trip, he describes the voyage to, and his first impressions of, New Guinea. Soon after their arrival, some of his colleagues displayed the nineteenth century explorers' usual propensity for shooting the first wildlife that they encountered in a new place.

PROCEEDING TO NEW GUINEA

On the 29th of October, *H.M.S. Nelson*, commanded by Commodore James Erskine, A.D.C., left Sydney for the purpose of proclaiming a protectorate over the South-eastern shores of New Guinea; she had on board as passengers, a member of the Royal Geographical Society of

New South Wales, an artist, a correspondent to the Australian papers, two photographers, a gentleman connected with the Government of New South Wales, and another civilian, a guest of the officers. We were all in good spirits, and looking forward to our trip, notwithstanding that we were obliged to forego the Melbourne Cup and all the festivities of that eminently gay city, which we were on the point of visiting when the orders came to proceed to New Guinea. We expected to be absent about two months, which for a small craft would not appear to be a very serious matter, but the departure of the flag ship from the fleshpots of Sydney for so long a period was an occurrence of no mean importance, especially as some of the officers were recently married, while others contemplated following their example at an early date.

After having called in at Brisbane, and duly performed the voyage to the town in our old friend *s.s. Kate*, we left for Port Moresby, New Guinea. The weather the whole way was as perfect as could be desired, and on Sunday, Nov. 2nd, we reached our destination and anchored in the harbour, where we found lying *H.M.S. Harrier*, *Swinger*, and *Raven*, the *Espiègle* arriving a few hours later. The entrance to the bay was very beautiful, owing to the long ranges of hills on either side, and the opal green of the water among the reefs. Many were the remarks and speculations as to what we should find on shore; made by the idlers on the fore-bridge as we steamed up the harbour, and our oracle, who always has a large audience on these occasions, was, as usual, infallible, giving reasons for each strange sight that met our view and pointing out the fires along the shore, which he informed us were watch fires lit as signals of our approach.

As soon as we were at anchor, we heard to our astonishment that Lieut. Commander Willcox, of *H.M.S. Harrier*, had, by request of Mr Deputy Commissioner Romilly, hoisted the British flag ten day's previously, being unaware that the *Nelson* was coming to New Guinea, of course this led to wild speculation, and each one was eager to express an opinion as to what we should probably do. It was, however, decided by the powers, that the act of hoisting the flag was illegal, consequently the original programme remained unaltered. Accordingly the *Espiègle* and *Raven* were sent along the coast east and west to proclaim to the chiefs the approaching ceremony of establishing a Protectorate over this portion of New Guinea, and on board of the *Raven* went Mr Chalmers, one of the missionaries, a charming man, who is not only a good fellow, but probably knows more about New Guinea and its inhabitants than any man living. These ships were instructed to bring back on board as many chiefs from the neighbouring tribes as they could collect. They were away for two days, thus enabling us to have a look at the country about Port Moresby, and see something of its inhabitants.

The village is built on piles along the shore, and populated by men, women, dogs, pigs, and children in seemingly the most hopeless confusion. I place the children last, as, so far as we could judge, the pigs and mongrel dogs appeared to possess quite the front place in the estimation of their masters and mistresses. The houses are of two stories, and the canoes are moored off the entrance to the sea, thus affording a ready means of escape when attacked by foes from the hills. The country beyond the village consists of apparently endless ranges of hills, dry and barren looking, and uninviting in appearance to even the keenest sportsmen among us.

The day after our arrival a party went away in the jolly boat to Fisherman Island, distant about five miles; the island is merely a coral reef overgrown with scrub, and the walking was very severe, as one's feet occasionally got jammed in deep holes between sharp pieces of coral. The heat was something phenomenal, but this being a first visit to the shores of New Guinea, our sportsmen were full of ardour, and tramped about after quail regardless of coral and oblivious of heat. About eight brace of quail were bagged altogether, besides a wallaby and two large pigeons. The next morning the hills of the mainland were scoured for game, with no better result than a brace of New Guinea pheasants, which, however, were very good eating.

The natives whom we met in our wanderings struck us chiefly by the appearance of their heads, which were surmounted by enormous erections of hair, something in the Fiji fashion, though without their tidy, well cared for appearance. For ornaments they mostly wear a semicircle of mother-of-pearl shell round their neck, with a quill like that of a porcupine stuck through the nose, the curves of the quill upwards, thus giving them rather a fierce appearance. The men are small, and almost devoid of clothing, while the women wear short skirts of grass around their waist, about as deep as the evening dress of a Christmas columbine.

Our Cruise to New Guinea (1884)

JOHN LINDT
(1845–1926)

*German-born photographer. Lindt, who was based in Melbourne from
1876 to 1894, became very well known for his photographs of people and
places. His 'ardent desire to become personally acquainted with these mysterious shores of Papua and their savage inhabitants' was conceived while
passing through Torres Strait in 1868 and reawakened at later meetings
with Luigi D'Albertis. It was, one assumes, at least partly satisfied when
Lindt visited the newly-established protectorate of British New Guinea in
1885, as official photographer to Peter Scratchley's expedition to investigate
the territory. His illustrated book entitled* Picturesque New Guinea, *from
which this piece comes, was published in 1887. Lindt moved to Narbethong,
in the Victorian countryside, in 1895, where he developed his 'Hermitage'
pleasure resort. It boasted, among other features, three New Guinea-style
treehouses designed by Baron Ferdinand von Mueller.*

'AN EXPEDITION INLAND'

At daybreak on Monday, September 28th, all was astir on the
'Governor Blackall.' Sir Peter Scratchley, Mr Fort, Mr Chalmers,
myself, the Doctor, and one or two others started in the dingy, towed
by the launch, for shore, which, owing to the low tide, we reached by
a circuitous route, and had to be carried through the shallows pick-a-
back. Once landed, we commenced our work, which was nothing
more or less than a pedestrian excursion under the guidance of Mr
Chalmers, to the village of Kalo, some miles inland, making Hula,
where we landed, our base. A crowd of natives surrounded us on landing, anxious to earn a little tobacco by assisting to transport our baggage. A dozen were told off to carry the Governor's effects, and four
more took my apparatus and wardrobe on their brawny shoulders.
After getting clear of the village I counted over fifty brothers, sisters,
cousins, and aunts of the bearers following our party on the chance of
a stray bit of tobacco. The country through which we passed was
richly cultivated, containing miles of native plantations devoted to
bananas, sweet potatoes and yams. Some of the gardens were in splendid order, and cultivated with Chinese minuteness, the young shoots
of the yams being sheltered from the sun by husks and leaves. We

found numbers of women at work, and at every cocoa-nut grove we passed we were offered a refreshing drink. The cocoa-nut is very abundant here, and consequently very cheap. Forty young nuts or twenty full grown ones can be purchased for a fig of trade tobacco, a price at which the 'three sticks a penny' fraternity might invest to a fabulous profit, could they but get their goods delivered at Epsom. After traversing three or four miles of fertile country, we arrived at the inland villages of Babaga and Kamali. The buildings here differ from the marine dwellings considerably. The piles on which they are built are mostly strong timber up to eighteen inches in diameter, and how with their primitive appliances they manage to move these huge logs is a mystery. I took views of some of these houses, which have two platforms, or rather a large platform and verandah in front, the latter corresponding to the upper story of the structure. The chiefs' houses are further decorated with a fanciful spire at the apex of the gable, sometimes with poles projecting from their sides ornamented with streamers or pennants of bark. The inland people suffer terribly from skin diseases, far more so than the coast tribes, who are by no means exempt, but here, where water is not abundant, two persons out of three are more or less affected. A great mortality must have prevailed lately, as we saw numbers of people in mourning and observed charnel houses and graves in the streets, under the dwellings, and in fact anywhere and everywhere, while the odour of decomposing heaps of vegetable matter rendered the atmosphere anything but savoury, and quickly drove us away. On the outskirts of Kamali we came upon a picturesque dwelling which I photographed, while Dr Doyle Glanville employed his pencil in sketching a woman in mourning. Kamali being more attractive than the village we had just quitted I remained to get a few studies, while the rest of the party went on ahead. The arrangement was that Sir Peter was to meet a boat at the crossing of the Kemp Welch river and be ferried to the launch which would rejoin the 'Governor Blackall' at her fresh anchorage at Kerepunu. I felt some misgivings as to getting sitters, being as I was unable to communicate with the people except by signs, but to my astonishment all the inhabitants turned out, evidently with the object of being photographed, and Mr Chalmers subsequently informed me that such is their vanity that had they but money, a photographic artist in New Guinea would rapidly accumulate a fortune. After an hour's rest I started with my four bearers in pursuit of the rest of the party who had preceded me to Kalo. The road lay through yam plantations and luxuriant groves of cocoanut palms, left to grow as they pleased, the native merely collecting the crops. The rapidity with which a Papuan can ascend a palm tree is marvellous. On an indication that a drink would be appreciated, up he goes, and in an incredible short space of time throws down half-a-dozen young nuts just fit for tapping. His method of ascending is to take anything that will spin into a lanyard, such as a bit of rattan, the rib of a cocoa-nut leaf, or even a handful of long grass. This he ties over his feet near the instep, connecting the feet by a pliable link, then by alternate movements of hands and feet he ascends the straight stem of the palm. Arrived underneath the fronds he holds on with one hand, and with the other twists the nut round the stem till it drops. Boys eight or ten years old can do this as well as the men, and I have no doubt the girls are equally agile, though as yet I have not seen them mount a tree. I arrived at Kalo just in time for lunch in the house of Tau the Rarotongan teacher, changing my clothes immediately, a precaution against fever which should always be taken after a fatiguing journey. After a rest and a smoke the General and his party walked to the river bank, where the boat was in waiting to proceed to Kerepunu, while I and my assistant made ourselves comfortable at Tau's house, where we were to spend the night. The Kalo people were in a state of great delight at the presents their chiefs had received from the General, whose visit tended to efface the sanguinary reprisals made by the blue-jackets of H.M.S. 'Wolverine' after the murder of ten teachers in the place. We were shown the marks of the bullets in the cocoa-nut trees, and altogether the people seemed to cherish a healthy recollection of the chastisement inflicted upon them, which was severe, the village being surrounded and several men shot before the rest were allowed to escape into the bush. The chief's house was razed to the ground. The teacher, Tau, informed us that the people are still somewhat predatory in their habits, his chest having on one occasion been broken open and eight pounds of tobacco stolen. On complaint being made to the chief, he compelled restitution of all the unconsumed tobacco and gave Tau a large pig to make up the difference. A large portion of the village was recently destroyed by fire, and is now in course of re-building. Among other curious sights we were shown the price or dowry of a wife heaped up on the platform of one of the houses. It consisted of a quantity of all kinds of New Guinea goods and chattels, pots, earthenware, and wooden weapons, bird of paradise plumes, baskets of yams, bunches of bananas and other produce. Among the articles were two pigs tied up underneath the house. The bride herself sat all smiles on the verandah above, over her earthly treasures, with as much pride as any white sister might feel on exhibiting her trousseau. I regretted that owing to the lateness of the evening I could not secure a picture of this curious scene, but managed to give the lady a prominent place in a group next morning. Skin disease is also rife here. We saw a young man walking about the village with his arm round his sweetheart's neck, both of them frightfully afflicted. He had a sore on his leg above the ankle, laying bare the bone, while she, not naturally ill-favoured, was covered with large patches which made her look positively mangy. Still, neither of them seemed to mind it in the least, and looked supremely happy. The head-dresses of marriageable girls are picturesque, their hair being frizzed and decorated with pink shells from Port Moresby, highly valued by them, strings of Venetian glass beads procured from the traders being woven in. All the women are tattooed from head to foot, and a peculiar necklace-like V-shaped mark, ending in a peak between the breasts, indicated those engaged or married. These cuticular devices, although obvious enough to the eye, do not show in a photograph unless picked out with black or some colour, a proceeding too tedious to perform even if they should be willing to submit to it. During our stay with Tau the house, doorways, and ladders on both sides were constantly crowded with natives attracted by motives of curiosity, and anxious to get a bit of tobacco or even the stump of a cigar. I commissioned Tau to buy me some bird of paradise plumes, leaving him a quantity of tobacco for the purpose, and making him a present of print and other articles for himself and wife. He told me that so long as the ship was in sight, the price of all curios was forced up to a fancy value, but that after her departure the beloved 'Kuku' would purchase anything at reasonable rates. The commercial ways of savages are very like those of civilized beings to be sure! The tobacco I brought — the best American Raven twist — was too good for the market; anything will do, if black and strong.

On the 29th, although it was still blowing hard, I managed to get some nice groups, and especially one of two women in mourning, keeping watch at a hut erected over the remains of some departed relative; I was obliged to go to leeward for the view, and as photography appeals to the eye and not the nose, I deemed the public had the best of it. Numbers of women sat outside the houses busy making ramis (petticoats) out of strips of fibrous leaves spread out in the sun to dry, and performing certain duties for each other often mentioned by previous travellers. After breakfast we started for Kerepunu, crossing the Kemp Welch river in a native canoe close to where the massacre of the teachers took place. The river is about a hundred yards wide and being shallow at its mouth can only be entered by boats of light draught.

Once across the bar there is water enough to float a big ship. About a mile from its mouth the stream bifurcates, the smaller affluent being nearly dry at low water, while the larger is navigable for about fifteen miles, and is supposed to take its rise in the neighbourhood of the Laloki, but on the eastern side of the water shed, running along the back of the Astrolabe range, until it reaches the level land at the back of Hula. The vegetation here is extremely rich, and the luxuriant condition of the native gardens indicates the great fertility of the soil. Dismissing our ferry men with a small present of tobacco, we proceeded with our bearers along the sandy beach. The glare of the sun on the shore and water was oppressive and I was thankful that I had provided myself with a pair of Mr Gaunt's smoked goggles before leaving Melbourne, as they saved my eyes, not only from the sun's rays but from the sand and grit blown up by the strong wind, to say nothing of the protection they afford against flies in the scrub. The teacher was rather uneasy about a little river named 'Alerai' which had to be crossed before reaching Kerepunu. At dead low water it is only about knee deep, but on reaching it we found that the rising tide had extended its width about sixty yards. We shot a couple of brace out of a flock of curlews we found at its mouth. Having no mind to follow the example of Horace's peasant and sit down half-a-dozen hours in the broiling sun, 'Expectantes dum defluit amnis,' we stripped and prepared to wade across, braving the alligators, which the teacher informed us were plentiful and possessed good appetites. First went the boys carrying their burdens over their heads and fortunately keeping them dry, though the water reached up to their shoulders. The teacher and myself followed, and last of all came Mr Bubb, my assistant. With my broad-brimmed straw hat, and goggles, and singlet, rolled up under my armpits, but otherwise in a state of nature, I must have presented a picturesque appearance, at any rate, I caused some amusement to our bearers, who sat waiting for us on the opposite side. The bottom was soft sand, sinking a foot with every step, but we got across without mishap and felt refreshed with our bath. Along the remaining two miles of hard beach I walked barefooted, but was compelled to resume my boots on crossing a neck of land covered with cocoa-nut trees and brushwood. Emerging from the thicket we found our ship snug at anchor in Hood Lagoon, with the village of Kerepunu as a background. The mouth of Hood Lagoon is about a mile wide and at high water sufficiently deep to allow vessels of fifteen feet draught to enter. Further inland it widens considerably and appears about eight miles long by six in diameter. The depth in some places is considerable, but the best anchorage is just within the narrow neck at the entrance. We got on board without loss of time and were glad of a bath and change of clothes. Tau, our guide, crossed over to Kerepunu to visit Manu, the teacher there, at whose house the teacher of Hula was also staying. Their wives had come with the ship to Kerepunu to assist in the ship's washing, fresh water being more abundant here than at Kalo or Hula.

Picturesque New Guinea (1887)

HUBERT MURRAY
(1861–1940)

Australian-born colonial administrator. Murray was educated in Sydney and England. Shortly after being called to the Bar in London in 1886, he returned to New South Wales, where he pursued a legal career, interrupted by service in South Africa during the Boer War. He was appointed chief judicial officer of British New Guinea in 1904, became acting administrator of the area in 1907, and served as the first lieutenant-governor of Papua under Australian rule from 1908 until his death. While in office, Murray went on a number of small expeditions, several of which are mentioned in this brief section from one of his publications.

'FLY AND STRICKLAND RIVERS'

Further to the West, the Fly and Strickland Rivers have been frequently visited of recent years; the lower parts of the Fly, for about 80 or 100 miles from the mouth, are regularly patrolled from the Government station at Daru, and the higher regions and the Strickland River have been examined by Messrs Massey Baker and Burrows, Messrs Ryan and Burrows, Messrs Lyons and Austen, Messrs Austen and Logan, and myself and Mr H. L. Murray, on three occasions, as well as by private expeditions of Sir Rupert Clarke and Messrs Pryke Brothers, two very well-known prospectors. The Prykes found traces of gold, but nothing more, and indeed, with the exception of the Herbert River and Lake Murray, between the Fly and the Strickland, which were discovered by Messrs Baker and Burrows in 1913, and the explorations of Messrs Austen and Logan between the Alice, a tributary of the

Upper Fly, and the Dutch border, nothing very much has been found on either River since the original visits of D'Albertis and Everill to the Fly and Strickland in 1877 and 1885 respectively. Mr Murray and myself, with Mr Burrows, who accompanied us on that occasion, were fortunate in finding a village of natives who were living in a peculiar kind of tree house, and were wearing cuirasses of rattan (called Irim), as a protection against arrows, but otherwise no new type of native was discovered until the visit of Messrs Austen and Logan in 1922. A cuirass of the kind to which I refer had been found by D'Albertis in a deserted house on the Alice River, but the tribe who wore them had not been met with (at any rate in Papua) until our visit in 1914.

Mr Massey Baker was patrolling the Upper Fly and the Strickland, in order to ascertain whether there was sufficient population to justify a new station, and if so, where the station should be placed. He left Daru on June 2nd, 1913, and on the 5th of the following month was ascending the Strickland, about 45 miles from Everill junction, when he 'entered a wide river on the Western bank.' At first he thought that this was the Western channel of the Strickland passing round an island, 'but,' he continues in his report, 'it turned out to be a previously undiscovered river. At its junction with the Strickland it is about 120 yards wide, but varies in its course, being in some parts nearly 200 yards wide. I have taken the liberty of calling the river after the Honourable Mr Justice Herbert. Immense flocks of geese and other wild fowl rose out of the reeds fringing the banks; there was no apparent current, and the depth varied from two to four fathoms. Bordered with tall cane grass, with occasional clumps of bamboo and small timber, it had all the appearance of the main river.' After a course of some 30 miles West from the Strickland, the Herbert 'opens out in to a magnificent lake, dotted with islands of bamboo.' 'The scene,' Mr Baker adds, 'was enchanting.' This lake he called Lake Murray. On the question of population, Mr Baker reports that the country 'bordering the West bank of the Strickland, as far as Latitude 6° 50' and the West and East banks of the Fly from the junction to approximately 7° 20' was thoroughly investigated,' and the conclusion he comes to is that on the Strickland there is a very sparse population, considerably scattered, and not exceeding 3,000 at the outside, and that there is no population at all on the part of the Fly that was investigated. Mr Baker excludes the people of the lake from his estimate for the Strickland; these people number some hundreds. Mr Baker found them hostile, and so did I when I was there in 1914 and 1917; but on my visit in 1922 they were quite friendly.

On our visit to the Strickland in 1917 we had a more powerful launch, and therefore succeeded in ascending the river rather higher than Mr Baker, and, with the exception of the people of Lake Murray and thereabouts, we saw no one. We went rather more than 100 miles beyond the Herbert River, and throughout the whole of that 100 miles we saw no trace of any human being. The inhabitants may have moved higher up the river, or it may be that they had exterminated each other. Their habits, as Mr Baker found them, rather suggests the latter explanation. About three days above the Herbert River he arrived at a large native camp or village. 'We counted,' he says, 'between 50 and 60 large canoes at the village and along the bank on the opposite side in a bend in the bank. There were very few men about, but a considerable number of women, some of them making sago.' There was a general scatter when the white men arrived, and Mr Baker investigated the camp. It was a large encampment, with accommodation for from 500 to 600 people. A large quantity of tobacco was lying about, done up into bales measuring from 2 feet to 2 feet 6 inches in length, and 12 inches in diameter, but the most striking thing about the camp was the large number of fresh heads 'in process of preparation,' which, according to Mr Baker, 'consisted primarily of tying them up in leaves, and allowing the cockroaches to do the rest.' Further up the river the party met the men of this village coming home from a raid, and fortunately got past them without an actual collision, and the next day came upon the scene from which the raiders were returning. 'A fair-sized native encampment appeared in sight on the West bank, and on coming close it was seen to be deserted. It had evidently been a sago making place. The mud bank was cut up by feet, as if there had been a considerable number of people, and as if there had been struggling, and on the beach close to the water's edge were the bodies of two or three women, minus heads and arms, and from the condition of things the massacre could only have happened a short time previously. In addition the bodies were horribly mutilated, stakes about 3 inches in diameter having been driven down from the neck through the trunk. The bodies were also flayed below the breasts. The camp was stripped of everything.'

Practices such as these are not conducive to an increase of population, and perhaps it is not to be wondered at that the banks of the Strickland, when I was there, bore no trace of human existence.

Recent Exploration in Papua (*c.* 1920s)

Part Three

—

THE ANTARCTIC

POSSESSION ISLAND.

Page 139.

LOUIS BERNACCHI

(1876–1942)

Australian scientist and explorer. Belgian-born Bernacchi migrated to Tasmania with his family in 1884, where his Italian entrepreneur father set about establishing a flamboyant settlement on Maria Island. Bernacchi took part, as physicist and astronomer, in Carsten Borchgrevink's 1898–1900 expedition to the Antarctic, the purpose of which was to make meteorological and magnetic observations for a year. The party was the first to winter on that continent. 'Bunny' Bernacchi is considered to be the first Australian to have set foot on Antarctica. He returned there with Captain Robert Scott's 1901–04 expedition, but sensibly, as it turned out, declined to join the latter's ill-fated 1910–12 venture.

'FIRST IMPRESSIONS'

We were now in the open sea to the south, for not a particle of ice was visible in any direction. Large flocks of brown-backed petrels were seen, and numbers of whales of the finner type. A sharp look-out was kept for land, and at 7 p.m. on the 15th of February [1899] it was sighted; but it was only a glimpse we caught of it through the dense canopy of clouds. Since noon the wind had increased steadily in force, until towards evening it was blowing a furious gale from the south-east and was accompanied by clouds of drifting snow. All that night and the following day the storm raged with full fury and the ship laboured heavily in the heavy seas. She lay to under half topsails, plunging fiercely into the seas and sometimes burying her whole bows beneath the waves, whilst ever and anon mighty green billows would pour over our decks and rush down into the cabins below. Our horizon was narrowly limited by the sheets of spray borne by the wind and the drifting snow, so we could see no land although we were not far from it.

The storm gradually abated towards the afternoon of the 17th, and we were able to stand in once more for the coast. The weather continued to improve and the dense mist cleared a little. At two o'clock in the afternoon land was again sighted distant some twenty-five miles, and we headed for a dark and high mass of rock which was evidently Cape Adare. It was a Cape of a very dark basaltic appearance, with scarcely any snow laying upon it, thus forming a strong contrast to the rest of the snow-covered coast. This lack of snow is principally due to the very exposed position of the Cape to the south-east winds, and, perhaps, also to the steep and smooth nature of its sides, which afford no hold for any snowfall. As we approached the coast it changed continually in aspect. Sometimes dense clouds of mist would envelop it; at other times the clouds would roll up like a great curtain, disclosing to our eyes a long chain of snow-clad mountains, the peaks of which tapered up one above the other like the tiers of an amphitheatre or those of the Great Pyramid of Cheops; but it was only a momentary vision, quickly disappearing, then all was again sombre, nothing but the heaving mass of waters, the whistle of the wind in the cordage, and the blinding snow across our decks.

Although we were certainly twenty miles distant from the land, the intervening space seemed infinitely less; in those high latitudes the eye is constantly liable to be deceived in the estimate it forms of distances. Apart from the contrast of light and shade, the great height of the mountain ranges and their bareness (they being destitute of any trees, etc., whereby to afford a point of comparison) augment this singular deception.

The wind decreased in fury as we got under the lee of the shore, but the whole heavens were still overcast with a dark mantle of tempestuous clouds, which now and then enshrouded the land in its folds, hiding it entirely from our view. The Bay (Robertson Bay) was clear of ice excepting for a huge stranded and weather beaten iceberg in its centre, into the cavities of which the seas ever and anon rushed with a great roar. As we drew closer, the coast assumed a most formidable aspect. The most striking features were the stillness and deadness and impassibility of the new world. Nothing around but ice and rock and water. No token of vitality anywhere; nothing to be seen on the steep sides of the excoriated hills. Igneous rocks and eternal ice constituted the landscape. Here and there enormous glaciers fell into the sea, the extremities of some many miles in width. Afterwards, when the mist had cleared away, we counted about a dozen of them around the Bay, rising out of the waters like great crystal walls. Approaching this sinister coast for the first time, on such a boisterous, cold and gloomy day, our decks covered with drift snow and frozen sea water, the rigging encased in ice, the heavens as black as death, was like approaching some unknown land of punishment, and struck into our hearts a feeling preciously akin to fear when calling to mind that there, on that terrible shore, we were to live isolated from all the world for many long months to come. It was a scene, terrible in its austerity, that can

only be witnessed at that extremity of the globe; truly, a land of un-
surpassed desolation.

To the South Polar Regions (1901)

DOUGLAS MAWSON

(1882–1958)

*Australian geologist and explorer. In 1909 Mawson and two companions
became the first people to reach the area of the south magnetic pole, doing so
in Ernest Shackleton's 1907–09 expedition. Mawson himself led the
Australasian Antarctic Expedition of 1911–14, which established three
bases, conducted major scientific investigations, and mapped a large part of
the coastline. Tragedy struck when Mawson was on a trip with Belgrave
Ninnis and Xavier Mertz to explore the far eastern coast. Ninnis fell into a
crevasse with a dog team and sledge and died. Mawson and Mertz were
forced to eat some of their dogs in order to survive, but in doing so may have
unwittingly contributed to Mertz's death in early 1913, because of the
potential toxicity of the dogs' livers. Mawson somehow managed to struggle
back to the base. Professor of geology at the University of Adelaide from
1920 to 1952, he also led the British–Australian–New Zealand Antarctic
Research Expedition of 1929–31. One of the bases in the Australian
Antarctic Territory is named after him.*

THE DEATH OF MERTZ

On talking things over with Mertz, I found that, though he had said
little on the subject in the past, he had found the dog meat very disagreeable and felt that he was getting little nutriment from it. He suggested that we should abstain for a time from eating any further of this
meat and draw solely upon the ordinary food of which we still had
some days' supply carefully husbanded. This plan was adopted as it was
expected to act beneficially on our health. I will always remember the
wonderful taste that the food had in those days. Acute hunger
enhances the taste and smell of food beyond all ordinary conception.
The flavour of food under such conditions is a miracle altogether
unsuspected by the millions of mortals who daily eat their fill. Cocoa
was almost intoxicating and even plain beef suet, such as we had in

fragments in our hoosh mixture, had acquired a sweet and aromatic taste scarcely to be described, but by contrast with the suet of our days of repletion it was certainly as different as chalk is from the richest chocolate cream.

The march that morning, the last day in the year, was under wretched conditions, for the light was atrocious and the surface slippery and ridged. The wind, tending to blow the sledge along sideways, only added to our troubles and assisted to bring us to 'earth' at frequent intervals. After stumbling along for two and a half miles we were obliged to give up and camp.

At 9.30 p.m. the sun appeared for a brief space gleaming through a pall of clouds, but was lost a moment afterwards. It was sufficient, however, to give us a bearing and as the wind subsided another stage was attempted. It was a costly performance, however, for on the polished surface in snow-blind light we literally staggered along, continually falling over unseen sastrugi. Of the latter, two sets crossing one another soon appeared confounding the only means of maintaining a course to march on, so camp was pitched after five miles.

Snow continued to fall all day long throughout New Year's day and the light remained as bad as ever. We waited anxiously for a glimpse of the sun to give us direction, in the meantime we decided not to attempt a move as Mertz was not up to his usual form and the rest might recuperate him. He had not been himself since the early morning hours of the 30th and had not responded to the change of diet. On the other hand, it was difficult to discover exactly what was the matter beyond exhaustion and the depressing effect of our continued bad fortune in the matter of weather. He did not complain, but endeavoured to be as cheerful as possible. I found that, like myself, he had from time to time a dull painful gnawing sensation in the abdomen; it may well have been that his was more acute than in my case. I had discovered that the pain was greatly relieved by frequently changing position as one rested. My theory, at the time, was that the gastric secretions, especially under the influence of food dreams, were so active in search of food as actually to attack the wall of the stomach itself. By turning over at intervals the damage would be distributed and less severe.

Later in the day I had another surprise finding that Mertz had lost appreciation of the biscuit; it was then that I first began to realize that something really serious was the matter and that his condition was worse than my own. As he expressed a desire for glaxo our small stock was made over to him, a larger proportion of biscuit and dog-meat falling to my share.

The wretched conditions persisted on January 2. It was decided that the few odd miles that might be covered were not worth attempting for the expenditure entailed would be out of all proportion to the result. In the first place we could not expect to make satisfactory course unless the sun were visible at least at intervals, for we had already found that thereabouts the trend of the sastrugi and the direction of the prevailing wind were considerably influenced locally by the depression ahead forming the upper part of the Mertz Glacier Valley. This confusion as to the direction of the sastrugi left us with only a rough notion of the bearing of the Hut. Secondly, owing to our reduced state and the awkwardness of the makeshift gear, an undue time was absorbed on every occasion when we got under way or pitched camp. Thus for the paltry gain of several miles we sometimes worked hours breaking and making camp, getting our clothes loaded with snow into the bargain. We longed for a good fine day when we could tramp on by the hour and appreciably lessen the distance ahead. While we lay in the bags weather-bound we felt constrained to eat less than ever.

At length in the evening of January 3 the clouds broke and the sun peered through for a time. We were not long in packing and getting on the way. It was an exceptionally cold night and the wind pierced our emaciated frames like a knife. Alas, before five miles were covered we were again in camp for Mertz had suddenly developed dysentery. To make matters worse his fingers had been badly frost-bitten, which for a moment he himself could scarcely believe, for so resistant to cold was he that he had never before suffered in this way. To convince himself he bit a considerable piece of the fleshy part off the end of one of them.

Though the wind howled and the drift flew past unceasingly throughout January 4, the sun shone brightly in the sky. We had intended rising at 10 a.m. to push on once more, but the condition of my companion called for a rest. I spent the day improving some of the gear, mending Mertz's and my own clothing and cooking a quantity of meat.

The day following was most depressing, for instead of improving the weather had relapsed. All day long in a gale of wind, falling snow lashed against the tent. The question of marching was referred to Mertz and he decided that we should remain in camp.

I busied myself cooking more meat and making appetizing broths which, however, my companion did not appreciate as I had hoped, furnishing additional evidence of the weakness of his digestive arrangements. Then followed wretched hours lying in the wet sleeping-bags — how we longed to get them properly dry!

January 6 was a great improvement on its predecessors, but the sky still remained overcast. Mertz agreed to try another stage. The grade was slightly downhill and the wind well behind, but these advantages were offset by an extremely slippery surface and awkward sastrugi ridges. Falls were frequent and they soon told severely upon my companion in his weak condition. At last, after consistently demurring, he consented to ride on the sledge. With a wind blowing from behind, it required no great exertion to bring the load along, though it would often pull up suddenly against sastrugi. After we had covered two and a half miles, Mertz became so chilled through inaction in the wind that, though otherwise all was going smoothly, there was nothing to do but pitch the tent.

Mertz was depressed and, after a little refreshment, sank back into his bag without saying much. He was troubled from time to time with recurrences of dysentery and had no power to hold in his stomach the broth which he was prevailed upon to swallow at intervals. Occasionally, during the day, I would ask him how he felt, or we would return to the old subject of food. Even then the conversation often led to the discussion of what we would do on arrival on board the *Aurora*, though I doubt if either of us at that time really expected to get through. I recollect that it was agreed that once on board the ship Mertz was to spend the day making penguin-egg omelettes, for the excellence of those he had made just prior to leaving the Hut had not been forgotten.

Starvation combined with superficial frost-bite, alternating with the damp conditions in the sleeping-bags, had by this time resulted in a wholesale peeling of the skin all over our bodies; in its place only a very poor unnourished substitute appeared which readily rubbed raw in many places. As a result of this, the chafing of the march had already developed large raw patches in just those places where they were most troublesome. As we never took off our clothes, the peelings of hair and skin from our bodies worked down into our under-trousers and socks, and regular clearances were made from the latter.

Our hair and beards, where exposed to the weather, were now bleached to a light sandy colour. A curious effect which, however, is noticed in greater or less degree by all sledging parties.

The night of the 6th was long and wearisome as I tossed about sleeplessly, mindful that for both of us our chances of reaching succour were now slipping silently and relentlessly away. I was aching to get on, but there could be no question of abandoning my companion whose condition now set the pace.

The morning of January 7th opened with better weather, for there was little wind and no snow falling; even the sun appeared gleaming through the clouds.

In view of the seriousness of the position it had been agreed overnight that at all costs we would go on in the morning, sledge-sailing with Mertz in his bag strapped on the sledge. It was therefore a doubly sad blow that morning to find that my companion was again touched with dysentery and so weak as to be quite helpless. After tucking him into the bag again, I slid into my own in order to kill time and keep warm, for the cold had a new sting about it in those days of want.

At 10 a.m. hearing a rustle from my companion's bag I rose to find him in a fit. Shortly afterwards he became normal and exchanged a few words, but did not appear to realize that anything out of the way had happened.

The information that this incident conveyed fell upon me like a thunderbolt, for it was certain that my companion was in a very serious state with little hope of any alleviation, for he was already unable to assimilate the meagre foods available.

There was no prospect of proceeding so I settled myself to stand by my stricken comrade and ease his sufferings as far as possible. It would require a miracle to bring him round to a fit travelling condition, but I prayed that it might be granted.

After noon he improved and drank some thick cocoa and soup.

Later in the afternoon he had several more fits and then, becoming delirious, talked incoherently until midnight. Most of that time his strength returned and he struggled to climb out of the sleeping-bag, keeping me very busy tucking him in again. About midnight he appeared to doze off to sleep and with a feeling of relief I slid down into my own bag, not to sleep, though weary enough, but to get warm again and to think matters over. After a couple of hours, having felt no movement, I stretched out my arm and found that my comrade was stiff in death. He had been accepted into 'the peace that passeth all understanding.'

It was unutterably sad that he should have perished thus, after the splendid work he had accomplished not only on that particular sledging journey but throughout the expedition. No one could have done better. Favoured with a generous and lovable character, he had been a general favourite amongst all the members of the expedition. Now all was over, he had done his duty and passed on. All that remained was his mortal frame which, toggled up in his sleeping-bag, still offered some sense of companionship as I threw myself down for the remainder of the night, revolving in my mind all that lay behind and the chances of the future.

The Home of the Blizzard (abridged popular edition 1930, first published in full 1915)

———

ERIC WEBB

(dates unknown)

New Zealand-born magnetician and explorer. Webb, a member of the main base party of Mawson's 1911–14 expedition, composed this tribute to his former leader in 1976. It was published at the end of Lennard Bickel's account of Mawson's tragic journey, This Accursed Land *(1977).*

'AN APPRECIATION'

Douglas Mawson is a giant figure in the history of the exploration of the southern continent. He led one of the greatest exploratory expeditions of all time in terms of territory covered on foot — a coastline of 2,000 miles, penetrated to a depth of nearly 400 miles by a handful of men — and made massive contributions to knowledge of our planet with resources which must be considered niggardly by modern standards.

However, it is for other reasons that I am happy to contribute this appreciation of the man who enriched my life, perhaps more than any other, by his personality, by his example and by his admirable leadership; and whose life-long friendship I prized above all others. I never had a stauncher friend; and, throughout his long life, he could stand and be compared with any explorer in history for courage, fortitude, endurance, resolve and loyalty to his fellows.

For these reasons, Douglas Mawson was always held in the highest regard among polar travellers, both in the age of heroics in Antarctica during the early decades of this century, and in more modern times. Yet, I fear his greatness as a man and as an explorer is too little known publicly, especially in Britain, merely because his feats were overshadowed by the Scott tragedy in 1912 and the Shackleton drama of 1914. There is today a strong need for a resurgence of interest, especially among young people, in his feats and fortitude and in the example of bravery which this book presents.

To me, when I was a young man in my early twenties, Mawson was already a hero. As a boy I had watched the Scott expeditions go out from my home town of Lyttelton, in New Zealand, in 1902 and in 1910; so, I was thrilled in July 1911, when I was invited to join Mawson's expedition as a magnetician. In preparation for this role I worked on the magnetic survey of Australia by the Carnegie Institution of Washington, DC, USA, which took me to the outback late in August where, at the tiny railway halt of Farina in the north of South Australia, I first saw Douglas Mawson — quite by chance.

Mawson arrived at that station to join the train in which I was travelling. He came in a Model T Ford — widely known as a 'Tin Lizzy' — which was loaded with boxes of uranium samples (pitchblende) collected from the first deposits (which he had discovered and identified) in Australia. I knew he was in the district and at once recognized this tall, tough-looking man in bush clothes. He was rangy and very strong. I saw him bend down and lift those boxes, which were heavier than lead, and heave them with his long arms into the rail wagon. I at once introduced myself and, from then on until the end of his life, I knew him as a man always straightforward who would not put up with nonsense, and who at once attracted respect.

My admiration for him was confirmed when I joined the expedition and we went south to Commonwealth Bay. His leadership was unobtrusive, capable, and highly appropriate to the personnel from 'down under' and for such a scientific venture.

He was not a Shackleton, nor a Scott — but he was no ordinary leader. Shackleton had a magnetic personality of the kind which is physical rather than intellectual, while Scott was, in the main, a naval martinet with scientific leanings. Mawson was, above everything, an intellectual leader with utter motivation and selfless dedication to his objective which he handed out to all of us in his party so that, by common consent, it became accepted and promoted as the policy of the expedition. Thus, when we saw how he was completely committed, so each one of us became committed to his own particular discipline. Mawson's dedication to scientific objectives infused a like spirit into us with the determination to emulate and excel the results of our peers. Other factors of great importance in this regard were his thorough and effective planning, his organization, and his contagious enthusiasm.

I am confident that his motivation and dedication to objective was a prime element in his ability to endure the terrible journey back to winter quarters following the loss of Ninnis down the crevasse. This was a very great and awful shock to his mental equilibrium, but I believe that his objective and resolve were then more firmly fixed in his mind than ever. Mawson normally weighed 15 stone (210 lbs) and this was all muscle and bone — no fat. When he got back to the hut, from what I heard he was skin and bone and weighed something less than 8 stone.

To me, and I have had some experience of what he suffered in my own journey to the South Magnetic Pole, his survival was the outstanding feat of any lone traveller in polar history. I have no hesitation in saying that. It showed him to be a great man in many senses, but mostly in that he could face the ultimate challenge and not flinch. We have to remember that he had already spent a whole winter in the base hut under the most blistering gales ever experienced by men. In the month of May alone, the average wind velocity (the mean strength of the wind for the whole of the month) was more than 60 m.p.h. which is something like six times the average for Europe. On many occasions, for several days together, the *average* wind velocity exceeded 80 m.p.h. with gusts peaking 200 m.p.h. and more. He was only too correct in saying that we had found 'the windiest place on the face of the earth.' Moreover, he had marched with Ninnis and Mertz more than 300 miles over territory of the most unimaginable difficulty in uncertain weather and poor light. They met falls of snow which covered and masked the areas of ice ridged beyond belief by sastrugi. These are waves and ridges of compacted snow produced by strong wind laden with drift snow and are shaped like an upturned boat but upwind tailing away to nothing. They may be only a few inches high, or go on right up to six feet, sharp-ridged at the top running out to merge into the general plateau surface, hard and smooth as polished ebony — nearly solid ice.

The cracks or crevasses underfoot largely ran across their path, both going out and coming back. Mawson's sufferings from starvation must have been horrendous. On my own journey coming back from the South Magnetic Pole, I had a glimpse of what he endured when, already debilitated by inadequate rations and extremely arduous hauling, my party hauled the last 70 miles in three days on one fifth of the standard ration.

I was aboard the *Aurora* when he returned to the hut and thus did not see him again until late in 1914 when he was already married to Paquita and had been knighted by King George V. He came to talk with me on the scientific accomplishments of the expedition, the compilation of data, and analysis. The Expedition's researches covered geo-magnetism, oceanography, meteorology, geology, biology, while the finding of traces of coal, copper, and valuable minerals had evoked considerable interest. It was a mountain of work calling for years of effort; moreover, he, himself, had to undertake public lectures, travel, and the writing of his account of the whole expedition in his book *The Home of the Blizzard* in order to pay off the debts which had accumulated steeply because of the second winter he was compelled to spend in the Antarctic.

When we met in New Zealand, he was the same tough, self-reliant character I had first seen loading the boxes of uranium samples at Farina. He was still purposeful, but he was a noticeably chastened man — quieter, humble, and I think very much closer to his God. To me, he was a superman — the marvel that had survived — and he took it as a matter of course, but that was his modesty, underlaid by his faith. I asked him about this and he told me that there was some other power he had borrowed on that journey which was superior to the willpower that pulled him through. His faith steeled him; he drew his personal strength from this faith. Yet, I saw he had aged, was worn, had lost much of his hair, and I fear he was never again the same iron man who started on that fateful journey. I am now convinced his terrible sufferings left scars on his physique and his constitution, and that he would have lived a lot longer than he did but for his awesome ordeal.

One other factor which must be mentioned in relation to his escape from death on the ice was character. He had always led a frugal life and had learned in his early years in Australia to meet difficulties and rugged conditions and to put up with limitations. He was a marvellous innovator, and improviser, and always extremely resourceful in the most practical way. Perhaps these qualities led to the saving of his life; his innovation prompted him to choose alcohol as the priming spirit for our primus stoves instead of methylated spirits, and I know this was of much help to my party. He was, as I have said, a great man in many senses; yet, the timing of the release of his story so close to the Scott tragedy meant it was almost completely eclipsed. This seems a wholly unfair quirk of fate which put his great performance in the shadows. World reaction to the Scott epic obliterated public interest in Mawson and left him with a daunting struggle, when he did get back, to win the interest and support he needed to pay off the debts caused by the disastrous delay. I am afraid that this disinterest and ignorance of this great man still persists in many places, even in his homeland of Australia. I deplore this utterly, because his epic belongs not to any single country but to all men, as a triumph of the human spirit over the most formidable adversity.

Strangely, the Antarctic maintained its hold on his mind for the rest of his life, though he never again made a long sledging journey. Like me, he joined the Services during the First World War, and then took up again his most distinguished academic career in geology. By the mid-1920s the south was again calling him, and he sought to extend the complex operation of charting the coast of Antarctica westward from the Shackleton ice shelf, where Wild had landed in 1912, along the quadrant below the Indian Ocean into the area south of South Africa. He was unable to obtain the kind of modern ship he wanted and his choice fell on the old, but worthy, *Discovery*, the same ship in which Scott had sailed south in 1901. He asked me to join him on the voyages he made along this vast strip of territory in 1929–31, but I was unable to do so since I was already committed to civil engineering and involved in hydro-electric schemes in India and elsewhere.

His work, by these expeditions, established Australian interest in the Antarctic over a vast sweep of the earth's surface. But, his contribution included an awareness of the resources and the wildlife in that region which is only today bearing some fruit.

He has done much to promote a world-wide awareness of the plight of the greatest mammal on earth, the whale. It is a world contribution arising from his anxiety over the plunder of the whale populations as early as 1911. He had great concern for all wildlife but, at that time, he became acutely conscious of the dangerous position in which man had placed these wonderful creatures. In later life, he never ceased his efforts to bring the plight of the whale to the attention of all nations and all peoples. Also he protested ceaselessly against the senseless slaughter of penguins for their oil which gave so little commercial return for the carnage that was inflicted.

For young generations today, the feat by this tremendous man, of surviving his epic, lone journey might have less appeal than the movement which he worked to set in motion, which was preservation of the unique wildlife in our oceans and our skies, so essential to our very existence. I have said he enriched my life; I hope that his story has like effect on many other people.

Lennard Bickel, *This Accursed Land* (1978 edition, first published 1977)

FRANK HURLEY

(1885–1962)

Australian photographer and film-maker. Hurley, who had worked from 1911 to 1913 with Mawson's Australasian Antarctic Expedition, was the official photographer with Shackleton's 1914–16 expedition, the aim of which was to cross the Antarctic continent. The expedition's ship, the Endurance, *however, became trapped in pack ice and drifted for more than nine months in 1915, before having to be abandoned. Shackleton and two others then made an extraordinary 800-mile voyage in an open boat to South Georgia for help. Here is Hurley's written account of the men's last days on the ship. Despite such off-putting experiences, Hurley made two more visits to the Antarctic, during Mawson's 1929–31 expedition.*

'THE SHIP IS DOOMED'

October 24th — The floes, which have been in motion during the afternoon, are assailing the ship on the starboard quarter with great energy. At 6 p.m. all hands go down on to the floe with picks, shovels and chisels, and cut trenches to try and relieve the strain, but we are miserably impotent. As fast as the ice can be hacked away new masses are hurled forward. At 7 p.m. an oncoming floe impinges on the helm, forcing it hard over to port and wrenching the rudder-post. The ship's sternpost is seriously damaged, and the hidden ends of the planking started. Soundings in the well announce the gloomy tidings that we are rapidly taking water. The pumps are manned, but it is a great task keeping them going as the water continually freezes and clogs the valve. The carpenter sets to work on a coffer-dam in the shaft tunnel in the hope of sealing-off the damaged stern of the vessel. Watches keep the pumps going vigorously. Their clickety-clack resounds throughout the night above the ominous creaking of timbers. The position is serious.

October 25th — Went down into the engine-room this morning to see the progress made by Chips on the coffer-dam. The water is level with the engine-room floor but is still being held in check and we still hope to bring our staunch craft through. Outside, the configuration of the ice has undergone another complete change, most of the pools in our vicinity have been converted into pressure-ridges, while there is an extensive lake half a mile away. Heavy pressure-ridges menace us on starboard quarter and astern. The ship is in a highly dangerous situation, with a heavy list to starboard. If the ridge advances it is obvious that the assailing ice will impinge above the sheer of the bilge and, as the ship is beset on every side by great masses of shattered ice, she will be unable to rise above the pressure. However, all is quiet for the present.

October 26th — Fine clear day. The ice in a state of turmoil all the morning subjected the ship to terrific strains. I was assisting Chips on the coffer-dam down in the shaft tunnel when the pressure set in and the creaking and groaning of timbers mingled with the pounding and scrunching against the ship's sides produced a hideous deafening din and warned us to make for safety. As there was a likelihood of the ship's sides crushing in and trapping us in the tunnel we hurried up on deck. All were actively engaged clearing the lowering-gear of the boats and stacking the emergency stores in case of compulsory disembarkation, which now seems inevitable.

The dogs, instinctively conscious of the imminent peril, set up distressed wails of uneasiness and fear. Sir Ernest stands on the poop, surveying the movements of the ice, and giving an occasional peremptory order. Sledges and all gear are being rapidly accumulated on deck, without confusion, as though it were ordinary routine duty. At 6 p.m. the pressure develops terrific energy; apparently our vicinity is the focus, as the ice, a short distance off, remains motionless. The ship shrieks and quivers, windows splinter, while the deck timbers gape and twist. The brunt of the pressure assails our starboard quarter and the damaged stern-post. The ship is forced ahead by a series of pulsating jerks, and with such force that the bows are driven wedgewise into the solid floe ahead. This frightful strain bends the entire hull some ten inches along its length. At 7 p.m. the order is given to lower the boats. They are hauled some distance away from the *Endurance* and out of the zone of immediate danger. At 8.15 p.m. there is a welcome cessation in the ice movement, and all go on board to take their turn at the pumps and get what rest they can.

October 27th — Chips expects to complete the coffer-dam tonight and great hopes are still entertained that he will be able to. All, including Sir Ernest, continue turns with the pumps, which are able to keep pace with the inflowing water. We have just finished lunch and the ice-mill is in motion again. Closer and closer the pressure-wave approaches. Immense slabs are rafted, balance a moment, then topple down and are over-ridden by a chaos of crunched fragments.

Irresistibly this stupendous power marches onward, grinding through the five-foot ice-floe surrounding us. Now it is within a few yards of the vessel. We are the embodiment of helpless futility and can only look impotently on. I am quickly down on the moving ice with the cinema, expecting every minute to see the sides of the ship, which are springing and buckling, stave in. The line of pressure now assaults the ship and she is heaved up to the crest of the ridge like a toy. Immense fragments are forced under the counter and wrench away the stern-post. Sir Ernest and Captain Worsley are surveying the ship's position from the floe when the carpenter announces that the water is gaining rapidly on the pumps. All hands are ordered to stand by to discharge equipment and stores on to the ice. The pumps work faster and faster and someone is singing a chanty to their beat. The dogs are rapidly passed out down a canvas chute and secured on the floe, followed by cases of concentrated sledging rations, sledges and equipment. The ship is doomed.

By 8 p.m. all essential gear is 'floed', and though the destruction of the ship continues, smoke may be observed issuing from the galley chimney — the cook is preparing supper. All hands assemble in the wardroom to partake of the last meal aboard the good old ship. The meal is taken in silent gravity, whilst the crushing is in progress and an ominous sound of splintering timbers arises from below. We have grown indifferent to dangers, for we have lived amongst them so long, and our sadness is for the familiar surroundings from which we are being expelled. The clock is ticking away on the wall as we take our final leave of the cosy ward-room, that has for over twelve months been connected with pleasant associations and fraternal happiness. Before leaving, I went below into the old winter quarters, the Ritz, and found the waters swirling in and already a foot above the floor, the ribs disrupting and tongues of ice driving through the sides. Our ship has put up a valiant fight and done honour to her noble name, *Endurance*.

Sir Ernest hoists the blue ensign on the mizzen-gaff to three lusty cheers and is the last to leave. All the equipment and boats are moved some three hundred yards away, as the floes are in active commotion in the vicinity of the ship. During the dim hours of midnight, the calm frigid atmosphere is resonant with the grinding of the pressure-ice, and the hideous noises coming from the dying vessel. By some electrical oddity the emergency light becomes automatically switched on and for an hour an intermittent making and breaking of the circuit seems to transmit a final sad signal of farewell.

Shackleton's Argonauts (1979 edition, first published 1948)

———

THOMAS KENEALLY

(1935–)

Australian novelist. Keneally was studying for the priesthood, but left the seminary in 1960, subsequently becoming a teacher and writer. His best-known novels include Bring Larks and Heroes *(1967),* Three Cheers for the Paraclete *(1968), and* Schindler's Ark *(1982), which inspired Steven Spielberg's film* Schindler's List *(1993). He visited the Antarctic in November 1968, not long before the publication of his novel* The Survivor *(1969). One of its main characters is Dr Leeming, the leader of a 1926 expedition to the south geomagnetic pole, whose death is described below. He has been cuckolded by Alec Ramsey, his friend and fellow expedition member. Keneally later wrote another novel with an Antarctic setting,* A Victim of the Aurora *(1977).*

THE DEATH OF LEEMING

After his first collapse, Leeming lived six days. He was irascible, resisted being loaded onto the sledge like baggage, tried to march. Often they let him. They too were weary, Ramsey wearied for life. And Lloyd thought that to struggle with Leeming to make him accept passenger status on the sledge would be more dangerous to him than to let him march. Ramsey suffered from finding himself aggressive against the leader who shambled through those days, the sort of brute wreckage that makes you want both to succour and lash out with your fists. Ramsey could sense perversity in the dying man's stamina, and condemned himself for sensing it, whenever he ceased hating him totally.

He felt liberated on the man's second and lethal collapse.

It was the end of March, 1926.

They were on fairly open ice with ridges running west-east. This counted as a good travelling surface: in fact, someone had surveyed the glacier earlier in the summer and recommended it as such.

Ramsey had loaded the tank on the sledge while the polar wigwam still stood upright, and had to work pieces of cooker and Lloyd's and his own sleeping-bags and the provision box up the funnel-entrance to the outside. He worked in this overdone way so that he could find it easier to build up a good head of resentment against Lloyd.

The canvas box they called the tank was frozen and the tank strap no more pliable than, say, a medium-tensile metal.

There was a terrible flesh-eating wind and he began and kept on whimpering for his fingers in useless inner gloves. The drift was beside the point, since they had to travel.

Without cease he swore against Lloyd.

The reason was that Lloyd was a doctor and had the, for the moment, soft work of attending Leeming inside and nodding over Leeming's feet. These had become especially liable to frostbite since Leeming took his first stroke.

Lloyd was competent, and called the strokes cerebral vascular accidents. Ramsey told himself that Lloyd used these terms to give a technical grandeur to his reasons for not strapping up the tank.

When he had packed, he wormed back under canvas, full of bad weather news.

'There,' he intended to say and show Lloyd his mitts. 'Freezing up already.'

Lloyd was toggling Leeming's sleeping-bag at the neck and face. Ramsey could see through for a second to the face within. It was livid and elsewhere canvas-coloured. Shredded skin hung from the lips like a moustache.

He asked if the man had moved. Lloyd said he had died. Lloyd seemed self-disgusted, as if his lack of skill had brought on the death. He was, in fact, an expert physician.

Ramsey's scalding hands engrossed him. Therefore he postponed any grief. If would have been better, he could remember thinking, if he had had time to speak to Leeming about his wife. And he had a woolly sense that Lloyd was wrapping up a wronged body. He felt that to be sure he ought to listen to Leeming's heart, but that meant a job of untying and untoggling and un-press-studding Leeming's clothing — the zip-fastener era had not dawned — and he was still bending over his hands, which were stuck into his clothes against his Jaeger fleece, returning to life and to their million daily pains that were all to do with chafing and split skin.

He was afraid besides that he might find the heart had begun beating again — and then they would have had to put up with his shambling again and waste food on him.

They removed the tent from him and folded it — it took forcing, and went together like a metal concertina. Ramsey thought Leeming looked hateful. Exposed like that in his grey sleeping-bag, he looked like some animal's hateful excreta.

Lloyd said they mustn't waste strength by the body. But he ran through some of the service for the dead — he'd learned it in France and knew it was the acceptable thing at such a time, as one sends cards at Christmas.

Then he went to the sledge and stood stiffly looking east, where, the maps had it, was the ice-tongue and the sound still ice-free (perhaps) and the *Westralis*. If the *Westralis* had not been there they would have made a hole in the ice and lived off seal-meat. And Ramsey would easily have gone mad.

He found he could not leave Leeming straightaway. Though he avoided looking at him, he put some markers at his head.

The Survivor (1969)

PHILLIP LAW

(1912–)

Australian scientist and explorer. Previously a lecturer in physics at the University of Melbourne, Law was the director of the Antarctic Division of the Department of External Affairs from 1949 to 1966, during which time he established the Mawson, Davis, and Casey bases and led many exploratory expeditions. From 1966 to 1980, he chaired the Australian National Committee on Antarctic Research. These terrifying events occurred in 1954, during a voyage back to Australia.

'THIS IS IT!'

I lay in my bunk, rolling from side to side with the violent motion of the ship, wedged into place as well as I could manage it with my knees pressed against the bulkhead on one side and my back against a rolled-up blanket laid lengthwise down the outer edge of the side board.

Squadron Leader Doug Leckie called me at 0130 hours on Friday 5 March to tell me that our Auster aircraft, lashed down on the deck, had been wrecked. The wind was now blowing at Force 14 and the ship was hove-to into the wind and rolling and pitching violently in heavy seas.

Doug and I stumbled along the heaving passage and pushed through the door at the end onto the boat deck. It was wild out there. We clung to the handrails as the wind buffeted us and freezing spray lashed our faces. The scream of the wind and the flapping of our parka hoods around our ears made conversation impossible, so I just stood and looked. The aircraft certainly was a mess. Gusts of wind under the starboard wing had caused the main strut, connecting the port float to the fuselage, to collapse and the plane had lurched over on one side, crumpled and twisted, with the port wing tangled up in the lifeboat davits.

There was nothing we could do except to hope that it would remain where it was. With the ship hove-to, there was a reasonable chance that it would. So we retreated inside and climbed the companionway to the bridge to inform the Captain of the accident.

Captain Petersen looked grim. He was having great difficulty holding the ship into the wind. Relieved of her cargo, *Kista Dan* was floating high in the water and, as each gust struck her starboard quarter, she would shudder and shy off to port, only to be hauled back into the wind by the helmsman. The wind was now blowing at hurricane force, well over 100 m.p.h. The pitching ship would bury its bows into each giant wave and send a sheet of water and spray slashing over the foredeck and across the windows of the bridge. Spray was freezing on the deck and the rigging and the windscreen wipers on the bridge windows were clogging with sludge ice.

There was little conversation on the darkened bridge. The helmsman's repetition of the Captain's steering orders and an occasional comment in a low voice by the First Mate or myself were the only words spoken. The radar shone green under its hood and the First Mate seldom left it. The crewman operating the depth sounder watched silently as the recorder swept around, sketching a profile of the sea floor, while out on each wing of the bridge a sailor, huddled up in waterproofs and mittens, peered out into the darkness on the lookout for ice floes and growlers.

The bows were riding so high out of the water that I asked the Chief Engineer whether the forward tanks had been ballasted. He said no; they had tried, but the pipes had frozen up.

A ship returning without cargo from a long voyage can be ballasted by pumping sea water into empty fuel tanks and, at a pinch, into the depleted fresh water tanks. Fuel can also be transferred between various tanks to trim the ship.

In *Kista Dan* the fuel in the deep tank forward had been used, as also had much of the fresh water from the forepeak tank. If the pipes had not frozen up, sea water could have been pumped into these tanks, or fuel could have been transferred from the double bottom tanks to the deep forward tank.

About 0200 hours the Captain lost control of the ship. No combination of rudder and engine revolutions could counteract the force of the wind on the bows and *Kista Dan* broached to, with her starboard side to the wind. Lying over on her port side, she drifted helplessly, pounded by every breaking wave and held in a permanent list by the hurricane.

Realizing that in this position the aircraft would be exposed, I again ventured out onto the boat deck and about 0300 hours I watched dejectedly as another spar collapsed and the 'plane toppled forward onto its nose on the deck. The propeller was bent back under the fuselage and the starboard wing crumpled up in a horrible, grinding mess. Shortly afterwards, the wind blew the whole lot over the ship's side and the Second Mate cut the lashings to let the wreckage drift away. As he did so, petrol from the fuel tank spilled over his hands and he writhed in agony as his fingers froze up. (As petrol does not freeze until its temperature is very low, it can become much colder than water.)

From this point on it was a nightmare. *Kista Dan* lay on her side, held to a permanent list of 30° by the force of the wind and rolling from there, so that the limits of the rolls were vertical or 10° to starboard, then 60° or 70° to port.

We knew the stability of the ship was marginal. In earlier voyages I had been used to very stiff, highly stable Polar vessels with rolling periods of five to eight seconds. *Kista Dan* during this voyage had demonstrated a rolling period of 14 seconds. As far back as 13 December, on the voyage to Macquarie Island, I had written in my diary: 'The ship feels top-heavy; she has a long period of roll and tends to hang over at the end of the roll. It makes for a comfortable ride, but I shall not feel very safe if she hangs over like this in a big storm.' (After she returned to Denmark at the end of the voyage the owners added 70 tons to her keel.)

I have never been so terrified. A gust of wind and a huge wave would strike the ship and she would heel over to 70°. There would hang and shudder as though debating whether to continue on or to return. For what seemed like a minute I would hold my breath, saying 'No, no!' with my heart thumping against my ribs; then she would lurch back to the 30° mark, only to be hurled over again to lie flat on her side. When in my bunk, I was lying on the bulkhead for half the time instead of on the mattress.

There have been a number of occasions in my life when I have been afraid, but never have I experienced, either before or since, terror extending unrelieved over such a long period of time. I don't think anyone on the ship really expected to survive and, over a period of 12 hours, each large roll seemed likely to be the last.

There was nothing for me to do. I felt superfluous on the bridge and was reluctant to intrude with unnecessary comments or questions. Most of my men were in their bunks and, although this was far from comfortable, it was much more comfortable than trying to maintain balance standing up, so I followed their example, only rising periodically to gaze through the porthole or occasionally to show my face for a minute or two on the bridge.

The most horrible moment of the whole night was when I stood in my cabin, in the semi-darkness, leaning against the bulkhead, with my face pressed against the porthole, peering out on the port side over the tormented water. All was confusion: the near-darkness, the spray slashing the glass, the blown spume streaking the tossing surface of the sea; the crashings and bangings around the ship, the high-pitched scream of the wind, and the violent movements as the ship reared and plunged like a frightened horse. Suddenly, struck by a fierce gust of wind and a particularly high wave, the ship heeled over until I was lying on my stomach on the bulkhead, practically horizontal, with my nose flattened against the submerged glass of the porthole, gazing down into the green-black depths. There I waited and waited for the recovery that would not come, as successive waves ground the ship further and further down on its side and my terror mounted. Finally, after shaking and shuddering and deliberating, the vessel slowly moved back to the 30° list position and I stood once again on the deck, with pounding heart and sweat pouring down my face.

In my imagination I could feel the ship go over again, shuddering at the horizontal mark and then turning right over. I could hear myself saying 'This is it!' as I was tossed onto the ceiling along with every loose article in the cabin. I could imagine the roar of water rushing into the ship and rising steadily around me as I floundered to reach the door of my cabin. Beyond that I was not sure. Would I struggle futilely against the flood, or would I resign myself to die slowly as the water rose higher and higher against my chest? Few prospects can be more horrible.

I recall quite clearly my emotion when confronting what then seemed like certain death. It was one of intense anger and resentment. Here I was, the successful expedition leader, returning home with a story of accomplishment and a load of important scientific records and photographs. Was all this to be lost? Was all our work to be wasted? And no one would ever know exactly what had happened to us!

Antarctic Odyssey (1983)

BIBLIOGRAPHY

Australian Dictionary of Biography, vols 1–13, Melbourne University Press, Carlton, 1966–93.

Australian Encyclopedia, 3rd edn, 6 vols, Grolier Society of Australia, Sydney, 1977.

Binks, C.J., *Explorers of Western Tasmania*, Mary Fisher Bookshop, Launceston, 1980.

Bonyhady, Tim, *Burke & Wills: From Melbourne to Myth*, David Ell Press, Balmain, 1991.

Borchardt, D.H. (ed.), *Australians: A Guide to Sources*, Fairfax, Syme & Weldon Associates, Broadway, 1987.

Carter, Paul, *The Road to Botany Bay: An Essay in Spatial History*, Faber & Faber, London, 1988 (1987).

Clancy, Robert, *The Mapping of Terra Australis*, Universal Press, Sydney, 1995.

Cowley, Des (guest ed.), *La Trobe Library Journal*, vol. 11, no. 41, autumn 1988, special issue, *The Great South Land*.

Dunmore, John, *Who's Who in Pacific Navigation*, Melbourne University Press, Carlton, 1992.

Feeken, E. H. V. & Feeken, G. E., *The Discovery and Exploration of Australia ... with an Introduction by O. H. K. Spate*, Nelson, Melbourne, 1970.

Fitzpatrick, Kathleen (ed.), *Australian Explorers: A Selection from their Writings*, Oxford University Press, London, 1958.

Gibson, Ross, *The Diminishing Paradise: Changing Literary Perceptions of Australia*, Sirius Books, Angus & Robertson Publishers, Sydney, 1984.

Hanbury-Tenison, Robin (ed.), *The Oxford Book of Exploration*, Oxford University Press, Oxford and New York, 1993.

Lansbury, Coral, *Arcady in Australia: The Evocation of Australia in Nineteenth Century English Literature*, Melbourne University Press, Carlton, 1970.

McLaren, Ian F., *Australian Explorers by Sea, Land and Air 1788–1988*, 9 vols, University of Melbourne Library, Melbourne, 1988–91.

Martin, Stephen, *A New Land: European Perceptions of Australia 1788–1850*, Allen & Unwin, Sydney, 1993.

Millar, Ann, *'I see no end to travelling': Journals of Australian Explorers 1813–1876*, Bay Books, Sydney, 1986.

BIBLIOGRAPHY

Moyal, Ann, *A Bright and Savage Land*, Penguin, Melbourne, 1993 (1986).

Perry, T. M., *The Discovery of Australia: The Charts and Maps of the Navigators and Explorers*, Nelson, Melbourne, 1982.

Whittaker, J.L., Gash, N.G., Hookey, J.F. & Lacey, J.R, *Documents and Readings in New Guinea History: Prehistory to 1889*, The Jacaranda Press, Brisbane, 1975.

SOURCES AND ACKNOWLEDGMENTS

Anonymous extract (re Lasseter): *Argus*, 29 April 1931.

Anonymous, 'Lines to T. L. Mitchell, Esq., M.R.G.S. & F.G.S. on His Leaving Sydney for the Interior on an Expedition of Discovery', *Sydney Gazette and New South Wales Advertiser*, 10 March 1836.

Anonymous, *Our Cruise to New Guinea*, Turner & Henderson, Sydney, 1884, pp. 5–9.

Janis Balodis, *Too Young For Ghosts*, Currency Press, Sydney, 1991 (1985), pp. 3–7.

Nicolas Baudin, *The Journal of Post-Captain Nicolas Baudin, Commander-in-Chief of the Corvettes* Géographe *and* Naturaliste: *Assigned by Order of the Government to a Voyage of Discovery*, trans. Christine Cornell, Libraries Board of South Australia, Adelaide, 1974, pp. 379–80.

Louis Bernacchi, *To the South Polar Regions: Expedition of 1898–1900*, Hurst & Blackett Ltd, London, 1901, pp. 62–5.

Gregory Blaxland, 'A Journal of a Tour of Discovery Across the Blue Mountains, New South Wales, in the Year 1813', in *Fourteen Journeys Over the Blue Mountains of New South Wales 1813–1841*, ed. George Mackaness, Horwitz-Grahame, Sydney, Melbourne and London, 1965, pp. 9–11.

George Caley, *Reflections on the Colony of New South Wales*, ed. J.E.B. Currey, Lansdowne Press, Melbourne, 1966, pp. 54–5.

David W Carnegie, *Spinifex and Sand. A Narrative of Five Years' Pioneering and Exploration in Western Australia*, C. Arthur Pearson Ltd, London, 1898, pp. 316–20. Facsimile edition published by Penguin, Harmondsworth and Melbourne, 1973.

William Clark extract: F. M. Bladen (ed.), *Historical Records of New South Wales*, vol. III, Charles Potter, Government Printer, Sydney, 1895, pp. 765–6. Facsimile edition published by Lansdown Slattery & Co., Sydney, 1978.

Kevin Coate, 'Quest in Wandjina Land', *Australian Geographic*, no. 21, March 1991, pp. 32–41.

James Cook extract: J. C. Beaglehole (ed.), *The Journals of Captain James Cook on his Voyages of Discovery*, vol. 1, *The Voyage of the* Endeavour, *1768–1771*, published for the Hakluyt Society at the University Press, Cambridge, 1955, pp. 204–6.

Allan Cunningham extract: *The Journal of the Royal Geographical Society of London*, vol. II, John Murray, London, 1832, pp. 111–13.

L. M. D'Albertis, *New Guinea: What I Did and What I Saw*, vol. II, Sampson Low, Marston, Searle, & Rivington, London, 1880, pp. 94–5.

William Dampier, *A New Voyage Round the World*, Adam & Charles Black, London, 1937 (1697), pp. 311–16.

Robyn Davidson, *Tracks*, Vintage, London, 1992 (first published by Jonathan Cape Ltd, 1980), pp. 189–92. Reproduced with permission of Jonathan Cape Ltd.

Louis de Rougemont, *The Adventures of Louis de Rougemont: As Told by Himself*, William Heinemann, London, 1899, pp. 122–5.

Willem de Vlamingh, *Voyage to the Great South Land, Willem de Vlamingh, 1696–1697*, ed. Günter Schilder and trans. C. de Heer, Royal Australian Historical Society, Sydney, 1985, p. 123. First published in Dutch by Martinus Nijhoff, The Hague, 1976.

Robert Drewe, 'The Last Explorer', in his *The Bodysurfers*, Picador, Sydney, 1987 (first published by James Fraser Publishing Pty Ltd, 1983), pp. 148–55.

Laurie Duggan, *The Ash Range*, Picador, Sydney, 1987, pp. 33–6.

Geoffrey Dutton, *Edward John Eyre: The Hero as Murderer*, Penguin, Harmondsworth, 1977, pp. 129–31. Originally published as *The Hero as Murderer: Edward John Eyre*, William Collins Ltd and F. W. Cheshire Publishing Pty Ltd, 1967.

Ray Ericksen, *West of Centre: A Journey of Discovery into the Heartland of Australia*, paperback students' edition, Heinemann Educational Australia, Melbourne, 1973 (1972), pp. 179–81. Reproduced with permission of Reed Books Australia.

George William Evans extract: *Historical Records of Australia*, series 1, vol. VIII, The Library Committee of the Commonwealth Parliament, Sydney, 1916, pp. 169–73.

Edward John Eyre, *Journals of Expeditions of Discovery into Central Australia, and Overland from Adelaide to King George's Sound, in the Years 1840–1; Sent by the Colonists of South Australia, With the Sanction and Support of the Government: Including an Account of the Manners and Customs of the Aborigines and the State of their Relations with Europeans*, vol. 1, T. & W. Boone, London, 1845, pp. 352–8. Facsimile edition published by the Libraries Board of South Australia, Adelaide, 1964.

Ernest Favenc, *The History of Australian Exploration from 1788 to 1888*, Turner & Henderson, Sydney, 1888, pp. 184–8. Facsimile edition published by Golden Press, Sydney, 1983.

H. H. Finlayson, *The Red Centre: Man and Beast in the Heart of Australia*, Angus & Robertson Ltd, Sydney, 1935, pp. 100–4. Facsimile edition published by the Libraries Board of South Australia, Adelaide, 1979.

Charles Augustus FitzRoy extract: *Historical Records of Australia*, series 1, vol. XXVI, The Library Committee of the Commonwealth Parliament, Sydney, 1925, pp. 440–3.

Matthew Flinders, *Observations on the Coasts of Van Diemen's Land, on Bass's Strait and its Islands, and on Part of the Coasts of New South Wales; Intended to Accompany the Charts of the Late Discoveries in those Countries*, Printed by John Nichols, London, 1801, pp. 33–4. Facsimile edition published by the Libraries Board of South Australia, Adelaide, 1965.

John Forrest, *Explorations in Australia*, Sampson Low, Marston, Low, & Searle, London, 1875, pp. 114–18. This is a facsimile edition published in 1969.

Jane Franklin extract: *Some Private Correspondence of Sir John and Lady Jane Franklin (Tasmania, 1837–1845)*, part II, introduction, notes and commentary by George Mackaness, D.S. Ford, Sydney, 1947, pp. 47–50.

Ernest Giles, *Geographic Travels in Central Australia from 1872 to 1874*, McCarron, Bird & Co., Melbourne, 1875, pp. 173–4. Facsimile edition published by Corkwood Press, Bundaberg, 1993.

W. C. Gosse, *Report and Diary of Mr W. C. Gosse's Central and Western Exploring Expedition, 1873: Ordered by the House of Assembly to be Printed, 2nd June, 1874*, Government Printer, Adelaide, 1874, p. 1. Facsimile edition published by the Libraries Board of South Australia, Adelaide, 1973.

Francis Thomas Gregory extract: Augustus Charles Gregory & Francis Thomas Gregory, *Journals of Australian Explorations*, James C. Beal, Government Printer, Brisbane, 1884, pp. 86–7. Facsimile edition published by Hesperian Press, Perth, 1981.

George Grey, *Journals of Two Expeditions of Discovery in North-West and Western Australia, During the Years 1837, 38, and 39, Under the Authority of Her Majesty's Government, Describing Many Newly Discovered, Important, and Fertile Districts, With Observations on the Moral and Physical Condition of the Aboriginal Inhabitants, &c. &c.*, vol. 1, T. & W. Boone, London, 1841, pp. 201–7. Facsimile edition published by Hesperian Press, Perth, 1983.

Arthur Groom, *I Saw a Strange Land: Journeys in Central Australia*, Angus & Robertson, Sydney, 1950, pp. 152–5.

Lawrence Hargrave, Private Papers of Lawrence Hargrave, letter from Lawrence Hargrave to the Chairman of the meeting of the Geographical Society of Australasia held on 19 June at the Protestant Hall, Pitt Street,

Sydney, dated at North Shore, 18 June 1883, microfilm, Mitchell Library FM 4/1060, in J.L. Whittaker, N.G. Gash, J.F. Hookey & J.R. Lacey, *Documents and Readings in New Guinea History: Prehistory to 1889*, The Jacaranda Press, Brisbane, 1975, pp. 258–9.

Joseph Hawdon, *The Journal of a Journey from New South Wales to Adelaide Performed in 1838*, Georgian House, Melbourne, 1952, pp. 48-53.

Barry Hill, *The Rock: Travelling to Uluru*, Allen & Unwin, Sydney, 1994, pp. 85–8.

Ernestine Hill, *My Love Must Wait: The Story of Matthew Flinders*, Angus & Robertson, Sydney and London, 1942 (1941), pp. 459–63.

John Ainsworth Horrocks extract: *Proceedings of the Royal Geographical Society of Australasia: South Australian Branch*, sessions 1904–05, 1905–06, vol. VIII, Vardon & Sons Ltd, Adelaide, 1906, pp. 44–6.

Hamilton Hume & William Hovell extract: W. Bland, *Journey of Discovery to Port Phillip, New South Wales; By Messrs W. H. Hovell and Hamilton Hume: in 1824 and 1825*, A. Hill, Printer, Sydney, 1831, pp. 37–41. Facsimile edition published by the Libraries Board of South Australia, Adelaide, 1965.

Frank Hurley, *Shackleton's Argonauts: The Epic Tale of Shackleton's Voyage to Antarctica in 1915*, McGraw-Hill Book Co., Sydney, 1979 (first published by Angus & Robertson, 1948), pp. 87–98.

Ion Idriess, *Lasseter's Last Ride: An Epic of Australian Discovery*, Angus & Robertson, Sydney, 1950 (1931), pp. 113–20.

Jackey Jackey extract: John MacGillivray, *Narrative of the Voyage of H.M.S. Rattlesnake, Commanded by the Late Captain Owen Stanley, R.N., F.R.S. &c, During the Years 1846–1850, Including Discoveries and Surveys in New Guinea, the Louisiade Archipelago etc., To which is Added the Account of Mr. E. B. Kennedy's Exploration of the Cape York Peninsula*, vol. II, T. & W. Boone, London, 1852, pp. 228–36.

Thomas Keneally, *The Survivor*, Belmont/Tower Books, New York City, 1977 (1969), pp. 136–9.

Phillip P. King, *Narrative of a Survey of the Intertropical and Western Coasts of Australia, Performed between the Years 1818 and 1822*, vol. I, John Murray, London, 1827, pp. 165–74.

William Landsborough, *Journal of Landsborough's Expedition from Carpentaria, In Search of Burke and Wills*, F.F. Bailliere, Melbourne, 1862, pp. 56–9.

Phillip Law, *Antarctic Odyssey*, William Heinemann Australia, Melbourne, 1983, pp. 149–52. Reproduced with permission of Reed Books Australia.

Robert Lawrence extract: T. E. Burns & J.R. Skemp, *Van Diemen's Land Correspondents: Letters from R.C. Gunn, R.W. Lawrence, Jorgen Jorgenson, Sir John Franklin and Others to Sir William J. Hooker, 1827–1849*, Queen Victoria Museum, Launceston, 1961, pp. 26–8.

J. A. Lawson, *Wanderings in the Interior of New Guinea*, Chapman & Hall, London, 1875, pp. 155–61.

F. W. Ludwig Leichhardt, *The Letters of F. W. Ludwig Leichhardt: Collected and Newly Translated by M. Aurousseau*, vol. III, Cambridge University Press for the Hakluyt Society, Cambridge, 1968, pp. 860–3.

John Lhotsky, *A Journey from Sydney to the Australian Alps, Undertaken in the Months of January, February and March 1834*, Innes, Sydney, 1835, pp. 3–5. Reprinted in facsimile, under the same title, ed. Alan E. J. Andrews, Blubber Head Press, Hobart, 1979.

William Light, *William Light's Brief Journal and Australian Diaries*, introduction and notes by David Elder, Wakefield Press, Adelaide, 1984, pp. 136–9.

J. W. Lindt, *Picturesque New Guinea: With an Historical Introduction and Supplementary Chapters on the Manners and Customs of the Papuans*, Longman, Green, & Co., London, 1887, pp. 64–9.

John MacGillivray, *Narrative of the Voyage of H.M.S. Rattlesnake, commanded by the late Captain Owen Stanley, R.N., F.R.S. &c. during the Years 1846–1850: Including Discoveries and Surveys in New Guinea, the Louisiade Archipelago, etc. ...*, vol. 1, T. & W. Boone, London, 1852, pp. 207–9.

Angus McMillan extract: Thomas Francis Bride (ed.), *Letters from Victorian Pioneers: Being a Series of Papers on the Early Occupation of the Colony, the Aborigines, etc.*, edited with an introduction and notes by C. E. Sayers, Heinemann, Melbourne and London, 1969, pp. 202–8. The original edition of this work was published for the Trustees of the Public Library, Museums, and National Gallery of Victoria by Robt S. Brain, Government Printer, Melbourne, 1898.

Catherine Martin extract: M.C., *The Explorers and Other Poems*, George Robertson, Melbourne, 1874, pp. 1–9.

Douglas Mawson, *The Home of the Blizzard: Being the Story of the Australasian Antarctic Expedition, 1911–1914*, abridged popular edition, Hodder & Stoughton, London, 1930 (first published in full 1915), pp. 180–5.

T. L. Mitchell, *Journal of an Expedition into the Interior of Tropical Australia, In Search of a Route from Sydney to the Gulf of Carpentaria*, Longman, Brown, Green, & Longmans, London, 1848, pp. 308–14. Facsimile edition published by Greenwood Press, New York, 1969.

T. L. Mitchell, *Three Expeditions into the Interior of Eastern Australia; With Descriptions of the Recently Explored Region of Australia Felix, And of the Present Colony of New South Wales*, vol. 1, 2nd edn, T. & W. Boone, London, 1839 (1838), pp. 269–75. Facsimile edition published by the Libraries Board of South Australia, Adelaide, 1965.

Alan Moorehead, *Cooper's Creek*, Nelson, Melbourne, 1985 (first published by Hamish Hamilton, 1963), pp. 202–9.

John Moresby, *Discoveries & Surveys in New Guinea and the D'Entrecasteaux Islands: A Cruise in Polynesia and Visits to the Pearl-Shelling Stations in Torres Straits of H.M.S. Basilisk*, John Murray, London, 1876, pp. 153–7.

George Ernest Morrison extract: *Age*, 21 November 1883.

J.H.P. Murray, *Recent Exploration in Papua*, Turner & Henderson Ltd, Sydney, c. 1920s, pp. 35–8.

George [*sic*] Neumayer, *Results of the Magnetic Survey of the Colony of Victoria: Executed During the Years 1858–1864*, J. Schneider, Mannheim, Germany, 1869, pp. 76–80.

Barry Oakley, 'O'Hara 1861', *Southerly*, vol. 20, no. 3, 1959, pp. 147–9.

John Oxley extract: *Historical Records of Australia*, series 1, vol. X, The Library Committee of the Commonwealth Parliament, Sydney, 1917, pp. 26–31.

A.B. Paterson, 'The Lost Leichhardt', in *The Oxford Book of Australian Light Verse*, eds R.F. Brissenden & Philip Grundy, Oxford University Press, Melbourne, 1991, pp. 7–8.

François Pelsaert, *The Voyage of the Batavia*, Hordern House, Sydney, 1994, pp. 91–6. This book includes a facsimile of the account of Pelsaert's journal by Jan Jansz, which was first published in Dutch as *Ongeluckige Voyagie, Van't Ship Batavia* in 1647, and Willem Siebenhaar's English translation of *Ongeluckige...*, which appeared in the *Western Mail* as 'The Abrolhos Tragedy' in 1897. The extract is taken from 'The Abrolhos Tragedy'.

John Price extract: F.M. Bladen (ed.), *Historical Records of New South Wales*, vol. III. Charles Potter, Government Printer, Sydney, 1895, pp. 820–3. Facsimile edition published by Lansdown Slattery & Company, Sydney, 1978.

Archibald John Richardson extract: *The Journal of the Royal Geographical Society*, vol. 36, John Murray, London, 1866, pp. 21–3.

Anne Robertson, 'The Little Explorer', *Sydney Morning Herald*, 13, 14, 20 May 1976. Reproduced with permission of the author.

George Augustus Robinson extract: N.J.B. Plomley (ed.), *Friendly Mission: The Tasmanian Journals and Papers of George Augustus Robinson, 1829–34*, Tasmanian Historical Research Association, Hobart, 1966, pp. 127–8.

Kenneth Slessor, *Five Visions of Captain Cook*, from his *Selected Poems*, Harper Collins Australia/Angus & Robertson, Sydney, 1977 (first published as *Selected Poems* in 1975, previously published as *One Hundred Poems* by Angus & Robertson, 1944), pp. 67–8.

J. Lort Stokes, *Discoveries in Australia: With an Account of the Coasts and Rivers Explored and Surveyed during the Voyage of H.M.S. Beagle, in the Years 1837–38–39–40–41–42–43, By Command of the Lords Commissioners of the Admiralty, Also a Narrative of Captain Owen Stanley's Visits to the Islands in the Arafura Sea*, vol. II, T. & W. Boone, London, 1846, pp. 5–13. Facsimile edition published by the Libraries Board of South Australia, Adelaide, 1969.

Paul Edmund de Strzelecki extract: British Parliamentary Papers, House of Commons, paper 120, session 26 January–22 June 1841, vol. 17, 1841, pp. 11–12.

John McDouall Stuart, *J. M'Dougall Stuart's Explorations Across the Continent of Australia, 1861–62*, F. F. Bailliere, Melbourne, 1863, pp. 56–7. Facsimile edition published by the Libraries Board of South Australia, Adelaide, 1963.

Charles Sturt, *Journal of the Central Australian Expedition 1844–5*, ed. Jill Waterhouse, Caliban Books, London, 1984, pp. 54–7. This book is a facsimile edition of pp. 145–286 of Charles Sturt's *Narrative of an Expedition into Central Australia*, vol. 2, 1849.

Charles Sturt, *Two Expeditions into the Interior of Southern Australia During the Years 1828, 1829, 1830, and 1831: With Observations on the Soil, Climate, and General Resources of the Colony of New South Wales*, vol. II, Smith, Elder & Co., London, 1833, pp. 106–10. Facsimile edition published by Doubleday Australia, Sydney, 1982.

Abel Tasman, *Discovery of Tasmania (24 November 1642)*, trans. J.E. Heeres, Government Printer, Hobart, 1985, pp. 29–30. Facsimile reprint. First published by the Government Printer, Hobart, 1942.

Martin Thomas, *The Roan*, Random House, Sydney, 1994, pp. 170–2.

Jules Verne, *Mistress Branican*, new and cheaper edition, Sampson Low, Marston & Co., London, *c.* 1892 (1891), pp. 299–302.

Alexander Vesper, 'The Three Brothers', in *The Man Who Sold His Dreaming*, Roland Robinson, Currawong Publishing Co., Sydney, 1965, pp. 40–4.

Peter Egerton Warburton extract: *Proceedings of the Royal Geographical Society*, vol. XIX, 1874–75, London, 1875, pp. 44–6.

Eric Webb, 'An Appreciation', in *This Accursed Land*, Lennard Bickel, Sun Books, The Macmillan Company of Australia, Melbourne and Sydney, 1978 (first published by The Macmillan Company of Australia, 1977), pp. 201–6.

Francis Webb, *Eyre All Alone*, in his *Socrates and Other Poems*, HarperCollins Australia/Angus & Robertson, London and Sydney, 1961, pp. 70–1.

Richard Whately extract: Lady Mary Fox (ed.), *Account of an Expedition to the Interior of New Holland*, Richard Bentley, London, 1837, pp. 1–9.

Patrick White, *Voss*, Penguin, Harmondsworth, 1960 (first published by Eyre & Spottiswoode, 1957), pp. 443–5.

William John Wills, *A Successful Exploration through the Interior of Australia, From Melbourne to the Gulf of Carpentaria, From the Journals and Letters of*

William John Wills, ed. William Wills, Richard Bentley, London, 1863, pp. 302–3.

C. Winnecke, *Journal of the Horn Scientific Exploring Expedition, 1894*, C.E. Bristow, Government Printer, Adelaide, 1897, pp. 61–5.

ILLUSTRATIONS

Page 1

From T.L. Mitchell, *Journal of an Expedition into the Interior of Tropical Australia, In Search of a Route from Sydney to the Gulf of Carpentaria*, Longman, Brown, Green, & Longmans, London, 1848, title page.

Page 257

From L.M. D'Albertis, *New Guinea: What I Did and What I Saw,* vol. II, Sampson Low, Marston, Searle, & Rivington, London, 1880, between pp. 46 & 47.

Page 238

From Anonymous, *Summer in the Antarctic Regions; A Narrative of Voyages of Discovery towards the South Pole*, Society for Promoting Christian Knowledge, London, 1848, p. 124.

INDEX

Antarctic, the 283–304
Arthur, George 68
Ayers Rock *see* Uluru

Balodis, Janis xi, 142–5
Banks, Joseph 18–19, 45, 62
Barcoo River 130–4, 176, 177
Bass, George 21
Bass Strait 21–2
Baudin, Nicolas 26–9
Baxter, John 104, 106–8, 109, 110–13
Bernacchi, Louis 284–6
Blaxland, Gregory ix, 47–9, 53
Blue Mountains ix, 45–7, 47–9, 49–54
Borchgrevink, Carsten 284
Botany Bay 18–19
Burke, Robert O'Hara viii, x, xi, 157–8, 159–64, 164–8, 168–75 *passim*, 177, 179

Caley, George 45–7
Calvert, Albert Frederick 242
Cape York Peninsula ix, 145–8, 148–53
Carnegie, David 241–5
Clarence River 3
Clark, William ix, 39–41
Coate, Kevin 218–23
Cook, James 17–19, 19–20
Cooper Creek 157–8, 164–8, 168–75 *passim*, 178

Creaghe, Emily Caroline 183–91
Cunningham, Allan 31, 62–64

D'Albertis, Luigi x, 266–7, 275, 281
Dampier, William 11–16
Darling Downs 62–4, 135
Darling River 65–7, 83–8, 169, 175
Darwin, Charles 34
Davidson, Robyn x, 247–50
De Grey River 224–5
de Rougemont, Louis xii, 245–7
de Vlamingh, Willem 16–17
Drewe, Robert 250–5
Duggan, Laurie 76–9
Dutton, Geoffrey 109–12

Elder, Thomas 232, 237
Encounter Bay 26–8
Ericksen, Ray ix, 239–41
Erskine, James 272
Evans, George 49–54
Eyre, Edward John vii, x, xiii, 37, 38, 104–8, 108–9, 109–12, 128

Favenc, Ernest 154–7, 183–90 *passim*
Finlayson, Hedley Herbert 203–6
Fitzpatrick, Kathleen vii–xiii *passim*
FitzRoy, Charles Augustus 145–8
Fitzroy River 243, 245

[315]

Flinders, Matthew x, 21–2, 22–6, 27–8
Fly River x, 266–7, 280–1
Forrest, John 226–9, 230
Fox, Lady Mary *see* Whately, Richard
Franklin, Jane x, 112–15
Franklin, John 112–15
Franklin River 113–14

Gibson's Desert ix
Giles, Ernest ix, 206, 212, 230, 237–9, 250
Gill, S. T. 127–30
Gipps, George 97
Gippsland 76, 97–102
Gosse, William 230–1
Goyder, George Woodroofe 230
Gray, Charles 157–8
Gregory, Augustus Charles 154–7, 175–6, 224
Gregory, Francis Thomas 224–5
Grey, George vii, 214–18, 218–23
Grey Range 122–5
Groom, Arthur 206–9, 209–13
Guérard, Eugene von 115–21 *passim*

Hargrave, Lawrence 266, 267–9
Hawdon, Joseph 90–3
Hill, Barry xi, 209–13
Hill, Ernestine x, 22–6
Hooker, William Jackson 70
Horn, William 191–2
Horrocks, John Ainsworth xii, 127–30
Houtman Abrolhos 5
Hovell, William 60–2
Howitt, A. W. 158, 175, 178
Hume, Hamilton 60–2
Hunter, John 21, 41
Hurley, Frank 296–8

Idriess, Ion xii, 198–203

Jackey Jackey xi, 145, 148–53
Jardine, Alexander and Frank ix, 181–3

Kata Tjuta (Olgas, the) 206–9 *passim*, 211, 212
Keneally, Thomas 299–301
Kennedy, Edmund xi, 130, 145–8, 148–53, 177
Kimberley 214–18, 218–23
King, John 157–8, 166–8, 172–3, 174
King, Phillip Parker 29–33, 62

Lake Amadeus 206–9, 211, 212
Lake Bonney 90–1
Landsborough, William 175–9
Lasseter, Lewis Hubert (Harold Bell) 196–8, 198–203
Law, Phillip 301–4
Lawrence, Robert 69–74
Lawson, J. A. 263–6
Lawson, William ix, 47–9
Leichhardt, Ludwig vii, xi, 134–7, 138–9, 140, 142–5, 146, 154, 156, 157, 226
Lhotsky, John xii, 74–6, 78–9
Light, William 93–7
Lindt, John 275–80
Louisiade Archipelago 258–9

MacDonnell Ranges 194–6
MacGillivray, John 258–9
McKinlay, John 175
McMillan, Angus 97–102
Macquarie, Lachlan 49, 54
Macquarie Harbour 112–15 *passim*
Macquarie River 49–54 *passim*, 54–7
Martin, Catherine x, 159–64
Mawson, Douglas x, 286–91, 291–5
Melbourne 159–64

Mertz, Xavier 286–91, 293
Mitchell, Thomas Livingstone vii,
   xiii, 83–8, 88–90, 99, 130–4, 146
Moorehead, Alan 168–75
Moresby, John 259–62
Morrison, George Ernest 269–72
Mount Kosciusko xiii, 102–4,
   115–20 *passim*
Mueller, Ferdinand von 154–7
   passim, 207, 275
Murray, Hubert 280–2
Murray River 60–1, 65, 90–3

Neumayer, Georg 115–21
New Guinea x, 257–82
Ninnis, Belgrave 286, 292, 293
Nullarbor Plain x, 104–8, 110–12,
   226–9

Oakley, Barry xi, 164–8
Olgas, the *see* Kata Tjuta
Oxley, John 29–33, 54–9, 62

Paterson, A. B. 138–9
Pelsaert, François 5–8
Petermann Ranges 197
Poole, James 122–5
Port Darwin 34–6
Port Macquarie 29–33, 58
Port Moresby 260–2, 273–4
Preservation Island 39
Price, John ix, 41–5

Richardson, Archibald John ix,
   181–3
Robertson, Anne 183–91
Robinson, George Augustus 68–9
Robinson, Roland 1
Rottnest Island 16–17

Scratchley, Peter 275–80 *passim*
Shackleton, Ernest 286, 291, 292,
   296–8
Slessor, Kenneth xiii, 19–20

Spencer, Walter Baldwin 191
Stanley, Owen 258
Stokes, John Lort 33–8, 146, 156,
   225
Strickland River 280–2
Strzelecki, Paul Edmund de xiii,
   97, 101, 102–4
Stuart, John McDouall 122–5
   passim, 179–81
Sturt, Charles vii, xii, 65–7, 83,
   122–5, 126, 179
Sydney 75, 135–6

Tasman, Abel 9–11
Thomas, Martin xii, 125–7
Thomson River 177, 178
Tillers, Imants 116
Tjalkalyiri, Tiger 206–9, 211–13

Uluru (Ayers Rock) 206–9,
   209–13, 230, 240

Van Diemen's Gulf 180–1
Verne, Jules xii, 234–7
Vesper, Alexander xi, 2–5
Victoria River (Northern Territory)
   154–6

Walker, Frederick 175, 176, 177
Warburton, Peter Egerton vii, xii,
   230, 232–4, 234–5
Webb, Eric 291–5
Webb, Francis xiii, 108–9
Wells, Larry 241–5
Wentworth, William Charles ix,
   47–9
Whately, Richard 79–83
White, Patrick xi, 139–41
Wills, William John viii, x, 157–8,
   159–64, 164–8 *passim*, 168–75
   passim, 177, 179
Wilson, John 41–5 *passim*
Winnecke, Charles 191–6
Wylie 104, 108–9, 110–12